Gravity at the International Criminal Court

OXFORD MONOGRAPHS IN INTERNATIONAL LAW

General Editors

PROFESSOR CATHERINE REDGWELL

*Chichele Professor of Public International Law at the University of Oxford
and Fellow of All Souls College, Oxford*

PROFESSOR ROGER O'KEEFE

Professor of International Law, Bocconi University, Milan

The aim of this series is to publish important and original pieces of research on all aspects of international law. Topics that are given particular prominence are those which, while of interest to the academic lawyer, also have important bearing on issues which touch the actual conduct of international relations. Nonetheless the series is wide in scope and includes monographs on the history and philosophical foundations of international law.

RECENT TITLES IN THE SERIES

International Law Obligations on Climate Change Mitigation
Benoit Mayer

**International Human Rights and Islamic Law
Second Edition**
Mashood Baderin

Coastal State Jurisdiction over Living Resources in the Exclusive Economic Zone
Camille Goodman

International Law and Corporate Actors in Deep Seabed Mining
Joanna Dingwall

The Concept of an International Organization in International Law
Lorenzo Gasbarri

Necessity and Proportionality and the Right of Self-Defence in International Law
Chris O'Meara

Neutrality in Contemporary International Law
James Upcher

Geographical Change and the Law of the Sea
Kate Purcell

Statehood and the State-Like in International Law
Rowan Nicholson

Confronting the Shadow State
Henri Decoeur

Irresolvable Norm Conflicts in International Law: The Concept of a Legal Dilemma
Valentin Jeutner

Gravity at the International Criminal Court

Admissibility and Prosecutorial Discretion

PRIYA URS

Great Clarendon Street, Oxford, OX2 6DP,
United Kingdom

Oxford University Press is a department of the University of Oxford.
It furthers the University's objective of excellence in research, scholarship,
and education by publishing worldwide. Oxford is a registered trade mark of
Oxford University Press in the UK and in certain other countries

© Priya Urs 2024

The moral rights of the author have been asserted

First Edition published in 2024

All rights reserved. No part of this publication may be reproduced, stored in
a retrieval system, or transmitted, in any form or by any means, without the
prior permission in writing of Oxford University Press, or as expressly permitted
by law, by licence or under terms agreed with the appropriate reprographics
rights organization. Enquiries concerning reproduction outside the scope of the
above should be sent to the Rights Department, Oxford University Press, at the
address above

You must not circulate this work in any other form
and you must impose this same condition on any acquirer

Public sector information reproduced under Open Government Licence v3.0
(http://www.nationalarchives.gov.uk/doc/open-government-licence/open-government-licence.htm)

Published in the United States of America by Oxford University Press
198 Madison Avenue, New York, NY 10016, United States of America

British Library Cataloguing in Publication Data

Data available

Library of Congress Control Number: 2023947969

ISBN 978-0-19-888295-4

DOI: 10.1093/oso/9780198882954.001.0001

Printed and bound by
CPI Group (UK) Ltd, Croydon, CR0 4YY

Links to third party websites are provided by Oxford in good faith and
for information only. Oxford disclaims any responsibility for the materials
contained in any third party website referenced in this work.

In loving memory of my father

General Editors' Preface

Not all cases falling within the jurisdiction of the International Criminal Court (ICC) are necessarily admissible before the Court. A case may be inadmissible where, among other things, it 'is not of sufficient gravity to justify further action by the Court', in the laconic formulation of Article 17(1)(*d*) of the Rome Statute. As the Appeals Chamber of the ICC has affirmed, the application of the deliberately vague or, in Hart's terminology, 'open-textured' standard of 'sufficient gravity' involves an exercise of discretion, even if the breadth of this discretion has been narrowed, in the usual interests of the rule of law, by the Court's enunciation of criteria or 'indicators' to be weighed in the assessment. Where the admissibility of a potential or actual case is to be taken into account in deciding whether to investigate a situation or, later, to prosecute a case, it is to the Prosecutor of the ICC that the discretionary assessment of gravity falls, although this assessment is subject to review by a Pre-Trial Chamber of the Court. The Appeals Chamber has taken the minimalist view that the function of the gravity requirement in Article 17(1)(*d*) of the Rome Statute is 'not to oblige the Court to choose only the most serious cases, but merely to oblige it not to prosecute cases of marginal gravity'.

The most fundamental claim of Priya Urs's *Gravity at the International Criminal Court: Admissibility and Prosecutorial Discretion* is—*pace* the Appeals Chamber— that, when applied in the context of the Prosecutor's decisions whether to investigate a situation or to prosecute a case, the function of the admissibility requirement that a case be 'of sufficient gravity to justify further action by the Court' is to facilitate the discretionary allocation by the Prosecutor of their Office's finite investigative and prosecutorial resources. In other words, the gravity assessment provides a statutory basis on which to justify the inevitable selectivity of the Prosecutor's work, enabling them, where appropriate, to decline to investigate or prosecute more than just 'those rather unusual cases', in the words of the Appeals Chamber, 'of marginal gravity only'. On the way to this conclusion, Dr Urs suggests more coherent indicators of the gravity of a crime within the Court's jurisdiction than those inconsistently applied to date by the ICC. She also argues for more deferential standards of Pre-Trial Chamber review of the Prosecutor's decisions, setting these against the backdrop of the judicial deference shown in international human rights law, international investment law, and international trade law.

Gravity at the International Criminal Court represents the best sort of legal formalism, in which a faithful account of the positive law is set in systemic and comparative legal context to reveal insufficiencies, inconsistencies, and fallacies, creating space for normative argument in what Julius Stone called 'the leeways of the law'. It combines attentive reading of the ICC's case-law with insightful identification and judicious weighing of legal policy considerations. It is rigorously analytical, tightly and attractively argued, and discerning. It will be of value not only to students, researchers, and practitioners of international criminal law but also to all those interested in the many and varied debates over the intensity of international judicial oversight of discretionary decision-making.

RO'K, CR
Milan and Oxford
October 2023

Acknowledgements

The work for this book began during my PhD at University College London (UCL) and was completed during my Junior Research Fellowship in Law at St John's College, University of Oxford. It has benefitted from the generous financial support of both institutions, in particular the Faculty Research Scholarship and the Joseph Hume Scholarship at the UCL Faculty of Laws. In less tangible ways, the book has also benefitted from my studies at the University of Cambridge and those who taught me public international law there, especially the late James Crawford.

I am grateful first and foremost to Roger O'Keefe, my PhD supervisor and mentor, who taught me international criminal law at the University of Cambridge and has since taught me much more. In many ways, not least while reading and re-reading various parts of this work, Roger showed me what it is to commit to the highest standards of academic rigour. In this, he has left an indelible mark. I would also like to thank Kimberley Trapp, who, as my second PhD supervisor, went above and beyond in support of both this work and my academic career. I do not take for granted her gentle but well-timed reminders not to miss the forest for the trees.

The manuscript for the book was vastly improved by many comments and conversations. I returned time and again to the thoughtful reflections of my PhD examiners, Miles Jackson and Megan Donaldson, and I am grateful to them for keeping the conversation going. Martins Paparinskis, Alex Mills, and Danae Azaria helped me view this research through a public international law lens and, to the same end, Katie Johnston kindly lent her time to read a chapter of the book. Dapo Akande was a tremendous support during the final stages. The constructive suggestions of the anonymous peer reviewers served as valuable guidance throughout.

At Oxford University Press, thanks to Merel Alstein and Robert Cavooris for facilitating the publication of the book and to Jaqueline Larabee for her constant support. Thanks to Reyman Joseph, Sally Evans-Darby, and the production team at Newgen.

I am grateful to Andrew McLean, Antonio Coco, Astrid Wiik, Devang Ram Mohan, Dina Elabd, Ed Robinson, Eleni Methymaki, Elisa Novic, Gaiane Nuridhzanian, Joe Crampin, Mariam Titus, Niccolò Ridi, Niko Pavlopoulos, Siddharth de Souza, Špela Kunej-Dælhi, Swantje Batista-Pabst, Talita Dias, and Tushar Menon for friendships that sustained me.

My most improbable family, Rani Batra, Pooja and Akshay Rathore, and my late parents, Usha and Shridhar Urs, have been variously inspirational and instrumental; I owe them each a debt I can never repay. Stephen Kastoryano's belief in my abilities has not yet seen any limits.

London

March 2023

Contents

Table of Cases	xv
List of Abbreviations	xxi

1. Introduction	1
1.1 The Selectivity of Investigations and Prosecutions at the International Criminal Court	1
1.2 The Gravity Criterion for Admissibility in Article 17(1)(*d*) of the Rome Statute	5
1.3 Methodology	11
1.4 Contributions to Practice and Scholarship	14
1.5 Scope and Limitations	16
1.5.1 Gravity in the Jurisdiction *Ratione Materiae* of the Court	17
1.5.2 The Interests of Justice and the Gravity of the Crime	19
1.5.3 Gravity and the Court's Sentencing Criteria	20
1.6 Terminological Clarifications	20
1.6.1 'Situation'	20
1.6.2 'Case'	21
1.7 Outline	22
2. The Application of the Gravity Criterion for Admissibility in Article 17(1)(*d*) of the Rome Statute	24
2.1 Introduction	24
2.2 The Function of the Gravity Criterion According to the Court	26
2.3 The Articulation of the Gravity Criterion	29
2.3.1 The Application of Article 17(1)(*d*) of the Statute to a Situation	29
2.3.1.1 The Assessment of the Admissibility of a Situation	29
2.3.1.1.1 The number of sufficiently grave potential cases	31
2.3.1.1.2 The assessment of gravity beyond the jurisdictional scope of the situation	34
2.3.1.2 The Application of Article 17(1)(*d*) to a Situation in Practice	35
2.3.1.2.1 Overview	35
2.3.1.2.2 In detail	36
2.3.1.2.2.1 Scale	38
2.3.1.2.2.2 Nature	40
2.3.1.2.2.3 Manner of commission	42
2.3.1.2.2.4 Impact	44
2.3.1.2.2.5 Those who bear the greatest responsibility	45
2.3.1.2.3 Recapitulation	48

xii CONTENTS

2.3.2 The Application of Article 17(1)(*d*) of the Statute to a Case 48
    2.3.2.1 The Assessment of the Admissibility of a Case 48
    2.3.2.2 The Application of Article 17(1)(*d*) to a Case in Practice 50
        2.3.2.2.1 Overview 50
        2.3.2.2.2 In detail 51
            2.3.2.2.2.1 Scale 56
            2.3.2.2.2.2 Nature 57
            2.3.2.2.2.3 Manner of commission 57
            2.3.2.2.2.4 Impact 60
            2.3.2.2.2.5 Those who bear the greatest
                    responsibility 61
        2.3.2.2.3 Recapitulation 61
2.4 The Assessment of Gravity under Article 17(1)(*d*) of the
Rome Statute 62
    2.4.1 The Appropriate Indicators of Gravity under Article 17(1)(*d*) 62
        2.4.1.1 The Indicator of 'Scale' 63
        2.4.1.2 The Indicator of 'Nature' 64
        2.4.1.3 The Indicator of 'Manner of Commission' 66
        2.4.1.4 The Indicator of 'Impact' 68
        2.4.1.5 The Indicator of 'Those Who Bear the Greatest
            Responsibility' 68
    2.4.2 The Subjective Nature of the Gravity Assessment under
Article 17(1)(*d*) 72
        2.4.2.1 As Viewed by the Court 72
        2.4.2.2 In Principle 74
2.5 Conclusion 79

3. Pre-Trial Chamber Review of the Admissibility of 'Situations' 81
3.1 Introduction 81
3.2 Pre-Trial Chamber Review of the Prosecutor's Assessment of
Admissibility 83
    3.2.1 Pre-Trial Chamber Review under Article 53(3)(*a*) 83
        3.2.1.1 Article 53(3)(*a*) 83
        3.2.1.2 Pre-Trial Chamber Review to Date under Article 53(3)(*a*) 85
            3.2.1.2.1 Overview 85
            3.2.1.2.2 In detail 85
            3.2.1.2.3 Recapitulation 90
    3.2.2 Pre-Trial Chamber Review under Article 15(4) 91
        3.2.2.1 Article 15(4) 91
        3.2.2.2 Pre-Trial Chamber Review to Date under Article 15(4) 95
            3.2.2.2.1 Overview 95
            3.2.2.2.2 In detail 96
            3.2.2.2.3 Recapitulation 101
3.3 The Appropriate Limits of Pre-Trial Chamber Review in
the Initiation of Investigations 101
    3.3.1 Prosecutorial Discretion in the Initiation of Investigations 102

CONTENTS xiii

3.3.2 Judicial Review of Prosecutorial Discretion in the Initiation of Investigations 105
3.3.3 Standards of Review under Article 53(3)(*a*) and Article 15(4) 107
3.4 Conclusion 114

4. Pre-Trial Chamber Review and Pre-Trial or Trial Chamber Determination of the Admissibility of 'Cases' 116
4.1 Introduction 116
4.2 Pre-Trial Chamber Review of the Prosecutor's Assessment of Admissibility 119
    4.2.1 Pre-Trial Chamber Review under Article 53(3)(*a*) of the Statute 119
        4.2.1.1 Article 53(3)(*a*) 119
        4.2.1.2 Pre-Trial Chamber Review to Date under Article 53(3)(*a*) 122
            4.2.1.2.1 Overview 122
            4.2.1.2.2 In detail 123
            4.2.1.2.3 Recapitulation 124
    4.2.2 The Appropriate Limits of Pre-Trial Chamber Review in the Initiation of Prosecutions 125
        4.2.2.1 Prosecutorial Discretion in the Initiation of Prosecutions 125
        4.2.2.2 Judicial Review of Prosecutorial Discretion in the Initiation of Prosecutions 129
        4.2.2.3 Standard of Review under Article 53(3)(*a*) 130
4.3 Pre-Trial or Trial Chamber Determination of Admissibility 134
    4.3.1 Pre-Trial or Trial Chamber Decision under Article 19 of the Statute 134
        4.3.1.1 Article 19 134
        4.3.1.2 Pre-Trial Chamber Decisions to Date under Article 19 137
            4.3.1.2.1 Overview 137
            4.3.1.2.2 In detail 138
            4.3.1.2.3 Recapitulation 144
    4.3.2 Assessment of Admissibility under Article 19 of the Statute 144
        4.3.2.1 Assessment of Admissibility during Proceedings under Article 58 144
            4.3.2.1.1 Judicial economy and related considerations 145
            4.3.2.1.2 Interest of the suspect in the question of admissibility 146
            4.3.2.1.3 The permissibility of the assessment of admissibility under Article 19(2)(*c*) and (3) 148
        4.3.2.2 Assessment of Gravity during Proceedings under Article 58 150
4.4 Conclusion 152

5. The Function of the Gravity Criterion for Admissibility in Article 17(1)(*d*) of the Rome Statute 155
5.1 Introduction 155

xiv CONTENTS

5.2 The Application of the Gravity Criterion in Article 17(1)(*d*) of the
Rome Statute and the Initiation of Investigations and Prosecutions   157
    5.2.1 The Appropriate Indicators of Gravity and the Subjective
Nature of the Gravity Assessment under Article 17(1)(*d*)   157
    5.2.2 Prosecutorial Discretion and Pre-Trial Chamber Review during
the Initiation of Investigations   158
    5.2.3 Prosecutorial Discretion and Pre-Trial Chamber Review during
the Initiation of Prosecutions   160
5.3 The Function of the Gravity Criterion in Article 17(1)(*d*) of the
Rome Statute and the Initiation of Investigations and Prosecutions   162
    5.3.1 The Independent Expert Review   163
    5.3.2 The Existing Scholarship   164
        5.3.2.1 A Policy Criterion of 'Relative Gravity'   164
        5.3.2.2 The Interests of Justice   165
    5.3.3 Rejecting the Approaches in the Existing Scholarship   166
        5.3.3.1 A Policy Criterion of 'Relative Gravity'   166
        5.3.3.2 The Interests of Justice   168
5.4 Recommendations for Practice   170
    5.4.1 At the ICC   170
    5.4.2 At Other International and National Criminal Courts   173
5.5 Conclusion   175

Bibliography   177
Index   187

Table of Cases

Prosecutor v Abu Garda, ICC-02/05-02/09-243-Red, Pre-Trial Chamber I,
Decision on the Confirmation of Charges, 8 February 2010. . . . . 54–55, 60–61

Prosecutor v Al Hassan, ICC-01/12-01/18-35-Red2-tENG, Pre-Trial Chamber I,
Decision on the Prosecutor's Application for the Issuance of a Warrant of
Arrest for Al Hassan Ag Abdoul Aziz Ag Mohamed Ag Mahmoud,
22 May 2018 . . . . 59, 137–38, 143–44

Prosecutor v Al Hassan, ICC-01/12-01/18-459-tENG, Pre-Trial Chamber I,
Decision on the Admissibility Challenge Raised by the Defence for
Insufficient Gravity of the Case, 27 September 2019 . . . . . . 54–55, 56, 57, 58, 59, 60–61

Prosecutor v Al Hassan, ICC-01/12-01/18-601-Red, Appeals Chamber, Judgment
on the Appeal of Mr Al Hassan Against the Decision of Pre-Trial Chamber I
Entitled 'Décision relative a l'exception d'irrecevabilité pour insufficiance de
gravité de l'affaire soulevée par la défense', 19 February 2020 . . . . 11, 28, 49–51, 55,
56–57, 58–59, 60, 61–62, 73–74, 143–44, 162, 164–65, 170

Prosecutor v Al-Werfalli, ICC-01/11-01/17-13, Pre-Trial Chamber I, Second
Warrant of Arrest, 4 July 2018. . . . . .58, 59, 61

Prosecutor v Banda and Jerbo, ICC-02/05-03/09-121-Corr-Red, Pre-Trial
Chamber I, Corrigendum of the 'Decision on the Confirmation of Charges',
7 March 2011. . . . . 54–55, 60–61

Prosecutor v Bemba and others, ICC-01/05-01/13-2276-Red, Appeals Chamber,
Judgment on the Appeals of the Prosecutor, Mr Jean-Pierre Bemba Gombo,
Mr Fidèle Babala Wandu and Mr Narcisse Arido against the Decision of Trial
Chamber VII entitled 'Decision on Sentence Pursuant to Article 76 of the
Statute', 8 March 2018. 58

Prosecutor v Bemba, ICC-01/05-01/08-14-tENG, Pre-Trial Chamber III, Decision
on the Prosecutor's Application for a Warrant of Arrest against Jean-Pierre
Bemba Gombo, 10 June 2008 141–42

Prosecutor v Bemba, ICC-01/05-01/08-424, Pre-Trial Chamber II, Decision
Pursuant to Article 61(7)(*a*) and (*b*) of the Rome Statute on the Charges of
the Prosecutor against Jean-Pierre Bemba Gombo, 15 June 2009 141–42

Prosecutor v Bemba, ICC-01/05-01/08-453, Pre-Trial Chamber II, Decision on
Request for Leave to Submit *Amicus Curiae* Observations Pursuant to
Rule 103 of the Rules of Procedure and Evidence, 17 July 2009 129–30

Prosecutor v Bemba, ICC-01/05-01/08-802, Trial Chamber III, Decision on the
Admissibility and Abuse of Process Challenges, 24 June 2010 141

Prosecutor v Charles Blé Goudé, ICC-02/11-02/11-185, Pre-Trial Chamber I,
Decision on the Defence Challenge to the Admissibility of the Case Against
Charles Blé Goudé for Insufficient Gravity, 12 November 2014. . . . . . .54–55, 56, 58, 59

Prosecutor v Gaddafi and Al-Senussi, ICC-01/11-01/11-129, Pre-Trial Chamber I,
Decision on OPCD Requests, 27 April 2012. 140–41

Prosecutor v Gaddafi and Al-Senussi, ICC-01/11-01/11-134, Pre-Trial Chamber I,
Decision on the Conduct of Proceedings Following the 'Application on Behalf of
the Government of Libya Pursuant to Article 19 of the Statute', 4 May 2012 140–41

xvi   TABLE OF CASES

Prosecutor v Gaddafi and Al-Senussi, ICC-01/11-01/11-325, Pre-Trial Chamber
I, Decision on the Conduct of the Proceedings Following the 'Application on
Behalf of the Government of Libya Relating to Abdullah Al-Senussi Pursuant
to Article 19 of the ICC Statute', 26 April 2013 140–41

Prosecutor v Gaddafi and Al-Senussi, ICC-01/11-01/11-547-Red, Appeals Chamber,
Judgment on the Appeal of Libya against the Decision of Pre-Trial Chamber I
of 31 May 2013 Entitled 'Decision on the Admissibility of the Case against Saif
Al-Islam Gaddafi', 21 May 2014 30

Prosecutor v Katanga and Ngudjolo, ICC-01/04-01/07-1213-tENG, Trial Chamber II,
Reasons for the Oral Decision on the Motion Challenging the Admissibility of
the Case (Article 19 of the Statute), 16 June 2009 145–46

Prosecutor v Kenyatta, ICC-01/09-02/11-1032, Appeals Chamber, Judgment on the
Prosecutor's Appeal against Trial Chamber V(B)'s 'Decision on Prosecution's
Application for a Finding of Non-Compliance under Article 87(7) of the
Statute', 19 August 2015 137–38

Prosecutor v Kony and others, ICC-02/04-01/05-320, Pre-Trial Chamber II, Decision
Initiating Proceedings under Article 19, Requesting Observations and
Appointing Counsel for the Defence, 21 October 2008 142–43

Prosecutor v Kony and others, ICC-02/04-01/05-377, Pre-Trial Chamber II,
Decision on the Admissibility of the Case under Article 19(1) of the Statute,
10 March 2009 . . . . 142–43, 151

Prosecutor v Kony and others, ICC-02/04-01/05-408, Appeals Chamber, Judgment
on the Appeal of the Defence against the 'Decision on the Admissibility of the
Case under Article 19 of the Statute' of 10 March 2009, 16 September 2009 137–38

Prosecutor v Lubanga, ICC-01/04-01/06-1084, Trial Chamber I, Decision on
the Status Before the Trial Chamber of the Evidence Heard by the Pre-Trial
Chamber and the Decisions of the Pre-Trial Chamber in Trial Proceedings,
and the Manner in Which Evidence Shall be Submitted, 13 December 2007 49–50

Prosecutor v Muthaura and others, ICC-01/09-02/11-382-Red, Pre-Trial
Chamber II, Decision on the Confirmation of Charges Pursuant to
Article 61(7)(*a*) and (*b*) of the Rome Statute, 23 January 2012 . . . . 49–50, 54–55, 59

Prosecutor v Ntaganda, ICC-01/04-02/06-1-Red-tENG, Pre-Trial Chamber I, Decision
on the Prosecution Application for a Warrant of Arrest, 6 March 2007 140–41

Prosecutor v Ruto and others, ICC-01/09-01/11-307, Appeals Chamber, Judgment on
the Appeal of the Republic of Kenya against the Decision of Pre-Trial Chamber
II of 30 May 2011 Entitled 'Decision on the Application by the Government of
Kenya Challenging the Admissibility of the Case Pursuant to Article 19(2)(b)
of the Statute', 30 August 2011 . . . . 30–31, 137–38

Prosecutor v Simone Gbagbo, ICC-02/11-01/12-15, Pre-Trial Chamber I, Decision
on the Conduct of the Proceedings Following Côte d'Ivoire's Challenge to the
Admissibility of the Case against Simone Gbagbo, 15 November 2013 140–41

Situation in Afghanistan, ICC-02/17-138, Appeals Chamber, Judgment on the
Appeal against the Decision on the Authorisation of an Investigation into the
Situation in the Islamic Republic of Afghanistan, 5 March 2020 . . . 92–95, 99–100, 114

Situation in Afghanistan, ICC-02/17-33-Anx, Pre-Trial Chamber II, Concurring
and Separate Opinion of Judge Antoine Kesia-Mbe Mindua, 31 May 2019 99–100

Situation in Afghanistan, ICC-02/17-33, Pre-Trial Chamber II, Decision Pursuant to
Article 15 of the Rome Statute on the Authorisation of an Investigation into the
Situation in the Islamic Republic of Afghanistan, 12 April 2019 . . . . 37, 39–40, 42,
43–44, 45, 93–95, 99–100, 101, 106, 110–11

Situation in Afghanistan, ICC-02/17-62, Pre-Trial Chamber II, Decision on the
Prosecutor and Victims' Requests for Leave to Appeal the 'Decision Pursuant to
Article 15 of the Rome Statute on the Authorisation of an Investigation into the
Situation in the Islamic Republic of Afghanistan', 17 September 2019 93–95

TABLE OF CASES xvii

Situation in Bangladesh/Myanmar, ICC-01/19-27, Pre-Trial Chamber III, Decision Pursuant to Article 15 of the Rome Statute on the Authorisation of an Investigation into the Situation in the People's Republic of Bangladesh/Republic of the Union of Myanmar, 14 November 2019 .... 31–32, 39–40, 100, 101

Situation in Bangladesh/Myanmar, ICC-RoC46(3)-01/1-Anx-ENG, Pre-Trial Chamber I, Partially Dissenting Opinion of Judge Marc Perrin de Brichambaut, 6 September 2018. 138–39

Situation in Bangladesh/Myanmar, ICC-RoC46(3)-01/18-37, Pre-Trial Chamber I, Decision on the 'Prosecution's Request for a Ruling on Jurisdiction under Article 19(3) of the Statute', 6 September 2018 .... 34–35, 48–49, 100, 138–39

Situation in Burundi, ICC-01/17-9-Red, Pre-Trial Chamber III, Public Redacted Version of 'Decision Pursuant to Article 15 of the Rome Statute on the Authorization of an Investigation into the Situation in the Republic of Burundi', 9 November 2017 ....39–40, 41–42, 43–44, 46, 98–99, 101, 106

Situation in Côte d'Ivoire, ICC-02/11-14, Pre-Trial Chamber III, Decision Pursuant to Article 15 of the Rome Statute on the Authorization of an Investigation into the Situation in the Republic of Côte d'Ivoire, 3 October 2011.........27–28, 30–31, 39–40, 41–42, 43–44, 46, 96–97, 101

Situation in Côte d'Ivoire, ICC-02/11-15, Pre-Trial Chamber III, Separate and Partially Dissenting Opinion of Judge Silvia Fernández de Gurmendi, 3 October 2011 ....96–97, 106, 109–10, 113–14

Situation in Côte d'Ivoire, ICC-02/11-36, Pre-Trial Chamber III, Decision on the 'Prosecution's Provision of Further Information Regarding Potentially Relevant Crimes Committed Between 2002 and 2010', 22 February 2012 .... 39–40, 96–97

Situation in Georgia, ICC-01/15-12-Anx1, Pre-Trial Chamber I, Separate Opinion of Judge Péter Kovács, 27 January 2016 97–98

Situation in Georgia, ICC-01/15-12, Pre-Trial Chamber I, Decision on the Prosecutor's Request for Authorization of an Investigation, 27 January 2016 .... 39–40, 41–42, 43–44, 45, 46, 97–98, 101, 106

Situation in Kenya, ICC-01/09-19, Pre-Trial Chamber II, Decision Pursuant to Article 15 of the Rome Statute on the Authorization on an Investigation into the Situation in the Republic of Kenya, 31 March 2010 .... 6–7, 27–28, 30–32, 39–40, 41–42, 43, 45–46, 92–93, 96

Situation in Kenya, ICC-01/09-19, Pre-Trial Chamber II, Dissenting Opinion of Judge Hans-Peter Kaul, 31 October 2010 96

Situation in Kenya, ICC-01/09-42, Pre-Trial Chamber II, Decision on the 'Application for Leave to Participate in the Proceedings before the Pre-Trial Chamber relating to the Prosecutor's Application under Article 58(7)', 11 February 2011 135–36

Situation in Palestine, ICC-01/18-143, Pre-Trial Chamber I, Decision on the 'Prosecution Request pursuant to Article 19(3) for a Ruling on the Court's Territorial Jurisdiction in Palestine, 5 February 2021 .... 48–49, 138–39

Situation in the Democratic Republic of the Congo, ICC-01/04-02/06-20-Anx2, Pre-Trial Chamber I, Decision on Prosecutor's Application for Warrants of Arrest, Article 58, 10 February 2006 ....27–28, 51–52, 68–69, 139–40

Situation in the Democratic Republic of the Congo, ICC-01/04-101-tEN-Corr, Pre-Trial Chamber I, Decision on the Applications for Participation in the Proceedings of VPRS 1, VPRS 2, VPRS 3, VPRS 4, VPRS 5 and VPRS 6, 17 January 2006.........138–39

Situation in the Democratic Republic of the Congo, ICC-01/04-169, Appeals Chamber, Judgment on the Prosecutor's Appeal against the Decision of Pre-Trial Chamber I entitled 'Decision on the Prosecutor's Application for Warrants of Arrest, Article 58', 13 July 2006...... 27–28, 137–38, 140–41, 144, 146–49, 150, 151

Situation in the Democratic Republic of the Congo, ICC-01/04-169, Appeals Chamber, Separate and Partly Dissenting Opinion of Judge Georghios M. Pikis, 13 July 2006 ....53–54, 140–41, 147–48

xviii   TABLE OF CASES

Situation in the Democratic Republic of the Congo, ICC-01/04-373, Pre-Trial
Chamber I, Decision on the Request Submitted Pursuant to Rule 103(1)
of the Rules of Procedure and Evidence, 17 August 2007 .123–24

Situation in the Democratic Republic of the Congo, ICC-01/04-399, Pre-Trial
Chamber I, Decision on the Requests of the Legal Representative for
Victims VPRS 1 to VPRS 6 regarding 'Prosecutor's Information on Further
Investigation', 26 September 2007. 123–24

Situation in the Democratic Republic of the Congo, ICC-01/04-556, Appeals
Chamber, Judgment on Victim Participation in the Investigation Stage of
the Proceedings in the Appeal of the OPCD against the Decision of Pre-Trial
Chamber I of 7 December 2007 and in the Appeals of the OPCD and the
Prosecutor against the Decision of Pre-Trial Chamber I of 24 December 2007,
19 December 2008 . . . . 104–5, 128–29

Situation in the Democratic Republic of the Congo, ICC-01/04-93, Pre-Trial Chamber
I, Decision Following the Consultation Held on 11 October 2005 and the
Prosecution's Submission on Jurisdiction and Admissibility Filed on
31 October 2005, 9 November 2005. . . . . 21–22, 138–39

Situation in the Philippines, ICC-01/21-12, Pre-Trial Chamber I, Decision on the
Prosecutor's Request for Authorisation of an Investigation Pursuant to
Article 15(3) of the Statute, 15 September 2021 100–1

Situation in Uganda, ICC-02/04-01/05-1-US-Exp, Pre-Trial Chamber 505II,
Decision on the Prosecutor's Application for Warrants of Arrest under
Article 58, 8 July 2005 138

Situation in Uganda, ICC-02/04-01/05-52, Pre-Trial Chamber II, Decision on the
Prosecutor's Application for Unsealing of the Warrants of Arrest, 13 October 2005. 123

Situation in Uganda, ICC-02/04-01/05-68, Pre-Trial Chamber II, Decision to
Convene a Status Conference on the Investigation in the Situation in Uganda in
Relation to the Application of Article 53, 2 December 2005. .123

*Situation on the Registered Vessels of the Union of the Comoros, the Hellenic Republic
and the Kingdom of Cambodia*, ICC-01/13-111, Pre-Trial Chamber I, Decision
on the 'Application for Judicial Review by the Government of the Comoros',
16 September 2020. . . . . 28, 41, 44–45, 46–47, 90

*Situation on the Registered Vessels of the Union of the Comoros, the Hellenic Republic and
the Kingdom of Cambodia*, ICC-01/13-34-Anx-Corr, Pre-Trial Chamber I, Partly
Dissenting Opinion of Judge Péter Kovács, 16 July 2015 . . . . . . 34–35, 38–39, 41, 46–47, 86–87

*Situation on the Registered Vessels of the Union of the Comoros, the Hellenic Republic
and the Kingdom of Cambodia*, ICC-01/13-34, Pre-Trial Chamber I, Decision
on the Request of the Union of the Comoros to Review the Prosecutor's
Decision Not to Initiate an Investigation, 16 July 2015 . . . . 31–32, 34–35, 38–39, 41,
43, 44–45, 46–47, 85–87, 108–9, 111–13, 129

*Situation on the Registered Vessels of the Union of the Comoros, the Hellenic Republic
and the Kingdom of Cambodia*, ICC-01/13-68, Pre-Trial Chamber I, Decision
on the 'Application for Judicial Review by the Government of the Union of the
Comoros', 15 November 2018. 88

*Situation on the Registered Vessels of the Union of the Comoros, the Hellenic Republic
and the Kingdom of Cambodia*, ICC-01/13-68-Anx, Pre-Trial Chamber I, Partly
Dissenting Opinion of Judge Péter Kovács, 15 November 2018. 88

*Situation on the Registered Vessels of the Union of the Comoros, the Hellenic Republic
and the Kingdom of Cambodia*, ICC-01/13-51, Appeals Chamber, Decision
on the Admissibility of the Prosecutor's Appeal Against the 'Decision on the
Request of the Union of the Comoros to Review the Prosecutor's Decision Not
to Initiate an Investigation', 6 November 2015 . . . . . . 87–88, 105–6, 108–9, 129, 130–31

TABLE OF CASES   xix

Situation on the Registered Vessels of the Union of the Comoros, the Hellenic Republic and the Kingdom of Cambodia, ICC-01/13-51-Anx, Appeals Chamber, Joint Dissenting Opinion of Judge Silvia Fernández de Gurmendi and Judge Christine van den Wyngaert, 6 November 2015............... 87–88, 108–9, 130–31

Situation on the Registered Vessels of the Union of the Comoros, the Hellenic Republic and the Kingdom of Cambodia, ICC/01/13-98, Appeals Chamber, Judgment on the Appeal of the Prosecutor against Pre-Trial Chamber I's 'Decision on the "Application for Judicial Review by the Government of the Union of the Comoros"', 2 September 2019 .... 72–73, 89–90, 105–6, 107–9, 126–28, 131

Situation on the Registered Vessels of the Union of the Comoros, the Hellenic Republic and the Kingdom of Cambodia, ICC-01/13-98-Anx, Appeals Chamber, Partly Dissenting Opinion of Judge Eboe-Osuji, 2 September 2019 89–90

Situation on the Registered Vessels of the Union of the Comoros, the Hellenic Republic and the Kingdom of Cambodia, ICC-01/13-98-AnxI, Appeals Chamber, Separate and Partly Dissenting Opinion of Judge Luz del Carmen Ibáñez Carranza, 4 November 2019 89–90

List of Abbreviations

AMIS	African Union Mission in Sudan
ASP	Assembly of States Parties
CAR	Central African Republic
CUP	Cambridge University Press
DRC	Democratic Republic of the Congo
FPLC	Forces Patriotiques pour la Libération du Congo
GA	General Assembly
ICC	International Criminal Court
ICTR	International Criminal Tribunal for Rwanda
ICTY	International Criminal Tribunal for the former Yugoslavia
IDF	Israel Defense Forces
IDP	internally displaced person
ILC	International Law Commission
ISIS	Islamic State of Iraq and al-Sham/the Levant
MONUC	United Nations Organization Mission in the Democratic Republic of the Congo
OTP	Office of the Prosecutor
OUP	Oxford University Press
RPE	Rules of Procedure and Evidence
SC	Security Council
SCSL	Special Court for Sierra Leone
UK	United Kingdom
UN	United Nations
UPC	Union des Patriotes Congolais
US	United States
VCLT	Vienna Convention on the Law of Treaties

1

Introduction

> The gravity threshold issue is far more complex and difficult of solution than may be immediately apparent, and it will ... have to engage the attention of the next Prosecutor.[1]

1.1 The Selectivity of Investigations and Prosecutions at the International Criminal Court

Great expectations burden international criminal courts. Such courts are asked to fulfil the objectives of retribution, deterrence, rehabilitation, and expressivism, to contribute to international peace and security, to create a historical record,[2] and to 'end[] impunity, outlaw[] evil, incapacitat[e] political leaders, or provid[e] catharsis for victims',[3] all while protecting the rights of the accused.[4] In no case is this burden more pronounced than in that of the International Criminal Court (ICC, the Court).

With substantial support from states, the ICC was established, with the adoption in 1998 and the entry into force in 2002 of the Rome Statute of the International Criminal Court (Rome Statute, the Statute), as the first permanent international criminal court for the prosecution of crimes under international law.[5] The preamble to the Statute declares that 'the most serious crimes of concern to the

---

[1] Overall Response of the International Criminal Court to the 'Independent Expert Review of the International Criminal Court and the Rome Statute System—Final Report': Preliminary Analysis of the Recommendations and Information on Relevant Activities undertaken by the Court, 14 April 2021 (hereafter 'Overall Response to the Independent Expert Review') para 413.

[2] M Damaška, 'What Is the Point of International Criminal Justice?' (2008) 83 Chicago-Kent Law Review 329, 331–40; C Stahn, 'The Future of International Criminal Justice' (2009) 4 Hague Justice Journal 257, 261–64; MM deGuzman and WA Schabas, 'Initiation of Investigations and Selection of Cases' in S Zappalà and others (eds), *International Criminal Procedure: Principles and Rules* (OUP 2013) 163.

[3] C Stahn, *Justice as Message: Expressivist Foundations of International Criminal* Justice (OUP 2020) 410.

[4] F Guariglia, 'Investigation and Prosecution' in RS Lee (ed), *The International Criminal Court: The Making of the Rome Statute—Issues, Negotiations, Results* (Kluwer Law International 1999) 234.

[5] For Cassese, the ICC, 'with its drive to universality, constitutes the only true and fully-fledged realization of the ideal of justice'. A Cassese, 'The International Criminal Court Five Years On: *Andante* or *Moderato*?' in C Stahn and G Sluiter (eds), *The Emerging Practice of the International Criminal Court* (Martinus Nijhoff 2009) 22–23.

Gravity at the International Criminal Court. Priya Urs, Oxford University Press. © Priya Urs 2024.
DOI: 10.1093/oso/9780198882954.003.0001

2 GRAVITY AT THE INTERNATIONAL CRIMINAL COURT

international community as a whole must not go unpunished' and emphasizes the need to 'put an end to impunity for the perpetrators of these crimes'.[6] This might be taken to imply 'a strong imperative' on the part of the Court to investigate and prosecute all crimes within its jurisdiction.[7] Such an imperative would also find support in a principled commitment to the equal application of the law.[8]

Yet preambular commitments notwithstanding, elsewhere the Rome Statute suggests that the investigation and prosecution of crimes within the jurisdiction of the Court represent exercises in selectivity. Relevant provisions of the Statute confer on the Prosecutor of the Court the discretion to choose whether to investigate and whether to prosecute.[9] That the ICC's jurisdiction is not restricted to one 'situation' in which crimes have been committed,[10] as has been the case with other international criminal courts, such as those established in relation to the situations in the former Yugoslavia, Rwanda, and Sierra Leone, further suggests a need for discrimination.[11] Speaking more generally, it is accepted in both the common law and the civil law traditions, in one form or another, that the exercise

---

[6] Paras 4–5, preamble, Rome Statute of the International Criminal Court 1998 (Rome Statute). It was ultimately agreed that the crimes within the jurisdiction of the Court would comprise genocide, crimes against humanity, war crimes, and the crime of aggression. See art 5, Rome Statute. The exclusion of treaty-based crimes during the work of the Preparatory Committee on the Establishment of an International Criminal Court (Preparatory Committee) resulted in part from concerns among some delegations that their inclusion would have the undesirable effect of 'overburdening the limited financial and personnel resources of the court or trivializing its role and functions'. UN General Assembly, 'Report of the Preparatory Committee on the Establishment of an International Criminal Court, Volume I (Proceedings of the Preparatory Committee During March–April and August 1996)' (13 September 1996) UN Doc A/51/22 (hereafter 'Preparatory Committee Report 1996') 25 para 103. See also draft art 20, International Law Commission's Draft Statute for an International Criminal Court 1994; UN General Assembly, 'Report of the Ad Hoc Committee on the Establishment of an International Criminal Court, General Assembly, Fiftieth Session' (6 September 1995) UN Doc A/50/22 (hereafter 'Ad Hoc Committee Report 1995') paras 38, 54–56, 81; H von Hebel and D Robinson, 'Crimes within the Jurisdiction of the Court' in RS Lee (ed), *The International Criminal Court: The Making of the Rome Statute—Issues, Negotiations, Results* (Kluwer Law International 1999) 80–81.

[7] P Webb, 'The ICC Prosecutor's Discretion Not to Proceed in the "Interests of Justice"' (2005) 50 Criminal Law Quarterly 305, 307. See also ibid 307–09.

[8] R Cryer, *Prosecuting International Crimes: Selectivity and the International Criminal Law Regime* (CUP 2005) 193. The equal application of the law is in turn a manifestation of a commitment to the rule of law. ibid 194–95.

[9] The Statute recognizes the limited capacity of the ICC to investigate, if not also to prosecute, all allegations of criminality. G Turone, 'Powers and Duties of the Prosecutor' in A Cassese, P Gaeta, and JRWD Jones (eds), *The Rome Statute of the International Criminal Court* (OUP 2002) 1174; AM Danner, 'Enhancing the Legitimacy and Accountability of Prosecutorial Discretion at the International Criminal Court' (2003) 97 American Journal of International Law 510, 518–19; M Brubacher, 'Prosecutorial Discretion within the International Criminal Court' (2004) 2 Journal of International Criminal Justice 71, 75. For some commentators, the ICC's capacity constraints also imply that the Prosecutor's obligation to 'investigate incriminating and exonerating circumstances equally' cannot be carried out in relation to all potential prosecutions. See art 54(1)(*a*), Rome Statute. Danner, ibid 519; Brubacher, ibid 76.

[10] For the definition of a 'situation' at the ICC, see Section 1.6.1.

[11] Brubacher (n 9) 76; L Moreno Ocampo, 'The International Criminal Court in Motion' in C Stahn and G Sluiter (eds), *The Emerging Practice of the International Criminal Court* (Martinus Nijhoff 2009) 14.

INTRODUCTION 3

of prosecutorial power involves the exercise of discretion,[12] thereby 'promot[ing] fairness, efficiency and transparency' in the allocation of limited resources.[13] In light of the considerable expectations that have been placed on the ICC, this selectivity is frequently described as 'the Achilles' heel' of the Court,[14] and it is in the light of these expectations that the Court's various forms of selectivity are scrutinized.

Scrutiny to date of the selection of investigations and prosecutions at the ICC has been overwhelmingly critical of prosecutorial decisions. Commentators from various quarters have levelled allegations of inconsistency, bias, or politicization on the part of the Prosecutor[15] or the favouring of 'institutional interests'[16] over 'geopolitical egalitarianism in who or what is prosecuted'[17]—leaving only 'the illusion of universality'.[18] They have questioned, amongst other things, the investigation of some situations and not others, the prosecution of certain crimes and cases to the exclusion of others,[19] and the near exclusive focus on the alleged perpetrators of crimes belonging to non-state groups as the price of securing the cooperation of states in investigations and prosecutions.[20]

Against this backdrop, the question how to justify, in a manner faithful to the Rome Statute and its supporting instruments, the selectivity of investigations and prosecutions at the Court has been posed. This question, among others, was taken up, at the request of the ICC's Assembly of States Parties, by the Independent Expert Review of the International Criminal Court and the Rome Statute System (Independent Expert Review), which published its report in 2020. The report, noting the scarce investigative and prosecutorial resources at the disposal of the Prosecutor, suggested the use of the Rome Statute's admissibility criterion of

---

[12] See K Ligeti, 'The Place of the Prosecutor in Common Law and Civil Law Jurisdictions' in DK Brown and others (eds), *The Oxford Handbook of Criminal Process* (OUP 2019) 150–53; Cryer (n 8) 192, footnotes 5–6; Turone (n 9) 1174–75; deGuzman and Schabas (n 2) 157–63.

[13] Webb (n 7) 307.

[14] C Stahn and G Sluiter, 'From "Infancy" to Emancipation? A Review of the Court's First Practice' in C Stahn and G Sluiter (eds), *The Emerging Practice of the International Criminal Court* (Martinus Nijhoff 2009) 5. See also W Burke-White, 'Proactive Complementarity: The International Criminal Court and National Courts in the Rome System of International Justice' (2008) 49 Harvard International Law Journal 53, 53–54.

[15] See eg SMH Nouwen and WG Werner, 'Doing Justice to the Political: The International Criminal Court in Uganda and Sudan' (2011) 21 European Journal of International Law 941; CN Ezennia, 'The *Modus Operandi* of the International Criminal Court System: An Impartial or a Selective Justice Regime?' (2016) 16 International Criminal Law Review 448; CC Jalloh, 'Regionalizing International Criminal Law?' (2009) 9 International Criminal Law Review 445, 452; M Kersten, 'Taking the Opportunity: Prosecutorial Opportunism and the International Criminal Court' in M deGuzman and V Oosterveld (eds), *The Elgar Companion to the International Criminal Court* (Edward Elgar 2020) 181–82.

[16] Kersten (n 15) 182.

[17] J Reynolds and S Xavier, ' "The Dark Corners of the World": TWAIL and International Criminal Justice' (2016) 14 Journal of International Criminal Justice 959, 963.

[18] ibid 960.

[19] For definitions of a 'situation' and a 'case', see Section 1.6.

[20] See A Kiyani, 'Group-Based Differentiation and Local Repression: The Custom and Curse of Selectivity' (2016) 14 Journal of International Criminal Justice 939.

4   GRAVITY AT THE INTERNATIONAL CRIMINAL COURT

the sufficient gravity of a case[21] to facilitate the allocation of these resources and thereby to justify the Prosecutor's decisions whether to investigate and whether to prosecute.[22] As a contribution to the ongoing debate, this book examines the application and function of the admissibility criterion of sufficient gravity in the selection of investigations and prosecutions at the Court.

The gravity or seriousness of a crime or case features in various legal frameworks, at both the international and national levels, for the investigation and prosecution of international crimes. It serves as a basis on which to divide the task of prosecuting such crimes as between international and national criminal courts and, at the national level, as between ordinary and specialized criminal courts. This demarcation function is reflected in the circumscribed jurisdiction *ratione materiae* of international criminal courts, which may be limited to 'serious violations of international humanitarian law'[23] or, in the case of the ICC, to 'the most serious crimes of concern to the international community as a whole'.[24] At the national level, the gravity of the crimes is commonly used to draw the line between the respective mandates of ordinary and specialized criminal courts, as with the recently constituted Kosovo Specialist Chambers,[25] and between courts and truth and reconciliation mechanisms, as was the case in post-independence East Timor.[26] In addition to defining the jurisdiction *ratione materiae* of different courts, the allocative function served by the gravity of a crime or case may be reflected in referral procedures that use such criteria to apportion the investigation and prosecution of

---

[21] See art 17(1)(*d*), Rome Statute.

[22] See Final Report of the Independent Expert Review of the International Criminal Court and the Rome Statute System, 30 September 2020 (hereafter 'Independent Expert Review') paras 647, 650, R227.

[23] See art 1, Statute of the International Criminal Tribunal for the former Yugoslavia 1993; art 1, Statute of the International Criminal Tribunal for Rwanda 1994; art 1(1), Statute of the Special Court for Sierra Leone 2002.

[24] art 5, Rome Statute. This is not to say that the same conduct cannot constitute both an international crime and an ordinary crime under national law. SMH Nouwen and DA Lewis, 'Jurisdictional Arrangements and International Criminal Procedure' in G Sluiter and others (eds), *International Criminal Procedure: Principles and Rules* (OUP 2013) 116.

[25] The jurisdiction *ratione materiae* of the Kosovo Specialist Chambers includes crimes against humanity, war crimes, and 'other crimes under Kosovo law'. See arts 13–15, Law No 05/L-053 on Specialist Chambers and Specialist Prosecutor's Office (3 August 2015). Additionally, the Chamber has the power to 'order the transfer of proceedings within its jurisdiction from any other prosecutor or any other court in the territory of Kosovo'. art 10(2), Law No 05/L-053 on Specialist Chambers and Specialist Prosecutor's Office (3 August 2015).

[26] The special panels in the District Court of Dili in East Timor had exclusive jurisdiction over 'serious criminal offences', which were defined to include genocide, war crimes, crimes against humanity, murder, sexual offences, and torture. In contrast, the Commission for Reception, Truth and Reconciliation in East Timor was responsible for the reintegration of individuals responsible for 'the commission of minor criminal offences and other harmful acts'. Section 3(1)(*h*), United Nations Transitional Administration in East Timor (UNTAET) Regulation No 2001/10 (13 July 2001). Like the Specialist Chambers in Kosovo, the special panels in the District Court of Dili enjoyed the power to require other panels or courts in East Timor to defer to them in the prosecution of a case. Section 1, UNTAET Regulation No 2000/15 (6 June 2000). The Commission for Reception, Truth and Reconciliation in East Timor could also refer 'matters of serious criminal offences' to 'the appropriate authority', presumably the special panels. Section 38(1), UNTAET Regulation No 2001/10 (13 July 2001).

INTRODUCTION 5

international crimes as between the international and national levels. The completion strategy of the International Criminal Tribunal for the former Yugoslavia, for example, adopted with a view to the efficiency of the Tribunal's operation,[27] provided for the referral of cases to relevant national jurisdictions on the basis of 'the gravity of the crimes charged'.[28] Conversely, a national criminal court was obliged to defer a case to the International Criminal Tribunal for Rwanda if '[t]he seriousness of the offences' warranted it.[29]

In the context of the ICC, the criterion of the sufficient gravity of a case, specified in Article 17(1)(*d*) of the Rome Statute, sits alongside the complementarity criteria in Article 17(1)(*a*)–(*c*) to determine the admissibility of a case before the Court. The complementarity criteria stipulate conditions for the inadmissibility of a case at the ICC where investigations or prosecutions have been undertaken or are being undertaken by a state with jurisdiction over the case, including where a trial has concluded. Article 17(1)(*d*) obliges the Court to determine that a case is inadmissible where '[t]he case is not of sufficient gravity to justify further action by the Court'. It is the application and function of the admissibility criterion of the sufficient gravity of a case in the selection of investigations and prosecutions by the Prosecutor of the ICC which constitutes the focus of this book.

1.2 The Gravity Criterion for Admissibility in Article 17(1)(*d*) of the Rome Statute

This book was written against the backdrop of the ongoing debate as to how to justify, in legal terms, the selectivity of investigations and prosecutions at the ICC. In this light, it addresses the question of how the admissibility criterion of 'sufficient gravity' specified in Article 17(1)(*d*) of the Rome Statute is to be applied in the context of the Prosecutor's decisions whether to investigate and whether to prosecute. The question is answered in two ways. First, the book ascertains how the gravity criterion has been applied in the Court's twenty years of practice. On the basis of this analysis, it proposes a more coherent and persuasive application of the criterion as part of the Prosecutor's respective decisions whether to investigate and to prosecute. Second, the book clarifies the respective roles of the Prosecutor and the relevant Chambers of the Court during admissibility proceedings to arrive at an appropriate balance in this context between prosecutorial discretion and

---

[27] O Bekou, 'Rule 11 BIS: An Examination of the Process of Referrals to Nationals Courts in ICTY Jurisprudence' (2009) 33 Fordham International Law Journal 723, 726; S Williams, 'ICTY Referrals to National Jurisdictions: A Fair Trial or a Fair Price?' (2006) 17 Criminal Law Forum 177, 178.

[28] Rule 11bis(C), Rules of Procedure and Evidence of the International Criminal Tribunal for the former Yugoslavia 1994 (as amended in 2009).

[29] Rule 9(ii)(*a*), Rules of Procedure and Evidence of the International Criminal Tribunal for Rwanda 1995 (as amended in 1997).

6 GRAVITY AT THE INTERNATIONAL CRIMINAL COURT

judicial oversight. The answer to the question of the application of the gravity criterion bears in turn on the question of its function in the context of the Prosecutor's decisions whether to investigate and whether to prosecute, including any role for the gravity criterion in justifying the selectivity of investigations and prosecutions at the Court.

The Rome Statute provides for various assessments of admissibility as part of the respective decisions by the Prosecutor whether to investigate a situation, encompassing multiple potential cases,[30] and to prosecute an individual case.[31] In accordance with Article 53(1)(*b*) of the Statute, the Prosecutor is required to undertake an assessment of admissibility in relation to a situation when deciding whether to initiate an investigation into it. Where, under Article 15 of the Statute, the Prosecutor decides to initiate an investigation into a situation *proprio motu*, Pre-Trial Chamber authorization is required, as provided for in Article 15(3) and (4), the latter of which requires the Pre-Trial Chamber to review the Prosecutor's admissibility assessment. Pursuant to Article 53(2)(*b*), the Prosecutor may decide, upon investigation, not to proceed with a prosecution on the basis that the case is inadmissible. Conversely, the admissibility of a case which has been selected by the Prosecutor for prosecution may be determined by the Pre-Trial Chamber or the Trial Chamber, whether *proprio motu*, in accordance with Article 19(1), upon a challenge by any of the parties listed under Article 19(2), in accordance with the same provision, or at the request of the Prosecutor himself or herself, in accordance with Article 19(3). Where a situation has been referred to the Prosecutor by a state party or the United Nations (UN) Security Council, any decision by the Prosecutor not to initiate an investigation or not to prosecute a case, including on the basis of inadmissibility, may be reviewed by the Pre-Trial Chamber at the request of the referring state or the Council, as provided for in Article 53(3)(*a*).

All these assessments of admissibility are conducted by reference to the admissibility criteria specified in Article 17 of the Rome Statute. These include the criterion in Article 17(1)(*d*) of the sufficient gravity of a case.[32] In the context of the admissibility of a situation, the reference in Article 17(1)(*d*) to a 'case' is to the

---

[30] For the definition of a 'situation', see Section 1.6.1.

[31] For the definition of a 'case', see Section 1.6.2.

[32] Exceptionally, the Pre-Trial Chamber's assessment of admissibility under Article 18(2) and the Pre-Trial Chamber or the Trial Chamber's assessment of admissibility under Article 19(2)(*b*) of the Rome Statute do not include a consideration of gravity. Under Article 18(2), the Pre-Trial Chamber may, at the request of the Prosecutor, determine the admissibility of the situation in the event that a state informs the Chamber that it is investigating or has investigated crimes in relation to the situation in question. Rule 55(2) of the Court's Rules of Procedure and Evidence 1998 provides that the assessment of admissibility under Article 18(2) is made by reference to the criteria in Article 17. Since, however, Article 18(2) specifically addresses ongoing or completed investigations at the national level, it excludes considerations of gravity. The reference in Rule 55(2) is only to Article 17(1)(*a*), (*b*), and perhaps also (*c*). Similarly, under Article 19(2)(*b*), a state with jurisdiction over a case may challenge its admissibility only 'on the ground that it is investigating or prosecuting the case or has investigated or prosecuted' it.

multiple potential cases arising out of the situation.[33] In the context of the admissibility of a case, the reference is to that individual case.

The text of Article 17(1)(*d*) of the Rome Statute provides no more than that a case shall be inadmissible where it is 'not of sufficient gravity to justify further action by the Court'. There is little guidance in the Statute or its supporting instruments as to the application of this open-textured[34] criterion in the context of the Prosecutor's decisions whether to investigate and whether to prosecute. The open texture of Article 17(1)(*d*) is the inevitable result of the limitations of the use of such terms as 'sufficient' and 'gravity'. No doubt 'there is a limit, inherent in the nature of language, to the guidance which general language can provide'.[35] The consequence of such drafting, whether deliberate or otherwise, is that the 'discretion ... left ... by language may be very wide', so much so that the application of the provision, 'even though it may not be arbitrary or irrational, is in effect a choice'.[36] In short, the application of the gravity criterion requires that 'something in the nature of a choice between open alternatives must be made'.[37]

As a consequence of the open-textured nature of Article 17(1)(*d*), which calls for the exercise of discretion, the application of the gravity criterion may give rise to a lack of consistency and attendant predictability in the assessment of admissibility, as demonstrated by the practice of the Court to date.[38] In the absence of statutory guidance, moreover, the application by the Prosecutor of the gravity criterion as part of the decisions whether to investigate and prosecute respectively may expose the Prosecutor to allegations of arbitrariness or, worse, abuse of discretion.[39] In light especially of the international crimes at issue, '[e]ach choice is open

---

[33] *Situation in Kenya*, ICC-01/09-19, Pre-Trial Chamber II, Decision Pursuant to Article 15 of the Rome Statute on the Authorization on an Investigation into the Situation in the Republic of Kenya, 31 March 2010, para 48.

[34] For the idea of the 'open texture' of legal language, see HLA Hart, *The Concept of Law* (3rd edn, OUP 2012) 124–36. As Hart explains, all rules will 'at some point ... prove indeterminate; they will have what has been termed an *open texture*'. ibid 128.

[35] ibid 126. On 'linguistic indeterminacy' in international law, see E Shirlow, *Judging at the Interface: Deference to State Decision-Making Authority in International Adjudication* (Cambridge University Press 2021) 249–50.

[36] Hart (n 34) 127. On the deliberate use of open-textured legal language, or 'vagueness', see T Endicott, 'The Value of Vagueness' in A Marmor and S Soames (eds), *Philosophical Foundations of Language in the Law* (OUP 2011).

[37] ibid. That the application of the gravity criterion for admissibility involves the exercise of discretion was acknowledged in the report of the Independent Expert Review. Independent Expert Review (n 22) para 649.

[38] As remarked by the Defence in a recent case, 'the Court has yet to enunciate clearly what th[e] [gravity] threshold is'. *Prosecutor v Al Hassan*, ICC-01/12-01/18-475-Red, Defence, Public Redacted Version of Appeal of the Pre-Trial Chamber's 'Décision relative à l'exception d'irrecevabilité pour insuffisance de gravité de l'affaire soulevée par la défence' (ICC-01/12-01/18-459), 21 October 2019, para 2.

[39] S Fernández de Gurmendi, 'The Role of the International Prosecutor' in RS Lee (ed), *The International Criminal Court: The Making of the Rome Statute—Issues, Negotiations, Results* (Kluwer Law International 1999) 181–82; Danner (n 9) 521; G-JA Knoops, 'The Legitimacy of Initiating Contemporary International Criminal Proceedings: Rethinking Prosecutorial Discretionary Powers from a Legal, Ethical and Political Perspective' (2004) 1 International Studies Journal 1, 10.

8 GRAVITY AT THE INTERNATIONAL CRIMINAL COURT

to controversy and claims of politicization.[40] Conversely, any argument for consistency and predictability in the assessment of the gravity of a case in the specific context of the Prosecutor's respective decisions whether to investigate and to prosecute must be mindful of the balance to be struck between prosecutorial accountability and prosecutorial independence.[41] As one commentator observes, '[p]ure discretion is too unpredictable and easily politicized', while complete judicial control of its exercise compromises the Statute's carefully negotiated commitment to prosecutorial independence.[42] In short, the appropriate balance between prosecutorial discretion and judicial oversight calls for context-specific analysis.

Only limited evidence as to the application and function of the admissibility criterion of sufficient gravity in Article 17(1)(*d*) can be found in the drafting history of the Rome Statute. This drafting history includes the draft statute for an

---

[40] D Robinson, 'Inescapable Dyads: Why the International Criminal Court Cannot Win' (2015) 28 Leiden Journal of International Law 323, 333. See also F Cowell, 'Inherent Imperialism: Understanding the Legal Roots of Anti-Imperialist Criticism of the International Criminal Court' (2017) 15 Journal of International Criminal Justice 667, 683–84; A Kiyani, 'Afghanistan and the Surrender of International Criminal Justice' TWAIL Review 2019, https://twailr.com/wp-content/uploads/2019/09/Kiyani-Afghanistan-the-Surrender-of-International-Criminal-Justice.pdf, accessed 18 March 2023; Nouwen and Werner (n 15) 951; Ezennia (n 15) 460.

[41] During the drafting of the Rome Statute, states disagreed on the appropriate scope of the Prosecutor's discretionary powers until the very last minute. On one side were those states that, owing to a fear of the politicization of the Court through investigations initiated only on the referral of a state party or the Security Council and with a view to guaranteeing prosecutorial independence, favoured the conferral on the Prosecutor of a power to initiate investigations *proprio motu*. On the other side were those states keen to avoid enabling a politicized prosecutor, a 'lone ranger running wild'. Fernández de Gurmendi (n 39) 181. The power to initiate an investigation *proprio motu* was eventually included in the Statute but was subjected to judicial oversight. In the words of one commentator, '[t]he debate over the role of the Prosecutor's *proprio motu* powers was essentially a fight over the proper scope of the Prosecutor's discretion'. Danner (n 9) 518. See further Fernández de Gurmendi (n 39) 183–84; M Bergsmo, J Pejic, and D Zhu, 'Article 15' in O Triffterer and K Ambos (eds), *Rome Statute of the International Criminal Court: A Commentary* (3rd edn, CH Beck 2016) 726–9; Brubacher (n 9) 72–74; D Scheffer, 'False Alarm about the *Proprio Motu* Prosecutor' in M Minow, C Cora True-Frost, and A Whiting (eds), *The First Global Prosecutor* (University of Michigan Press 2015).

[42] Webb (n 7) 307. The issue was debated at the UN Diplomatic Conference of Plenipotentiaries on the Establishment of an International Criminal Court (Rome Conference) at which the Rome Statute was eventually adopted. Generally speaking, delegations from the common law tradition feared that prosecutorial independence would be compromised by judicial oversight, while delegations from the civil law tradition countered that justice and the avoidance of abuse of prosecutorial power called for 'at least some degree of judicial supervision'. Guariglia (n 4) 228. In 2020, one Pre-Trial Chamber remarked that, notwithstanding the jurisprudence of the Appeals Chamber on the issue, it remained unclear 'whether and to what extent it may request the Prosecutor to correct errors' relating to her assessment of gravity. *Situation on the Registered Vessels of the Union of the Comoros, the Hellenic Republic and the Kingdom of Cambodia*, ICC-01/13-111, Pre-Trial Chamber I, Decision on the 'Application for Judicial Review by the Government of the Comoros', 16 September 2020, para 110. In the absence of agreement as to a suitable balance between prosecutorial independence and prosecutorial accountability, the tendency within the Office of the Prosecutor and in existing scholarship has been to favour the elaboration by the Prosecutor of *ex ante* guidelines for the application of the relevant criteria, including the criteria of independence, impartiality, and objectivity articulated by the Office of the Prosecutor. See eg Policy Paper on Preliminary Examinations, Office of the Prosecutor, 2013, 7–8; Policy Paper on Case Selection and Prioritisation, Office of the Prosecutor, 2016, 7–9. See also Danner (n 9); Webb (n 7) 317; JA Goldston, 'More Candour about Criteria' (2010) 8 Journal of International Criminal Justice 383; deGuzman and Schabas (n 2) 169.

INTRODUCTION 9

international criminal court adopted by the International Law Commission (ILC) in 1994, which doubtless had an influence on subsequent developments.[43] The earliest articulation of what would eventually become Article 17(1)(*d*) of the Rome Statute was draft article 35(*c*) of the ILC's 1994 draft statute, which would have rendered a case inadmissible on the basis that the crime was 'not of such gravity to justify further action by the Court'.[44] The gravity of the crime had already acquired a certain significance, however, in the proposed court's jurisdiction *ratione materiae*,[45] leading some members of the Commission,[46] as well as some states,[47] to question the need for its additional consideration in the context of admissibility.[48] That the Commission nevertheless saw fit to restrain the exercise of the Court's jurisdiction through a gravity-based criterion of admissibility suggests that the limited scope of the court's jurisdiction *ratione materiae* was perceived as an insufficient filter, including by states in the UN General Assembly.[49] Indeed, it was thought that 'the court might be swamped by peripheral complaints involving minor offenders, possibly in situations where the major offenders were going free'.[50] Since,

[43] See R O'Keefe, 'The ILC's Contribution to International Criminal Law' (2006) 49 German Yearbook of International Law 201, 234–52.

[44] The term 'sufficient gravity', which appears in Article 17(1)(*d*) of the Rome Statute, appeared in the commentary to the ILC's 1994 draft statute. ILC, 'Report of the International Law Commission on the Work of Its Forty-Sixth Session' (2 May–22 July 1994) UN Doc A/49/10 (hereafter 'ILC Report 1994') 52.

[45] The inclusion in the ILC's 1994 draft statute of jurisdiction *ratione materiae* over treaty-based crimes was only to the extent that the latter constituted 'exceptionally serious crimes of international concern'. Draft art 20(*e*), Draft Statute for an International Criminal Court 1994. See also ILC, 'Summary Records of the Meetings of the Forty-Sixth Session' (2 May–22 July 1994) UN Doc A/CN.4/SER.A/1994 (hereafter 'ILC Summary Records 1994') 226–7, para 40.

[46] See ILC Report 1994 (n 44) 52.

[47] See ILC, 'Report of the International Law Commission on the Work of Its Forty-Sixth Session (1994), Topical Summary of the Discussion Held in the Sixth Committee of the General Assembly during Its Forty-Ninth Session Prepared by the Secretariat, Addendum' (22 February 1995), UN Doc A/CN.4/464/Add.1 (hereafter 'ILC Topical Summary 1995') para 147; Ad Hoc Committee Report 1995 (n 6) para 162; Preparatory Committee Report 1996 (n 6) para 169; UN General Assembly, 'United Nations Diplomatic Conference of Plenipotentiaries on the Establishment of an International Criminal Court, Report of the Preparatory Committee on the Establishment of an International Criminal Court, Addendum' (14 April 1998) UN Doc A/CONF.183/2/Add.1, 40–41.

[48] For an overview, see S SáCouto and K Cleary, 'The Gravity Threshold of the International Criminal Court' (2007) 23(5) American University International Law Review 807, 817–22. See also H Olásolo, *The Triggering Procedure of the International Criminal Court* (Martinus Nijhoff 2005) 183–84.

[49] Draft article 35, which included the gravity criterion for admissibility, was incorporated into the ILC's 1994 draft statute to 'respond[] to the concerns expressed by many States that the court might exercise jurisdiction in cases that were not of sufficient international significance'. ILC Summary Records 1994 (n 45) 193. This was because, notwithstanding the limits of the court's jurisdiction *ratione materiae*, 'there could still be cases in which no action was warranted'. J Crawford, 'The ILC Adopts a Statute for an International Criminal Court' (1995) 89 American Journal of International Law 404, 413.

[50] ILC Summary Records 1994 (n 45) 9. More general concerns about the resource implications of the Court's activities were subsequently expressed in the Sixth Committee of the UN General Assembly and in the Ad Hoc Committee on the Establishment of an International Criminal Court (Ad Hoc Committee). One representative in the Sixth Committee cautioned that 'the demands on scarce resources for prosecutions and especially for investigations were dependent on the scope and reach of the Court's jurisdiction'. ILC Topical Summary 1995 (n 47) para 15. See ibid para 14. In the Ad Hoc Committee, 'some representatives ... drew attention to the far-reaching legal and financial implications of the project'. Ad Hoc Committee Report 1995 (n 6) para 12.

10   GRAVITY AT THE INTERNATIONAL CRIMINAL COURT

according to some members of the Commission, 'the circumstances of particular cases could vary widely',[51] the consideration of the gravity of the crime as an admissibility criterion would 'ensur[e] that the court would deal solely with the most serious crimes' and 'adapt its caseload to the resources available'.[52] Accordingly, it was not only in the conferral of jurisdiction but also in its exercise that the ILC laid emphasis on 'the limited function of the Court, which [was] intended to exercise jurisdiction only over the most serious crimes of concern to the international community as a whole'.[53] Despite the subsequent substantial narrowing of the Court's jurisdiction *ratione materiae* in what would eventually become the Rome Statute, the admissibility criterion of the gravity of a case, as opposed to a crime, was retained through the drafting discussions in the Ad Hoc Committee on the Establishment of an International Criminal Court (Ad Hoc Committee) and the Preparatory Committee on the Establishment of an International Criminal Court (Preparatory Committee) constituted by the General Assembly.[54] In the Preparatory Committee, the need for 'a minimum threshold, a screening mechanism or a judicial filter to distinguish between well-founded complaints of sufficiently serious crimes and frivolous or vexatious complaints' was affirmed.[55] The text of the Preparatory Committee's draft article 15(*d*), which was reproduced verbatim in Article 17(1)(*d*) of the Rome Statute, made a finding of inadmissibility where the case was not of 'sufficient gravity' mandatory.[56] At the UN Diplomatic Conference of Plenipotentiaries on the Establishment of an International Criminal Court (Rome Conference), the suggestion that greater clarity was needed as to the application of this admissibility criterion of sufficient gravity went unheeded.[57]

---

[51] ILC Report 1994 (n 44) 52.

[52] ibid 22.

[53] Crawford (n 49) 409.

[54] Draft article 35(*c*) of the ILC's draft referred to the gravity of a 'crime', while the Preparatory Committee's draft article 15(1)(*d*) and Article 17(1)(*d*) of the Rome Statute refer to the gravity of a 'case'. On the crimes ultimately excluded from the jurisdiction of the ICC, see note 6.

[55] Preparatory Committee Report 1996 (n 6) para 224.

[56] UN General Assembly, 'United Nations Diplomatic Conference of Plenipotentiaries on the Establishment of an International Criminal Court, Volume II' (15 June–17 July 1998) UN Doc A/CONF.183/13 (hereafter 'Rome Conference II') 40–41. Even earlier, in the Ad Hoc Committee, 'the view was widely held that there should be no discretion for the court to declare a case admissible if the grounds for inadmissibility had been duly made out'. Ad Hoc Committee Report 1995 (n 6) para 159. See also ibid para 42. In contrast, the ILC's draft article 35 would not have obliged the court to declare inadmissible a case which did not satisfy the gravity criterion. O'Keefe, *The ILC's Contribution to International Criminal Law* (n 43) 248.

[57] See eg Rome Conference II (n 56) 215, para 29. The point had also been raised in the Ad Hoc Committee by the US representative, who suggested that the draft statute, including draft article 35(*c*), 'lack[ed] the specificity or emphasis required to avoid burdening the international criminal court with individual crimes that do not satisfy the requirement for seriousness'. UN Secretary-General, 'Comments Received Pursuant to Paragraph 4 of General Assembly Resolution 49/53 on the Establishment of an International Criminal Court, Report of the Secretary-General' (31 March 1995) UN Doc A/AC.244/1/Add.2, 13, paras 24–5. As one commentator has remarked, '[s]tates could agree that the ICC's work should be limited to "the most serious crimes ..." without having to agree on what that include[d]'. MM deGuzman, 'Gravity Rhetoric: The Good, the Bad, and the "Political" ' (2013) American Society of International Law Proceedings 421, 422.

INTRODUCTION 11

In spite of the limited attention it received at the Rome Conference, there is little doubt now that '[t]he term "gravity" has come to life and [has] turned into one of the central themes for the selection of situations and cases'.[58] This is not to say that the practice of the Court has brought any clarity to the application of the admissibility criterion of the sufficient gravity of a case eventually specified in Article 17(1)(*d*) of the Rome Statute. The same goes for the criterion's purpose. The Appeals Chamber considers the purpose of the gravity criterion in Article 17(1)(*d*) of the Rome Statute—whether applied by the Prosecutor when deciding whether to investigate and to prosecute respectively or by the Pre-Trial or Trial Chamber when determining the admissibility of a case—to be to exclude cases 'of marginal gravity only'.[59] The Independent Expert Review constituted by the ICC Assembly of States Parties, however, recommended the application by the Prosecutor of a 'higher threshold' of gravity than that articulated by the Appeals Chamber, with a view to the judicious allocation of scarce investigative and prosecutorial resources.[60] As the Court noted in its response to the Independent Expert Review: '[t]he gravity threshold issue is far more complex and difficult of solution than may be immediately apparent'.[61]

In its final analysis, this book argues for a recalibration of the application and a reconsideration of the function of the gravity criterion in the context of the Prosecutor's decisions whether to investigate and whether to prosecute. It finds that the function of the gravity criterion in Article 17(1)(*d*) of the Rome Statute is not only the exclusion of 'marginal cases' from investigation and prosecution, as is suggested by the Court.[62] In reality, the application of the gravity criterion in Article 17(1)(*d*) facilitates the allocation of investigative and prosecutorial resources by the Prosecutor and offers the most convincing basis on which to justify the selectivity of investigations and prosecutions at the ICC.

1.3 Methodology

The book uses a doctrinal methodology to address the question of the application and function of the admissibility criterion of the sufficient gravity of a case in the selection of investigations and prosecutions by the Prosecutor.[63] It proceeds on the

---

[58] Stahn and Sluiter (n 14) 3.

[59] *Prosecutor v Al Hassan*, ICC-01/12-01/18-601-Red, Appeals Chamber, Judgment on the Appeal of Mr Al Hassan Against the Decision of Pre-Trial Chamber I Entitled 'Décision relative a l'exception d'irrecevabilité pour insufficiance de gravité de l'affaire soulevée par la défense', 19 February 2020 (hereafter '*Al Hassan*, Appeals Chamber Decision 2020') para 53.

[60] Independent Expert Review (n 22) para R227. See ibid paras 647, 650.

[61] Overall Response to the Independent Expert Review (n 1) para 413.

[62] *Al Hassan*, Appeals Chamber Decision 2020 (n 59) para 53.

[63] As one commentator has remarked, the Rome Statute's admissibility provisions leave 'some of the most critical and disputed questions to be resolved though [*sic*] judicial determination and prosecutorial discretion'. AKA Greenawalt, 'Admissibility as a Theory of International Criminal Law' in MM deGuzman and V Oosterveld (eds), *The Elgar Companion to the International Criminal Court* (Edward

12   GRAVITY AT THE INTERNATIONAL CRIMINAL COURT

basis that the question is chiefly one of the application, rather than the interpretation, of Article 17(1)(*d*) of the Rome Statute. Very little is made in the existing scholarship of the distinction between the 'interpretation' and the 'application' of treaty provisions.[64] The practical difference is a fine one: '[l]a première fixe le sens et le contenu de la norme, la deuxième en tire les conséquences en visant la mis on œuvre pratique'.[65] In other words, interpretation 'refers to a mental process' whereby 'the meaning of a treaty, including of one or more of its provisions, is clarified',[66] while application is the legal characterization of facts in light of the meaning of the provision.[67] Where 'the meaning of the treaty [provision] is clear', therefore, it is not the interpretation but the application of the provision that is in question.[68] Application is the process of 'determining the consequences which the rule attaches to the occurrence of a given fact' or 'the action of bringing about the consequences which, according to a rule, should follow a fact'.[69]

When it comes to Article 17(1)(*d*) of the Rome Statute, the relevant question is one of the application of law to facts.[70] Customary and conventional rules on the interpretation of treaties may assist with the clarification of the meaning of the provision, that is, in declaring what it means in general terms for a case to be 'of sufficient gravity' to justify further action by the Court. Limited support is lent by the rules of treaty interpretation, however, when asking whether a particular case is of sufficient gravity.[71] These rules are not especially helpful in determining the application to facts of open-textured legal language, as with the term 'sufficient gravity'.[72] Simply put, '[t]here cannot be a rule to tell us how to apply every rule: sooner or later one simply makes a judgment'.[73] That being said, some of the

---

Elgar 2020) 63. Another commentator observes more generally that '[the] lion's share of the normative content of [international criminal law] is an outgrowth of judicial law-ascertainment'. S Vasiliev, 'The Making of International Criminal Law' in C Brölmann and Y Radi (eds), *Research Handbook on the Theory and Practice of International Lawmaking* (Edward Elgar 2016) 386.

[64] See M Bos, *A Methodology of International Law* (North-Holland 1984) 110–14; F Berman, 'International Treaties and British Statutes' (2005) 26(1) Statute Law Review 1, 10.

[65] 'The former sets the meaning and content of the norm, the latter draws consequences in relation to its practical implementation' (author's translation). R Kolb, *Interprétation et Création du Droit International* (Editions Bruylant 2006) 26.

[66] ILC, 'Text of the Draft Conclusions on Subsequent Agreements and Subsequent Practice in Relation to the Interpretation of Treaties with Commentaries' (2018) UN Doc A/73/10, 43, para 3.

[67] R O'Keefe, 'Interpretation versus Application of Treaties: A Question of Character' (forthcoming).

[68] A McNair, *The Law of Treaties* (OUP 1986) 365.

[69] *Case Concerning the Factory at Chorzow (Claim for Indemnity) (Germany v Poland)* (Jurisdiction) PCIJ Rep Series A No 9 (1927) 39 (Dissenting Opinion of Judge Ehrlich).

[70] Relevant Chambers of the ICC have, for their part, characterized much of the task of application as the 'interpretation' of Article 17(1)(*d*) of the Statute. *Situation in the Democratic Republic of the Congo*, ICC-01/04-02/06-20-Anx2, Pre-Trial Chamber I, Decision on Prosecutor's Application for Warrants of Arrest, Article 58, 10 February 2006 (hereafter '*Situation in the Democratic Republic of the Congo*, Pre-Trial Chamber Decision 2006') paras 44–55.

[71] 'Canons of "interpretation" cannot eliminate, though they can diminish, these uncertainties.' Hart (n 34) 126.

[72] O'Keefe, *Interpretation versus Application of Treaties: A Question of Character* (n 67).

[73] J Waldron, 'Vagueness in Law and Language: Some Philosophical Issues' (1994) 82 California Law Review 509, 511. As Waldron explains, '[t]he mere fact that terms like "unreasonable" or "excessive"

INTRODUCTION 13

considerations reflected in the rules on the interpretation of treaty provisions also logically inform, *mutatis mutandis*, the distinct but closely related question of the application of treaty provisions. These are the text of Article 17(1)(*d*) and other relevant provisions of the Rome Statute and its supporting instruments, read in context and with a view to structural considerations, alongside their drafting history.[74] Conversely, limited assistance is lent by the object and purpose of the Rome Statute, any definitive articulation of which is contestable.[75]

It is worth stating at the outset that the existing literature does not consider the gravity criterion for admissibility in Article 17(1)(*d*) of the Rome Statute as open-textured. Nor does it assume, as this book does, that the application of the provision calls for the exercise of discretion. Instead, it is widely agreed that Article 17(1)(*d*) is meant to exclude cases 'of marginal gravity only',[76] an exercise deemed to require little or no discretion. For this reason, among others, the scholarship to date has overwhelmingly excluded the central claim of this book, that the subjective[77] and discretionary application by the Prosecutor of the gravity criterion in Article 17(1)(*d*) facilitates the allocation by him or her of scarce investigative and prosecutorial resources. It is instead suggested that the allocation of these resources, which commentators all acknowledge as being a necessary part of the Prosecutor's decisions whether to investigate and prosecute respectively, is or must be situated elsewhere. Some commentators propose including an additional policy consideration of gravity ('relative gravity') over and above the admissibility criterion under Article 17(1)(*d*), which they suggest permits regard for resource constraints and other practical concerns such as the likelihood of state cooperation, the availability of evidence, and the ability to apprehend suspects.[78] Alternatively, others argue that practical considerations, including resource constraints, may be better accounted for in the 'interests of justice' assessments under Article 53(1)(*c*) and (2)(*c*) respectively of the Statute.[79] The book scrutinizes and ultimately rejects these views.[80]

---

invite us to make value judgments does not in itself undermine the determinacy of their meanings. On the contrary, it is part of the meaning of these words to indicate that a value judgment is required, a function which the words perform quite precisely'. ibid 527. The same applies to the term 'sufficient' in Article 17(1)(*d*) of the Rome Statute.

[74] See arts 31–32, Vienna Convention on the Law of Treaties 1969.
[75] On the diversity of objectives, see Damaška (n 2) 331–40; deGuzman and Schabas (n 2) 163–64.
[76] *Al Hassan*, Appeals Chamber Decision 2020 (n 59) para 53.
[77] On whether the assessment of gravity is 'objective' or 'subjective', see Chapter 2, Section 2.4.2.
[78] The term 'relative gravity' does not appear in the Rome Statute. MM deGuzman, 'Gravity and the Legitimacy of the International Criminal Court' (2008) 32(5) Fordham International Law Journal 1400, 1432–33; MM deGuzman, *Shocking the Conscience of Humanity: Gravity and the Legitimacy of International Criminal Law* (OUP 2020) 113–14; A Pues, 'Discretion and the Gravity of Situations at the International Criminal Court' (2017) 17 International Criminal Law Review 960, 982–84; SáCouto and Cleary (n 48) 813–14; I Stegmiller, 'The Gravity Threshold under the ICC Statute: Gravity Back and Forth in *Lubanga* and *Ntaganda*' (2009) 9 International Criminal Law Review 547, 557.
[79] See C Davis, 'Political Considerations in Prosecutorial Discretion at the International Criminal Court' (2015) 15 International Criminal Law Review 170, 182; deGuzman, *Shocking the Conscience of Humanity* (n 78) 136; deGuzman and Schabas (n 2) 146.
[80] See Chapter 5, Section 5.3.

14   GRAVITY AT THE INTERNATIONAL CRIMINAL COURT

As a point of methodology, it should suffice to say that this book characterizes the requirement of sufficient gravity in Article 17(1)(*d*) of the Rome Statute as open-textured and assumes that its application involves the exercise of discretion.[81]

Given the limited utility of the rules of treaty interpretation in this context, the application of the gravity criterion in Article 17(1)(*d*) of the Rome Statute proposed in this book relies in large part on what the book argues is the appropriate balance between prosecutorial discretion and judicial oversight under various admissibility provisions. In the context of each provision, the question is asked whether the Pre-Trial Chamber must defer to the Prosecutor's discretionary assessment of the sufficient gravity of a case in Article 17(1)(*d*) and what the extent of any such deference might be. Answering the question involves the consideration of the desire for consistency and predictability in the application of the provision and of the interests underlying relevant provisions, notably those of the referring state party or the UN Security Council, where relevant, and victims. It also requires the clarification of the respective institutional competences of the Prosecutor and the Pre-Trial Chambers, as provided in the Rome Statute and its supporting instruments, as gleaned from their drafting history, and through the consideration more generally of judicial economy. The analysis relies further on the justifications for deference by other international courts, notably in international human rights law, international investment law, and international trade law, where relevant, and the justifications for deference to prosecutors and other administrative authorities in the common law and civil law traditions, elements of which are represented in the Rome Statute.

1.4 Contributions to Practice and Scholarship

In common with the recommendation of the Independent Expert Review, and in contrast with the Court's case-law to date, the book argues for a recalibration of the application and ultimately a reconsideration of the function of the criterion of the sufficient gravity of a case in Article 17(1)(*d*) of the Rome Statute, when applied in the context of the Prosecutor's respective decisions whether to investigate and to prosecute. First, by identifying appropriate indicators of the gravity of potential or actual cases, it contends that the application in all contexts of Article 17(1)(*d*), whether by the Prosecutor or the Pre-Trial Chamber, involves a subjective, case-by-case assessment that calls for the exercise of discretion. When it comes specifically to the assessment by the Prosecutor of sufficient gravity, this discretion facilitates the judicious allocation by him or her of scarce investigative and prosecutorial resources. Second, by clarifying the respective roles of the Prosecutor and

---

[81] Recall Section 1.2.

the Pre-Trial Chamber in the assessment of the gravity of potential or actual cases in different contexts, the book argues that the considerable discretion conferred on the Prosecutor in the making of this assessment, compared with the limited powers of judicial oversight conferred on the Pre-Trial Chamber, allows the Prosecutor to decline to investigate or prosecute for purposes beyond merely the exclusion of cases 'of marginal gravity only'.[82] By facilitating the allocation by the Prosecutor of limited investigative and prosecutorial resources, the application of the gravity criterion in the context of the Prosecutor's decisions whether to investigate and whether to prosecute provides a legal basis for the selection of investigations and prosecutions.

First, as a contribution to practice and scholarship in international criminal law, the book clarifies how Article 17(1)(*d*) of the Rome Statute has been applied to date and how the provision should be applied, both in the context of the Prosecutor's respective decisions whether to investigate and to prosecute and, in contradistinction, as part of the Pre-Trial Chamber's determination of the admissibility of a case. Second, the book contributes to the scholarship on the exercise of prosecutorial discretion during the initiation of investigations and prosecutions at the Court. This literature has so far addressed neither squarely nor comprehensively the applicable standard or standards of Pre-Trial Chamber review of the Prosecutor's decisions whether to investigate and whether to prosecute.[83] The competing pulls of prosecutorial independence and prosecutorial accountability, and with them the respective interests of the referring state party or the Security Council, the Defence, and victims, all hang in this balance. Third, the book attempts to resolve the ongoing debate over how to justify in legal terms the selectivity of the Prosecutor's investigations and prosecutions. The utilization to this end of the admissibility criterion of the sufficient gravity of the case in Article 17(1)(*d*) of the Rome Statute may prove instructive in other contexts as well. It may offer a

---

[82] *Al Hassan*, Appeals Chamber Decision 2020 (n 59) para 53.

[83] The following contributions on this subject are noteworthy. Pues discusses the standard of Pre-Trial Chamber review under Article 53(3)(*a*) of the Statute of the Prosecutor's assessment of the admissibility of a situation. A Pues, *Prosecutorial Discretion at the International Criminal Court* (Hart Publishing 2020) 77–81. She does not address the standard of review of the same under Article 15(4). See ibid 71–76. Nor does she discuss the standard of review under Article 53(3)(*a*) of the Prosecutor's assessment of the admissibility of a case. Poltronieri Rossetti takes a different approach entirely, focusing on identifying the reasons for what he argues is a distinction between the 'law in the books' and the 'law in action'. L Poltronieri Rossetti, Prosecutorial Discretion and Its Judicial Review at the International Criminal Court: A Practice-Based Analysis of the Relationship between the Prosecutor and Judges (doctoral thesis, Università Degli Studi di Trento 2017–2018) 282. He does not propose suitable standards of Pre-Trial Chamber review of prosecutorial discretion under relevant provisions. See ibid 310–14. Finally, Zakerhossein limits himself to supporting 'a broad and inclusive judicial review system'. MH Zakerhossein, *Situation Selection Regime at the International Criminal Court: Law, Policy, Practice* (Intersentia 2017) 408. An earlier version of Chapter 3 of this book identifies suitable standards of review under Articles 53(3)(*a*) and 15(4) respectively of the Prosecutor's assessment of the gravity of potential cases arising out of a situation. See P Urs, 'Judicial Review of Prosecutorial Discretion in the Initiation of Investigations into Situations of "Sufficient Gravity"' (2020) 18(4) Journal of International Criminal Justice 851.

16 GRAVITY AT THE INTERNATIONAL CRIMINAL COURT

useful device to be deployed in the context of other international or national criminal courts as a means of effectively dividing the task of prosecuting international crimes between international and national criminal courts or, at the national level, between ordinary and specialized criminal courts or between courts and truth and reconciliation mechanisms.[84] As an ancillary fourth contribution, the book offers insights as to the application of other criteria relevant to the Prosecutor's decisions whether to investigate and whether to prosecute.[85] In particular, by contending that the application by the Prosecutor of the gravity criterion facilitates the allocation of limited investigative and prosecutorial resources, it refutes suggestions in the existing scholarship that the application of other criteria, such as the 'interests of justice',[86] better facilitates the allocation of these resources.

Beyond international criminal law, the book contributes to the wider scholarship in public international law on the role of international courts vis-à-vis discretionary decision-makers. This scholarship is focused heavily on the limits of judicial scrutiny of discretionary decisions by states and on the reasons for judicial deference in that context. Adding a new dimension to the discussion, the book identifies similarities across international criminal law and other areas of international law and teases out what emerge as the distinct justifications for and against judicial deference by international criminal courts. It also answers the analogous question of how international courts might address the exercise of discretion by entities other than states, in this case the Office of the Prosecutor of the ICC, an organ of an international court with a distinctive allocative function.

1.5 Scope and Limitations

The book does not assess the application of the admissibility criterion of sufficient gravity in Article 17(1)(d) of the Rome Statute against the various underlying objectives of international criminal law.[87] Nor does it investigate any effects the application of this gravity criterion may have on the legitimacy or effectiveness of the ICC as an institution, effects which are addressed at length elsewhere.[88] It does not propose either any broader conception of 'gravity' that transcends international criminal courts and their procedures.[89] These lines of inquiry together represent

---

[84] See Chapter 5, Section 5.4.2.

[85] In addition to the other three admissibility criteria specified in Article 17(1), all of which reflect the notion of the 'complementarity' of the ICC's jurisdiction, the criteria for the initiation of investigations and prosecutions include the jurisdictional requirements specified in Article 53(1)(a) and (2)(a) and the 'interests of justice' under Article 53(1)(c) and (2)(c) of the Statute.

[86] See art 53(1)(c) and (2)(c), Rome Statute.

[87] On the book's treatment of the object and purpose of the Rome Statute, see Section 1.3.

[88] See deGuzman, *Shocking the Conscience of Humanity* (n 78); deGuzman, *Gravity and the Legitimacy of the International Criminal Court* (n 78).

[89] See M Hacking, The Law of Gravity: The Role of Gravity in International Criminal Law (doctoral thesis, University of Cambridge 2014). For an even broader survey of notions of gravity across

INTRODUCTION   17

existing approaches to the gravity criterion, to which, it is hoped, the book adds a distinctive formalist perspective.

The focus being the admissibility criterion of sufficient gravity in Article 17(1) (d) of the Rome Statute, the book excludes the consideration, in addition to admissibility, of gravity-based limits on the Court's jurisdiction *ratione materiae*, the assessment of the gravity of the alleged crimes as part of an 'interests of justice' analysis, and the use of gravity as a sentencing criterion.[90] The necessary distinction between each of these articulations of gravity and the gravity criterion for admissibility in Article 17(1)(d) is drawn below.

1.5.1 Gravity in the Jurisdiction *Ratione Materiae* of the Court

In addition to the admissibility criterion of the sufficient gravity of the case in Article 17(1)(d) of the Rome Statute, varying notions of gravity have been used to define the crimes within the Court's jurisdiction *ratione materiae*. The line between these distinct considerations of gravity is at times blurred,[91] most evidently in the Statute's conferral of jurisdiction over war crimes 'in particular when committed as part of a plan or policy or as part of a large-scale commission of such crimes'.[92] This clause is widely regarded as a policy indication akin to the gravity criterion in Article 17(1)(d), rather than as a jurisdictional requirement, and is treated as such in the book.[93] Similarly, when it comes to genocide, the Elements of Crimes[94] indicate that the crime in question must have taken place 'in the context of a manifest

---

various areas of public international law, see R López, 'The Law of Gravity' (2020) 58 Columbia Journal of Transnational Law 565.

[90] For the additional consideration of these manifestations of gravity, see Pues, *Prosecutorial Discretion at the International Criminal Court* (n 83); deGuzman, *Shocking the Conscience of Humanity* (n 78); Hacking (n 89).

[91] C Stahn, 'Judicial Review of Prosecutorial Discretion: Five Years On' in C Stahn and G Sluiter (eds), *The Emerging Practice of the International Criminal Court* (Martinus Nijhoff 2009) 247, 268.

[92] art 8(1), Rome Statute.

[93] See WA Schabas, *The International Criminal Court: A Commentary on the Rome Statute* (2nd edn, OUP 2016) 225–28; L Arbour, 'The Need for an Independent and Effective Prosecutor in the Permanent International Criminal Court' (1999) 17 Windsor Yearbook of Access to Justice 207, 214; F Guariglia and E Rogier, 'The Selection of Situations and Cases by the OTP of the ICC' in C Stahn (ed), *The Law and Practice of the International Criminal Court* (OUP 2015) 359; M Longobardo, 'Factors Relevant for the Assessment of Sufficient Gravity in the ICC: Proceedings and the Elements of International Crimes' (2016) 33 Questions of International Law 21, 34; deGuzman, *Gravity and the Legitimacy of the International Criminal Court* (n 78) 1408; Cryer (n 8) 268–69. Conversely, Knoops and Zwart suggest that '[t]he lack of a plan or policy would … be a valid consideration to determine that no war crimes … were committed'. G-JA Knoops and T Zwart, 'The *Flotilla Case* before the ICC: The Need to Do Justice While Keeping Heaven Intact' (2015) 15 International Criminal Law Review 1069, 1089.

[94] See art 9, Rome Statute. The Elements of Crimes, adopted by a two-thirds majority in the ICC Assembly of States Parties, assist in the interpretation and application of the provisions of the Rome Statute which define the crimes within the jurisdiction *ratione materiae* of the Court; that is, Articles 6, 7, 8, and 8bis.

18   GRAVITY AT THE INTERNATIONAL CRIMINAL COURT

pattern of similar conduct'.[95] As one commentator points out, the inclusion of this contextual element, allegedly to avoid 'isolated hate crimes', is superfluous, since such crimes may in any event be filtered out through the use of the gravity criterion for admissibility.[96] The crime of aggression is defined by a more direct reference to gravity. The crime involves 'an act of aggression which, by its character, gravity and scale, constitutes a manifest violation of the Charter of the United Nations',[97] the focus being 'on the seriousness, rather than the plainness, of the violation'.[98] So also the jurisdictional requirement of 'a widespread or systematic attack' for crimes against humanity may equally be construed as an indicator of gravity for the purpose of admissibility.[99]

When it comes to the assessment of admissibility, the question arises as to the extent to which the satisfaction of these various gravity-based elements of jurisdiction *ratione materiae* bears on the satisfaction of the criterion of the sufficient gravity of the case under Article 17(1)(*d*). While it is in principle clear that the fulfilment of the admissibility criteria, including the gravity criterion in Article 17(1)(*d*), requires something more than the satisfaction of jurisdictional requirements[100] and, indeed, is 'always a function of the specific conduct alleged in a specific case, not of its formal legal characterization',[101] this distinction has not always been maintained in practice.

The book considers the gravity-based aspects of the Court's jurisdiction *ratione materiae* to the extent of their elision in practice with the admissibility requirement of the sufficient gravity of a case in Article 17(1)(*d*). Maintaining the conceptual distinction between jurisdiction *ratione materiae* and admissibility is key to the application of the provision it proposes.[102]

---

[95] art 6(*a*), element 4, Elements of Crimes 2002 ('Elements of Crimes'). According to one commentator, this contextual element 'align[s] genocide with crimes against humanity'. Schabas (93) 131.

[96] R O'Keefe, *International Criminal Law* (OUP 2016) 149–50.

[97] art 8bis(1), Rome Statute. See also art 8bis, element 5, Elements of Crimes; understandings 6–7, Understandings regarding the Amendments to the Rome Statute of the International Criminal Court on the Crime of Aggression 2010, RC/10/Add.1 (referring to 'the gravity of the acts concerned and their consequences' in a determination of whether an act of aggression has been committed and to 'the character, gravity and scale' to establish whether an act of aggression constitutes a manifest violation of the Charter of the United Nations).

[98] O'Keefe, *International Criminal Law* (n 96) 158. In the 2008 Assembly of States Parties, delegations noted that the definition 'would appropriately limit the Court's jurisdiction to the most serious acts of aggression under customary international law, thus excluding cases of insufficient gravity'. Official Records of the Assembly of States Parties to the Rome Statute of the International Criminal Court, Resumed Sixth Session, New York, 2–6 June 2008, ICC-ASP/6/20Add.1, 12. See also T Ruys, 'Criminalizing Aggression: How the Future of the Law on the Use of Force Rests in the Hands of the ICC' (2018) 29 European Journal of International Law 887, 906–10.

[99] art 7(1), Rome Statute. See Olásolo, *The Triggering Procedure of the International Criminal Court* (n 48) 183–84; MM deGuzman, 'The International Criminal Court's Gravity Jurisprudence at Ten' (2013) 12(3) Washington University Global Studies Law Review 475, 485–86.

[100] *Situation in the Democratic Republic of the Congo*, Pre-Trial Chamber Decision 2006 (n 70) para 42. See also Longobardo (n 93).

[101] O'Keefe, *International Criminal Law* (n 96) 161. See also Independent Expert Review (n 22) para 661; Longobardo (n 93) 29.

[102] See Chapter 2.

1.5.2 The Interests of Justice and the Gravity of the Crime

When it comes to the Prosecutor's decisions whether to investigate and whether to prosecute, the question arises whether the references in Article 53(1)(c) and (2)(c) of the Rome Statute to 'the gravity of the crime' as part of the assessment of the 'interests of justice' address the assessment of gravity for the purpose of admissibility under Article 53(1)(b) and (2)(b) of the Statute. Were this the case, the assessment of the interests of justice under Article 53(1)(c) and (2)(c) would be equally relevant to an inquiry into the application of the gravity criterion for admissibility.

That the admissibility criterion of 'sufficient gravity' under Article 53(1)(b) and 2(b) cannot be equated with 'the gravity of the crime' as part of the assessment of the interests of justice under Article 53(1)(c) and (2)(c) is evidenced by the distinct procedures that Article 53 outlines for Pre-Trial Chamber review of the Prosecutor's assessments of admissibility and the interests of justice respectively. While under Article 53(3)(a) the Pre-Trial Chamber may review the Prosecutor's assessment of admissibility, including his or her assessment as to the sufficiency of gravity, only at the request of the referring state party or the Security Council, the Pre-Trial Chamber may review the Prosecutor's assessment of the interests of justice under Article 53(3)(b) 'on its own initiative'. Moreover, while under Article 53(3)(a) the Pre-Trial Chamber may 'request' that the Prosecutor reconsider his or her assessment of admissibility and thereby of gravity under Article 53(1)(b) and (2)(b), under Article 53(3)(b) 'the decision of the Prosecutor shall be effective only if confirmed by the Pre-Trial Chamber'. Were the references to 'the gravity of the crime' in Article 53(1)(c) and (2)(c) intended to address the admissibility criterion of the gravity of the case, the distinction between Pre-Trial Chamber review under Article 53(3)(a) and Pre-Trial Chamber review under Article 53(3)(b) would be rendered meaningless. Indeed, the distinction between the gravity criterion, to be considered under Article 53(1)(b) and (2)(b), and the interests of justice, to be considered under Article 53(1)(c) and (2)(c), would be effaced.[103]

In this light, the book does not address 'the gravity of the crime', which is part of the distinct analysis of the interests of justice under Article 53(1)(c) and (2)(c). When discussing the function of the gravity criterion in Article 17(1)(d) in the context of the Prosecutor's decisions whether to investigate and whether to prosecute, however, the book addresses proposals in the existing scholarship for allocating investigative and prosecutorial resources through the assessment of the interests of justice.[104]

---

[103] This distinction is supported by the text of each provision. Stegmiller (n 78) 563.
[104] See Chapter 5, Sections 5.3.2.2 and 5.3.3.2.

20 GRAVITY AT THE INTERNATIONAL CRIMINAL COURT

1.5.3 Gravity and the Court's Sentencing Criteria

The Court's sentencing criteria, as specified in Rule 145 of its Rules of Procedure and Evidence, are discussed to the extent that the Court has considered them relevant to the articulation of the admissibility criterion of the sufficient gravity of the case in Article 17(1)(*d*) of the Statute.

1.6 Terminological Clarifications

The Rome Statute, in various provisions not limited to admissibility, sets out procedures relating to 'situations' and 'cases' respectively.[105] Neither the Statute nor its supporting instruments defines these terms. While the definition of a 'case' may be understood by analogical reference to national criminal law, the same cannot be said of a 'situation', which, even among international criminal courts, is a term employed exclusively by the ICC and which is 'a core feature of [its] procedural regime'.[106]

1.6.1 'Situation'

The exercise of the jurisdiction of the Court is conditioned on the referral by a state party or the Security Council of '[a] situation in which one or more ... crimes appears to have been committed' or on the initiation by the Prosecutor of an investigation *proprio motu*.[107] To this end, the Statute entitles a state party to the Rome Statute to refer to the Prosecutor 'a situation in which one or more crimes within the jurisdiction of the Court appear to have been committed' and to request that the Prosecutor 'investigate the situation'.[108] The analogous power of the Security Council to do so is conferred under the Charter of the United Nations.[109] When it comes to the initiation by the Prosecutor under Article 15 of the Rome Statute of an investigation *proprio motu*, the exercise of the Court's jurisdiction, and any subsequent investigation, is likewise in relation to a 'situation'.[110] These references to a 'situation' are to 'the overall factual context in which it is believed that "a crime within the jurisdiction of the court" ... has been committed'.[111] When it comes to

---

[105] The closely related question of how the assessment of admissibility is tailored to a 'situation' and a 'case' is addressed in Chapter 2, Sections 2.3.1.1 and 2.3.2.1.

[106] H Olásolo, 'The Lack of Attention to the Distinction between Situations and Cases in National Laws on Co-operation with the International Criminal Court with Particular Reference to the Spanish Case' (2007) 20 Leiden Journal of International Law 193, 194.

[107] See art 13, Rome Statute.

[108] art 14(1), Rome Statute. See also art 18(1), Rome Statute.

[109] M Cherif Bassiouni, *Introduction to International Criminal Law* (Martinus Nijhoff 2013) 680.

[110] See art 15(5)–(6), Rome Statute.

[111] Cherif Bassiouni (n 109) 680.

the exercise of the Court's jurisdiction on the basis of the acceptance by a non-state party of the jurisdiction of the Court, the reference in Article 12(3) of the Rome Statute to the 'crime', rather than to the 'situation', may be taken to be a drafting oversight.[112]

Notably, Article 53(1), the general provision on the initiation of investigations, does not itself refer to the investigation of a 'situation'. Nevertheless, its references to the Prosecutor's investigation must logically be, by analogical reference to Article 15 and by the fact of the referral by a state party or the Security Council of and the exercise of the Court's jurisdiction over a 'situation', to the investigation of a 'situation'. In this context, the 'situation' 'denotes the confines within which the Court determines whether there is a reasonable basis to initiate an investigation and the jurisdictional parameters of any ensuing investigation'.[113] It is circumscribed by the territorial, temporal, and, where relevant, personal limits of the Court's jurisdiction to the extent that the jurisdiction of the Court has been triggered by a referral, the declaration of a non-state party,[114] or the authorization by the Pre-Trial Chamber of an investigation *proprio motu*.[115] Where clarification as to the scope of a situation proves necessary, the task of delimiting its boundaries falls to the Pre-Trial Chamber.[116]

1.6.2 'Case'

Various provisions of the Rome Statute refer to a 'case'. A 'case' technically comes into existence upon the issuance of a warrant of arrest or a summons to appear in respect of a specific suspect in relation to specific conduct.[117] In contradistinction to a 'situation', thus, '[t]he parameters of "the case" ... are defined by the suspect under investigation and the conduct that gives rise to criminal liability under the

---

[112] ibid 681.

[113] R Rastan, 'Situation and Case: Defining the Parameters' in C Stahn and M El Zeidy (eds), *The International Criminal Court and Complementarity* (CUP 2011) 422.

[114] See art 12(2)–(3), Rome Statute.

[115] Where, however, the alleged commission of the crimes crosses state borders, the definition of a situation by reference to the Court's territorial jurisdiction in respect of individual states may create artificial boundaries within what would otherwise be one situation. This is a problem which remains to be addressed. See Rastan, *Situation and Case* (n 113) 426–28.

[116] For a detailed analysis of relevant practice, see R Rastan, 'The Jurisdictional Scope of Situations before the International Criminal Court' (2012) 23 Criminal Law Forum 1.

[117] See art 58, Rome Statute. See also *Prosecutor v Ruto and others*, ICC-01/09-01/11-307, Appeals Chamber, Judgment on the Appeal of the Republic of Kenya against the Decision of Pre-Trial Chamber II of 30 May 2011 Entitled 'Decision on the Application by the Government of Kenya Challenging the Admissibility of the Case Pursuant to Article 19(2)(b) of the Statute', 30 August 2011 (hereafter '*Ruto and others*, Appeals Chamber Decision 2011') para 39; *Situation in the Democratic Republic of the Congo*, ICC-01/04-93, Pre-Trial Chamber I, Decision Following the Consultation Held on 11 October 2005 and the Prosecution's Submission on Jurisdiction and Admissibility Filed on 31 October 2005, 9 November 2005, 4.

22   GRAVITY AT THE INTERNATIONAL CRIMINAL COURT

Statute[118] The Rome Statute nonetheless refers to a 'case' also in Article 53(2), in the context of a decision by the Prosecutor not to prosecute a specific suspect in relation to specific conduct.

1.7 Outline

Chapter 2 surveys the application to date of the criterion of the sufficient gravity of a case in Article 17(1)(*d*) of the Rome Statute with a view to identifying and evaluating the suitability of the various indicators of gravity articulated in the policy of the Office of the Prosecutor and in the decisions of the various Chambers of the ICC. On this basis, it determines whether the application of the relevant indicators under Article 17(1)(*d*) requires an objective or a subjective assessment of gravity and, accordingly, the extent of the discretion involved in their application.[119]

Chapters 3 and 4 aim to clarify the respective roles of the Prosecutor and the Pre-Trial Chamber in the assessment of the gravity of potential and actual cases in the contexts of 'situations' and 'cases' respectively. Chapter 3 analyses the intensity of Pre-Trial Chamber oversight of the Prosecutor's application of Article 17(1)(*d*) of the Statute as part of his or her decision whether to initiate an investigation into a 'situation'. It draws a distinction between the review procedure applicable under Article 53(3)(*a*) to the initiation of investigations generally and the initiation of investigations by the Prosecutor *proprio motu*, as reviewable by the Pre-Trial Chamber under Article 15(4). The chapter identifies what it argues is the most suitable standard of review of the Prosecutor's assessment of gravity under each provision.

The first part of Chapter 4 considers the intensity of Pre-Trial Chamber review under Article 53(3)(*a*) of the Prosecutor's application of Article 17(1)(*d*) of the Statute as part of his or her decision not to proceed with the prosecution of a 'case'. It proposes the appropriate standard of review of the Prosecutor's assessment of gravity in this context. In contradistinction to the Prosecutor's application of the gravity criterion in the context of his or her decision whether to prosecute, the second part of Chapter 4 addresses the assessment of the gravity of a case as part of the Pre-Trial or Trial Chamber's own determination of the admissibility of a case in accordance with the procedures specified in Article 19(1)–(3) of the Statute. The relevant question in this context is whether the Pre-Trial or Trial Chamber may assess the gravity of the case during proceedings pertaining to the issuance of a

---

[118] *Al Hassan*, Appeals Chamber Decision 2020 (n 59) para 127; *Prosecutor v Gaddafi and Al-Senussi*, ICC-01/11-01/11-547-Red, Appeals Chamber, Judgment on the Appeal of Libya against the Decision of Pre-Trial Chamber I of 31 May 2013 Entitled 'Decision on the Admissibility of the Case against Saif Al-Islam Gaddafi', 21 May 2014, para 1. See also *Ruto and others*, Appeals Chamber Decision 2011 (n 117) para 39.
[119] On the book's use of the terms 'objective' and 'subjective', see Chapter 2, Section 2.4.2.

warrant of arrest or a summons to appear; that is, before the appearance before the Court of the suspect.

Chapter 5 first recapitulates the analysis undertaken in Chapters 2, 3, and 4, offering guidance as to how to apply the criterion of the sufficient gravity of a case in Article 17(1)(*d*) in the context of the Prosecutor's decisions whether to investigate and whether to prosecute. It then scrutinizes by reference to the various strands of inquiry undertaken in Chapters 2, 3, and 4 the purpose of the gravity criterion in Article 17(1)(*d*) of the Statute as articulated by the Court. It examines whether the application of the gravity criterion requires a reconsideration of what has been stated by the Court and endorsed by the existing scholarship to be the purpose of the gravity assessment pursuant to Article 17(1)(*d*), namely to exclude only marginal cases from investigation and prosecution. On this basis, the chapter makes recommendations for practice at the ICC and reflects on the use of a comparable criterion of gravity at other courts, at both the international and national levels, for the investigation and prosecution of international crimes. It concludes by drawing attention to the contribution of international criminal courts to the wider literature on the interaction between international courts and discretionary decision-makers.

2

The Application of the Gravity Criterion for Admissibility in Article 17(1)(*d*) of the Rome Statute

2.1 Introduction

Various provisions of the Rome Statute call for the assessment by the Prosecutor or the Pre-Trial Chamber of the International Criminal Court (ICC, the Court), as the case may be, of admissibility. In accordance with Article 53(1)(*b*) of the Rome Statute, the Prosecutor is required to assess admissibility in relation to a situation when deciding whether to initiate an investigation into it. Pursuant to Article 53(2)(*b*), the Prosecutor may, upon investigation, decide not to proceed with a prosecution on the basis that the case is inadmissible. At both stages, admissibility falls to be assessed by reference to the criteria specified in Article 17 of the Statute, among them the criterion of sufficient gravity found in Article 17(1)(*d*). Where the Prosecutor decides to initiate an investigation into a situation *proprio motu*,[1] Pre-Trial Chamber authorization is required, as provided for in Article 15(3) and (4) of the Statute. The admissibility of any case eventually selected for prosecution by the Prosecutor may also be determined by the Pre-Trial Chamber or, exceptionally, the Trial Chamber,[2] whether *proprio motu*, in accordance with Article 19(1), upon a challenge by any of the parties listed under Article 19(2), in accordance with the same provision, or at the request of the Prosecutor, in accordance with Article 19(3). Conversely, where a situation has been referred to the Prosecutor by a state party or the United Nations (UN) Security Council, any decision by the Prosecutor not to initiate an investigation or not to prosecute a case, including on the basis of inadmissibility, may equally be reviewed by the Pre-Trial Chamber at the request of the state or the Council, as provided for in Article 53(3)(*a*).

Article 17(1)(*d*) of the Statute provides that 'a case is inadmissible' where 'it is not of sufficient gravity to justify further action by the Court'. Nowhere does it or any other provision of the Rome Statute specify relevant indicators of gravity, leaving to the Court the articulation of the open-textured criterion of 'sufficient gravity'. The criterion may be construed in objective or subjective terms.[3] On the

---

[1] See art 15(1), Rome Statute of the International Criminal Court 1998 (Rome Statute).
[2] See art 19(6), Rome Statute.
[3] See Section 2.4.2.

Gravity at the International Criminal Court. Priya Urs, Oxford University Press. © Priya Urs 2024.
DOI: 10.1093/oso/9780198882954.003.0002

one hand, an objective approach to the requirement of sufficient gravity involves the mechanistic application of quantifiable indicators of gravity, leading to the same result irrespective of the decision-maker and thus promoting consistency and attendant predictability in the application of Article 17(1)(*d*) in all contexts in which it is applied, whether by the Prosecutor or the Pre-Trial Chamber. On the other hand, a subjective approach to the requisite sufficiency of gravity, when Article 17(1)(*d*) is applied in the context of the Prosecutor's decisions whether to investigate and whether to prosecute, favours discretion in the initiation of investigations and prosecutions. It calls for the exercise of individual judgement in the weighing of quantitative and qualitative indicators, an assessment which may lead to a different result depending on the decision-maker, and which involves more or less discretion depending on the articulation of relevant indicators and their weight in the assessment.

The application of the same gravity criterion in Article 17(1)(*d*) under various admissibility provisions—some addressing a 'situation', others pertaining to a 'case'— also raises questions relating to the application of the same provision to a 'situation' and a 'case'. When it comes to the assessment of gravity in respect of a situation, it is unclear how many potential cases arising out of a situation must be sufficiently grave to justify the initiation of an investigation. It is equally unclear whether it is necessary or permissible for the Prosecutor, in his or her assessment of gravity in respect of a situation, to look at facts beyond the jurisdictional scope of the situation.

In their practice to date, the Pre-Trial Chambers have not addressed these issues clearly, resulting in persisting uncertainty and warranting the exhaustive assessment in this chapter of the application of Article 17(1)(*d*). The chapter scrutinizes the articulation by the Pre-Trial Chambers and the Appeals Chamber of the gravity criterion in Article 17(1)(*d*) of the Rome Statute over twenty years of the Court's practice. Drawing a distinction between the application of the criterion of sufficient gravity as part of the decision whether to initiate an investigation into a 'situation' under Articles 53(1) and 15(3)–(4) and as part of the assessment of the admissibility of a 'case' under Articles 53(2) and 19(1)–(3), it identifies the various indicators of gravity articulated in each context in the policy of the Office of the Prosecutor and in the decisions of the Pre-Trial Chambers and the Appeals Chamber. Based on this body of practice, in particular the authoritative decisions of the Appeals Chamber, the chapter suggests the appropriate indicators of 'sufficient gravity'. By reference to these indicators and other relevant considerations, in particular the desire for consistency and predictability in the application of Article 17(1)(*d*) and the competing need for discretion in the allocation of limited investigative and prosecutorial resources, it clarifies whether the application of Article 17(1)(*d*) in the context of the Prosecutor's decisions whether to investigate and prosecute respectively calls for an objective or a subjective assessment of gravity.[4]

---

[4] The analysis is in turn relevant to the question of the respective roles of the Prosecutor and the Pre-Trial Chamber in the assessment of gravity under various admissibility provisions discussed in Chapters 3 and 4.

26 GRAVITY AT THE INTERNATIONAL CRIMINAL COURT

Section 2.2 of the chapter prefaces this analysis by outlining what the Court has so far considered to be the function of the gravity criterion specified in Article 17(1)(d) of the Statute.[5] Section 2.3 examines the Pre-Trial Chambers' admissibility decisions to date in relation to situations and cases respectively and identifies the various indicators of gravity articulated in each context by the Office of the Prosecutor, the Pre-Trial Chambers, and the Appeals Chamber. It notes inconsistencies across the decisions of the Pre-Trial Chambers, revealing points of divergence not only in the application of Article 17(1)(d) to situations and cases respectively but also in the provision's application under different admissibility provisions. Section 2.4 assesses the relevance of various indicators to the gravity assessment and ultimately to the Prosecutor's decisions whether to investigate and whether to prosecute. On this basis, and through additional reflection upon other relevant considerations, it clarifies whether Article 17(1)(d) requires an objective or a subjective assessment of gravity in the context of the Prosecutor's respective decisions whether to investigate and to prosecute.

2.2 The Function of the Gravity Criterion According to the Court

The text of Article 17(1)(d) of the Rome Statute does not itself resolve the question of the function of the gravity assessment in the context of the Prosecutor's respective decisions whether to investigate and to prosecute.[6] The chapeau to Article 17(1) is of little assistance either, providing only that a determination of admissibility conducted in accordance with the criteria specified therein, including that of 'sufficient gravity' under Article 17(1)(d), shall '[h]av[e] regard' to 'paragraph 10' (meaning the tenth unnumbered recital) of the preamble to, and to Article 1 of, the Statute.[7] Of these provisions, only Article 1 refers, in general terms, to the exercise of the Court's jurisdiction over persons 'for the most serious crimes of international concern'. References elsewhere in the preamble to 'grave crimes' which threaten peace and security and 'the most serious crimes of concern to the international community as a whole' are not similarly cross-referenced in Article

---

[5] The question of the function of the gravity criterion in the context of the Prosecutor's decisions whether to investigate and whether to prosecute is addressed conclusively in the final analysis in Chapter 5.

[6] According to deGuzman, '[t]he Statute leaves the concept of gravity ambiguous, allowing states with divergent visions of the Court's role to believe, or at least hope, that their vision will prevail'. MM deGuzman, 'The International Criminal Court's Gravity Jurisprudence at Ten' (2013) 12(3) Washington University Global Studies Law Review 475, 477.

[7] Both preambular paragraph 10 and Article 1 mention the principle of complementarity, which is likely the reference that was intended in the chapeau to Article 17(1).

APPLICATION OF GRAVITY CRITERION FOR ADMISSIBILITY   27

17(1), suggesting, in accordance with the maxim *expressio unius exclusio alterius*, that they are not directly relevant to any assessment under that provision.[8] Beyond this, there is little indication in the Statute as to the purpose of the gravity assessment as part of either the decision whether to investigate a situation or the decision whether to prosecute a case.[9]

In the earliest decision addressing the application of Article 17(1)(*d*) of the Statute, in the cases arising out of the situation in the Democratic Republic of the Congo (DRC) against Thomas Lubanga Dyilo (*Lubanga*) and Bosco Ntaganda (*Ntaganda*), Pre-Trial Chamber I considered that, for the case to be admissible, the conduct must 'present particular features which render it especially grave'.[10] In contrast, the Pre-Trial Chambers that authorized investigations *proprio motu* in Kenya and Côte d'Ivoire concluded that 'the reference to the insufficiency of gravity ... prevents the Court from investigating, prosecuting and trying peripheral cases'.[11] The Appeals Chamber in *Ntaganda* preferred the latter approach, pointing, inter alia, to the fact that a formulation which would have excluded matters 'not of exceptional gravity such as to justify further action by the Court' had been rejected during the drafting of Article 17(1)(*d*).[12] In the Appeals Chamber's view, moreover, an overly

---

[8] See paras 3–4, 9, preamble, Rome Statute. Conversely, in relation to its 1994 draft statute for an international criminal court, the International Law Commission (ILC) had considered more generally that '[t]he purposes set out in the preamble are intended to assist in ... the exercise of the power conferred by [draft] article 35', which articulated relevant admissibility criteria. ILC, 'Report of the International Law Commission on the Work of its Forty-Sixth Session' (2 May–22 July 1994) UN Doc A/49/10 (hereafter 'ILC Report 1994') 27. In support of a more generalized reliance on the preamble to the Statute when reading Article 17, see R Murphy, 'Gravity Issues and the International Criminal Court' (2006) 17 Criminal Law Forum 281, 286. But see MM deGuzman and WA Schabas, 'Initiation of Investigations and Selection of Cases' in S Zappalà and others (eds), *International Criminal Procedure: Principles and Rules* (OUP 2013) 163–64.

[9] It has been suggested that the limited discussion during the drafting of the Rome Statute of the gravity criterion indicates of itself that only cases or potential cases of *de minimis* seriousness are excluded by Article 17(1)(*d*). MM deGuzman, 'Gravity and the Legitimacy of the International Criminal Court' (2008) 32(5) Fordham International Law Journal 1400, 1404, 1424–25, 1435.

[10] *Situation in the Democratic Republic of the Congo*, ICC-01/04-02/06-20-Anx2, Pre-Trial Chamber I, Decision on Prosecutor's Application for Warrants of Arrest, Article 58, 10 February 2006 (hereafter '*Situation in the Democratic Republic of the Congo*, Pre-Trial Chamber Decision 2006') para 46.

[11] *Situation in Kenya*, ICC-01/09-19, Pre-Trial Chamber II, Decision Pursuant to Article 15 of the Rome Statute on the Authorization of an Investigation into the Situation in the Republic of Kenya, 31 March 2010 (hereafter '*Situation in Kenya*, Pre-Trial Chamber Decision 2010') para 56; *Situation in Côte d'Ivoire*, ICC-02/11-14, Pre-Trial Chamber III, Decision Pursuant to Article 15 of the Rome Statute on the Authorization of an Investigation into the Situation in the Republic of Côte d'Ivoire, 3 October 2011 (hereafter '*Situation in Côte d'Ivoire*, Pre-Trial Chamber Authorization Decision 2011') para 201.

[12] *Situation in the Democratic Republic of the Congo*, ICC-01/04-169, Appeals Chamber, Judgment on the Prosecutor's Appeal against the Decision of Pre-Trial Chamber I entitled 'Decision on the Prosecutor's Application for Warrants of Arrest, Article 58', 13 July 2006 (hereafter '*Situation in the Democratic Republic of the Congo*, Appeals Chamber Decision 2006') para 81. It was relevant that during the drafting of Article 17(1)(*d*), the wording of which was taken in part from draft article 35 of the ILC's draft statute, a proposal to frame the gravity requirement more strictly had been rejected ('A case is inadmissible before the Court if ... (e) the matters of which complaint has been made were not of exceptional gravity such as to justify further action by the Court'). UN General Assembly, 'Summary of the Proceedings of the Preparatory Committee during the Period 25 March–12 April 1996' (7 May 1996) UN Doc A/AC.249/1, 100.

restrictive gravity threshold would risk unjustifiably narrowing the Court's jurisdiction *ratione materiae* and with it the Court's ability to deter.[13]

In its subsequent decision in the case against Al Hassan Ag Abdoul Aziz Ag Mohamed Ag Mahmoud (*Al Hassan*), arising out of the situation in Mali, the Appeals Chamber unanimously affirmed that the purpose of Article 17(1)(*d*) is 'not to oblige the Court to choose only the most serious cases, but merely to oblige it not to prosecute cases of marginal gravity'.[14] In short, the purpose of Article 17(1)(*d*), according to the Appeals Chamber in *Al Hassan*, is 'to exclude ... those rather unusual cases when conduct that technically fulfils all the elements of a crime under the Court's jurisdiction is nevertheless of marginal gravity only'.[15]

When reviewing the Prosecutor's decision not to initiate an investigation into the situation on the registered vessels of The Comoros, Greece, and Cambodia (the 'Mavi Marmara' incident),[16] Pre-Trial Chamber I relied on the Appeals Chamber's statements in *Al Hassan* to reject the Prosecutor's suggestion that the application of the gravity criterion in this context be informed by the 'selective mandate of the Court' and 'the Prosecutor's implicit duty to be a good steward of the limited resources of her Office'.[17] The purpose of the gravity criterion, when applied in the context of the Prosecutor's decisions whether to investigate and prosecute respectively, is not 'the selection of the most serious situations and cases'.[18] It is 'the exclusion of (potential) cases of marginal gravity'.[19]

---

[13] *Situation in the Democratic Republic of the Congo*, Appeals Chamber Decision 2006 (n 12) paras 69–79. See also MM deGuzman, *Shocking the Conscience of Humanity: Gravity and the Legitimacy of International Criminal Law* (OUP 2020) 120.

[14] *Prosecutor v Al Hassan*, ICC-01/12-01/18-601-Red, Appeals Chamber, Judgment on the Appeal of Mr Al Hassan Against the Decision of Pre-Trial Chamber I Entitled 'Décision relative a l'exception d'irrecevabilité pour insufficiance de gravité de l'affaire soulevée par la défense', 19 February 2020 (hereafter '*Al Hassan*, Appeals Chamber Decision 2020') para 59. The Appeals Chamber relied in support on the ILC's draft statute for an international criminal court, in which context the assessment of gravity had been included 'to ensure that the court only deals with cases in circumstances outlined in the preamble, that is to say where it is really desirable to do so'. ILC Report 1994 (n 8) 52; *Al Hassan*, Appeals Chamber Decision 2020 (n 14) para 58. In other words, for the Commission, the gravity criterion would determine whether 'the acts alleged were not of sufficient gravity to warrant trial at the international level' and thereby exclude 'peripheral complaints'. ILC, 'Summary Records of the Meetings of the Forty-Sixth Session' (2 May–22 July 1994) UN Doc A/CN.4/SER.A/1994, 9. Draft article 35(*c*) of the ILC's draft statute specified that a case would be inadmissible if 'the crime in question ... [i]s not of such gravity to justify further action by the Court'. The commentary to the provision used the term 'sufficient gravity', which appears in Article 17(1)(*d*) of the Rome Statute. While some members of the Commission believed that the inclusion of draft article 35(*c*) was unnecessary given that 'the relevant factors could be taken into account at the level of jurisdiction', others considered that 'the circumstances of particular cases could vary widely', warranting the inclusion of the admissibility criteria specified in draft article 35. ILC Report 1994 (n 8) 52.

[15] *Al Hassan*, Appeals Chamber Decision 2020 (n 14) para 53.

[16] See art 53(3)(*a*), Rome Statute.

[17] *Situation on the Registered Vessels of the Union of the Comoros, the Hellenic Republic and the Kingdom of Cambodia*, ICC-01/13-111, Pre-Trial Chamber I, Decision on the 'Application for Judicial Review by the Government of the Comoros', 16 September 2020 (hereafter '*Situation on the Registered Vessels of the Union of the Comoros, the Hellenic Republic and the Kingdom of Cambodia*, Pre-Trial Chamber Decision 2020') para 95 and footnote 190.

[18] ibid para 96.

[19] ibid para 96.

2.3 The Articulation of the Gravity Criterion

2.3.1 The Application of Article 17(1)(*d*) of the Statute to a Situation

2.3.1.1 The Assessment of the Admissibility of a Situation

As part of the assessment under Article 53(1) of the Rome Statute of whether there exists a 'reasonable basis to proceed under th[e] Statute'—that is, a reasonable basis to proceed with an investigation into a situation[20]—the Prosecutor is required under Article 53(1)(*b*) to undertake an assessment of admissibility. The assessment is conducted by reference to the admissibility criteria specified in Article 17 of the Statute, including the criterion of sufficient gravity found in Article 17(1)(*d*). Although the Prosecutor's decision under Article 53(1) pertains to the initiation or not of an investigation into a 'situation',[21] Article 53(1)(*b*) requires the Prosecutor to consider whether '[t]he case' is or would be admissible.[22] This incongruity in terminology arises equally in relation to the Prosecutor's decision whether to initiate an investigation into a situation *proprio motu*, since the Prosecutor's assessment of whether there exists a 'reasonable basis to proceed with an investigation' under Article 15(3), including his or her assessment of admissibility, is effectively taken under Article 53(1).[23] The chapeau to Article 17(1), by reference to which the Prosecutor's admissibility assessment is made, likewise speaks of the admissibility of a 'case', with Article 17(1)(*d*) specifying that '[t]he case is inadmissible if it is not of sufficient gravity to justify further action by the Court'.

What is required of the Prosecutor under Article 53(1)(*b*) of the Statute was first addressed in 2010 upon the Prosecutor's request for authorization to initiate an investigation into the situation in Kenya, the Prosecutor's first *proprio motu* investigation. Observing that the Prosecutor's assessment of admissibility under Article 53(1)(*b*) must be tailored to suit the functionally distinct stage at which it is undertaken,[24] Pre-Trial Chamber II considered that the assessment under this provision

---

[20] See Chapter 3, Section 3.2.1.1.

[21] See also arts 13(*a*)–(*b*), 14(1), 15(5)–(6), 18(1), Rome Statute; *Situation in Kenya*, Pre-Trial Chamber Decision 2010 (n 11) para 44.

[22] In the words of one Pre-Trial Chamber, 'the Court's jurisprudence has considered that a "case" falls within the ambit of the article 19 stage and it starts after the issuance of an arrest warrant or a summons to appear'. *Situation in Kenya*, Pre-Trial Chamber Decision 2010 (n 11) para 44. Recall Chapter 1, Section 1.6.2.

[23] See Rule 48, Rules of Procedure and Evidence 1998 (RPE); Chapter 3, Section 3.2.2.1.

[24] *Situation in Kenya*, Pre-Trial Chamber Decision 2010 (n 10) paras 41, 45–48. According to the Pre-Trial Chamber, the use of the term 'case' in Article 53(1) and other relevant provisions was 'advertently retained … leaving it for the Court to harmonize the meaning according to the different stages of the proceedings'. ibid para 47. Rastan suggests that the use of the term was 'the result of the disjunctive drafting process'. R Rastan, 'What Is a "Case" for the Purpose of the Rome Statute?' (2008) 19 Criminal Law Forum 435, 441.

30   GRAVITY AT THE INTERNATIONAL CRIMINAL COURT

must relate to 'one or more potential cases within the context of [the] situation'.[25] In the Chamber's view, this requires that admissibility be assessed by reference to

> (i) the groups of persons involved that are likely to be the object of an investigation for the purpose of shaping the future case(s); and (ii) the crimes within the jurisdiction of the Court allegedly committed during the incidents that are likely to be the focus of an investigation for the purpose of shaping the future case(s).[26]

The Appeals Chamber agreed that the assessment of admissibility was context-specific and, although not explicitly endorsing the approach of the Pre-Trial Chamber, observed that 'the contours of the likely cases will often be relatively vague' during proceedings under Articles 53(1) and 15(3)–(4), such that 'no individual suspects will have been identified ... nor will the exact conduct nor its legal classification be clear'.[27] The Prosecutor has subsequently followed the approach taken by Pre-Trial Chamber II in the Kenya authorization decision, claiming to carry out admissibility assessments under Article 53(1)(*b*) 'in relation to the most serious crimes allegedly committed by those who appear to bear the greatest responsibility' for them.[28] After initial confusion,[29] later Pre-Trial Chambers, in

---

[25] *Situation in Kenya*, Pre-Trial Chamber Decision 2010 (n 11) para 48.

[26] ibid para 59. An 'incident' has been defined by the Appeals Chamber as 'a historical event, defined in time and place, in the course of which crimes within the jurisdiction of the Court [a]re allegedly committed by one or more direct perpetrators'. *Prosecutor v Gaddafi and Al-Senussi*, ICC-01/11-01/11-547-Red, Appeals Chamber, Judgment on the Appeal of Libya against the Decision of Pre-Trial Chamber I of 31 May 2013 Entitled 'Decision on the Admissibility of the Case against Saif Al-Islam Gaddafi', 21 May 2014 (hereafter '*Gaddafi and Al-Senussi*, Appeals Chamber Decision 2014') para 62. See also *Al Hassan*, Appeals Chamber Decision 2020 (n 14) para 65.

[27] *Prosecutor v Ruto and others*, ICC-01/09-01/11-307, Appeals Chamber, Judgment on the Appeal of the Republic of Kenya against the Decision of Pre-Trial Chamber II of 30 May 2011 Entitled 'Decision on the Application by the Government of Kenya Challenging the Admissibility of the Case Pursuant to Article 19(2)(b) of the Statute', 30 August 2011 (hereafter '*Ruto and others*, Appeals Chamber Decision 2011') para 39. See also *Situation in Kenya*, Pre-Trial Chamber Decision 2010 (n 11) para 48; *Situation in Afghanistan*, ICC-02/17-33, Pre-Trial Chamber II, Decision Pursuant to Article 15 of the Rome Statute on the Authorisation of an Investigation into the Situation in the Islamic Republic of Afghanistan, 12 April 2019 (hereafter '*Situation in Afghanistan*, Pre-Trial Chamber Authorization Decision 2019') para 80; *Situation in Bangladesh/Myanmar*, ICC-01/19-27, Pre-Trial Chamber III, Decision Pursuant to Article 15 of the Rome Statute on the Authorisation of an Investigation into the Situation in the People's Republic of Bangladesh/Republic of the Union of Myanmar, 14 November 2019 (hereafter '*Situation in Bangladesh/Myanmar*, Pre-Trial Chamber Authorization Decision 2019') para 115; *Situation on the Registered Vessels of the Union of the Comoros, the Hellenic Republic and the Kingdom of Cambodia*, Pre-Trial Chamber Decision 2020 (n 17) para 44; Rastan, 'What Is a "Case" for the Purpose of the Rome Statute?' (n 24) 441; F Guariglia and E Rogier, 'The Selection of Situations and Cases by the OTP of the ICC' in C Stahn (ed), *The Law and Practice of the International Criminal Court* (OUP 2015) 361.

[28] See eg Article 53(1) Report, Office of the Prosecutor, 16 January 2013, para 134.

[29] The Pre-Trial Chamber in the Kenya authorization decision chose first to review the Prosecutor's assessment of the gravity of the 'entire situation' before 'undertaking its own assessment of the gravity of the potential cases'. *Situation in Kenya*, Pre-Trial Chamber Decision 2010 (n 11) para 189. Similarly, in respect of the situation in Côte d'Ivoire, Pre-Trial Chamber III considered that the gravity assessment should be conducted 'in a general sense, as regards the entire situation, but also against the backdrop of the potential case(s) within the context of a situation'. Ultimately, however, the Pre-Trial Chamber's evaluation was limited to a single paragraph that blurred the distinction it sought to draw. *Situation in Côte d'Ivoire*, Pre-Trial Chamber Authorization Decision 2011 (n 11) para 202.

their decisions to date under Articles 53(3)(*a*) and 15(4), have also adopted the approach taken by Pre-Trial Chamber II to the assessment of admissibility under Article 53(1)(*b*), even if they have not always implemented it in their application of the various indicators of gravity.[30]

The assessment of gravity in the context of the admissibility of one or more potential cases arising out of a situation raises two preliminary questions, namely how many potential cases need to be sufficiently grave in order to justify the initiation of an investigation into the situation and whether it is necessary or permissible for the Prosecutor to go beyond the jurisdictional scope of the situation in his or her assessment of gravity. Each is addressed here in turn.

2.3.1.1.1 *The number of sufficiently grave potential cases*

While clarifying that it is a potential case that is the object of the admissibility assessment under Article 53(1)(*b*) of the Statute, the decisions of the Pre-Trial Chambers have not addressed squarely how many potential cases need to be admissible to justify the initiation of an investigation into a situation. None of them has decided whether a finding in favour of the admissibility of one potential case alone arising out of the situation, including on the basis of the case's sufficient gravity, obliges the Prosecutor to initiate an investigation into the situation on the ground that there is a 'reasonable basis to proceed' under Article 53(1) or whether the satisfaction of the gravity criterion as part of the decision under Article 53(1) requires additional consideration of the number of potential cases that are admissible or even of the gravity of the situation considered as a whole.[31] The various formulae adopted by the Pre-Trial Chambers nonetheless appear to indicate that the admissibility of a single potential case suffices for the initiation of an investigation into a situation.

In the Kenya authorization decision, Pre-Trial Chamber II held that Article 53(1)(*b*) requires an assessment of gravity 'against the backdrop of a potential case within the context of a situation', suggesting that the situation may provide no more than relevant context for the assessment of the gravity of a potential case.[32] In its subsequent review of the Prosecutor's decision to decline, on the basis of

---

[30] See Section 2.3.1.2.2.

[31] Heller argues, for example, that the jurisdictional scope of the situation as a whole, while not determinative, bears on the assessment of gravity. KJ Heller, 'Could the ICC Investigate Israel's Attack on the Mavi Marmara?', Opinio Juris, 14 May 2013, http://opiniojuris.org/2013/05/14/could-the-icc-investig ate-the-mavi-marmara-incident, accessed 13 March 2023. This appears also to be the approach taken by the Prosecutor in declining to initiate an investigation into the situation on the registered vessels of The Comoros, Greece, and Cambodia (the 'Mavi Marmara' incident), which she described as 'limited' in scope. Article 53(1) Report, Office of the Prosecutor, 6 November 2014, para 143.

[32] *Situation in Kenya*, Pre-Trial Chamber Decision 2010 (n 11) para 188. See also *Situation on the Registered Vessels of the Union of the Comoros, the Hellenic Republic and the Kingdom of Cambodia*, ICC-01/13-34-Anx-Corr, Pre-Trial Chamber I, Partly Dissenting Opinion of Judge Péter Kovács, 16 July 2015 (hereafter '*Situation on the Registered Vessels of the Union of the Comoros, the Hellenic Republic and the Kingdom of Cambodia*, Kovács Partial Dissent 2015') paras 19–23.

32   GRAVITY AT THE INTERNATIONAL CRIMINAL COURT

insufficient gravity, to initiate an investigation into the Mavi Marmara incident, Pre-Trial Chamber I ruled that a reasonable basis to proceed with an investigation into a situation is established if 'at least one crime within the jurisdiction of the Court has been committed and ... the case would be admissible'.[33] The same approach was taken in respect of the situation in Bangladesh/Myanmar.[34]

Conversely, there are reasons to consider that a decision to initiate an investigation into a situation requires something more than the admissibility of one potential case. To be sure, initiating an investigation into a situation under Article 53(1)(*b*) on the basis of the admissibility of a single potential case is not inconsistent with the notion of a situation, which is defined by implication in the Rome Statute to include the commission of one or more crimes within the Court's jurisdiction.[35] Some commentators argue in this light that 'the ICC should not forgo prosecuting ... relevant cases solely on the ground that the situation does not involve a wider range of cases that could be prosecuted'.[36] Those, however, who disagree with the Pre-Trial Chambers' approach rightly point to the distinction between the gravity of a potential case and the gravity of the situation, contending that it is the latter which must satisfy the admissibility requirement

[33] *Situation on the Registered Vessels of the Union of the Comoros, the Hellenic Republic and the Kingdom of Cambodia*, ICC-01/13-34, Pre-Trial Chamber I, Decision on the Request of the Union of the Comoros to Review the Prosecutor's Decision Not to Initiate an Investigation, 16 July 2015 (hereafter '*Situation on the Registered Vessels of the Union of the Comoros, the Hellenic Republic and the Kingdom of Cambodia*, Pre-Trial Chamber Decision 2015') para 13. The Appeals Chamber, while not endorsing the approach of the Pre-Trial Chamber, considered that the Prosecutor had been bound by the Pre-Trial Chamber's conclusions on questions of law, which in the event included its articulation of a 'reasonable basis to proceed' under Article 53(1). *Situation on the Registered Vessels of the Union of the Comoros, the Hellenic Republic and the Kingdom of Cambodia*, ICC-01/13-98, Appeals Chamber, Judgment on the Appeal of the Prosecutor against Pre-Trial Chamber I's 'Decision on the "Application for Judicial Review by the Government of the Union of the Comoros"', 2 September 2019 (hereafter '*Situation on the Registered Vessels of the Union of the Comoros, the Hellenic Republic and the Kingdom of Cambodia*, Appeals Chamber Decision 2019') paras 87, 90. But see *Situation on the Registered Vessels of the Union of the Comoros, the Hellenic Republic and the Kingdom of Cambodia*, ICC-01/13-99-Anx1, Office of the Prosecutor, Final Decision of the Prosecutor Concerning the 'Article 53(1) Report' (ICC-01/13-6-AnxA), Dated 6 November 2014, as Revised and Refiled in Accordance with the Pre-Trial Chamber's Request of 15 November 2018 and the Appeals Chamber's Judgment of 2 September 2019, 2 December 2019 (hereafter '*Situation on the Registered Vessels of the Union of the Comoros, the Hellenic Republic and the Kingdom of Cambodia*, Final Decision of the Prosecutor 2019') footnote 20.

[34] *Situation in Bangladesh/Myanmar*, Pre-Trial Chamber Authorization Decision 2019 (n 27) para 127.

[35] See arts 13(*a*)–(*b*), 14, Rome Statute, each referring to a situation in which 'one or more' crimes appear to have been committed. As SáCouto and Cleary note, 'nothing from the drafting history clearly indicates that the negotiating states intended to *require* that a situation involve more than one case'. S SáCouto and K Cleary, 'The Relevance of a "Situation" to the Admissibility and Selection of Cases before the International Criminal Court' (2009) War Crimes Research Office 17. As Whiting elaborates, '[t]here could one day be a single-episode situation that would be sufficiently grave to warrant opening an investigation (think: Srebrenica)'. A Whiting, 'The ICC Prosecutor Should Reject Judges' Decision in Mavi Marmara Incident', Just Security, 20 July 2015 www.justsecurity.org/24778/icc-prosecutor-reject-judges-decision-mavi-marmara, accessed 13 March 2023.

[36] SáCouto and Cleary, 'The Relevance of a "Situation"' (n 35).

under Article 53(1)(*b*). Since what is ultimately being selected for investigation is a situation,[37]

> situational gravity is a function of all the potential cases in a situation that would be admissible before the Court: the greater the number of prosecutable crimes and the greater their individual gravity, the more situationally grave the situation.[38]

Accordingly, while the initiation of an investigation into a situation involving only one potential case is not excluded under Article 53(1), obliging the Prosecutor to initiate an investigation into every situation in which at least one potential case is admissible effectively lowers the standard of the 'reasonable basis to proceed' requirement in Articles 53(1) and 15(3) to the extent that it almost always compels the initiation of an investigation. In this way, the Pre-Trial Chambers' apparent approach not only restricts the Prosecutor's discretion to compare and choose among the various situations under consideration for investigation but also effectively eliminates prosecutorial discretion in the allocation of limited investigative resources.[39] Viewed in this light, the better approach would be to permit the

[37] WA Schabas, 'Selecting Situations and Cases' in C Stahn (ed), *The Law and Practice of the International Criminal Court* (OUP 2015) 366–67; MH Zakerhossein, 'A Concept without Consensus: Conceptualisation of the "Situation" Notion in the Rome Statute' (2018) 18 International Criminal Law Review 686, 688. For Jacobs, the initiation of an investigation into a situation comprising only one case blurs the distinction between a situation and a case, effectively permitting the referral by states parties or the Security Council of individual cases. See D Jacobs, 'The Comoros Referral to the ICC of the Israel Flotilla Raid: When a "Situation" Is Not Really a "Situation"', Spreading the Jam, 15 May 2013, https://dovjacobs.com/2013/05/15/the-comoros-referral-to-the-icc-of-the-israel-flotilla-raid-when-a-situation-is-not-really-a-situation, accessed 13 March 2023.

[38] KJ Heller, 'A Potentially Serious Problem with the Final Decision Concerning Comoros', Opinio Juris, 1 December 2017, http://opiniojuris.org/2017/12/01/33365, accessed 13 March 2023. Similarly, the 2020 report of the Independent Expert Review of the International Criminal Court and the Rome Statute System (Independent Expert Review) considered the number of potential cases to be relevant to the assessment of gravity. Final Report of the Independent Expert Review of the International Criminal Court and the Rome Statute System, 30 September 2020 (hereafter 'Independent Expert Review') para 648. In support, see G-JA Knoops and T Zwart, 'The *Flotilla Case* before the ICC: The Need to Do Justice While Keeping Heaven Intact' (2015) 15 International Criminal Law Review 1069, 1094–95; M Longobardo, 'Factors Relevant for the Assessment of Sufficient Gravity in the ICC: Proceedings and the Elements of International Crimes' (2016) 33 Questions of International Law 21, 28. In contrast, Mariniello argues that 'situational gravity' is an element of prosecutorial policy that lies outside the admissibility assessment under Article 53(1)(*b*) but nevertheless contributes to the Prosecutor's decision whether to initiate an investigation. T Mariniello, 'Judicial Control over Prosecutorial Discretion at the International Criminal Court' (2019) 19 International Criminal Law Review 979, 985–86, 1005. The limitation of this latter approach is that the discretion to use an additional policy consideration of situational gravity outside of the gravity assessment for admissibility is possible only through the exercise of the Prosecutor's discretion whether to request authorization for the initiation of an investigation *proprio motu*, under Article 15(3), precluding the use under Article 53(1) of situational gravity as part of the Prosecutor's decision whether to initiate an investigation into a situation upon referral.

[39] Heller predicts that this is in turn likely to increase disagreements between the Prosecutor and the Pre-Trial Chambers as to the application of gravity, as well as to create an incentive for states parties and the Security Council to refer situations comprising only one case, including with frivolity or for political reasons, thereby restricting the Prosecutor's discretion in the selection of cases for prosecution. Heller, *A Potentially Serious Problem with the Final Decision Concerning Comoros* (n 38). See also KJ Heller, 'The Pre-Trial Chamber's Dangerous Comoros Review Decision', Opinio Juris, 17 July 2015, http://opin iojuris.org/2015/07/17/the-pre-trial-chambers-problematic-comoros-review-decision, accessed 13

34   GRAVITY AT THE INTERNATIONAL CRIMINAL COURT

Prosecutor the discretion to decide whether to initiate an investigation into a situation through additional consideration of the number of potential cases that may be admissible, while still allowing, in line with the Rome Statute, the initiation of an investigation into a situation involving only one potential case.

2.3.1.1.2 *The assessment of gravity beyond the jurisdictional scope of the situation*

The second related question, which pertains to the scope of the gravity assessment under Article 53(1)(*b*) of the Statute, is whether it is necessary or permissible for the Prosecutor to go beyond the jurisdictional scope of the situation in his or her assessment of gravity. In relation to the Mavi Marmara incident, the majority of Pre-Trial Chamber I considered that the Prosecutor is not limited in his or her assessment of gravity to the jurisdictional scope of the situation. In other words, the Prosecutor 'has the authority to consider all necessary information, including as concerns extra-jurisdictional facts for the purpose of establishing ... gravity'.[40] The Pre-Trial Chamber did not determine, however, how far the gravity assessment could extend. It is unclear whether it went so far as to affirm the referring state party's assertion that the Prosecutor should have accounted for facts relating to the blockade, occupation, and conflict between Israel and Palestine in her application of the gravity threshold.[41] In dissent, Judge Kovács emphasized the need to maintain the distinction in his view between the gravity of the situation under consideration, which was 'confined to the crimes allegedly committed by IDF [Israeli

---

March 2023; L Poltronieri Rossetti, Prosecutorial Discretion and Its Judicial Review at the International Criminal Court: A Practice-Based Analysis of the Relationship between the Prosecutor and Judges (doctoral thesis, Università Degli Studi di Trento 2017–2018) 298–99.

[40] *Situation on the Registered Vessels of the Union of the Comoros, the Hellenic Republic and the Kingdom of Cambodia*, Pre-Trial Chamber Decision 2015 (n 33) para 17. The position was reiterated by Pre-Trial Chamber III when addressing the satisfaction of jurisdictional requirements in relation to the situation in Bangladesh/Myanmar. *Situation in Bangladesh/Myanmar*, Pre-Trial Chamber Authorization Decision 2019 (n 27) para 93. In support, see A Emrah Bozbayindir, 'The Venture of the Comoros Referral at the Preliminary Examination Stage' in C Stahn and M Bergsmo (eds), *Quality Control in Preliminary Examinations Volume 1* (Torkel Opsahl Academic EPublisher 2018) 634–36. In line with this approach, Pues proposes a reference to 'the broader situation of crisis that provides the background of the specific crime committed', including beyond the jurisdiction of the Court, on which basis she excludes 'isolated incidents that lack any context to a broader situation of crisis'. A Pues, 'Discretion and the Gravity of Situations at the International Criminal Court' (2017) 17 International Criminal Law Review 960, 977–79. See also WA Schabas, 'Prosecutorial Discretion and Gravity' in C Stahn and G Sluiter (eds), *The Emerging Practice of the International Criminal Court* (Martinus Nijhoff 2009) 245–46.

[41] *Situation on the Registered Vessels of the Union of the Comoros, the Hellenic Republic and the Kingdom of Cambodia*, ICC-01/13-3-Red, Government of The Comoros, Application for Review pursuant to Article 53(3)(a) of the Prosecutor's Decision of 6 November 2014 Not to Initiate an Investigation in the Situation, 29 January 2015 (hereafter '*Situation on the Registered Vessels of the Union of the Comoros, the Hellenic Republic and the Kingdom of Cambodia*, Application for Review 2015') paras 13–15. See also C Meloni, 'The ICC Preliminary Examination of the Flotilla Situation: An Opportunity to Contextualise Gravity' (2016) 33 Questions of International Law 3, 20; AKA Greenawalt, 'Admissibility as a Theory of International Criminal Law' in MM deGuzman and V Oosterveld (eds), *The Elgar Companion to the International Criminal Court* (Edward Elgar Publishing 2020) 89.

Defense Forces] soldiers on board the vessels' registered to states parties,[42] and 'the *overall* humanitarian crisis suffered by the Palestinian civilian population which in fact resulted from the entirety of the ongoing Palestinian-Israeli conflict'.[43] The concern that Judge Kovács seems to have alluded to, although not expressly articulated, is that the consideration of the latter would inflate the gravity of the otherwise limited situation. Similar concerns could be said to arise in respect of the situation in Bangladesh/Myanmar, in which context the jurisdiction of the Court and the scope of the situation are limited to crimes committed in part on the territory of Bangladesh, a state party. An assessment of gravity that accounts also for facts beyond the scope of the situation, such as those pertaining to crimes committed exclusively on the territory of Myanmar, a non-state party, might support a finding of sufficient gravity based on the consideration of extra-jurisdictional facts.[44] The Pre-Trial Chamber's approach in the Mavi Marmara proceedings is problematic if taken to require the initiation of an investigation even into a situation in respect of which much of what renders the situation sufficiently grave lies beyond the scope of the proposed investigation and of any eventual prosecution or prosecutions which the assessment of gravity is intended to justify. It is doubtful whether considerations beyond the jurisdictional scope of the situation could be relevant to the assessment of gravity in the context of the initiation of an investigation that is limited by the jurisdiction of the Court.

2.3.1.2 The Application of Article 17(1)(*d*) to a Situation in Practice
2.3.1.2.1 *Overview*
When it comes to the Prosecutor's decision whether to initiate an investigation into a situation, whether under Article 53(1) of the Statute alone or by additional reference to Article 15(3), the understanding of the Office of the Prosecutor of the gravity criterion in Article 17(1)(*d*) is articulated in Regulation 29(2) of the 2009 Regulations of the Office of the Prosecutor. The four indicators cited therein of the scale, nature, manner of commission, and impact of the crimes are elaborated on further in the Office of the Prosecutor's 2013 Policy Paper on Preliminary

---

[42] *Situation on the Registered Vessels of the Union of the Comoros, the Hellenic Republic and the Kingdom of Cambodia*, Kovács Partial Dissent 2015 (n 32) para 22.

[43] ibid para 21. See also D Jacobs, 'ICC Judges Ask the Prosecutor to Reconsider Decision Not to Investigate Israeli Gaza Flotilla Conduct', Spreading the Jam, 20 July 2015, https://dovjacobs.com/2015/07/20/icc-judges-ask-the-prosecutor-to-reconsider-decision-not-to-investigate-israeli-gaza-flotilla-conduct, accessed 13 March 2023.

[44] See *Situation in Bangladesh/Myanmar*, ICC-RoC46(3)-01/18-37, Pre-Trial Chamber I, Decision on the 'Prosecution's Request for a Ruling on Jurisdiction under Article 19(3) of the Statute', 6 September 2018 (hereafter '*Situation in Bangladesh/Myanmar*, Pre-Trial Chamber Decision 2018') paras 73–74; KJ Heller, 'Three Cautionary Thoughts on the OTP's Rohingya Request', Opinio Juris, 9 April 2018, http://opiniojuris.org/2018/04/09/some-thoughts-on-the-otps-rohingya-request, accessed 13 March 2023. Another example is the situation in Iraq, whose scope is limited to crimes allegedly committed by UK nationals in Iraq. The additional consideration of other events in the territory of Iraq may inflate the assessment of the gravity of the arguably more limited situation.

36   GRAVITY AT THE INTERNATIONAL CRIMINAL COURT

Examinations. In their respective reviews to date, under Articles 53(3)(*a*) and 15(4) of the Statute, of the Prosecutor's assessments of admissibility, the Pre-Trial Chambers have in principle endorsed the relevance of these indicators to the gravity assessment. When it has come, however, to the application of the same indicators, the approach of the Pre-Trial Chambers has at times differed from that of the Prosecutor. Since the decision authorizing the initiation of the Prosecutor's first *proprio motu* investigation, in Kenya, the Pre-Trial Chambers have also included a fifth indicator of gravity in relation to situations, requiring that the potential case or cases arising out of a situation implicate the person or persons bearing the greatest responsibility for the alleged crimes. The Appeals Chamber has, for its part, shed limited light on the application of Article 17(1)(*d*) in relation to situations, even though the disagreement between the Prosecutor and the Pre-Trial Chamber as to the application of gravity came before it twice during the Mavi Marmara proceedings.[45]

2.3.1.2.2 In detail

In the early practice of the Court, there was little indication as to how the Prosecutor reached a decision under Article 53(1) of the Statute.[46] This was probably in part a result of the fact that the Prosecutor had decided to initiate an investigation into every situation referred to him, whether by a state party or the Security Council, and felt no need rigorously to justify decisions that conformed to the views of the referring entities. These decisions pertained to the situations in the DRC, Uganda, and Darfur, Sudan.[47] It was only in relation to the first situation in the Central African Republic (CAR), referred to the Prosecutor by the government of the CAR

---

[45] A more detailed analysis of the Appeals Chamber's decisions is provided in Chapter 3.

[46] For an overview, see Schabas, *Prosecutorial Discretion and Gravity* (n 40) 229–31.

[47] In the Prosecutor's first ever investigation, in the situation in the DRC, the only statement addressing the application of Article 53(1) was as follows: 'my Office has conducted analysis and sought additional information in order to support a determination under Article 53 on the DRC situation. Having considered all of the criteria, I have determined that there is a reasonable basis to initiate an investigation'. See the letter of the Office of the Prosecutor dated 17 June 2004, annexed to *Situation in Uganda*, ICC-02/04-1, Presidency, Decision Assigning the Situation in Uganda to Pre-Trial Chamber II, 5 July 2004. Similarly, in relation to the situation in Darfur, the Prosecutor 'determined that there is a reasonable basis to initiate an investigation into the situation in Darfur, The Sudan'. Letter of the Office of the Prosecutor dated 1 June 2005, *Situation in Darfur, Sudan*, ICC-02/05-2, Office of the Prosecutor, 1 June 2005, www.icc-cpi.int/CourtRecords/CR2007_01519.PDF, accessed 13 March 2023. A 2006 report summarizing the first three years of the Prosecutor's activities is only slightly more helpful. It confirmed that '[t]he situations in the Democratic Republic of the Congo ... and Northern Uganda were the gravest admissible situations under the jurisdiction of the Court' and that '[t]he situation in Darfur, the Sudan ... also clearly met the gravity standard'. Report on the Activities Performed During the First Three Years (June 2003–June 2006), Office of the Prosecutor, 12 September 2006, 6–7. In the absence of judicial oversight, details regarding these determinations under Article 53(1), which we can only presume included assessments of gravity, were not made publicly available. For the view that considerations of gravity did not play a role in these decisions to investigate, see D Scheffer, 'False Alarm about the *Proprio Motu* Prosecutor' in M Minow, C Cora True-Frost, and A Whiting (eds), *The First Global Prosecutor* (University of Michigan Press 2015) 35.

in 2004, that the Prosecutor published a report detailing his decision under Article 53(1), and even then only when in 2006 the government of the CAR sought information as to his failure to decide 'within a reasonable time' whether to initiate an investigation.[48] The report did not include a consideration of gravity.[49]

The first occasion on which the Prosecutor had explicit recourse to the gravity criterion in the context of a situation was when justifying his decision in 2006 not to proceed with an investigation into the situation in Iraq on the basis of insufficient gravity. While asserting that various unspecified indicators were relevant to the assessment of gravity under Article 53(1)(*b*), the 'key consideration' for the Prosecutor was 'the number of victims of particularly serious crimes, such as wilful killing or rape'.[50] Contrasting on this basis the situation in Iraq, on the one hand, and the situations already under investigation in the DRC, Uganda, and Darfur, on the other, the Prosecutor concluded that the requirement of gravity had not been satisfied in relation to the situation in Iraq.[51] Since the decision pertained to the initiation of an investigation *proprio motu*, it was not subjected to review by a Pre-Trial Chamber.[52] Not long after the decision in respect of the situation in Iraq, the Prosecutor advanced the position that, conditional upon the satisfaction of jurisdictional requirements, the initiation or not of an investigation into a situation would be 'guided by the standard of gravity'.[53]

The Prosecutor's approach to the application under Article 53(1)(*b*) of the criterion of gravity was eventually codified in the 2009 Regulations of the Office of the Prosecutor. The Regulations explain that

[i]n order to assess the gravity of the crimes allegedly committed in the situation the Office shall consider various factors including their scale, nature, manner of commission, and impact.[54]

---

[48] *Situation in the Central African Republic I*, ICC-01/05-5-Anx3, Government of the CAR, Réception par le Procureur d'un renvoi concernant la République Centrafricaine, 27 September 2006.

[49] See *Situation in the Central African Republic I*, ICC-OTP-BN-20070522-220-A_EN, Office of the Prosecutor, Background: Situation in the Central African Republic, 22 May 2007, 2–3.

[50] Letter of the Office of the Prosecutor dated 9 February 2006, *Situation in Iraq*, 9 February 2006, www.icc-cpi.int/sites/default/files/NR/rdonlyres/04D143C8-19FB-466C-AB77-4CDB2FDEBEF7/143 682/OTP_letter_to_senders_re_Iraq_9_February_2006.pdf, accessed 13 March 2023, 8–9.

[51] ibid 9.

[52] The Prosecutor reopened the preliminary examination into the situation in Iraq in 2014 and closed it in 2020 based on considerations of complementarity. As for gravity, the Prosecutor concluded that the criterion had been satisfied, including on the basis of supervisory failings at various levels, which contributed in her opinion to the gravity of the manner of the commission of the crimes. See Situation in Iraq/UK: Final Report, Office of the Prosecutor, 9 December 2020, paras 128–48.

[53] Report on the Activities Performed During the First Three Years (June 2003–June 2006), Office of the Prosecutor, 12 September 2006, para 2(*a*).

[54] Reg 29(2), Regulations of the Office of the Prosecutor 2009 (OTP Regs).

38 GRAVITY AT THE INTERNATIONAL CRIMINAL COURT

The four indicators cited, namely the scale, nature, manner of commission, and impact of the crimes allegedly committed, are further developed in the Prosecutor's 2013 Policy Paper on Preliminary Examinations.[55]

For their part, the Pre-Trial Chambers have endorsed in principle the use of these indicators in their decisions under Articles 53(3)(a) and 15(4) of the Statute, even if they have not always agreed with the Prosecutor's articulation of each indicator in policy or with its application in practice. When it has come to their own application of the four indicators, moreover, the Pre-Trial Chambers have at times disagreed among themselves as to their content. In addition, Pre-Trial Chambers acting under both Article 53(3)(a) and Article 15(4) have required, as part of the assessment of gravity, consideration of whether the potential case or cases arising out of the situation implicate the person or persons bearing greatest responsibility for the alleged crimes. Each of the indicators is discussed in turn below.

2.3.1.2.2.1 Scale The scale of the crimes allegedly committed is the first indicator considered relevant in assessing the gravity of a situation. According to the Office of the Prosecutor, the scale of the crimes

> may be assessed in light of, *inter alia*, the number of direct and indirect victims, the extent of the damage caused by the crimes, in particular the bodily or psychological harm caused to the victims and their families, or their geographical or temporal scope (high intensity of the crimes over a brief period or low intensity of crimes over an extended period).[56]

In their decisions to date under Articles 53(3)(a) and 15(4) of the Statute, the Pre-Trial Chambers have endorsed the relevance of this indicator to the assessment of gravity. While claiming, since the Kenya authorization decision, to conduct the assessment by reference to one or more potential cases arising out of the situation, they have not always limited the assessment of scale to the potential case or cases arising out of the situation.

In the first decision issued under Article 53(3)(a) of the Statute, Pre-Trial Chamber I, in its 2015 review of the Prosecutor's decision not to initiate an investigation into the Mavi Marmara incident, considered—in relation to the situation as a whole, rather than any potential cases arising out of it[57]—that 'ten killings, 50–55

---

[55] Since 2011, the Office of the Prosecutor has also published annual reports detailing its preliminary examination activities, including, to a limited extent, its application of the gravity criterion in respect of situations under consideration for investigation.

[56] Policy Paper on Preliminary Examinations, Office of the Prosecutor, 2013, para 62.

[57] One possible explanation for this is that the Pre-Trial Chamber considered the situation—which had been confined to three vessels registered to states parties—as being so limited in scope as to comprise only one potential case. This was evidently not the view taken by the Prosecutor. See Article 53(1) Report, Office of the Prosecutor, 6 November 2014, para 148. See also Jacobs, *The Comoros Referral to the ICC of the Israel Flotilla Raid* (n 37).

APPLICATION OF GRAVITY CRITERION FOR ADMISSIBILITY   39

injuries, and possibly hundreds of instances of outrages upon personal dignity, or torture or inhuman treatment', satisfied the requirement of scale.[58] It was relevant for the Chamber that the scale of the alleged crimes, in its estimate, 'exceed[ed] the number of casualties in actual cases that were previously not only investigated but even prosecuted by the Prosecutor'.[59] Judge Kovács disagreed on the point and sought to make his own comparison between the Mavi Marmara incident and the situations—as opposed to cases—that were already under investigation by the Prosecutor at the time. In his view, 'the underlying incidents in the Kenya situation' were, for instance, 'much broader in scope and magnitude', and the number of deaths in relation to the Mavi Marmara incident did not compare to 'the death of about 1,220 and the serious injury of 3,561 persons in six out of the eight Kenyan provinces'.[60] He made a similar comparison with the incidents arising out of the situation in Côte d'Ivoire.[61]

The Pre-Trial Chambers have also endorsed the scale of the alleged crimes as an indicator of gravity in their decisions, under Article 15(4) of the Statute, on the initiation of investigations *proprio motu*. The 2010 decision authorizing the initiation of the investigation in Kenya relied on the sentencing criteria in the Court's Rules of Procedure and Evidence to support its consideration of the scale of the alleged crimes, including 'the extent of the damage caused', in particular 'the harm caused to the victims and their families', and the 'geographical and temporal intensity' of the crimes.[62] In line with this approach, Pre-Trial Chamber III, in its 2011 decision authorizing the initiation of an investigation in Côte d'Ivoire, found that the requirement of scale had been satisfied by the alleged large-scale commission of 'serious crimes such as murder, rape and enforced disappearance'.[63] The subsequent authorization by Pre-Trial Chamber I of an investigation into the situation in Georgia was similarly supported by the consideration of '51–113 killings, the

---

[58] *Situation on the Registered Vessels of the Union of the Comoros, the Hellenic Republic and the Kingdom of Cambodia*, Pre-Trial Chamber Decision 2015 (n 33) para 26.

[59] ibid.

[60] *Situation on the Registered Vessels of the Union of the Comoros, the Hellenic Republic and the Kingdom of Cambodia*, Kovács Partial Dissent 2015 (n 32) para 19.

[61] The situation in Côte d'Ivoire had pertained, among other things, to 'the killings of *hundreds* of civilians in the town of Duékoué', a figure incomparable in the view of Judge Kovács to the number of deaths that resulted from the Mavi Marmara incident as a whole. *Situation on the Registered Vessels of the Union of the Comoros, the Hellenic Republic and the Kingdom of Cambodia*, Kovács Partial Dissent 2015 (n 32) para 23.

[62] The Pre-Trial Chamber cited, inter alia, Rule 145(1)(c) of the RPE. *Situation in Kenya*, Pre-Trial Chamber Decision 2010 (n 11) para 62. It pointed to the number of 'deaths, documented rapes, displaced persons, and acts of injury', as well as the widespread geographical scope of their commission, to establish their scale. ibid para 191.

[63] *Situation in Côte d'Ivoire*, Pre-Trial Chamber Authorization Decision 2011 (n 11) para 205. Notably, neither the Prosecutor in the submission of additional information on the request of the Pre-Trial Chamber nor the Chamber itself in its second decision expanding the temporal scope of the authorized investigation conducted an additional assessment of gravity. See *Situation in Côte d'Ivoire*, ICC-02/11-36, Pre-Trial Chamber III, Decision on the 'Prosecution's Provision of Further Information Regarding Potentially Relevant Crimes Committed Between 2002 and 2010', 22 February 2012, para 38.

destruction of over 5,000 dwellings and the forced displacement of 13,400–18,500 persons', which had, in the Prosecutor's estimate, collectively resulted in a 75 per cent decrease in the ethnic Georgian population in South Ossetia.[64] In the same vein, Pre-Trial Chamber II, in the first decision rejecting a request for the authorization of an investigation *proprio motu* on the grounds of the 'interests of justice',[65] nevertheless found in its decision of 2019 on the situation in Afghanistan that the gravity requirement had been satisfied by the large numbers of direct and indirect victims of the alleged crimes and the latter's 'large-scale commission over a prolonged period of time'.[66] The Chamber that authorized the initiation of the investigation in Burundi believed more generally that 'the many thousands of victims' of the crimes[67] allegedly committed within the situation satisfied the requirement of scale, while noting that even 'a limited number of casualties' coupled with qualitative indicators might satisfy the gravity criterion.[68] So also Pre-Trial Chamber III, in its authorization of an investigation into the situation in Bangladesh/Myanmar, relied solely on the scale of the crimes allegedly committed within the situation as a whole to satisfy the gravity criterion, which it evidenced by the 'estimated 600,000 to one million' victims of displacement.[69]

In contrast with their endorsement in principle of the assessment of gravity by reference to one or more potential cases arising out of the situation, none of the Pre-Trial Chambers has clearly restricted its assessment of scale to the potential case or cases arising out of the situation under consideration for investigation, instead assessing the scale of the crimes by reference to the situation as a whole.

2.3.1.2.2.2 Nature The second indicator of the gravity of the crimes allegedly committed within a situation is their nature. In the policy of the Office of the Prosecutor, the nature of the crimes

> refers to the specific elements of each offence such as killings, rapes and other
> crimes involving sexual or gender violence and crimes committed against

---

[64] *Situation in Georgia*, ICC-01/15-12, Pre-Trial Chamber I, Decision on the Prosecutor's Request for Authorization of an Investigation, 27 January 2016 (hereafter '*Situation in Georgia*, Pre-Trial Chamber Authorization Decision 2016') para 54.

[65] See art 53(1)(*c*), Rome Statute.

[66] *Situation in Afghanistan*, Pre-Trial Chamber Authorization Decision 2019 (n 27) para 81. See also ibid para 82. While satisfying the gravity criterion in relation to crimes allegedly committed by US nationals, however, the Chamber did not appear to address the scale of the crimes. ibid para 83.

[67] *Situation in Burundi*, ICC-01/17-9-Red, Pre-Trial Chamber III, Public Redacted Version of 'Decision Pursuant to Article 15 of the Rome Statute on the Authorization of an Investigation into the Situation in the Republic of Burundi', 9 November 2017 (hereafter '*Situation in Burundi*, Pre-Trial Chamber Authorization Decision 2017') para 188.

[68] ibid para 184.

[69] *Situation in Bangladesh/Myanmar*, Pre-Trial Chamber Authorization Decision 2019 (n 27) para 118.

children, persecution, or the imposition of conditions of life on a group calculated to bring about its destruction.[70]

The Pre-Trial Chambers have endorsed the nature of the crimes as a relevant indicator of gravity. In only a handful of decisions, however, have they actually considered the nature of the alleged crimes as part of their assessment of gravity. In some of these decisions, the Pre-Trial Chambers have adopted an approach different from that of the Prosecutor, relying on the legal characterization of the conduct as the basis for the assessment. In others, they have focused on the vulnerability of the victims as the relevant indicator of the nature of the alleged crimes.

In its review under Article 53(3)(*a*) of the Statute of the Prosecutor's decision not to initiate an investigation into the Mavi Marmara incident, Pre-Trial Chamber I found that the nature of the alleged crimes 'revolves around ... the possible legal qualifications of the apparent facts, *i.e.* the crimes that are being or could be prosecuted'.[71] Considering that it was the legal characterization of the conduct that was relevant to the assessment of the nature of the crimes, the Pre-Trial Chamber found that the Prosecutor's assessment, which had been based on what the Chamber considered to be her premature characterization of relevant conduct as the war crime of 'outrages upon personal dignity', excluded the potential characterization of the conduct as the arguably more serious war crime of 'torture or inhuman treatment', which would have supported a finding of sufficient gravity, and was therefore erroneous.[72]

Only three of the Pre-Trial Chambers acting under Article 15(4) of the Statute have referred to the nature of the alleged crimes when reviewing the Prosecutor's assessments of the gravity of a situation, relying in this context variously on the legal characterization of conduct and the vulnerability of the victims to demonstrate gravity.[73] Pre-Trial Chamber II, in its decision authorizing the *proprio motu*

---

[70] Policy Paper on Preliminary Examinations, Office of the Prosecutor, 2013, para 63. As Seils explains, it was perhaps assumed that 'while there is no explicit hierarchy of crimes in the Rome Statute, it is generally accepted that most national systems of law enforcement will prioritize certain kinds of crimes, in particular those dealing with loss of life or serious violation of physical integrity'. P Seils, 'The Selection and Prioritization of Cases by the Office of the Prosecutor' in M Bergsmo (ed), *Criteria for Prioritizing and Selecting Core International Crimes* (Torkel Opsahl Academic EPublisher 2010) 73–74.

[71] *Situation on the Registered Vessels of the Union of the Comoros, the Hellenic Republic and the Kingdom of Cambodia*, Pre-Trial Chamber Decision 2015 (n 33) para 28. See also *Situation on the Registered Vessels of the Union of the Comoros, the Hellenic Republic and the Kingdom of Cambodia*, Pre-Trial Chamber Decision 2020 (n 17) para 58. Conversely, Judge Kovács considered that the majority went beyond the scope of its review in 'enter[ing] new findings under jurisdiction (war crimes of torture or inhuman treatment) instead of reviewing the existing ones'. *Situation on the Registered Vessels of the Union of the Comoros, the Hellenic Republic and the Kingdom of Cambodia*, Kovács Partial Dissent 2015 (n 32) para 11.

[72] See Article 53(1) Report, Office of the Prosecutor, 6 November 2014, para 139.

[73] Other Pre-Trial Chambers made only passing references to the nature of the alleged crimes. Pre-Trial Chamber III in its decision authorizing the investigation in Côte d'Ivoire referred to the commission of 'serious crimes' such as murder and rape. *Situation in Côte d'Ivoire*, Pre-Trial Chamber Authorization Decision 2011 (n 11) para 205. So also, when Pre-Trial Chamber I authorized the initiation of an investigation into the situation in Georgia, no mention was made of the nature of the crimes

42 GRAVITY AT THE INTERNATIONAL CRIMINAL COURT

investigation in Kenya, relied again on sentencing criteria to endorse 'the nature of the unlawful behaviour or of the crimes allegedly committed' as an indicator of gravity, even if it did not apply the indicator to the situation at hand.[74] Pre-Trial Chamber III, in its 2017 authorization of the investigation in Burundi, referred to the crimes of murder, rape, and imprisonment as having allegedly been committed against children to support a finding of sufficient gravity.[75] Similarly, in the subsequent 2019 decision in respect of the situation in Afghanistan, Pre-Trial Chamber II characterized certain alleged crimes as having involved 'the recurrent targeting of women, even very young, and vulnerable civilians' to justify their gravity.[76] Much like the Pre-Trial Chamber that had addressed the Mavi Marmara incident, Pre-Trial Chamber II also invoked the legal characterization of certain other conduct to conclude that 'the gravity per se of the crime of torture' itself satisfied the requirement of sufficient gravity.[77]

2.3.1.2.2.3 Manner of commission The third indicator of the gravity of a situation is the manner of commission of the crimes allegedly committed. In the view of the Office of the Prosecutor, this

> may be assessed in light of, *inter alia*, the means employed to execute the crime, the degree of participation and intent of the perpetrator (if discernible at this stage), the extent to which the crimes were systematic or result from a plan or organised policy or otherwise resulted from the abuse of power or official capacity, and elements of particular cruelty, including the vulnerability of the victims, any motives involving discrimination, or the use of rape and sexual violence as a means of destroying groups.[78]

The Pre-Trial Chambers have endorsed the relevance of this indicator to the assessment of gravity, highlighting in particular the means employed to execute the crimes and elements of particular cruelty in their commission. None of the Pre-Trial Chambers acting under either Article 53(3)(*a*) or Article 15(4) has considered, however, the degree of participation and intent of the potential perpetrators of the crimes to be factors relevant to the assessment of the gravity of a situation.

---

beyond the superfluous observation that 'the potential cases could encompass an array of war crimes and crimes against humanity'. *Situation in Georgia*, Pre-Trial Chamber Authorization Decision 2016 (n 64) para 53.

[74] See Rule 145(1)(*c*), RPE. *Situation in Kenya*, Pre-Trial Chamber Decision 2010 (n 11) para 62.
[75] *Situation in Burundi*, Pre-Trial Chamber Authorization Decision 2017 (n 67) para 188.
[76] *Situation in Afghanistan*, Pre-Trial Chamber Authorization Decision 2019 (n 27) para 84.
[77] ibid para 85.
[78] Policy Paper on Preliminary Examinations, Office of the Prosecutor, 2013, para 64.

Proceeding under Article 53(3)(a) of the Statute, the Pre-Trial Chamber that considered the Mavi Marmara incident examined in detail the manner of commission of the alleged crimes as an indicator of gravity. Placing particular emphasis on the existence of a plan to commit the crimes,[79] it suggested that unnecessary cruelty in the commission of the crimes might, in addition to itself supporting a finding of sufficient gravity, evidence the existence of such a plan.[80]

Conversely, proceeding under Article 15(4) of the Statute, the Pre-Trial Chamber that authorized the initiation of the investigation *proprio motu* in Kenya articulated the manner of commission of the alleged crimes as an indicator of gravity more narrowly than did the Office of the Prosecutor, equating it only with 'the employed means for the execution of the crimes', a term that appears among the sentencing criteria specified in the Court's Rules of Procedure and Evidence.[81] Accordingly, the Chamber considered that the particular brutality with which the crimes had allegedly been committed had been 'pertinent to the means used to execute the violence'.[82] Notwithstanding their inclusion in the same sentencing provision, the Chamber did not refer—as the Office of the Prosecutor appeared to do—to the sentencing criteria of 'the degree of participation of the convicted person' and 'the degree of intent'.[83] Neither was the existence of a plan to commit the crimes nor systematicity in their alleged commission considered relevant.

Subsequent Pre-Trial Chambers issuing decisions under Article 15(4) have not limited themselves to brutality in the alleged execution of the crimes.[84] Pre-Trial

---

[79] The Pre-Trial Chamber considered that the possible use of live fire by the Israeli Defense Forces (IDF) prior to their boarding of the Mavi Marmara, a fact the Prosecutor had been unable to establish, should have contributed to the Prosecutor's gravity assessment as it was 'material to the determination of whether there was a prior intent and plan to attack and kill unarmed civilians'. *Situation on the Registered Vessels of the Union of the Comoros, the Hellenic Republic and the Kingdom of Cambodia,* Pre-Trial Chamber Decision 2015 (n 33) para 34. For the Chamber, the use of live fire 'may reasonably suggest that there was, on the part of the IDF forces who carried out the identified crimes, a prior intention to attack and possibly kill'. ibid para 36. But see Whiting, '*The ICC Prosecutor Should Reject Judges' Decision in Mavi Marmara Incident*' (n 35).

[80] *Situation on the Registered Vessels of the Union of the Comoros, the Hellenic Republic and the Kingdom of Cambodia,* Pre-Trial Chamber Decision 2015 (n 33) para 41. Accordingly, the Prosecutor's failure to account for the possibility of a plan adversely affected the outcome of her gravity assessment. *Situation on the Registered Vessels of the Union of the Comoros, the Hellenic Republic and the Kingdom of Cambodia,* Pre-Trial Chamber Decision 2015 (n 33) para 34.

[81] See Rule 145(1)(c), RPE. *Situation in Kenya,* Pre-Trial Chamber Decision 2010 (n 11) para 62.

[82] *Situation in Kenya,* Pre-Trial Chamber Decision 2010 (n 11) para 193. The Chamber relied on the material supporting the Prosecutor's request to illustrate 'many instances of cutting and hacking, including amputations, and reports of forced circumcision and genital amputation inflicted upon members of the Luo community', as well as 'high numbers of reported gang rapes, including by a group of over 20 men, and the cutting of the victims or the insertion of crude weapon [sic] and other objects in the vagina'. *Situation in Kenya,* Pre-Trial Chamber Decision 2010 (n 11) para 193. When addressing the gravity of potential cases arising from the situation, additional elements of brutality noted by the Chamber included 'burning victims alive, attacking places sheltering IDPs [internally displaced persons], beheadings, and using pangas and machetes to hack people to death'. ibid para 199.

[83] See Rule 145(1)(c) and (2)(b)(ii)–(v), RPE.

[84] For the Pre-Trial Chambers' approaches to brutality in the commission of the crimes, see eg *Situation in Georgia,* Pre-Trial Chamber Authorization Decision 2016 (n 64) para 54; *Situation in Burundi,* Pre-Trial Chamber Authorization Decision 2017 (n 67) para 188; *Situation in Afghanistan,* Pre-Trial Chamber Authorization Decision 2019 (n 27) para 84.

44   GRAVITY AT THE INTERNATIONAL CRIMINAL COURT

Chamber III, for instance, in relation to the situation in Côte d'Ivoire, pointed as evidence of the gravity of the alleged crimes to their commission 'as part of a plan or in furtherance of a policy'.[85] For Pre-Trial Chamber II, in respect of the situation in Afghanistan, it was also relevant that crimes allegedly committed by US personnel had been executed 'by public officials in [the exercise of] their functions'.[86]

2.3.1.2.2.4 Impact The final indicator of gravity articulated by the Office of the Prosecutor in respect of situations is the impact of the crimes allegedly committed. According to the Prosecutor, the impact of the crimes

> may be assessed in light of, *inter alia*, the sufferings endured by the victims and their increased vulnerability; the terror subsequently instilled, or the social, economic and environmental damage inflicted on the affected communities.[87]

The Pre-Trial Chambers have likewise considered as relevant to the assessment of gravity the impact of the alleged crimes, with the majority of the Chambers placing emphasis on the impact of the crimes on their victims.

For its part, Pre-Trial Chamber I, in its review under Article 53(3)(*a*) of the Statute of the Prosecutor's decision not to proceed with an investigation into the Mavi Marmara incident, seemed to disagree with the Prosecutor's articulation of the impact of the alleged crimes, which in its view wrongly assigned equal weight to their impact on victims, on the one hand, and on society as a whole, on the other. In the Chamber's view, 'before attempting a determination of the impact of the identified crimes on the lives of the people in Gaza', which the Prosecutor had considered as militating against the satisfaction of the gravity criterion, the Prosecutor should have accounted for 'the significant impact of such crimes on the lives of the victims and their families'.[88] This required a consideration of the 'physical,

---

[85] *Situation in Côte d'Ivoire*, Pre-Trial Chamber Authorization Decision 2011 (n 11) para 205.

[86] *Situation in Afghanistan*, Pre-Trial Chamber Authorization Decision 2019 (n 27) para 85.

[87] Policy Paper on Preliminary Examinations, Office of the Prosecutor, 2013, para 65.

[88] *Situation on the Registered Vessels of the Union of the Comoros, the Hellenic Republic and the Kingdom of Cambodia*, Pre-Trial Chamber Decision 2015 (n 33) para 47. The Prosecutor's approach raises the question of whether it is permissible for the assessment of the impact of the alleged crimes to include any impact the crimes may have had beyond the jurisdictional scope of the situation. While the assessment of gravity should generally be restricted by the confines of the situation, the reasons for doing so, discussed in Section 2.3.1.1.2, do not seem to extend to the assessment of impact as long as the alleged crimes themselves fall within the jurisdictional scope of the situation under consideration for investigation. Whether the crimes allegedly committed during the course of the Mavi Marmara incident had the kinds of impact articulated by the Prosecutor is a separate question. In a subsequent decision of 2020, the Pre-Trial Chamber in its review of the Prosecutor's decision, on reconsideration, not to initiate an investigation found that the Prosecutor had failed to assess the impact of the alleged crimes on the victims and their families and had thus failed to assign any weight to impact as an indicator of gravity. *Situation on the Registered Vessels of the Union of the Comoros, the Hellenic Republic and the Kingdom of Cambodia*, Pre-Trial Chamber Decision 2020 (n 17) para 80. See also Bozbayindir (n 40) 647–48.

psychological or emotional harm suffered by the direct and indirect victims', which in the Chamber's opinion were sufficient in and of themselves to evidence 'sufficient gravity'.[89] The impact on the victims of the alleged crimes did not need to be supported by the 'more general impact of [the] crimes' such that the absence of the latter 'could be taken into account as outweighing the significant impact of the crimes on the victims'.[90]

Similarly, and once again citing the Court's sentencing criteria, the Pre-Trial Chamber that authorized the initiation of the *proprio motu* investigation in Kenya emphasized 'the impact of the crimes and the harm caused to victims and their families' as an indicator of gravity.[91] It offered a detailed account of 'the individual impact of the violence on the victims',[92] including the 'psychological trauma, social stigma, abandonment', contraction of HIV/AIDS,[93] and pregnancy[94] among victims of rape and sexual assault, and the precarious conditions under which victims of displacement, having lost their homes, livelihoods, and possessions, lived.[95] Likewise, in the situation in Georgia, the impact of the alleged crimes was evidenced by the overwhelming reduction in the ethnic Georgian population in South Ossetia as a result of '51–113 killings, the destruction of over 5,000 dwellings and the forced displacement of 13,400–18,500 persons'.[96] With reference to attacks against peacekeepers, the Pre-Trial Chamber made special note of 'the detriment to their ability to execute their mission'.[97] Only Pre-Trial Chamber II emphasized, in relation to the situation in Afghanistan, the 'devastating and unfinished systemic consequences on the life of innocent people', 'for a prolonged period of time', resulting from the alleged commission of the crimes.[98]

2.3.1.2.2.5 Those who bear the greatest responsibility In addition to the scale, nature, manner of commission, and impact of the crimes allegedly committed,

---

[89] *Situation on the Registered Vessels of the Union of the Comoros, the Hellenic Republic and the Kingdom of Cambodia*, Pre-Trial Chamber Decision 2015 (n 33) para 47.

[90] ibid. On the facts, the Pre-Trial Chamber nevertheless concluded that the alleged crimes had had broader forms of impact. ibid para 48. The Chamber also eventually considered that the Prosecutor should have accounted for the 'international concern' caused by the incident in her assessment of impact. ibid para 48. See also *Situation on the Registered Vessels of the Union of the Comoros, the Hellenic Republic and the Kingdom of Cambodia*, Pre-Trial Chamber Decision 2020 (n 17) para 78.

[91] See Rule 145(1)(*c*), RPE; *Situation in Kenya*, Pre-Trial Chamber Decision 2010 (n 11) para 62.

[92] *Situation in Kenya*, Pre-Trial Chamber Decision 2010 (n 11) para 196.

[93] ibid para 194.

[94] ibid para 195.

[95] ibid paras 195–96.

[96] *Situation in Georgia*, Pre-Trial Chamber Authorization Decision 2016 (n 64) para 54.

[97] ibid para 55.

[98] *Situation in Afghanistan*, Pre-Trial Chamber Authorization Decision 2019 (n 27) para 84.

46   GRAVITY AT THE INTERNATIONAL CRIMINAL COURT

Pre-Trial Chamber II, in its authorization in 2010 of the investigation in Kenya, required

> a generic examination of ... whether such groups of persons that are likely to form the object of the investigation capture those who may bear the greatest responsibility for the alleged crimes committed.[99]

In respect of the situation in Kenya, the Chamber considered that the requirement had been satisfied by the reference in the material supporting the Prosecutor's request to the high-ranking positions of 'the groups of persons likely to be the focus of the Prosecutor's investigations' and their roles in 'inciting, planning, financing, colluding with criminal gangs, and otherwise contributing to the organization of the violence'.[100] With the exception of the decisions pertaining to the situations in Afghanistan and Bangladesh/Myanmar, which make no mention of the level of responsibility of the possible perpetrators of the alleged crimes, subsequent Pre-Trial Chambers proceeding under Article 15(4) of the Statute have taken the same approach. In its authorization of the investigation in Côte d'Ivoire, for instance, Pre-Trial Chamber III endorsed the Prosecutor's submission that 'the individuals likely to be the focus of ... future investigations [we]re high-ranking political and military figures'.[101] Pre-Trial Chamber I did the same in respect of the situation in Georgia,[102] while a differently composed Pre-Trial Chamber III was likewise satisfied that 'high-ranking officials of the Burundian government, the police, the intelligence service and the military services, [as well as] the *Imbonerakure*', all of whom appeared to be the most responsible for the alleged crimes, were the focus of the proposed investigation in Burundi.[103]

While endorsing the relevance of this fifth indicator of gravity, Pre-Trial Chamber I, in its review of the Prosecutor's decision not to initiate an investigation into the Mavi Marmara incident, took a different approach. In its view, while it was necessary for the potential cases identified by the Prosecutor to address 'those persons who may bear the greatest responsibility for the identified crimes',[104] this did

---

[99] *Situation in Kenya*, Pre-Trial Chamber Decision 2010 (n 11) para 188. This was on the basis that the parameters of a potential case include 'the groups of persons involved that are likely to be the object of an investigation for the purpose of shaping the future case(s)'. ibid para 50.

[100] ibid para 198.

[101] *Situation in Côte d'Ivoire*, Pre-Trial Chamber Authorization Decision 2011 (n 11) para 205.

[102] *Situation in Georgia*, Pre-Trial Chamber Authorization Decision 2016 (n 64) para 52. As per the Prosecutor's submissions, the persons likely to be the focus of the investigation held 'political or command positions' and had a role in 'ordering, facilitating or otherwise contributing to the commission of the alleged crimes'. *Situation in Georgia*, ICC-01/15-4-Corr2, Office of the Prosecutor, Corrected Version of 'Request for Authorisation of an Investigation Pursuant to Article 15', 16 October 2015, ICC-01/15-4-Corr, 17 November 2015, para 337.

[103] *Situation in Burundi*, Pre-Trial Chamber Authorization Decision 2017 (n 67) para 187.

[104] *Situation on the Registered Vessels of the Union of the Comoros, the Hellenic Republic and the Kingdom of Cambodia*, Pre-Trial Chamber Decision 2015 (n 33) para 24. The government of The Comoros, as the referring state party seeking review under Article 53(3)(*a*), raised the issue of the Prosecutor's failure to apply this indicator as part of her gravity assessment, arguing that a potential

not warrant a consideration of 'the seniority or hierarchical position of those who may be responsible for such crimes', as is the approach preferred by the Pre-Trial Chambers when acting under Article 15(4).[105] Instead, what was required was an assessment of the Prosecutor's ability to investigate and prosecute whoever was 'the most responsible for the crimes under consideration' irrespective of their level of seniority or hierarchical position.[106] Judge Kovács, in agreement with the majority on the point, explained that the Prosecutor had erroneously 'limit[ed] the gravity assessment to the seniority of the alleged suspect(s) rather than their actual role in the commission of the crimes'.[107] In his view, as in the view of the majority, while those who bear the greatest responsibility are 'quite often at the top of the hierarchy', in some instances 'mid-level perpetrators could also bear the greatest responsibility', which would equally justify the initiation of an investigation.[108] In a later decision addressing the Mavi Marmara incident, the Pre-Trial Chamber added the qualification that it was not necessary at this stage of the proceedings to identify which potential perpetrators allegedly perpetrated which crimes.[109]

In contrast to the Pre-Trial Chambers acting under both Article 53(3)(*a*) and Article 15(4) of the Statute, neither the 2009 Regulations of the Office of the Prosecutor nor the 2013 Policy Paper on Preliminary Examinations—the latter specifying the Prosecutor's 'stated policy of focussing on those bearing the greatest responsibility for the most serious crimes'[110]—lists among the indicators of the gravity of a situation the involvement of those who may bear the greatest responsibility for the alleged crimes.

perpetrator's 'level of command in the political and military hierarchy' could support a finding of sufficient gravity. *Situation on the Registered Vessels of the Union of the Comoros, the Hellenic Republic and the Kingdom of Cambodia*, Application for Review 2015 (n 41) paras 85–86. The Prosecutor contended that 'the potential perpetrators of the identified crimes were among those who carried out the boarding of the Mavi Marmara, and subsequent operations aboard, but not necessarily other persons further up the chain of command'. Thus, '[t]he Prosecution's strategic interest in bringing to justice those who appear to be most responsible for crimes within the Court's jurisdiction cannot detract from the facts indicating who those persons might actually be'. *Situation on the Registered Vessels of the Union of the Comoros, the Hellenic Republic and the Kingdom of Cambodia*, ICC-01/13-14-Red, Office of the Prosecutor, Public Redacted Version of Prosecution Response to the Application for Review of Its Determination under Article 53(1)(b) of the Rome Statute, 30 March 2015, para 60.

[105] *Situation on the Registered Vessels of the Union of the Comoros, the Hellenic Republic and the Kingdom of Cambodia*, Pre-Trial Chamber Decision 2015 (n 33) para 23. See also *Situation on the Registered Vessels of the Union of the Comoros, the Hellenic Republic and the Kingdom of Cambodia*, Pre-Trial Chamber Decision 2020 (n 17) para 19.

[106] *Situation on the Registered Vessels of the Union of the Comoros, the Hellenic Republic and the Kingdom of Cambodia*, Pre-Trial Chamber Decision 2015 (n 33) para 23.

[107] *Situation on the Registered Vessels of the Union of the Comoros, the Hellenic Republic and the Kingdom of Cambodia*, Kovács Partial Dissent 2015 (n 32) para 28.

[108] ibid.

[109] *Situation on the Registered Vessels of the Union of the Comoros, the Hellenic Republic and the Kingdom of Cambodia*, Pre-Trial Chamber Decision 2020 (n 17) para 44.

[110] Policy Paper on Preliminary Examinations, Office of the Prosecutor, 2013, para 45.

2.3.1.2.3 *Recapitulation*

While agreeing on the relevance of the scale, nature, manner of commission, and impact of the alleged crimes to the assessment of gravity in respect of a situation, the Pre-Trial Chambers have to date been inconsistent in the articulation and application of each indicator. When it has come to the scale of the crimes, they have often contradicted their stated approach to admissibility under Article 53(1)(*b*) of the Statute, which requires an assessment of the gravity of one or more potential cases arising out of the situation, and instead assessed the scale of the crimes committed within the situation as a whole. In all situations to date, this has supported a finding of sufficient gravity, most notably in the Pre-Trial Chamber's 2015 decision in the Mavi Marmara proceedings. As to the nature of the crimes, the few Pre-Trial Chambers that have addressed the contribution of this indicator to the gravity assessment have disagreed as to its application. Some have focused on the legal characterization of the relevant conduct, which has tended by definition to satisfy the gravity criterion, while others have instead assessed the nature of the crimes by reference to the vulnerability of the victims. The treatment by the Pre-Trial Chambers of the manner of commission of the crimes as an indicator of gravity has included a variety of factors barring the degree of participation and intent of the alleged perpetrator. In their assessments of impact, the majority of the Pre-Trial Chambers have focused their attention on the impact of the crimes on their victims to the exclusion of wider considerations, with this approach contributing more easily to the satisfaction of the gravity criterion. Beyond the four indicators articulated by the Office of the Prosecutor, Pre-Trial Chambers acting under both Article 53(3)(*a*) and Article 15(4) have consistently included a fifth indicator of gravity, requiring that the potential cases identified by the Prosecutor implicate the person or persons bearing greatest responsibility for the crimes allegedly committed. As with the other indicators of gravity, however, the Chambers have not agreed upon its content. While those acting under Article 15(4) have addressed the seniority or hierarchical status of the potential perpetrators of the crimes, the sole Pre-Trial Chamber acting under Article 53(3)(*a*) preferred to focus on the 'actual role' of the potential perpetrators in the commission of the crimes. The latter approach is capable of satisfying the gravity criterion even in respect of situations in which the potential perpetrators may not be high-ranking.

2.3.2 The Application of Article 17(1)(*d*) of the Statute to a Case

2.3.2.1 The Assessment of the Admissibility of a Case

Following the investigation of a situation, the Prosecutor may conclude under Article 53(2)(*b*) of the Rome Statute that '[t]he case is inadmissible under article 17' and that there is, as a result, 'not a sufficient basis for a prosecution'.[111] Under

---

[111] art 53(2), Rome Statute. For a detailed analysis of what is required of the Prosecutor under Article 53(2)(*b*), see Chapter 4, Section 4.2.1.1.

Article 53(3)(*a*), the Pre-Trial Chamber may, at the request of the referring state party or the Security Council, where relevant, review the decision of the Prosecutor and request that he or she reconsider it. Conversely, where the Prosecutor has elected to proceed with the prosecution of a case, the Pre-Trial Chamber may determine the admissibility of the case on its own initiative, in accordance with Article 19(1), or upon a challenge by any of the parties listed in Article 19(2), in accordance with that provision, or at the request of the Prosecutor, in accordance with Article 19(3).[112]

Distinguishing the assessment of the admissibility of a 'case' from that of a 'potential case', the policy of the Office of the Prosecutor explains that

> case selection requires the application of a more focused test than the one conducted at the situation stage. For each case selected for investigation and prosecution ... admissibility ... will be considered in relation to identified incidents, persons and conduct.[113]

The Appeals Chamber has confirmed that '[t]he parameters of "the case" for the purpose of article 17(1)(d) of the Statute are defined by the suspect under investigation and the conduct that gives rise to criminal liability under the Statute'.[114] The assessment is not, however, limited to the suspect's individual conduct but includes '[a]n evaluation of the factual allegations underpinning the contextual elements of the ... crimes',[115] notwithstanding that 'the contextual elements may be the same for [all] cases arising from the same conflict or attack'.[116] Depending on the stage of the proceedings, the assessment of admissibility may pertain to the case as described in the warrant of arrest or summons to appear, in the document containing the

---

[112] To date, the Prosecutor has not resorted to Article 19(3) to seek a ruling on the admissibility of a case with which he or she has wished to proceed. Instead, Article 19(3) has been invoked to clarify the jurisdiction of the Court in respect of certain contentious situations. The Prosecutor first invoked Article 19(3) to this end in 2018 to ascertain the Court's jurisdiction over crimes committed in part on the territory of a state party, Bangladesh, before initiating a preliminary examination into the situation in Bangladesh/Myanmar. The proceedings having not yet reached the stage of a 'case', the Pre-Trial Chamber rejected this reliance on Article 19(3), although this did not prevent it from rendering a decision on other grounds. See *Situation in Bangladesh/Myanmar*, Pre-Trial Chamber Decision 2018 (n 44) paras 26–29. Similarly, in 2020, the Prosecutor sought a ruling under Article 19(3) to clarify the territorial scope of the situation in Palestine, again without having initiated the prosecution of a case or even an investigation into the situation. In this context, the Pre-Trial Chamber permitted the request on the basis of an expansive reading of Article 19(3). See *Situation in Palestine*, ICC-01/18-143, Pre-Trial Chamber I, Decision on the 'Prosecution Request Pursuant to Article 19(3) for a Ruling on the Court's Territorial Jurisdiction in Palestine', 5 February 2021, paras 63–86.

[113] Policy Paper on Case Selection and Prioritisation, Office of the Prosecutor, 15 September 2016, para 25.

[114] *Al Hassan*, Appeals Chamber Decision 2020 (n 14) para 127. See also *Ruto and others*, Appeals Chamber Decision 2011 (n 27) para 40; *Gaddafi and Al-Senussi*, Appeals Chamber Decision 2014 (n 26) para 1.

[115] *Al Hassan*, Appeals Chamber Decision 2020 (n 14) para 69.

[116] ibid para 72.

50   GRAVITY AT THE INTERNATIONAL CRIMINAL COURT

charges, or, exceptionally, in the charges as confirmed by the Pre-Trial Chamber.[117] In other words, the assessment is carried out in relation to 'the document that is statutorily envisaged as defining the allegations against the person at a given stage of proceedings.'[118] In addition to distinguishing the assessment of admissibility of a 'case' from that of a 'potential case', the Pre-Trial Chambers have sought to separate the assessment of admissibility from any subsequent proceedings, in particular by excluding from the gravity assessment any requirement of supporting evidence of the kind necessary for the trial.[119]

2.3.2.2 The Application of Article 17(1)(d) to a Case in Practice
2.3.2.2.1 Overview

Regulation 29(5) of the 2009 Regulations of the Office of the Prosecutor specifies that the assessment of gravity for the purpose of deciding whether to prosecute a case requires the consideration of the same indicators, mutatis mutandis, of scale, nature, manner of commission, and impact of the alleged crimes as considered when deciding whether to investigate a situation.[120] The Office of the Prosecutor's 2016 Policy Paper on Case Selection and Prioritisation elaborates on each of these indicators in the specific context of the potential prosecution of a case. To date, the Prosecutor is yet to issue a decision not to prosecute under Article 53(2) of the Statute. When it has come to Pre-Trial Chamber determination under Article 19 of the Statute of the admissibility of a case that the Prosecutor does wish to prosecute, ever since a controversial decision of 2006 relating to the cases against *Lubanga* and

---

[117] *Ruto and others*, Appeals Chamber Decision 2011 (n 27) para 40. On the permissibility of an admissibility assessment after the confirming of the charges, Article 19(4) of the Statute provides that an admissibility challenge 'shall take place prior to or at the commencement of the trial'. The Chambers have taken varied approaches to the question whether the trial may be said to commence upon the confirmation of the charges or at a later point in time. See *Prosecutor v Lubanga*, ICC-01/04-01/06-1084, Trial Chamber I, Decision on the Status Before the Trial Chamber of the Evidence Heard by the Pre-Trial Chamber and the Decisions of the Pre-Trial Chamber in Trial Proceedings, and the Manner in Which Evidence Shall Be Submitted, 13 December 2007, para 39; *Prosecutor v Katanga and Ngudjolo*, ICC-01/04-01/07-1213-tENG, Trial Chamber II, Reasons for the Oral Decision on the Motion Challenging the Admissibility of the Case (Article 19 of the Statute), 16 June 2009, para 47; *Prosecutor v Bemba*, ICC-01/05-01/08-802, Trial Chamber III, Decision on the Admissibility and Abuse of Process Challenges, 24 June 2010, para 210.

[118] *Prosecutor v Charles Blé Goudé*, ICC-02/11-02/11-185, Pre-Trial Chamber I, Decision on the Defence Challenge to the Admissibility of the Case Against Charles Blé Goudé for Insufficient Gravity, 12 November 2014 (hereafter '*Charles Blé Goudé*, Pre-Trial Chamber Decision 2014') para 9.

[119] In *Al Hassan*, the Pre-Trial Chamber clarified that it would not, during the assessment of the admissibility of the case, 'exclude certain aspects of the Prosecutor's allegations on the basis of a purported lack of evidence, as to do so would amount to assessing the available evidence and would, therefore, be part of the determination on the merits of the charges presented by the Prosecutor'. *Prosecutor v Al Hassan*, ICC-01/12-01/18-459-tENG, Pre-Trial Chamber I, Decision on the Admissibility Challenge Raised by the Defence for Insufficient Gravity of the Case, 27 September 2019 (hereafter '*Al Hassan*, Pre-Trial Chamber Decision 2019') para 52. See also *Prosecutor v Muthaura and others*, ICC-01/09-02/11-382-Red, Pre-Trial Chamber II, Decision on the Confirmation of Charges Pursuant to Article 61(7)(a) and (b) of the Rome Statute, 23 January 2012 (hereafter '*Muthaura and others*, Pre-Trial Chamber Decision 2012') para 48; *Charles Blé Goudé*, Pre-Trial Chamber Decision 2014 (n 118) para 17.

[120] See Reg 29(2), OTP Regs.

Ntaganda, both arising out of the situation in the DRC, the Pre-Trial Chambers have endorsed the Prosecutor's articulation of the four indicators of gravity, even if they have not always applied them in practice. As for the Appeals Chamber, to date it has reviewed the Pre-Trial Chambers' assessments of gravity and clarified the application of Article 17(1)(*d*) in the context of a case in two instances, first in *Ntaganda* and more recently in *Al Hassan*, the latter arising out of the situation in Mali.

2.3.2.2.2 *In detail*

The first occasion on which the Pre-Trial Chamber applied the gravity criterion in relation to a case was in response, acting *proprio motu* under Article 19(1) of the Statute, to the Prosecutor's request in 2006 for the issuance of warrants for the arrest of Thomas Lubanga Dyilo (*Lubanga*) and Bosco Ntaganda (*Ntaganda*) for their alleged involvement in the situation in the DRC.[121] Observing that the gravity criterion for admissibility under Article 17(1)(*d*) of the Statute was 'in addition to the gravity-driven selection of the crimes within the material jurisdiction of the Court', the Pre-Trial Chamber considered that the conduct in question must, in order for the case to be admissible, 'present particular features which render it especially grave'.[122] Using what it referred to as literal,[123] contextual,[124] and teleological[125] approaches to the interpretation rather than the application of the provision, the Chamber required that the following questions be answered affirmatively for Article 17(1)(*d*) to be satisfied:

(i) Is the conduct which is the object of a case systematic or large-scale (due consideration should also be given to the social alarm caused to the international community by the relevant type of conduct)?;

(ii) Considering the position of the relevant person in the State entity, organisation or armed group to which he belongs, can it be considered that such person falls within the category of most senior leaders of the situation under investigation?; and

(iii) Does the relevant person fall within the category of most senior leaders suspected of being most responsible, considering (1) the role played by the relevant person through acts or omissions when the State entities, organisations or armed groups to which he belongs commit systematic or

---

[121] While the Pre-Trial Chamber invoked its *proprio motu* power under Article 19(1) to justify its assessment of admissibility, the proceedings took place under Article 58(1), the provision for the issuance of arrest warrants. The question of the permissibility of an admissibility assessment before the issuance of an arrest warrant or summons to appear under Article 58 is discussed in Chapter 4, Section 4.3.

[122] *Situation in the Democratic Republic of the Congo*, Pre-Trial Chamber Decision 2006 (n 10) para 46.

[123] ibid para 44.

[124] ibid paras 45–47.

[125] ibid paras 48–55.

52   GRAVITY AT THE INTERNATIONAL CRIMINAL COURT

large-scale crimes within the jurisdiction of the Court, and (2) the role played by such State entities, organisations or armed groups in the overall commission of crimes within the jurisdiction of the Court in the relevant situation?[126]

In its application of the test in *Lubanga*, the Pre-Trial Chamber found that the case met all three requirements and was admissible.[127] In contrast, when applying the test in *Ntaganda*, it concluded that the case did not satisfy the second and third limbs and was therefore inadmissible.[128]

Appealing the Pre-Trial Chamber's decision in *Ntaganda*, the Prosecutor contested the Chamber's application of Article 17(1)(*d*) on the grounds, inter alia, that the Chamber's narrow circumscription of the category of senior leaders, which emphasized, for instance, the authority to negotiate peace agreements, 'inappropriately limited his prosecutorial discretion and would make it impossible to investigate and prosecute perpetrators lower down the chain of command'.[129] The Appeals Chamber agreed that the Pre-Trial Chamber's approach to Article 17(1) (*d*) had been too strict. It considered the first limb of the Pre-Trial Chamber's test, namely that the conduct in question must be systematic or large-scale, particularly problematic. In the Appeals Chamber's view, the requirement blurred the distinction between jurisdiction *ratione materiae* and admissibility. While the definition of crimes against humanity under Article 7(1) specifically required the existence

---

[126] ibid para 64.

[127] Satisfying the first limb of the test, the Chamber found that the case included Lubanga's alleged responsibility in the Union des Patriotes Congolais (UPC)/Forces Patriotiques pour la Libération du Congo's (FPLC's) 'alleged policy/practice of enlisting into the FPLC, conscripting into the FPLC and using to participate actively in hostilities children under the age of fifteen'. *Situation in the Democratic Republic of the Congo*, Pre-Trial Chamber Decision 2006 (n 10) para 66. These practices not only met the 'systematic or large-scale' requirement but also resulted in a degree of social alarm at the international level. ibid para 67. Turning to the second limb, the Chamber relied on Lubanga's status as president of the UPC and as founder of its military wing, the FPLC, as well as his de facto authority to negotiate, sign, and implement ceasefires/peace agreements and to participate in negotiations relating to access of UN personnel in Ituri, to conclude that he was one of the most senior leaders involved in the situation. ibid paras 68–69. Satisfying the third limb of the test, the Chamber concluded that Lubanga was 'the man with ultimate control over the policies/practices adopted and implemented by the UPC/ FPLC'. ibid para 71. While acknowledging that the UPC/FPLC was operating only in Ituri, the Chamber ultimately found that the UPC/FPLC's role in the conflict had been an important one. ibid paras 72, 74.

[128] As he held no official position or role in the UPC, Ntaganda was not, in the opinion of the Chamber, among the most senior leaders involved in the situation. *Situation in the Democratic Republic of the Congo*, Pre-Trial Chamber Decision 2006 (n 10) paras 82–83. It was also relevant that within the FPLC hierarchy, Ntaganda ranked only third. ibid para 79. In accordance with the third limb of its test, the Chamber further found that Ntaganda lacked '*de jure* or *de facto* authority to negotiate, sign and implement ceasefires or peace agreements' and had not participated in 'negotiations relating to controlling access of MONUC and other UN personnel to Bunia and other parts of the territory of Ituri under the control of the UPC/FPLC'. ibid para 86. The Prosecutor had also failed to establish reasonable grounds to believe that Ntaganda had de jure or de facto autonomy to change such policies/practices or to prevent their implementation. ibid para 87. In the Chamber's view, thus, Ntaganda had not been a core actor in the decision-making process of the UPC/FPLC.

[129] Cf *Situation in the Democratic Republic of the Congo*, Appeals Chamber Decision 2006 (n 12) para 66.

APPLICATION OF GRAVITY CRITERION FOR ADMISSIBILITY   53

of 'a widespread or systematic attack' against a civilian population, Article 8(1), through the use of the term 'in particular', made the existence of a plan or policy in the commission of war crimes or their commission as part of a large-scale commission of such crimes optional. It would thus be

> inconsistent with article 8(1) of the Statute if a war crime that was not part of a plan or policy or part of a large-scale commission could not, under any circumstances, be brought before the International Criminal Court because of the gravity requirement of article 17(1)(d) of the Statute.[130]

The Appeals Chamber also discarded the Pre-Trial Chamber's 'social alarm' requirement, which 'depend[ed] upon the subjective and contingent reactions to crimes rather than upon their objective gravity'.[131] When addressing the second and third limbs of the Pre-Trial Chamber's test, the Appeals Chamber was emphatic in its rejection of the lower court's proposition that an exclusive focus on senior leaders suspected of being most responsible for the crimes was justified by the objective of maximizing deterrence:

> It may indeed have a deterrent effect if high-ranking leaders who are suspected of being responsible for having committed crimes within the jurisdiction of the Court are brought before the International Criminal Court. But that the deterrent effect is highest if all other categories of perpetrators cannot be brought before the Court is difficult to understand. It seems more logical to assume that the deterrent effect of the Court is highest if no category of perpetrators is per se excluded from potentially being brought before the Court.[132]

The majority concluded that, while the Court's jurisdiction *ratione materiae* was limited to the most serious crimes, it was not similarly limited to the most senior leaders suspected of being most responsible for the crimes.[133] On the contrary, 'individuals who are not at the very top of an organization may still carry considerable influence and commit, or generate the widespread commission of, very serious crimes'.[134] Ultimately, the Appeals Chamber was not convinced that the factors comprising the second and third limbs of the Pre-Trial Chamber's test were indicators of gravity at all. Since the proceedings in *Ntaganda* had taken place *ex parte*, however, it declined itself to 'identify the correct legal principle to be applied'

---

[130] ibid para 70.

[131] ibid para 72.

[132] ibid para 73.

[133] ibid paras 77–79. See also *Situation in the Democratic Republic of the Congo*, ICC-01/04-169, Appeals Chamber, Separate and Partly Dissenting Opinion of Judge Georghios M. Pikis, 13 July 2006 (hereafter '*Situation in the Democratic Republic of the Congo*, Pikis Partial Dissent 2006') para 35.

[134] *Situation in the Democratic Republic of the Congo*, Appeals Chamber Decision 2006 (n 12) para 77.

under Article 17(1)(*d*).[135] Instead, the Appeals Chamber remanded the case to the Pre-Trial Chamber for reconsideration,[136] but not before clarifying that

> [the] [c]riteria considered by the Pre-Trial Chamber such as the national or regional scope of activities of a group or organization, the exclusively military character of a group, the capacity to negotiate agreements, the absence of an official position, [and] the capacity to change or prevent a policy, are not necessarily directly related to gravity as set out in Article 17(1)(d).[137]

Agreeing with the majority on these points, Judge Pikis, in his partly dissenting opinion, was alone in rejecting altogether an objective articulation of the gravity criterion.[138] While Article 17(1)(*d*) was aimed at excluding 'borderline cases' or 'cases insignificant in themselves', in which '[b]oth ... the inception and the consequences of the crime [are] negligible',[139] 'the weightiness of a case' was not referable to 'any objective criteria of seriousness on any scale of gravity'.[140]

Following the Appeals Chamber's decision in *Ntaganda*, the Office of the Prosecutor sought to clarify the application of the gravity criterion in the context of its assessment of the admissibility of a case under Article 53(2)(*b*) of the Statute, as part of the decision whether 'there is not a sufficient basis for a prosecution' under Article 53(2). Regulation 29(5) of the 2009 Regulations of the Office of the Prosecutor extends mutatis mutandis to the assessment under Article 53(2)(*b*) of the Statute the four indicators of gravity to be applied under Article 53(1)(*b*), namely the scale, nature, manner of commission, and impact of the alleged crimes. The same indicators were subsequently elaborated on in the Office of the Prosecutor's 2016 Policy Paper on Case Selection and Prioritisation.

Subsequent to the Appeals Chamber's decision in *Ntaganda*, the Pre-Trial Chambers have addressed the application of the gravity criterion to a case in a range of proceedings under Article 19(1)–(3) of the Statute.[141] When assessing the admissibility of the case against Bahr Idriss Abu Garda (*Abu Garda*) in connection

---

[135] ibid para 89.

[136] ibid para 90.

[137] ibid para 77. See also *Situation in the Democratic Republic of the Congo*, Pikis Partial Dissent 2006 (n 133) para 41.

[138] On an objective approach to the assessment of gravity, see Section 2.4.2.

[139] *Situation in the Democratic Republic of the Congo*, Pikis Partial Dissent 2006 (n 133) para 40. As a commentator, Judge Pikis has noted that '[t]he lack of gravity ... must stem from the insignificance or immateriality of the *mens rea* or *actus reus*, or both, in the commission of the offence'. GM Pikis, *The Rome Statute of the International Criminal Court: Analysis of the Rome Statute, the Rules of Procedure and Evidence, the Regulations of the Court and Supplementary Instruments* (Martinus Nijhoff 2010) 59.

[140] *Situation in the Democratic Republic of the Congo*, Pikis Partial Dissent 2006 (n 133) para 39.

[141] The Prosecutor has to date issued no decision under Article 53(2). See Chapter 4, Section 4.2.1.2.

with war crimes in Darfur, Pre-Trial Chamber I endorsed the Prosecutor's enumeration of the quantitative and qualitative indicators of scale, nature, manner of commission, and impact.[142] Relying on the sentencing criteria in the Court's Rules of Procedure and Evidence, it found 'the extent of the damage caused, in particular, the harm caused to victims and their families, the nature of the unlawful behaviour and the means employed to execute the crime' to be 'useful guidelines' for the application of Article 17(1)(d) of the Statute.[143] Subsequent Pre-Trial Chambers have taken the same approach.[144] The Pre-Trial Chamber that addressed the case against Charles Blé Goudé (*Blé Goudé*) arising out of the situation in Côte d'Ivoire made additional reference to the 'degree of participation of the convicted person; the degree of intent; the circumstances of manner, time and location', the '[c]ommission of the crime where the victim is particularly defenceless', the '[c]ommission of the crime with particular cruelty or where there were multiple victims', and the '[c] ommission of the crime for any motive involving discrimination'.[145] It further suggested that the assessment is 'not limited to particular factors taken in isolation' but must be 'based on all relevant aspects of the Prosecutor's allegations ... considered as a whole'.[146] The same factors were deemed relevant by a differently composed Pre-Trial Chamber I in Al Hassan Ag Abdoul Aziz Ag Mohamed Ag Mahmoud (*Al Hassan*).[147]

When the Defence appealed the Pre-Trial Chamber's decision in *Al Hassan*, the Appeals Chamber had a second opportunity to address the application of the gravity criterion to a case. The Appeals Chamber in its decision of 2020 confirmed that the assessment 'involves a holistic evaluation of all relevant quantitative and qualitative criteria' and that '[q]uantitative criteria alone, including the number of victims, are not determinative of the gravity of a given case'.[148] Each of the relevant criteria is addressed in turn below.

---

[142] *Prosecutor v Abu Garda*, ICC-02/05-02/09-243-Red, Pre-Trial Chamber I, Decision on the Confirmation of Charges, 8 February 2010 (hereafter '*Abu Garda*, Pre-Trial Chamber Decision 2010') para 31.

[143] See Rule 145(1)(c), RPE. *Abu Garda*, Pre-Trial Chamber Decision 2010 (n 142) para 32.

[144] See eg *Prosecutor v Banda and Jerbo*, ICC-02/05-03/09-121-Corr-Red, Pre-Trial Chamber I, Corrigendum of the 'Decision on the Confirmation of Charges', 7 March 2011 (hereafter '*Banda and Jerbo*, Pre-Trial Chamber Decision 2011') paras 27–28; *Muthaura and others*, Pre-Trial Chamber Decision 2012 (n 119) para 50; *Al Hassan*, Pre-Trial Chamber Decision 2019 (n 119) para 47.

[145] See Rule 145(1)(c), (2)(b)(iii)–(v), RPE. *Charles Blé Goudé*, Pre-Trial Chamber Decision 2014 (n 118) paras 11–12.

[146] *Charles Blé Goudé*, Pre-Trial Chamber Decision 2014 (n 118) para 19. See also *Al Hassan*, Pre-Trial Chamber Decision 2019 (n 119) para 54.

[147] *Al Hassan*, Pre-Trial Chamber Decision 2019 (n 119) para 48.

[148] *Al Hassan*, Appeals Chamber Decision 2020 (n 14) para 2.

56 GRAVITY AT THE INTERNATIONAL CRIMINAL COURT

2.3.2.2.2.1 Scale The first indicator that the Office of the Prosecutor considers when assessing the gravity of a case is the scale of the crimes allegedly committed. According to the Prosecutor, this

> may be assessed in light of, *inter alia*, the number of direct and indirect victims, the extent of the damage caused by the crimes, in particular the bodily or psychological harm caused to the victims and their families, and their geographical or temporal spread (high intensity of the crimes over a brief period or low intensity of crimes over an extended period).[149]

The Pre-Trial Chambers have also, in their decisions under Article 19, recognized the scale of the crimes as an indicator of gravity. Pre-Trial Chamber I, in an earlier admissibility decision of 2014 in *Blé Goudé*, considered that the alleged commission by the defendant of 'at least 800 criminal acts' contributed to the satisfaction of the gravity criterion.[150] More recently, in 2019, a differently composed Pre-Trial Chamber I found in *Al Hassan* that the scale of the crimes had in the event been evidenced by '13 counts of crimes against humanity and war crimes allegedly committed against the civilian population in Timbuktu and its region over a period of around 10 months'.[151] The Chamber also took note of the 882 victims who had been admitted to participate in the proceedings.[152]

On appeal in *Al Hassan*, the Appeals Chamber confirmed that 'the number of participating victims may provide some indication of the scope of victimhood within the context of a case',[153] while at the same time noting that the Pre-Trial Chamber had not in fact afforded 'significant weight' in its assessment of scale to the number of participating victims.[154] The Appeals Chamber went on to demonstrate the scale of the alleged crimes by reference to the numbers of victims beyond those participating in the proceedings, which in respect of the crime against humanity of persecution included 'the entire population of Timbuktu and its

---

[149] Policy Paper on Case Selection and Prioritisation, Office of the Prosecutor, 15 September 2016, para 38.

[150] *Charles Blé Goudé*, Pre-Trial Chamber Decision 2014 (n 118) para 21. This included 'the murder of at least 184 persons, the rape of at least 38 women and girls, the infliction of bodily harm on at least 126 persons', and 'acts of persecution against at least 348 persons'. ibid. The Pre-Trial Chamber did not, however, respond to the Defence's contention that the incidents were 'extremely limited in temporal and geographical scope'. *Situation in Côte d'Ivoire*, ICC-02/11-02/11-171, Defence, Defence Application Pursuant to Articles 19(4) and 17(1)(d) of the Rome Statute, 27 September 2014, para 36.

[151] *Al Hassan*, Pre-Trial Chamber Decision 2019 (n 119) para 57.

[152] The Defence appealed the Pre-Trial Chamber's decision inter alia on the ground that victims' participation constitutes a procedural right to be heard and cannot be used to establish facts for the purpose of admissibility. *Situation in Mali*, ICC-01/12-01/18-475-Red, Defence, Public Redacted Version of Appeal of the Pre-Trial Chamber's 'Décision relative à l'exception d'irrecevabilité pour insuffisance de gravité de l'affaire soulevée par la défence', 21 October 2019, paras 41–48.

[153] *Al Hassan*, Appeals Chamber Decision 2020 (n 14) para 97.

[154] The Pre-Trial Chamber had 'also had regard to the alleged repercussions of the crimes on the direct victims and on the population of Timbuktu as a whole'. *Al Hassan*, Appeals Chamber Decision 2020 (n 14) para 100.

region'.[155] As to the 'large degree of overlap in the factual allegations supporting the 13 counts', the Appeals Chamber held that 'each count, amounting to a different crime under the Statute, represents distinct values of the international community that have allegedly been violated'.[156] As such, it was permissible in the assessment of scale to consider the various counts cumulatively.

2.3.2.2.2.2 Nature In the policy of the Office of the Prosecutor, the second indicator of gravity in relation to a case is the nature of the crimes. This

> refers to the specific factual elements of each offence such as killings, rapes, other sexual or gender-based crimes, crimes committed against or affecting children, persecution, or the imposition of conditions of life on a group calculated to bring about its destruction.[157]

The only Pre-Trial Chamber decision to date in which mention has been made of this indicator is *Al Hassan*, in which the point was not developed.[158]

2.3.2.2.2.3 Manner of commission According to the Office of the Prosecutor, the third indicator of gravity is the manner of commission of the crimes. This may be assessed

> in light of, *inter alia*, the means employed to execute the crime, the extent to which the crimes were systematic or resulted from a plan or organised policy or otherwise resulted from the abuse of power or official capacity, the existence of elements of particular cruelty, including the vulnerability of the victims, any motives involving discrimination held by the direct perpetrators of the crimes, the use of rape and other sexual or gender-based violence or crimes committed by means of, or resulting in, the destruction of the environment or of protected objects.[159]

This approach excludes 'the degree of participation and intent of the perpetrator', which had been included in the Office of the Prosecutor's prior articulation of the manner of commission of the crimes in respect of the gravity of a situation, rather than a case.[160]

---

[155] *Al Hassan*, Appeals Chamber Decision 2020 (n 14) para 101. The scale of the crimes had also been evidenced by 'at least 10 direct victims of forced marriage, sexual slavery and rape, 22 direct victims of torture and other ill treatment, 60 direct victims of the passing of sentences without due process, and the destruction of ten protected buildings'. ibid.

[156] ibid para 123.

[157] Policy Paper on Case Selection and Prioritisation, Office of the Prosecutor, 15 September 2016, para 39.

[158] *Al Hassan*, Pre-Trial Chamber Decision 2019 (n 119) para 57.

[159] Policy Paper on Case Selection and Prioritisation, Office of the Prosecutor, 15 September 2016, para 40.

[160] See Policy Paper on Preliminary Examinations, Office of the Prosecutor, 2013, para 64.

58   GRAVITY AT THE INTERNATIONAL CRIMINAL COURT

For their part, the Pre-Trial Chambers have considered both the degree of participation, by reference to the various modes of responsibility,[161] and the intent of the
alleged perpetrator in their assessments of the manner of commission of the crimes
as an indicator of the gravity of a case but not of a situation. Their consideration of
these factors has been alongside the closely related consideration of the role of the
suspect, in factual terms, in the commission of the alleged crimes, which the Pre-
Trial Chambers have deemed as equally relevant to the assessment of gravity. In *Blé
Goudé*, for example, the Pre-Trial Chamber found that the suspect had played a 'crucial role' in 'the adoption and implementation of the policy to carry out the attack and
in the plan that resulted in the commission of the crimes charged'.[162] Although the
Prosecutor had not yet settled on the applicable mode of responsibility, the Pre-Trial
Chamber also noted 'the degree of intent and participation' of the suspect in the commission of the alleged crimes.[163] It was especially relevant that the suspect had shared
as 'a prominent member of th[e] group of people that ... conceived, adopted and implemented the policy'[164] 'the intent to commit the crimes charged'.[165] In its assessment
of the gravity of the case when issuing an arrest warrant for Mahmoud Mustafa Busayf
Al-Werfalli (*Al-Werfalli*) for his involvement in the situation in Libya, the Pre-Trial
Chamber pointed to the fact that Al-Werfalli had enjoyed a 'commanding role'.[166] In
Al Hassan, the 'significant role' of the suspect 'in the execution of [the] crimes' and his
'degree of intent and degree of participation' in these crimes all served as evidence of
sufficient gravity.[167]

In its discussion of gravity on appeal in *Al Hassan*, the Appeals Chamber did
not rule out the relevance of these considerations to the assessment of gravity.[168]

---

[161]   See arts 25(3), 28, Rome Statute. There is considerable debate as to whether there exists a hierarchy of blameworthiness among the various modes of responsibility. See H Vest, 'Problems of
Participation—Unitarian, Differentiated Approach, or Something Else?' (2014) 12 Journal of
International Criminal Justice 295; E van Sliedregt, 'The ICC Ntaganda Appeals Judgment: The End of
Indirect Co-perpetration?', Just Security, 14 May 2021, www.justsecurity.org/76136/the-icc-ntaganda-
appeals-judgment-the-end-of-indirect-co-perpetration, accessed 13 March 2023. In the context of sentencing, international criminal courts have at times considered that 'criminal responsibility as principal
merits more severe punishment that [sic] criminal responsibility as accessory'. R O'Keefe, *International
Criminal Law* (OUP 2015) 167. At least in the context of sentencing, this appears not to be the position of the Appeals Chamber of the ICC. See *Prosecutor v Bemba and others*, ICC-01/05-01/13-2276-
Red, Appeals Chamber, Judgment on the Appeals of the Prosecutor, Mr Jean-Pierre Bemba Gombo,
Mr Fidèle Babala Wandu and Mr Narcisse Arido against the Decision of Trial Chamber VII Entitled
'Decision on Sentence Pursuant to Article 76 of the Statute', 8 March 2018, paras 60–61.
[162]   *Charles Blé Goudé*, Pre-Trial Chamber Decision 2014 (n 118) para 20.
[163]   ibid paras 20, 21(i).
[164]   ibid para 21(v).
[165]   ibid para 21(vi).
[166]   *Prosecutor v Al-Werfalli*, ICC-01/11-01/17-13, Pre-Trial Chamber I, Second Warrant of Arrest, 4
July 2018 (hereafter '*Al-Werfalli*, Pre-Trial Chamber Decision 2018') para 31.
[167]   *Al Hassan*, Pre-Trial Chamber Decision 2019 (n 119) para 57. See also *Prosecutor v Al Hassan*,
ICC-01/12-01/18-35-Red2-tENG, Pre-Trial Chamber I, Decision on the Prosecutor's Application for
the Issuance of a Warrant of Arrest for Al Hassan Ag Abdoul Aziz Ag Mohamed Ag Mahmoud, 22 May
2018 (hereafter '*Al Hassan*, Pre-Trial Chamber Decision 2018') paras 37–38.
[168]   *Al Hassan*, Appeals Chamber Decision 2020 (n 14) paras 112, 115–16. The Appeals Chamber affirmed the substantial role of the suspect in 'personally flogging three individuals; giving instructions

The only clarification it offered was that, as far as the assessment of gravity was concerned, the suspect's degree of participation was to be assessed by reference to the 'specific factual allegations' rather than the legal characterization of the facts as reflecting one or another mode of responsibility.[169]

Leaving aside the degree of participation, intent, and role of the perpetrator, the Pre-Trial Chambers' assessments of the manner of commission of the crimes differ little from the Prosecutor's approach. In its 2012 decision on the case against Francis Kirimi Muthaura, Uhuru Muigai Kenyatta, and Mohammed Hussein Ali (*Kenyatta and others*) arising out of the situation in Kenya, Pre-Trial Chamber II emphasized the 'particular brutality' in the execution of the crimes, which allegedly included the beheading and burning alive of victims.[170] Similarly, in *Al-Werfalli*, Pre-Trial Chamber I considered that, while the number of victims had been low, 'the manner in which the crime was committed and publicized was cruel, dehumanizing and degrading'.[171] In *Blé Goudé*, the Pre-Trial Chamber likewise considered the means by which the crimes had been executed, which included the use of 'heavy weaponry, fragmentation grenades, firearms or blade weapons' and, as in *Kenyatta and others*, the burning alive of victims.[172] It was relevant that the crimes had been committed as part of a widespread and systematic attack pursuant to a policy and plan,[173] and that there had been elements of particular cruelty in their commission, especially in the rape (including gang-rape) of women and young girls.[174] Discriminatory motives in the alleged commission of the crimes had also supported the targeting of victims based on real or perceived political affiliation.[175] In *Al Hassan*, as in *Blé Goudé*, the Pre-Trial Chamber took account of the widespread and systematic manner in which the crimes had allegedly been committed and the discriminatory motives, this time 'religious and/or gender-based' or based on 'the vulnerability of the victims', for their alleged commission.[176]

---

or transmitting orders to members of the Islamic Police; allegedly taking action against members of the Islamic Police, and making decisions concerning offences against them, or investigating complaints about them; allegedly taking part in policy patrols and the arrest and detention of members of the civilian population; allegedly leading and/or participating in the work of the police dealing with numerous cases of men and women accused of violating the new rules, such as the prohibition of adultery, theft, drinking or selling alcohol, smoking or selling cigarettes or tobacco, wearing talismans or practicing witchcraft, or violating the dress code imposed'. ibid para 112.

[169] ibid para 116. See also *Muthaura and others*, Pre-Trial Chamber Decision 2012 (n 119) paras 45–47.
[170] *Muthaura and others*, Pre-Trial Chamber Decision 2012 (n 119) para 49.
[171] *Al-Werfalli*, Pre-Trial Chamber Decision 2018 (n 166) para 31. 'The victims were lined up on a public street, kneeling down and with their hands tied behind their backs. They were shot dead one by one, in front of a crowd of onlookers who were chanting in apparent support for the killings'. ibid.
[172] *Charles Blé Goudé*, Pre-Trial Chamber Decision 2014 (n 118) para 21(ii).
[173] ibid paras 20, 21(iv).
[174] ibid para 21(ii).
[175] ibid para 21(iii).
[176] *Al Hassan*, Pre-Trial Chamber Decision 2019 (n 119) para 57. See also *Al Hassan*, Pre-Trial Chamber Decision 2018 (n 167) para 38 (referring to 'the harassment and systematic gender-based violence perpetrated against women and girls').

60   GRAVITY AT THE INTERNATIONAL CRIMINAL COURT

Going beyond both the Prosecutor's approach and the jurisprudence of the Pre-Trial Chambers, the Appeals Chamber in *Al Hassan* considered relevant to assessing the gravity of the manner of commission of the alleged crimes the violation of human rights resulting from this commission,

> including the physical and mental integrity of the victims and their human dignity, the right to a fair trial, the right to liberty and security of person, the human right of all persons deprived of their liberty to be treated with humanity and with respect for their inherent dignity, the right to freedom of thought, conscience and religion and the prohibition on discriminating on the grounds of religion or belief.[177]

For the Appeals Chamber, this was relevant to assessing 'the nature of the unlawful behaviour'.[178]

2.3.2.2.2.4 Impact The final indicator of gravity articulated by the Office of the Prosecutor in relation to a case is the impact of the crimes allegedly committed. According to the Prosecutor, this

> may be assessed in light of, *inter alia*, the increased vulnerability of victims, the terror subsequently instilled, or the social, economic and environmental damage inflicted on the affected communities.[179]

Additionally, the Prosecutor continues,

> the Office will give particular consideration to prosecuting Rome Statute crimes that are committed by means of, or that result in, *inter alia*, the destruction of the environment, the illegal exploitation of natural resources or the illegal dispossession of land.[180]

This articulation of impact differs slightly from the Prosecutor's prior articulation of the same indicator in respect of the assessment of the gravity of a situation, which had included the additional consideration of 'the sufferings endured by the victims'.[181]

For their part, the Pre-Trial Chambers have agreed that the assessment of the gravity of a case requires the consideration of the impact of the alleged crimes on

---

[177] *Al Hassan*, Appeals Chamber Decision 2020 (n 14) para 122.
[178] ibid para 124.
[179] Policy Paper on Case Selection and Prioritisation, Office of the Prosecutor, 15 September 2016, para 41.
[180] ibid.
[181] Policy Paper on Preliminary Examinations, Office of the Prosecutor, 2013, para 65.

both their victims and on affected communities. In the opinion of the Pre-Trial Chamber in *Abu Garda*, an assessment of impact is not limited to 'the direct victims of the attack'.[182] In that case, it was relevant that the local population in Darfur had been severely affected by the disruption of the operations of the African Union Mission in Sudan (AMIS), which had 'left a large number of civilians without AMIS protection, on which they had allegedly relied'.[183] The same reasoning was adopted in the case against Abdallah Banda Abakaer Nourain (*Banda*) and Saleh Mohammed Jerbo Jamus (*Jerbo*) relating to their alleged involvement in the situation in Darfur.[184] In *Al Hassan*, the Pre-Trial Chamber likewise considered the impact of the crimes on both 'the direct victims and on the population of Timbuktu as a whole'.[185]

Going beyond both the policy of the Prosecutor and the jurisprudence of the Pre-Trial Chambers, the Appeals Chamber in *Al Hassan* considered that human rights violations resulting from the alleged commission of the crimes were part of the assessment of the impact of the crimes on their victims.[186]

2.3.2.2.2.5 Those who bear the greatest responsibility According to the Appeals Chamber's *Ntaganda* decision, the assessment of the gravity of a case does not require a consideration of whether the suspect is a senior leader suspected of being most responsibility for the alleged crimes, which the Pre-Trial Chamber had in that case assessed by reference, among other things, to the role played by the suspect in the alleged commission of the crimes. Since then, only the Pre-Trial Chamber in *Al-Werfalli* has held that the application of Article 17(1)(*d*) of the Statute requires consideration of 'whether the case captures those persons who may bear the greatest responsibility for the alleged crimes', although the Pre-Trial Chamber did not elaborate on how this indicator was to be assessed.[187] Consistently with the decision of the Appeals Chamber and with its own policy in respect of the gravity of a situation, the Office of the Prosecutor has not considered it necessary to address, as part of the assessment of the gravity of a case, whether the suspect is among those who bear the greatest responsibility for the crimes.[188]

2.3.2.2.3 Recapitulation

Since the blanket rejection by the Appeals Chamber of the Pre-Trial Chamber's restrictive articulation of gravity in *Lubanga* and *Ntaganda*, the Pre-Trial

---

[182] *Abu Garda*, Pre-Trial Chamber Decision 2010 (n 142) para 33.

[183] ibid.

[184] *Banda and Jerbo*, Pre-Trial Chamber Decision 2011 (n 144) paras 27–28.

[185] *Al Hassan*, Pre-Trial Chamber Decision 2019 (n 119) para 57. Paying particular attention to the victims of rape, sexual slavery, and forced marriage, the Chamber also took note of the 'tragic consequences' of amputation upon one victim. ibid.

[186] *Al Hassan*, Appeals Chamber Decision 2020 (n 14) para 124.

[187] *Al-Werfalli*, Pre-Trial Chamber Decision 2018 (n 166) para 30.

[188] Instead, Regulation 34(1) of the OTP Regs states that the Prosecutor shall, as a matter of policy, identify 'the person or persons who appear to be the most responsible'.

62   GRAVITY AT THE INTERNATIONAL CRIMINAL COURT

Chambers, in their admissibility decisions under Article 19(1)–(3) of the Statute, have endorsed in principle the indicators of gravity articulated by the Office of the Prosecutor, namely the scale, nature, manner of commission, and impact of the crimes allegedly committed. As with their decisions under Articles 53(3)(*a*) and 15(4) of the Statute, however, the Pre-Trial Chambers have been inconsistent in their application of these indicators. Most conspicuously, they have not considered the nature of the crimes as an indicator of gravity, raising the question of its relevance as a matter of law. In contrast, a wide range of considerations pertaining to the scale, manner of commission, and impact of the crimes have contributed to the Pre-Trial Chambers' gravity assessments. When it has come to the assessment of the manner of commission of the alleged crimes, the Pre-Trial Chambers have taken a different approach from that of the Prosecutor by considering as relevant to the assessment the degree of participation, intent, and role of the alleged perpetrators, even if, following the Appeals Chamber's decision in *Ntaganda*, they have jettisoned their more onerous requirement that the case relate to the most senior leaders bearing the greatest responsibility for those crimes. The Pre-Trial Chambers' assessments in respect of cases of the impact of the alleged crimes have, unlike their decisions in relation to situations, considered the impact on affected communities as being equally relevant to the assessment of gravity as the impact on victims. To the assessments of both the manner of commission and the impact of the alleged crimes the Appeals Chamber in *Al Hassan* added human rights violations. Finally, since the Appeals Chamber's decision in *Ntaganda*, all but one Pre-Trial Chamber have excluded from the assessment of gravity the consideration of whether the case involves the persons bearing greatest responsibility for the alleged crimes.

2.4 The Assessment of Gravity under Article 17(1)(*d*) of the Rome Statute

2.4.1 The Appropriate Indicators of Gravity under Article 17(1)(*d*)

In relation to both situations and cases, the Pre-Trial Chambers and the Appeals Chamber have endorsed in principle the four indicators of scale, nature, manner of commission, and impact of the alleged crimes considered relevant by the Office of the Prosecutor to the criterion of sufficient gravity in Article 17(1)(*d*) of the Rome Statute. In practice, the Pre-Trial Chambers have emphasized in both contexts the scale, manner of commission, and impact of the crimes to the exclusion of their nature, the endorsement of which has not been matched in practice and which the Pre-Trial Chambers have addressed only rarely and inconsistently. When it has come to their assessments of scale, the assessment undertaken in respect of a situation has frequently been by reference to the crimes allegedly committed within the situation as a whole rather than in respect of any potential case or cases arising out of the situation, with the approach taken by the Pre-Trial Chambers being used ultimately to support a finding of sufficient gravity. As to the manner of commission of the crimes, the consideration by the Pre-Trial Chamber under admissibility provisions addressing cases but not situations of the alleged perpetrator's degree of participation, intent, and role raises the question of the relevance of these factors to the assessment of gravity. So too have the Pre-Trial Chambers taken different approaches in relation to situations and cases respectively in their assessments of impact. When addressing situations, they have deemed as adequate to support a finding of sufficient gravity the impact of the alleged crimes on their victims. Conversely, when addressing cases, they have accorded equal importance to wider forms of impact on affected communities. Finally, the consideration or not by the Pre-Trial Chambers, as a fifth indicator of gravity, of whether the situation or case captures those who bear the greatest responsibility for the alleged crimes likewise reveals a divergence in practice between situations and cases. In decisions on the initiation of investigations into situations, the Pre-Trial Chambers have consistently required consideration of this additional indicator of gravity, even if they have disagreed as to its content. In decisions on cases, in contrast, they have specifically excluded, since the Appeals Chamber's decision in *Ntaganda*, any such consideration.

Taken together, this seemingly confused body of Pre-Trial Chamber and, to a lesser extent, Appeals Chamber practice raises the question of the suitability of the various indicators of gravity suggested as relevant under Article 17(1)(*d*) of the Statute. The application of these various indicators in turn raises the question of the nature of gravity as a criterion of admissibility under Article 17(1)(*d*), that is, whether its application calls for an objective or a subjective assessment.[189]

2.4.1.1 The Indicator of 'Scale'

In principle, the Pre-Trial Chambers have, since the Kenya authorization decision, considered that the assessment of gravity in respect of a situation is to be conducted by reference to one or more potential cases arising out of the situation which are likely to be the focus of the proposed investigation. In their assessments of the scale of the alleged crimes, however, the Pre-Trial Chambers have frequently undertaken the assessment by reference to the crimes allegedly committed within the situation as a whole rather than in respect of any potential case or cases arising out of the situation. The approach they have taken to the assessment of scale allows the situation to more easily satisfy the requirement of sufficient gravity than it

---

[189] See Section 2.4.2.

64   GRAVITY AT THE INTERNATIONAL CRIMINAL COURT

would have done had the assessment been restricted to one or more potential cases arising out of the situation.[190]

Not only is the approach taken by the Pre-Trial Chambers to the assessment of scale inconsistent with their stated approach to the assessment of gravity, it is also problematic in requiring the Prosecutor to do the same in his or her own assessment, that is, to assess scale by reference to all the crimes allegedly committed within the situation. Under Article 53(1)(*b*), it is the Prosecutor who is obliged, in the first instance, to undertake the assessment of gravity as part of his or her decision whether there exists a reasonable basis to proceed with an investigation into the situation. All other things being equal, the relative ease with which the indicator of scale is satisfied when assessed in respect of all the crimes allegedly committed within the situation, rather than by reference to one or more potential cases, restricts the Prosecutor's discretion to decide whether to initiate an investigation into the situation, a discretion necessitated mainly by the limited investigative resources at his or her disposal.[191] Indeed, it is difficult to envisage a situation which will not, when considered as a whole, satisfy the indicator of scale. The point is illustrated by the conclusion of Pre-Trial Chamber I that the crimes allegedly committed within the relatively limited jurisdictional scope of the Mavi Marmara incident satisfied the requirement of scale, which the Prosecutor subsequently pointed out would not have been the case had the assessment been conducted by reference to each potential case arising out of the situation.[192] In order to preserve the Prosecutor's discretion to decide whether to initiate an investigation into a situation and to ensure consistency across the various indicators of gravity, the scale of the alleged crimes is better assessed by reference to one or more potential cases arising out of the situation rather than to the situation as a whole.

2.4.1.2 The Indicator of 'Nature'

When it has come to the initiation of both investigations and prosecutions, the Pre-Trial Chambers have attached little significance to the nature of the alleged crimes in their assessments of gravity. Indeed, the majority of their decisions omit consideration of the nature of the crimes altogether. This omission raises the question of the relevance of the nature of the alleged crimes to the assessment of gravity as a matter of law. The few decisions that have addressed the nature of the crimes have

---

[190] As Hacking suggests, the gravity of the situation has 'little to do with the gravity of the potential cases at hand', which will be more limited. M Hacking, The Law of Gravity: The Role of Gravity in International Criminal Law (doctoral thesis, University of Cambridge 2014) 120.

[191] See Chapter 3, Section 3.3.1.

[192] The issue was crucial in the Mavi Marmara proceedings, wherein the scale of the crimes committed within each potential case was arguably limited. The Prosecutor rightly noted in her decision of 2019 that 'it is not necessarily true that *any* potential case arising from this situation will encompass *all* the victimisation which has been identified in the situation as a whole'. *Situation on the Registered Vessels of the Union of the Comoros, the Hellenic Republic and the Kingdom of Cambodia*, Final Decision of the Prosecutor 2019 (n 33) para 34.

either relied on the legal characterization of the conduct, as in the Mavi Marmara proceedings, or emphasized the vulnerability of the victims, as in relation to the situation in Burundi. It is doubtful whether either of these approaches supports a consideration of the nature of the alleged crimes as a relevant indicator of gravity.

An approach to the gravity of the nature of the alleged crime based on the legal characterization of the conduct confuses admissibility and jurisdiction *ratione materiae*, in practice barring the Court from ever exercising the jurisdiction vested in it by the Rome Statute over those crimes deemed not to be of sufficient gravity.[193] In addition to the effective exclusion from the jurisdiction of the Court of the crimes that fail to satisfy the gravity criterion, addressing the legal characterization of the conduct as part of the assessment of gravity also effectively creates a gravity-based hierarchy among crimes, which is likewise not supported by the text of the Rome Statute.[194] Rather than being a function solely of its characterization as this or that crime, the gravity of acts or omissions punishable under the Statute is 'always a function of the specific conduct alleged in a specific case, not of its formal legal characterisation'.[195] This is not to say that the Prosecutor cannot account for the legal characterization of conduct as part of the decisions whether to investigate and whether to prosecute. Although irrelevant to the assessment of admissibility, the prioritization of certain crimes—such as those involving sexual and gender-based violence[196]—as a matter of prosecutorial policy may be otherwise justifiable. Any such reliance on the nature of the crimes, having been removed from the assessment of admissibility, is excluded from Pre-Trial Chamber review under relevant provisions. In this context, the need to avoid restricting the Court's jurisdiction *ratione materiae* takes priority over the desire for judicial oversight of the Prosecutor's prioritization of certain crimes to the exclusion of others.

As for an approach to the gravity of the nature of the alleged crime based on the vulnerability of the victims, the vulnerability of the victims is undoubtedly relevant to the gravity assessment, but it is equally accounted for in the manner

---

[193] A similar argument has been made in English criminal law. See J Rogers, 'Restructuring the Exercise of Prosecutorial Discretion in England' (2006) 26 Oxford Journal of Legal Studies 775, 785–86. Conversely, Hacking argues that including the nature of crimes as an indicator of gravity 'serve[s] the purpose of addressing perceptions' that certain Rome Statute crimes are 'not serious enough'. Hacking (n 190) 157–58. She does not elaborate, however, on how the nature of the crimes may be used to distinguish between admissible and inadmissible potential cases or cases.

[194] O'Keefe (n 161) 160–61.

[195] ibid 161. See also Independent Expert Review (n 38) para 661; Longobardo (n 38) 29. This is the preferred approach of the Office of the Prosecutor, which seeks to tailor the assessments of gravity to 'the specific factual elements' of the crimes. Policy Paper on Case Selection and Prioritisation, Office of the Prosecutor, 15 September 2016, para 39. See also *Situation on the Registered Vessels of the Union of the Comoros, the Hellenic Republic and the Kingdom of Cambodia*, Final Decision of the Prosecutor 2019 (n 33) para 43. As Seils observes, 'there appears to be an increasing tendency for the Office [of the Prosecutor] to avoid the suggestion of an inherent hierarchy of gravity in relation to the crimes themselves'. Seils (n 70) 75.

[196] Policy Paper on Sexual and Gender-Based Crimes, Office of the Prosecutor, 2014.

of commission of the crimes, the third indicator of gravity.[197] As accepted by the Pre-Trial Chambers, the latter takes account of 'elements of particular cruelty, including the vulnerability of the victims'.[198] This overlap of the nature and the manner of commission of the crimes renders one of the two indicators superfluous. Given the considerable weight placed on the manner of commission of the crimes in the gravity analysis[199] and the limited application in practice of the nature of the crimes, superfluity in the application of these indicators under Article 17(1)(*d*) would be better avoided by considering the vulnerability of the victims only in the assessment of the manner of the commission of the alleged crimes and by doing away with the nature of the alleged crimes as an indicator of gravity.

2.4.1.3 The Indicator of 'Manner of Commission'

Various factors have been considered by the Pre-Trial Chambers as relevant to the assessment, as an indicator of the gravity, of the manner of commission of the crimes. As regards specifically the alleged perpetrator's degree of participation, intent, and role in the commission of the crimes respectively, these have been considered relevant to the gravity of cases but not of situations. The exclusion of these factors from the assessment of the gravity of a situation is most likely because it is difficult to identify the perpetrators of the alleged crimes prior to the initiation of an investigation,[200] let alone to ascertain any criminal intent, the varying degrees of their participation, and the specific role of each perpetrator in the commission of the crimes.[201] This difference of treatment raises the question of the appropriateness of these factors in the first place.

To dispose first of the intent of the perpetrator, it is not clear how this factor could be relevant to the assessment of gravity, whether in respect of a situation or a case. Criminal intent either exists or it does not.[202] Where, by reference to the

---

[197] Longobardo goes further in suggesting that the nature of the crimes is evidenced also by brutality and cruelty in their commission, both elements that the Pre-Trial Chambers have recognized as part of the assessment of the manner of commission of the crimes. Longobardo (n 38) 37.

[198] Policy Paper on Case Selection and Prioritisation, Office of the Prosecutor, 15 September 2016, para 40.

[199] While the Pre-Trial Chambers have assigned particular weight to brutality in the commission of the crimes, the literature has emphasized systematicity in the commission of the crimes, the existence of 'a plan or organised policy', and 'the abuse of power or official capacity', since national courts are less likely to prosecute state officials and military personnel, particularly in weak or failed states. See eg KJ Heller, 'Situational Gravity under the Rome Statute' in C Stahn and L van den Herik (eds), *Future Perspectives on International Criminal Justice* (TM Asser Press 2010); Schabas, *Prosecutorial Discretion and Gravity* (n 40) 245–46.

[200] See note 27.

[201] See eg *Situation on the Registered Vessels of the Union of the Comoros, the Hellenic Republic and the Kingdom of Cambodia*, Final Decision of the Prosecutor 2019 (n 33) paras 25–26. On the difficulty of discerning the intent of the perpetrator at this stage, see D Jacobs and J Naouri, 'Making Sense of the Invisible: The Role of the "Accused" during Preliminary Examinations' in C Stahn and M Bergsmo (eds), *Quality Control in Preliminary Examinations Volume 2* (Torkel Opsahl Academic EPublisher 2018) 497.

[202] Jacobs and Naouri (n 201).

respective evidentiary standards applicable to the Prosecutor's decisions whether to investigate and whether to prosecute, criminal intent cannot be established, the relevant conclusion to be drawn is not that the potential case or case is of insufficient gravity but that the commission of the crime is not made out, even if the result is in either event a decision not to proceed with an investigation or prosecution, as the case may be.

More importantly, the fact that it is impossible for the Prosecutor to identify the respective degrees of participation, intent, and roles of the perpetrators of the crimes before the initiation of an investigation militates against the subsequent consideration of these factors during the investigation. The desire for consistency and predictability in the application of the gravity criterion in Article 17(1)(*d*) supports the application of the same indicators, identically construed, in the context of both a situation and a case.[203] The position is equally supported by considerations of judicial economy, which call for the assessment sooner rather than later of all factors relevant to the assessment, as an indicator of the gravity, of the manner of the commission of the crimes.[204] Simply put, any factors capable of rendering a case insufficiently grave must be equally capable of rendering a potential case insufficiently grave.

This is not to say, however, that the perpetrator's degree of participation, intent, and role in the commission of the alleged crimes are irrelevant to the decision whether to prosecute. As far as intent is concerned, this is the requisite mental element for the commission of a crime.[205] Whether the perpetrator was responsible for the perpetration of the crimes as a principal or an accessory,[206] or if their participation was as a superior,[207] and the perpetrator's role in the commission of the crimes in factual terms may be equally relevant to the Prosecutor's decision whether to prosecute. These considerations are more appropriately characterized, however, as elements of prosecutorial policy, rather than as factors relevant to the admissibility assessment of gravity.[208]

As a separate matter, the Appeals Chamber's reference to violations of human rights resulting from the alleged commission of the crimes as an indicator of the

---

[203] This is also the approach taken by the Office of the Prosecutor to the assessment of gravity across situations and cases. See eg Situation in Iraq/UK Final Report, Office of the Prosecutor, 9 December 2020, para 122. A desire for uniformity in the assessment of admissibility across situations and cases, including the assessment of gravity, is evidenced by the assessment of the admissibility of potential cases arising out of a situation rather than the situation taken as a whole. See Pues (n 40) 976–77.

[204] For the view that judicial economy supports the assessment of admissibility (including gravity) sooner rather than later, see Chapter 4, Section 4.3.2.1.1.

[205] O'Keefe (n 161) 168–69.

[206] See art 25(3), Rome Statute.

[207] See art 28, Rome Statute.

[208] The Independent Expert Review suggested, for example, that cases against mid-level perpetrators be pursued if 'their participation in the overall criminal conduct constitutes part of a strategic plan that is designed to facilitate the subsequent prosecution of those in leadership positions'. The report did not consider these factors to be part of the assessment of gravity. See Independent Expert Review (n 38) para 670.

68   GRAVITY AT THE INTERNATIONAL CRIMINAL COURT

manner of their commission is questionable given that non-state actors, which may be the focus of investigations and prosecutions, are not bound by international human rights law.

2.4.1.4 The Indicator of 'Impact'

When assessing the impact of the alleged crimes as an indicator of the gravity of a situation, all but one of the Pre-Trial Chambers have supported a finding of sufficient gravity by reference to the impact of the crimes on their victims alone. Pre-Trial Chamber I, for example, when addressing the Mavi Marmara incident, considered that the impact of the crimes on their victims was enough, conditional upon the satisfaction of other indicators, to satisfy the requirement of sufficient gravity. In contrast, in the context of the gravity of a case, the Pre-Trial Chambers have assigned equal importance to the impact of the alleged crimes on victims and on affected communities respectively. By excluding any requirement that the Prosecutor consider the wider impact of the crimes on affected communities, the approach taken by the Pre-Trial Chambers in the context of a situation has the consequence that the situation satisfies the gravity criterion more easily than it would have done had the Pre-Trial Chamber required consideration of wider forms of impact, as it has done in the context of a case.

That the consideration of wider forms of impact is relevant to the assessment of gravity, whether in respect of a situation or a case, is supported by the fact that there may be crimes the perpetration of which does not give rise to direct victims but which may nevertheless have an impact on affected communities. Nor is there a clear rationale for an approach that allows the situation to satisfy the gravity criterion with relative ease through consideration of the impact of the alleged crimes on their victims alone and only subsequently requiring, when the Prosecutor decides whether to prosecute a case arising out of that situation, the additional consideration of wider forms of impact on affected communities. The judicious use of limited investigative resources calls for the consideration sooner rather than later of all forms of impact relevant to the assessment of gravity. Consistency in the application of the gravity criterion across situations and cases also warrants the consideration of the same factors as part of the assessment of the impact of the crimes in both contexts.

As with the Appeals Chamber's inclusion of human rights violations as part of the assessment of the manner of commission of the crimes, the inclusion of this factor in the assessment of the impact of the crimes is questionable given that non-state actors are not bound by international human rights law.

2.4.1.5 The Indicator of 'Those Who Bear the Greatest Responsibility'

When it comes to the consideration, as a fifth indicator of gravity, of whether a potential case or a case implicates those who bear the greatest responsibility for the alleged crimes, the Court has taken different approaches to situations and cases

APPLICATION OF GRAVITY CRITERION FOR ADMISSIBILITY   69

respectively. As a factor relevant to the Prosecutor's decision whether to initiate an investigation into a situation, the Pre-Trial Chambers have all required that the potential case or cases identified implicate the person or persons who bear the greatest responsibility for the alleged crimes. In contrast, when it has come to the assessment of the gravity of a case, the Appeals Chamber in *Ntaganda* rejected the requirement that a case implicate 'the most senior leaders suspected of being most responsible' for the alleged crimes.[209] Whether the requirement that a potential case or case implicates those who bear the greatest responsibility for the alleged crimes is articulated as a requirement as to the seniority of the perpetrator[210] or as a requirement as to the actual role of the perpetrator, irrespective of any high-ranking status, in the commission of the crimes,[211] its consideration as an indicator of gravity is questionable. Such a requirement is simply not relevant to the gravity assessment, whether in the context of a situation or a case.

For the reasons explained by the Appeals Chamber in *Ntaganda*, any admissibility requirement that a potential case or a case implicates those who bear the greatest responsibility for the alleged crimes effectively restricts the Court's jurisdiction *ratione personae*,[212] which extends to 'persons' and not only to the 'most responsible' persons.[213] Through the inclusion of such an indicator, 'the admissibility threshold would become a permanent legal barrier providing permanent *ex ante* impunity to an entire class of perpetrators', thereby limiting the Court's ability to deter perpetrators other than those deemed to be the most responsible for the crimes, whether owing to their hierarchical status or their actual role in the commission of the crimes.[214] Such an approach would also exclude the initiation of

[209] *Situation in the Democratic Republic of the Congo*, Pre-Trial Chamber Decision 2006 (n 10) para 64.
[210] This is the preferred approach of the Pre-Trial Chambers under Article 15(4). In support of this approach and for a detailed critique of the approach taken by Pre-Trial Chamber I under Article 53(3) (*a*) on the basis that it prevents the Prosecutor from making any meaningful distinctions in the assessment of gravity, see Heller, '*The Pre-Trial Chamber's Dangerous Comoros Review Decision*' (n 39).
[211] This was the approach taken by Pre-Trial Chamber I in the Mavi Marmara proceedings under Article 53(3)(*a*). As del Ponte explains, 'some individuals who have no particularly important functional role may have distinguished themselves in committing numerous crimes in the most overt, systematic or widespread manner'. C del Ponte, 'Prosecuting the Individuals Bearing the Highest Level of Responsibility' (2004) 2 Journal of International Criminal Justice 516, 517. See also SE Smith, 'Inventing the Laws of Gravity: The ICC's Initial *Lubanga* Decision and Its Regressive Consequences' (2008) 8 International Criminal Law Review 331, 347–50.
[212] *Situation in the Democratic Republic of the Congo*, Appeals Chamber Decision 2006 (n 12) para 73.
[213] See art 1, Rome Statute. Various other provisions of the Statute and its preamble support this position. See *Situation in the Democratic Republic of the Congo*, Appeals Chamber Decision 2006 (n 12) paras 78–79. The suggestion in the ILC that the jurisdiction of a permanent international criminal court should be limited to 'the principal perpetrators', as has been done at some other international criminal courts, was ultimately rejected, including at the Rome Conference. See ILC, 'Summary Records of the Meetings of the Forty-Second Session' (1 May–20 July 1990) UN Doc A/CN.4/SER.A/1990, 37. In support, see S SáCouto and K Cleary, 'The Gravity Threshold of the International Criminal Court' (2007) 23(5) American University International Law Review 807, 812; deGuzman, *Shocking the Conscience of Humanity* (n 13) 121; Seils (n 70) 72.
[214] F Guariglia, 'The Selection of Cases by the Office of the Prosecutor of the International Criminal Court' in C Stahn and G Sluiter (eds), *The Emerging Practice of the International Criminal Court* (Martinus Nijhoff, 2009) 215. See also Pues (n 40) 981–82. Conversely, one commentary disagrees with the approach taken by the Appeals Chamber on the ground that the ICC was never intended to

70 GRAVITY AT THE INTERNATIONAL CRIMINAL COURT

investigations into situations in which the persons most responsible for the alleged crimes are outside the jurisdiction of the Court[215] or have died or absconded.[216]

Practical difficulties in determining who bears the greatest responsibility for the alleged crimes as part of the Prosecutor's decision whether to initiate an investigation into a situation, coupled with the need for consistency in the assessment of gravity across situations and cases, which supports the application of the same indicators in each context,[217] likewise call for the exclusion of this indicator from the assessment of gravity in both contexts. The question of who bears the greatest responsibility requires a 'thorough analysis of all available evidence' and is 'not one that can be properly answered *ex ante*'.[218] As has already been noted, including by the Appeals Chamber, the identities and precise contributions of the perpetrators of the alleged crimes may not be known prior to the commencement of an investigation.[219]

Practical considerations aside, nor is a focus on those most responsible for the alleged crimes during the initiation of an investigation effective if the same requirement is not also imposed during any subsequent investigation. Since the decision of the Appeals Chamber in *Ntaganda*, the Pre-Trial Chambers have rightly excluded any such requirement from the assessment of the gravity of a case. Requiring the Prosecutor to prosecute only the person or persons bearing greatest responsibility for the crimes would infringe on his or her investigative independence, guaranteed under Article 42 of the Statute.[220] This independence permits the Prosecutor the use of pyramidal prosecution strategies during case selection, allowing an initial focus on perpetrators other than those most responsible for the alleged crimes with a view to building a case or cases against the most responsible perpetrator or perpetrators.[221]

prosecute all the cases falling within its jurisdiction, arguably justifying the drawing of a distinction between sufficiently and insufficiently grave cases based on a consideration of the perpetrator's responsibility in the alleged commission of the crimes. According to these commentators, the deterrent effect of the Court is not lost by a focus on those most responsible for the alleged crimes, since low-level perpetrators may still be prosecuted at the national level. WA Schabas and MM El Zeidy, 'Article 17' in O Triffterer and K Ambos (eds), *The Rome Statute of the International Criminal Court: A Commentary* (3rd edn, CH Beck 2016) 814. Although these are valid considerations, the deterrent effect of the Court cannot depend on the prosecution of low-level perpetrators at the national level, which states parties to the Rome Statute are not obliged to undertake.

[215] See eg Statement of the Prosecutor of the International Criminal Court, Fatou Bensouda, on the Alleged Crimes Committed by ISIS, Office of the Prosecutor, 8 April 2015, www.icc-cpi.int/Pages/item.aspx?name=otp-stat-08-04-2015-1, accessed 13 March 2023.

[216] deGuzman, 'The International Criminal Court's Gravity Jurisprudence at Ten' (n 6) 485.

[217] See note 203.

[218] Guariglia and Rogier (n 27). See also Seils (n 70) 72; Rastan, 'What Is a "Case" for the Purpose of the Rome Statute?' (n 24) 441; deGuzman, 'Gravity and the Legitimacy of the International Criminal Court' (n 9) 1451.

[219] See note 27.

[220] deGuzman, 'The International Criminal Court's Gravity Jurisprudence at Ten' (n 6) 482–83; Hacking (n 190) 135.

[221] In fact, the Office of the Prosecutor has moved away from its initial policy focus on 'those who bear the greatest responsibility for the most serious crimes', namely 'those situated at the highest echelons

APPLICATION OF GRAVITY CRITERION FOR ADMISSIBILITY 71

The additional consideration of judicial economy that militates against the use of this indicator in relation to both situations and cases is that requiring a focus on those most responsible would, during any eventual prosecutions, 'enabl[e] perpetrators to bring legal challenges demanding evidence showing that they are not only guilty but the most guilty'.[222]

None of this is to say that considerations pertaining to the responsibility of the alleged perpetrators of the crimes are irrelevant to the decisions whether to investigate and whether to prosecute. Conditional on the satisfaction of all other requirements, there may be good reasons for the Prosecutor to invest his or her limited resources in the prosecution of those most responsibility for the crimes, whether owing to their seniority or their actual role in the commission of the crimes.[223] Any such factors are more appropriately characterized, however, as they have been by the Office of the Prosecutor, as policy considerations relevant to the exercise of other discretions conferred on the Prosecutor, rather than as an indicator of the gravity of the alleged crimes.[224] Precisely this distinction between the assessment of gravity under Article 17(1)(d) and the requirement that the Prosecutor focus his or her investigations on those bearing the greatest responsibility for the alleged crimes is also made by the Independent Expert Review of the International Criminal Court and the Rome Statute System (Independent Expert Review) in its report of 2020.[225] Any such consideration of the responsibility of the alleged

---

of responsibility, including those who ordered, financed, or otherwise organized the alleged crimes'. Prosecutorial Strategy 2009–2012, Office of the Prosecutor, 1 February 2010, para 19. Instead, prosecutorial policy favours prosecutions against mid-level perpetrators 'in order to ultimately have a reasonable chance to convict the most responsible'. Strategic Plan June 2012–2015, Office of the Prosecutor, 11 October 2013, para 22. In support of this revised approach, see Independent Expert Review (n 38) para R233; Guariglia and Rogier (n 27) 351; Guariglia (n 214) 210–11; M El Zeidy, 'The Gravity Threshold under the Statute of the International Criminal Court' (2008) 19 Criminal Law Forum 35, 49–50; A Whiting, 'A Program for the Next ICC Prosecutor' (2020) 52 Case Western Reserve Journal of International Law 479, 487–88; Smith (n 211) 343; SáCouto and Cleary, 'The Gravity Threshold of the International Criminal Court' (n 213) 812–13.

[222] Guariglia (n 214) 215.

[223] A variety of views have been expressed. See HB Jallow, 'Prosecutorial Discretion and International Criminal Justice' (2005) 3 Journal of International Criminal Justice 145, 152–53; 'Improving the Operations of the ICC Office of the Prosecutor: Reappraisal of Structures, Norms, and Practices', Outcome Report and Recommendations, Open Society Justice Initiative and Amsterdam Center for International Law/Department of Criminal Law, Amsterdam Law School, 15 April 2020, 9–11.

[224] For the Office of the Prosecutor, a focus on those bearing greatest responsibility for the crimes has always been a policy criterion over and above admissibility requirements. See eg Policy Paper on Case Selection and Prioritisation, Office of the Prosecutor, 15 September 2016, paras 34–44. In support of this view, see Schabas, 'Prosecutorial Discretion and Gravity' (n 40) 243; Pues (n 40) 981–82; Guariglia (n 214) 215; I Stegmiller, 'The Gravity Threshold under the ICC Statute: Gravity Back and Forth in *Lubanga* and *Ntaganda*' (2009) 9 International Criminal Law Review 547, 552; Hacking (n 190) 120–23; A Whiting, 'What to Look for in the Next ICC Prosecutor', Justice in Conflict, 17 April 2020, https://justiceinconflict.org/2020/04/17/what-to-look-for-in-the-next-icc-prosecutor, accessed 13 March 2023; Jacobs, '*ICC Judges Ask the Prosecutor to Reconsider Decision Not to Investigate Israeli Gaza Flotilla Conduct*' (n 43).

[225] Independent Expert Review (n 38) paras R234, 664.

72 GRAVITY AT THE INTERNATIONAL CRIMINAL COURT

perpetrators of the crimes is not reviewable by the Pre-Trial Chamber as part of the assessment of admissibility.

2.4.2 The Subjective Nature of the Gravity Assessment under Article 17(1)(*d*)

A question that remains to be addressed is whether the application of Article 17(1)(*d*) of the Statute, in the context of the Prosecutor's respective decisions whether to investigate and to prosecute, requires an objective or a subjective approach to the assessment of gravity. An objective approach implies the mechanistic application of quantifiable indicators of gravity to meet an objective threshold of sufficient gravity. It assumes that there is 'one "right" answer to the issues in dispute', suggesting a degree of automaticity in the assessment and leading to the same result irrespective of the decision-maker.[226] In contrast, a subjective approach involves the exercise of individual judgement in the case-by-case weighing of both quantitative and qualitative indicators. This exercise, and the application in particular of qualitative indicators of gravity, suggests that the assessment of gravity may differ as between decision-makers. It thus calls for the exercise of discretion, which may be limited by the consistent application of suitable indicators of gravity. Although these considerations are equally relevant to the application of the gravity criterion by the Pre-Trial Chamber, a necessary distinction must be made as to what an objective or a subjective approach to the assessment of gravity requires in each context.

2.4.2.1 As Viewed by the Court
An objective approach to the assessment of gravity, which calls for the application of quantifiable indicators,[227] might be thought to be supported by the Appeals Chamber's rejection in *Ntaganda* of the relevance of the subjective criterion of 'social alarm', which in its opinion did not capture the 'objective gravity' of the crimes.[228] On closer examination, however, an objective approach to the

---

[226] E Shirlow, *Judging at the Interface: Deference to State Decision-Making Authority in International Adjudication* (CUP 2021) 241.

[227] deGuzman proposes an objective assessment of gravity with a view to 'mark[ing] a lower boundary' that excludes 'instances of the proscribed conduct that cause minor harms' and 'crimes involving minimal moral culpability, even if they cause significant harm'. deGuzman, *Shocking the Conscience of Humanity* (n 13) 119–20. Even so, she concedes that 'the context-specific nature of the enterprise means that no rigid formula should be adopted' and that '[t]he Court must not ... set a particular number on the victims harmed or mandate a certain leadership rank for perpetrators'. deGuzman, 'Gravity and the Legitimacy of the International Criminal Court' (n 9) 1457.

[228] *Situation in the Democratic Republic of the Congo*, Appeals Chamber Decision 2006 (n 12) para 72. In support of social alarm as an indicator of gravity, see Heller, 'Situational Gravity under the Rome Statute' (n 199) 233–37; F Mégret, 'Beyond "Gravity": For a Politics of International Criminal Prosecutions' (2013) American Society of International Law Proceedings 428, 430; MH Zakerhossein, *Situation Selection Regime at the International Criminal Court: Law, Policy, Practice* (Intersentia 2017)

APPLICATION OF GRAVITY CRITERION FOR ADMISSIBILITY   73

assessment of gravity appears not to be the preferred approach of the Appeals Chamber. Its jurisprudence instead indicates that the assessment of gravity, in the context of both situations and cases, is a subjective undertaking involving the exercise of judgement or discretion. The Appeals Chamber posited a subjective approach to gravity in respect of the admissibility of a situation in its 2019 decision in relation to the Mavi Marmara incident, in which it stated that

> the assessment of gravity involves ... the evaluation of numerous factors and information relating thereto, which the Prosecutor has to balance in reaching her decision.[229]

As such, it was not the role of the Pre-Trial Chamber to

> direct the Prosecutor as to how the information made available to her should be analysed, which factual findings she should reach, how to apply the law to the available information, or what weight she should attach to the different factors in the course of a gravity assessment.[230]

In the context of the admissibility of a case, the Appeals Chamber explained in its 2020 decision in *Al Hassan* that the assessment of gravity 'must be made on a case-by-case basis having regard to the specific facts of a given case'.[231] That the assessment does not involve the application of 'exacting legal requirements'[232] is evidenced by the articulation in practice of various qualitative indicators of gravity, such as the manner of commission of the crimes and their impact, the application of which 'will always be relative'.[233] The absence of a fixed weighting of the indicators, both quantitative and qualitative, has also been said to make the application of Article 17(1)(*d*) of the Statute not a science but 'a craft, based on guiding principles but sufficiently flexible to address the infinite variety of factual scenarios that will present themselves'.[234] In other words, the various indicators of gravity 'cannot purport to dictate in advance the substance of each and every ... decision'.[235]

229–30. But see M Osiel, 'How Should the ICC Office of the Prosecutor Choose Its Cases? The Multiple Meanings of "Situational Gravity"', The Hague Justice Portal, 5 March 2009, www.haguejusticeportal. net/Docs/Commentaries%20PDF/Osiel_ICC_EN.pdf, accessed 28 October 2023, 5–6.

[229] *Situation on the Registered Vessels of the Union of the Comoros, the Hellenic Republic and the Kingdom of Cambodia*, Appeals Chamber Decision 2019 (n 33) para 81.
[230] ibid para 82.
[231] *Al Hassan*, Appeals Chamber Decision 2020 (n 14) para 53. See also *Situation in the Democratic Republic of the Congo*, Pikis Partial Dissent 2006 (n 133) paras 39–40; Greenawalt (n 41) 84.
[232] *Situation on the Registered Vessels of the Union of the Comoros, the Hellenic Republic and the Kingdom of Cambodia*, Pre-Trial Chamber Decision 2015 (n 33) para 14.
[233] Schabas and El Zeidy (n 214) 816.
[234] Seils (n 70) 73.
[235] JA Goldston, 'More Candour about Criteria' (2010) 8 Journal of International Criminal Justice 383, 403. Put differently, 'there will always be a myriad of complex but legitimate factors involved in

74 GRAVITY AT THE INTERNATIONAL CRIMINAL COURT

Rather, '[w]hether the particular circumstances of a given case are of sufficient gravity ... is always a case-specific assessment'[236] involving 'a high level of subjectivity'.[237] The task of weighing the various indicators of gravity is conferred on either the Prosecutor or the Pre-Trial Chamber, depending on the stage at which the assessment of admissibility is made.

2.4.2.2 In Principle

There are good reasons to support a subjective approach to the assessment of gravity under Article 17(1)(d) of the Statute, even if such reasons have not been articulated clearly by the Appeals Chamber. To begin with, any objective articulation of gravity is likely to be arbitrary. Without clear guidance in the Statute as to what the application of the gravity criterion requires, any objective articulation by the Court of a threshold of 'sufficient gravity', whether by reference to the object and purpose of the Statute[238] or a variety of policy considerations, could be objected to on the basis of different but equally valid readings of that object and purpose or of competing considerations of policy.[239] In other words, there is no self-evident basis in either law or policy on which to justify the drawing of a purportedly objective line beyond which cases would be deemed to be insufficiently grave. In a related vein, an objective approach to gravity could become 'quasi-jurisdictional' in that it would 'have a tendency to limit the Court's exercise of jurisdiction not only in the case at hand but also for future cases and situations'.[240]

---

making calls that, ultimately, are always case and context-specific'. B Kotecha, 'The International Criminal Court's Selectivity and Procedural Justice' (2020) 18 Journal of International Criminal Justice 107, 136.

[236] *Al Hassan*, Appeals Chamber Decision 2020 (n 14) para 58.

[237] Schabas and El Zeidy (n 214) 816. In support of a discretionary assessment of gravity, see also G Turone, 'Powers and Duties of the Prosecutor' in A Cassese, P Gaeta, and JRWD Jones (eds), *The Rome Statute of the International Criminal Court* II (OUP 2002) 1173; Schabas, 'Selecting Situations and Cases' (n 37) 380–81; Mariniello (n 38) 1002; Pues (n 40) 969; D Jacobs, 'The Gaza Flotilla, Israel and the ICC: Some Thoughts on Gravity and the Relevant Armed Conflict', Spreading the Jam, 11 November 2014, https://dovjacobs.com/2014/11/11/the-gaza-flotilla-israel-and-the-icc-some-thoughts-on-grav ity-and-the-relevant-armed-conflict, accessed 13 March 2023; Whiting, '*The ICC Prosecutor Should Reject Judges' Decision in Mavi Marmara Incident*' (n 35); Zakerhossein, *Situation Selection Regime at the International Criminal Court* (n 228) 229; Hacking (n 190) 112–20.

[238] For a reading of the various objectives outlined in the preamble to the Rome Statute, see O Triffterer, M Bergsmo, and K Ambos, 'Preamble' in O Triffterer and K Ambos (eds), *The Rome Statute of the International Criminal Court: A Commentary* (3rd edn, CH Beck 2016).

[239] See M Damaška, 'What Is the Point of International Criminal Justice?' (2008) 83 Chicago-Kent Law Review 329, 331–40. As deGuzman and Schabas note, it is difficult to evaluate the Prosecutor's admissibility assessments against the objectives articulated in the preamble, given the 'much wider range of objectives' that may be relevant to the assessment. deGuzman and Schabas (n 8) 163–64. For Mégret, 'even if one can come to an agreement that certain crimes are relatively less grave, some will still argue that they are, at least, based on an understanding of the Court's priorities, grave enough'. Mégret, 'Beyond "Gravity"' (n 228) 430, emphasis omitted. See also Osiel (n 228) 4–5.

[240] deGuzman, 'Gravity and the Legitimacy of the International Criminal Court' (n 9) 1457. More generally, '[p]recise standards are impossible when the law needs to regulate widely varying conduct with a general standard'. T Endicott, 'The Value of Vagueness' in A Marmor and S Soames (eds), *Philosophical Foundations of Language in the Law* (OUP 2011) 24.

APPLICATION OF GRAVITY CRITERION FOR ADMISSIBILITY   75

Admittedly, a subjective approach to the assessment of gravity could equally be objected to on grounds of the arbitrariness that may result from a lack of consistency and attendant predictability in the case-by-case application and weighing of the various indicators of gravity under Article 17(1)(*d*), whether by the Prosecutor or the Pre-Trial Chamber.[241] In light of the Appeals Chamber's endorsement of a subjective approach to gravity, however, the desire for consistency and predictability in the application of Article 17(1)(*d*) must be qualified by the discretionary nature of the assessment. That the conferral of this discretion does not amount to an endorsement of arbitrariness in the application of the provision is evidenced by the articulation of the relevant indicators of gravity, which may be required to be considered as a matter of law.[242] Although the application and weighing of these indicators is not uncontentious,[243] a subjective approach to the application of Article 17(1)(*d*) accommodates decisions that are made reasonably and in good faith.[244] As one commentator notes, '[a]s long as these criteria are applied genuinely and faithfully', there is 'nothing to fear from reasonable disagreement'.[245]

[241] On the choice between the two kinds of arbitrariness, see Endicott (n 240) 22–24. On the importance of consistency in the application of Article 17(1)(*d*), see deGuzman, 'Gravity and the Legitimacy of the International Criminal Court' (n 9) 1457; Pues (n 40) 983–84; M Delmas-Marty, 'Interactions between National and International Criminal Law in the Preliminary Phase of Trial at the ICC' (2006) 4 Journal of International Criminal Justice 2, 10; Kotecha (n 235) 121–22. These commentators nevertheless acknowledge 'the need for flexibility and fact-sensitivity in the face of the diverse situations that the ICC is confronted with'. Pues (n 40) 966.

[242] The indicators of gravity, as articulated by the Prosecutor and the Pre-Trial Chambers and as confirmed by the Appeals Chamber, may crystallize over time and become binding on the Prosecutor in the exercise of his or her discretion. Their application thus becomes a matter of law. See MS Davis, 'Standards of Review: Judicial Review of Discretionary Decisionmaking' (2000) 2(1) Journal of Appellate Practice and Process 47, 50–51. As Orentlicher explains, it is necessary to 'defend the Court's case load in terms of consistent baseline criteria' such that, if 'applied consistently and explained persuasively, the concept of gravity can ... help legitimate the selection of situations deemed to warrant the Court's attention'. D Orentlicher, 'Remarks of Diane Orentlicher' (2013) American Society of International Law Proceedings 425, 426. See also Mégret, 'Beyond "Gravity"' (n 228) 428. Conversely, Stahn observes that, in practice, '[m]any of the key factors guiding the selection of situations and cases were developed outside the box of legality requirements and thus moved from the domain of review to the area of prosecutorial policy'. C Stahn, 'Judicial Review of Prosecutorial Discretion: Five Years On' in C Stahn and G Sluiter (eds), *The Emerging Practice of the International Criminal Court* (Martinus Nijhoff 2009) 270.

[243] deGuzman objects that '[t]he result of this factor-based approach is that virtually any crime can be labelled "grave"'. MM deGuzman, 'Gravity Rhetoric: The Good, the Bad, and the "Political"' (2013) American Society of International Law Proceedings 421, 422. Schabas regrets that 'the "gravity" language strikes the observer as little more than obfuscation, a contrived attempt to make the determinations look objective and judicial'. WA Schabas, 'Victor's Justice: Selecting Situations at the International Criminal Court' (2010) 43 John Marshall Law Review 535, 549.

[244] The decisions whether to investigate and whether to prosecute will always be subject to disagreement. Robinson's view, shared here, is that this awareness paves the way for 'accord[ing] the Court's officials some "margin of appreciation" to make reasonable, good faith selections from the understandable yet inevitably imperfect and assailable options'. D Robinson, 'Inescapable Dyads: Why the International Criminal Court Cannot Win' (2015) 28 Leiden Journal of International Law 323, 345. See also F Mégret, 'The Anxieties of International Criminal Justice' (2016) 29 Leiden Journal of International Law 197, 204–05. The Office of the Prosecutor has identified independence, impartiality, and objectivity as the three principles governing the selection of situations and cases. See Guariglia (n 214) 212–13.

[245] Seils (n 70) 78. The discretionary application of any open-textured provision 'is in effect a choice'. This alone does not make its application arbitrary or irrational. HLA Hart, *The Concept of Law* (3rd edn, OUP 2012) 127.

76 GRAVITY AT THE INTERNATIONAL CRIMINAL COURT

Perhaps more significantly, a subjective approach to the assessment of gravity, when applied by the Prosecutor in the initiation of investigations and prosecutions, provides a legal basis on which to justify what are in the face of scarce investigative and prosecutorial resources highly selective investigations and prosecutions.[246] The underlying purpose of the gravity criterion articulated by the Court, namely to exclude only 'marginal', 'peripheral', or 'less serious' cases,[247] does not reflect the reality that the Prosecutor is in fact required 'to choose from many meritorious complaints the appropriate ones for international intervention, rather than to weed out weak or frivolous ones'.[248] In reality, '[t]he choice ... is not so much between grave and not-so-grave crimes, but between different shades of the most atrocious crimes'.[249] As early as 2003, the Office of the Prosecutor admitted that its 'limited resources ... mean that not every situation can be immediately investigated' and that 'prioritization based on the factors in article 53 is necessary'.[250] In its first ever annual report, of 2022, the Office affirmed its 'commitment to go deeper within a narrower range of situations, which will be prioritized on the basis of gravity and seek to optimise the use of the Office's finite resources'.[251] Viewed in this light, the subjective nature of the gravity assessment articulated by the Appeals Chamber makes gravity a criterion for the allocation of scarce investigative and prosecutorial resources. Even those commentators who oppose the inclusion of

---

[246] As one ILC member explained, the inclusion of the admissibility criteria in the 1994 draft statute for an international criminal court would 'ensur[e] that the court would deal solely with the most serious crimes ... and it would adapt its caseload to the resources available'. ILC Report 1994 (n 8) 22. Goldston supports this use of prosecutorial discretion as 'an essential means of rationalizing the use of scarce law enforcement resources'. Goldston (n 235) 389. See also R Rastan, 'Situation and Case: Defining the Parameters' in C Stahn and M El Zeidy (eds), *The International Criminal Court and Complementarity* vol I (CUP 2011) 455–56; Mégret, 'The Anxieties of International Criminal Justice' (n 244) 203; Orentlicher (n 242) 426. For a useful overview of the Office of the Prosecutor's budgetary constraints, see J O'Donohue, 'ICC Prosecutor Symposium: Wanted—International Prosecutor to Deliver Justice Successfully across Multiple Complex Situations with Inadequate Resources', Opinio Juris, 14 April 2020, http://opiniojuris.org/2020/04/14/icc-prosecutor-symposium-wanted-international-pro secutor-to-deliver-justice-successfully-across-multiple-complex-situations-with-inadequate-resour ces/?utm_source=feedburner&utm_medium=email&utm_campaign=Feed%3A+opiniojurisfeed+ %28Opinio+Juris%29, accessed 13 March 2023.

[247] Recall Section 2.2.

[248] L Arbour, 'The Need for an Independent and Effective Prosecutor in the Permanent International Criminal Court' (1999) 17 Windsor Yearbook of Access to Justice 207, 213. See also Robinson (n 244) 332–33.

[249] F Mégret, 'Three Dangers for the International Criminal Court' (2001) 12 Finnish Yearbook of International Law 193, 213.

[250] Annex to the 'Paper on Some Policy Issues before the Office of the Prosecutor': Referrals and Communications, Office of the Prosecutor, 2003, 4. The Office of the Prosecutor has further clarified that 'feasibility is not a separate factor under the Statute ... when determining whether to open an investigation'. Policy Paper on Preliminary Examinations, Office of the Prosecutor, 2013, para 70. The 2015 Report of the Court on the Basic Size of the Office of the Prosecutor referred more generally to the need for 'a reasonable degree of prioritization' in carrying out preliminary examinations, investigations, and prosecutions, even if it implied 'an insufficient response to the demand'. Report of the Court on the Basic Size of the Office of the Prosecutor, 17 September 2015, ICC-ASP/14/21, para 11.

[251] 'Towards a More Just World Every Day', Annual Report of the Office of the Prosecutor, Office of the Prosecutor, 1 December 2022, 52.

APPLICATION OF GRAVITY CRITERION FOR ADMISSIBILITY   77

any such consideration in the gravity assessment[252] recognize that the allocation of limited resources is an indispensable element of the Prosecutor's decisions whether to investigate and whether to prosecute, even if they propose situating this consideration elsewhere.[253] That resource considerations play at least a part in the application of the gravity criterion in Article 17(1)(d) of the Statute is evidenced by the Prosecutor's recent assertion that,

> although the drafters did not expressly include the proper allocation of the Court's resources among the article 53(1) criteria, such considerations cannot be ignored ... Indeed, it may be precisely in this context, at least in part, that the 'sufficient gravity' requirement was included as an express criterion for initiating any investigation.[254]

The consideration of resource constraints in the assessment of gravity is also supported by the report of the Independent Expert Review, which, in the light of these constraints, recommended the 'allocat[ion] [of] the limited resources of the [Office of the Prosecutor] to the situations that are the most serious'.[255] The same logic supports a subjective assessment of the gravity of a case as part of the decision whether to prosecute.

Although the allocation of resources is an important justification for a subjective approach to the assessment of gravity, a distinction must be drawn as regards the application of Article 17(1)(d) between assessment by the Prosecutor under Article 53(1)(b) and (2)(b) and assessment by the Pre-Trial Chamber under Article 19(1)–(3).[256]

---

[252] Some commentators do so by prioritizing consistency in the application of Article 17(1)(d). Pues (n 40) 983–84. Others invoke policy justifications for the exclusion of resource considerations from the gravity assessment. deGuzman and Stegmiller are concerned about the restriction of the Court's deterrence potential in relation to potential cases or cases which may be rendered inadmissible based on resource considerations. deGuzman, 'Gravity and the Legitimacy of the International Criminal Court' (n 9) 1433; Stegmiller (n 224) 557. The argument has merit if gravity is conceived as an objective criterion but is unconvincing if gravity is conceived, as it is by the Appeals Chamber, as requiring a subjective assessment. A second policy objection is that the consideration of resource constraints obscures the decision-making process. SáCouto and Cleary, 'The Gravity Threshold of the International Criminal Court' (n 213) 814; Stegmiller (n 224) 559. On the contrary, transparency will be better achieved by acknowledging that resource limitations play a role in the assessment of gravity.

[253] For a detailed critique of the distinction between the gravity criterion for admissibility in Article 17(1)(d) and the policy consideration of 'relative gravity' proposed by some commentators, see Chapter 5, Sections 5.3.2.1 and 5.3.3.1. An approach to the criterion of 'seriousness' that excludes the consideration of 'the various costs associated with bringing proceedings' has been considered equally problematic in English criminal law. Rogers (n 193) 785.

[254] *Situation on the Registered Vessels of the Union of the Comoros, the Hellenic Republic and the Kingdom of Cambodia*, ICC-01/13-57/Anx1, Office of the Prosecutor, Final Decision of the Prosecutor concerning the 'Article 53(1) Report' (ICC-01/13-6-AnxA), dated 6 November 2014, 29 November 2017, para 25. See also Strategic Plan 2019–2021, Office of the Prosecutor, 17 July 2019, 18.

[255] Independent Expert Review (n 38) para 650.

[256] The procedural aspects of this distinction are addressed in Chapter 4.

78 GRAVITY AT THE INTERNATIONAL CRIMINAL COURT

As far as the Prosecutor is concerned, given that any prosecutorial decision whether to initiate an investigation or prosecution is necessarily allocative, it is not clear how he or she could assess 'sufficient gravity' without comparing the situation or case before him or her with others that might also draw on his or her limited investigative resources at that point.[257] This is not to say, however, that a situation or case need be as serious as any which has previously already been investigated or prosecuted. There is no competition for resources between a situation which is yet to be investigated and one which has already been investigated or between a case which is yet to be prosecuted and one which has already been prosecuted. Rather, the subjective, case-by-case nature of the assessment suggests that any conclusion as to the sufficiency of the gravity of a situation or case is a matter of factual appreciation and cannot be binding as a matter of law on either the Prosecutor or the Court.[258]

When it comes to the determination by the Pre-Trial Chamber of the admissibility of a case under Article 19(1)–(3), the Pre-Trial Chamber, unlike the Prosecutor, is not responsible for assessing the allocative implications of any decision to prosecute. The management of investigative and prosecutorial resources is part of the independent mandate of the Office of the Prosecutor.[259] The assessment of admissibility by the Pre-Trial Chamber is different in this sense from the Prosecutor's assessments of admissibility, with the Pre-Trial Chamber being required only to approach each case on its subjective merits.

In sum, the subjective, case-by-case assessment of gravity reflected in the jurisprudence of the Appeals Chamber is supported by the application and weighing of relevant quantitative and qualitative indicators of gravity articulated in the decisions of the Pre-Trial Chambers and the Appeals Chamber, which call for the exercise of discretion. A subjective approach to the application of Article 17(1) (*d*) is equally supported by the balancing of this discretion against the desire for

---

[257] Accordingly, it should not be considered impermissible for the Prosecutor to compare the gravity of a situation with others currently under consideration for investigation. What is required is an assessment of whether the situation, comprising one or more admissible potential cases, is 'sufficiently grave *relative to other situations* to justify a formal investigation'. Heller, '*The Pre-Trial Chamber's Dangerous Comoros Review Decision*' (n 39). It should equally not be considered impermissible for the Prosecutor to compare a potential case or case arising out of a situation with other potential cases or cases arising out of the same or other situations under consideration for investigation and prosecution. Greenawalt (n 41) 85. This is not to say that the gravity of a situation as a whole (that is, of all the potential cases that satisfy the gravity requirement) can be compared to the gravity of a potential case or case. Heller, '*The Pre-Trial Chamber's Dangerous Comoros Review Decision*' (n 39); Mariniello (n 38) 993, 1002–03; Knoops and Zwart (n 38) 1094–95; Jacobs, '*The Gaza Flotilla, Israel and the ICC*' (n 237). Conversely, some commentators argue that this comparative assessment of gravity confers too much discretion on the Prosecutor. deGuzman and Schabas (n 8) 144–45; Kotecha (n 235) 121–22.

[258] Making the assessment binding would have the effect of ossifying the requirement of sufficient gravity over time, leaving little room for flexibility in addressing the different kinds of situations and cases which may arise in the future.

[259] art 42(2), Rome Statute; Rule 110.2 and Reg 1.4, Financial Regulations and Rules 2008. See also Shirlow (n 226) 23–24.

consistency and predictability in the application of the provision. When it comes to the initiation of investigations and prosecutions, this permits the Prosecutor the exercise of discretion reasonably and in good faith with a view to the consideration, as part of the assessment of relevant indicators of gravity, of the allocation of scarce investigative and prosecutorial resources.

2.5 Conclusion

On close examination, not all of the indicators of sufficient gravity articulated by the Office of the Prosecutor and endorsed by the Pre-Trial Chambers and the Appeals Chamber are relevant to the assessment under Article 17(1)(d) of the Statute. The scale, manner of commission, and impact of the alleged crimes are suitable indicators of gravity, whether in respect of a situation or a case, under Article 17(1)(d). With a view to the predictability of the assessment of gravity, and with due regard for the distinction between its assessment in relation to situations and cases respectively, these indicators must be applied consistently by the Prosecutor or the Pre-Trial Chamber, as the case may be, in relation to potential cases or cases. Conversely, to preserve the distinction between jurisdiction *ratione materiae* and admissibility and to avoid superfluity, the nature of the alleged crimes, which ought rightly to be assessed by reference to neither the legal characterization of the punishable conduct nor the vulnerability of the victims, should be excluded from the gravity assessment. Nor is any requirement that a potential case or case implicate the person or persons bearing greatest responsibility for the alleged crimes relevant to the assessment of gravity. The exclusion of this requirement from the application of Article 17(1)(d) maintains the Statute's distinction between jurisdiction *ratione personae* and admissibility and is also desirable for practical reasons. The nature of the alleged crimes and the level of responsibility may nevertheless be considered as a matter of prosecutorial policy.

In respect of the admissibility of both situations and cases, the Appeals Chamber has stated that the assessment of gravity is case-specific and fact-dependent, in essence subjective. This would seem to rule out an objective assessment of gravity, instead permitting the exercise of discretion in the application of Article 17(1)(d). Support for the exercise of this discretion, whether by the Prosecutor or the Pre-Trial Chamber, is lent by the endorsement of qualitative indicators of gravity by the Appeals Chamber. The indicators, moreover, both qualitative and quantitative, are each assigned such weight as the Prosecutor or the Pre-Trial Chamber, as the case may be, considers appropriate. Beyond the decisions of the Appeals Chamber, a subjective assessment of gravity in the specific context of the selection of investigations and prosecutions is supported by the fact that the Prosecutor is in reality required to choose from among many meritorious cases those that are suitable for investigation and prosecution, rather than merely to exclude cases 'of marginal gravity only'.[260] When it comes to the Prosecutor's decisions whether to investigate and whether to prosecute, this warrants the exercise of discretion in the allocation of limited investigative and prosecutorial resources through the application of the gravity criterion. What remains to be seen, and is addressed in Chapters 3 and 4, is the intensity of Pre-Trial Chamber oversight of the exercise of this discretion under relevant provisions.

---

[260] *Al Hassan*, Appeals Chamber Decision 2020 (n 14) para 53.

3

Pre-Trial Chamber Review of the Admissibility of 'Situations'

3.1 Introduction

Relevant provisions of the Rome Statute provide for judicial oversight of the assessment by the Prosecutor, as part of the decision whether to investigate a situation, of admissibility. In accordance with Article 53(1)(*b*) of the Statute, the Prosecutor is required to assess the admissibility of a situation when deciding whether to initiate an investigation into it. As indicated in Article 53(1)(*b*), admissibility falls to be assessed by reference to the criteria specified in Article 17 of the Statute, among them the criterion of sufficient gravity found in Article 17(1)(*d*).[1] Where a situation has been referred to the Prosecutor by a state party or the United Nations (UN) Security Council, any decision by the Prosecutor not to initiate an investigation, including any decision taken on the basis of inadmissibility, may be reviewed by the Pre-Trial Chamber at the request of the referring state or the Council, as provided for in Article 53(3)(*a*).[2] Where the Prosecutor decides to initiate an investigation into a situation *proprio motu*,[3] Pre-Trial Chamber authorization is required, as provided for in Article 15(3) and (4) of the Statute, the latter of which logically requires the Pre-Trial Chamber to review the Prosecutor's admissibility assessment.

To initiate an investigation into a situation, whether under Article 53(1) alone or by additional reference to Article 15(3), the Prosecutor must have concluded

---

[1] If, on referral of a situation or *proprio motu*, the Prosecutor concludes that there is a reasonable basis to proceed with the investigation of a situation, he or she must notify relevant states of his or her intention to proceed, as stipulated in Article 18(1) of the Rome Statute of the International Criminal Court 1998 (Rome Statute). Having received such notification, a state may inform the Court that it is investigating or has investigated crimes in relation to the situation. On this basis, the Pre-Trial Chamber may, on the application of the Prosecutor, determine the admissibility of the situation under Article 18(2). As per Rule 55(2) of the Rules of Procedure and Evidence 1998 (RPE), this determination is, like the Prosecutor's assessment, made by reference to the criteria in Article 17(1) of the Statute. As Article 18(2) relates to challenges on the basis of ongoing or complete investigations at the national level, an admissibility determination under this provision does not include considerations of gravity. The reference in Rule 55(2) is clearly, albeit implicitly, only to sub-paragraphs (*a*) and (*b*), and perhaps (*c*) of Article 17(1), the first two as elaborated on in Article 17(2) and (3).

[2] Where the Prosecutor's decision not to initiate an investigation is based solely on the interests of justice in Article 53(1)(*c*), the decision may be reviewed at the initiative of the Pre-Trial Chamber under Article 53(3)(*b*) and 'shall be effective only if confirmed by the Pre-Trial Chamber'.

[3] See art 15(1), Rome Statute.

Gravity at the International Criminal Court. Priya Urs, Oxford University Press. © Priya Urs 2024.
DOI: 10.1093/oso/9780198882954.003.0003

82 GRAVITY AT THE INTERNATIONAL CRIMINAL COURT

that there exists a 'reasonable basis to proceed' with the investigation. This assessment, in particular the application of the open-textured requirement of 'sufficient gravity' in Article 17(1)(*d*), involves the exercise of discretion on the part of the Prosecutor.[4] Pre-Trial Chamber oversight in Articles 53(3)(*a*) and 15(4) respectively is designed to discipline the exercise of this discretion. What is lacking, however, in the admissibility framework of the Rome Statute is any explicit indication of the standard of review to be applied in the course of judicial oversight of the Prosecutor's exercise of her discretion to initiate an investigation. That is, the Statute does not expressly direct the Pre-Trial Chamber only to ask, for example, whether the Prosecutor's assessment constitutes an abuse of discretion or reflects a manifest error of law or fact or is reasonable or instead to go further and engage in de novo or ex novo assessment or 'correctness' review by reference to the legal test applied by the Prosecutor him or herself, effectively substituting its forensic analysis and legal characterization of the facts for those of the Prosecutor. In the absence of any such explicit indication, the various Pre-Trial Chambers have themselves sought to articulate appropriate standards of judicial review under Articles 53(3)(*a*) and 15(4) respectively of the Prosecutor's admissibility assessment.

This chapter teases apart and scrutinizes what emerge as the distinct standards of review that the Pre-Trial Chambers purport to and actually apply when acting under Articles 53(3)(*a*) and 15(4) respectively. It also examines the decisions of the Appeals Chamber in this respect. To arrive at the most suitable standard of review under each provision, the chapter disaggregates the procedural contexts in which the Prosecutor's respective admissibility assessments are made and analyses in each context the underlying interests at stake. Various considerations are weighed to strike what the chapter suggests is a necessary balance between prosecutorial independence and prosecutorial accountability. On the one hand, the subjectivity of the criterion of 'sufficient gravity' in Article 17(1)(*d*) of the Rome Statute justifies the recognition of a broad discretion on the part of the Prosecutor.[5] The Prosecutor's exclusive fact-finding mandate vis-à-vis the Pre-Trial Chamber during the preliminary examination[6] of a situation and the limited resources at his or her disposal in the conduct of investigations similarly support judicial deference. The case for deference is assisted further by an examination of the justifications for deference to primary decision-makers at other international courts, including in international human rights law, international investment law, and international trade law. On the other hand, the desiderata of prosecutorial accountability, consistency, and predictability in the application of the criterion of 'sufficient gravity' favour closer scrutiny by the Pre-Trial Chambers, as does states'

[4] Recall Chapter 2, Section 2.4.2.
[5] Recall Chapter 2, Section 2.4.2.
[6] The term 'preliminary examination' appears in Article 15(6). It refers to the initial evaluation of a situation that serves as the basis for the Prosecutor's conclusion as to whether an investigation shall commence under Article 53(1) and Article 15(3).

interest in restraining the Prosecutor from proceeding with frivolous or politically motivated investigations. Whether the Prosecutor is bound to comply with the Pre-Trial Chamber's determinations under Articles 53(3)(a) and 15(4) respectively is also relevant to the analysis of their respective roles in the initiation of investigations and in the application of the gravity criterion in this context.[7]

Section 3.2 of the chapter examines the Pre-Trial Chambers' exercise of judicial review to date under Articles 53(3)(a) and 15(4) respectively of the Rome Statute. Section 3.3 highlights certain inconsistencies and problems with the exercise of review by the Pre-Trial Chambers and offers to resolve them by proposing the appropriate balance—in the form of a suitable standard or standards of review under Article 53(3)(a) and Article 15(4)—between prosecutorial discretion and judicial oversight in the assessment of admissibility, and in the application of the gravity criterion, in the context of the Prosecutor's decision whether to initiate an investigation.

3.2 Pre-Trial Chamber Review of the Prosecutor's Assessment of Admissibility

3.2.1 Pre-Trial Chamber Review under Article 53(3)(a)

3.2.1.1 Article 53(3)(a)

In the application of Article 53(1)(b) of the Rome Statute, the Prosecutor may, having evaluated the information available to him or her,[8] consider that the potential case or cases arising out of a situation are inadmissible and that there is as a result 'no reasonable basis to proceed under [the] Statute'. The provision is unclear on its face as to whether proceeding 'under [the] Statute' means proceeding with an investigation. This is particularly so when it is contrasted with Article 15(3), the provision addressing the Prosecutor's initiation of an investigation *proprio motu*, which requires explicitly that the Prosecutor establish a reasonable basis to proceed 'with an investigation'.[9] The title of Article 53 ('Initiation of an Investigation') and the substance of Article 53(1), which addresses the initiation or not of an investigation by the Prosecutor, nonetheless suggest that a reasonable basis to proceed

---

[7] A related question is whether it is permissible for the Chamber in its review under Article 53(3)(a) or Article 15(4) to go beyond the crimes identified by the Prosecutor and to order him or her to expand the scope of his or her investigation accordingly. The question is addressed in this chapter only to the extent that it assists in clarifying the respective roles of the Prosecutor and Pre-Trial Chamber in the initiation of investigations and in identifying the appropriate standards of judicial review of the Prosecutor's admissibility assessment.

[8] See also Rule 104(1), RPE, speaking of an 'analys[is] [of] the seriousness of the information received'.

[9] The Pre-Trial Chamber reviewing the Prosecutor's request under Article 15(4) is similarly required to determine whether there is a reasonable basis to proceed 'with an investigation'.

84   GRAVITY AT THE INTERNATIONAL CRIMINAL COURT

'under [the] Statute' in Article 53(1) refers to proceeding 'with an investigation'. Moreover, Rule 48 of the Rules of Procedure and Evidence, by requiring that the Prosecutor's assessments under Article 15(3) be made by reference to the criteria specified in Article 53(1)(*a*)–(*c*), confirms that the applicable standard is the same under Articles 53(1) and 15(3). In short, there is no material distinction between establishing a reasonable basis to proceed 'under [the] Statute', as per Article 53(1), and a reasonable basis to proceed 'with an investigation', as per Article 15(3).[10] This minor textual disparity may be attributed to an oversight during the fragmented drafting of the Rome Statute.[11]

Where the situation was referred to the Prosecutor by a state party or the Security Council, any decision by the Prosecutor, on the basis of inadmissibility or otherwise, not to proceed with an investigation into it is subject to judicial review pursuant to Article 53(3)(*a*), which provides:

> At the request of the State making a referral under article 14 or the Security Council under article 13, paragraph (b), the Pre-Trial Chamber may review a decision of the Prosecutor under paragraph 1 or 2 not to proceed and may request the Prosecutor to reconsider that decision.[12]

[10] In support, see H Olásolo, *The Triggering Procedure of the International Criminal Court* (Martinus Nijhoff 2005) 71–72; MJ Ventura, 'The "Reasonable Basis to Proceed" Threshold in the Kenya and Côte d'Ivoire *Proprio Motu* Investigation Decisions: The International Criminal Court's Lowest Evidentiary Standard?' (2013) 12 The Law and Practice of International Courts and Tribunals 49; I Stegmiller, 'Article 15' in M Klamberg (ed), *Commentary on the Law of the International Criminal Court* (Torkel Opsahl Academic EPublisher 2017) 188; K De Meester, 'Article 53' in M Klamberg (ed), *Commentary on the Law of the International Criminal Court* (Torkel Opsahl Academic EPublisher 2017) 388.

[11] Draft article 12 of the draft statute for an international criminal court prepared by the Preparatory Committee required the Prosecutor to establish a 'sufficient basis to proceed' with an investigation *proprio motu*. A note made alongside that text indicated an intention to harmonize its use of this term with the term 'reasonable basis' in draft article 54, which, like Article 53 of the Rome Statute, addressed the initiation of investigations generally. The distinction was rectified in the final draft. The remaining distinction discussed here is likely a result of the preparation of the text of the Rome Statute by different working groups of different committees set up by the UN Diplomatic Conference of Plenipotentiaries on the Establishment of an International Criminal Court ('Rome Conference'). UN General Assembly, 'United Nations Diplomatic Conference of Plenipotentiaries on the Establishment of an International Criminal Court, Report of the Preparatory Committee on the Establishment of an International Criminal Court, Addendum' (14 April 1998) UN Doc A/CONF.183/2/Add.1, 37, 75.

[12] Some commentators suggest that any decision by the Prosecutor not to proceed with an investigation on the ground of insufficient gravity is reviewable not only at the request of a referring state party or the Security Council under Article 53(3)(*a*) but also at the initiative of the Pre-Trial Chamber under Article 53(3)(*b*). G Turone, 'Powers and Duties of the Prosecutor' in A Cassese, P Gaeta, and JRWD Jones (eds), *The Rome Statute of the International Criminal Court II* (OUP 2002) 1154; MM deGuzman, 'Gravity and the Legitimacy of the International Criminal Court' (2008) 32(5) Fordham International Law Journal 1400, 1414. With respect, it is the Prosecutor's assessment of the interests of justice under Article 53(1)(*c*), which includes, inter alia, consideration of 'the gravity of the crime', that is reviewable by the Pre-Trial Chamber under Article 53(3)(*b*). The requirement of 'sufficient gravity' in relation to the situation is a discrete admissibility criterion under Article 53(1)(*b*) that cannot be equated with 'the gravity of the crime', an indicator of the interests of justice, under Article 53(3)(*b*). In accordance with the maxim *expressio unius exclusio alterius*, moreover, the express mention of Article 53(1)(*c*) in Article 53(3)(*b*)—to the exclusion of Article 53(1)(*b*)—excludes review of the Prosecutor's admissibility assessment under Article 53(1)(*b*) at the initiative of the Pre-Trial Chamber under Article 53(3)(*b*). Recall Chapter 1, Section 1.5.2.

Article 53(3)(*a*) does not specify the standard of judicial review that the Pre-Trial Chamber is expected to apply when reviewing the Prosecutor's decision under Article 53(1) that there is 'no reasonable basis' to proceed with an investigation into the situation and when determining whether to request that he or she reconsider that decision.[13]

3.2.1.2 Pre-Trial Chamber Review to Date under Article 53(3)(*a*)

3.2.1.2.1 Overview

To date, the Pre-Trial Chamber has had three occasions to review a prosecutorial decision not to proceed with an investigation into a situation, all in relation to the situation on the registered vessels of The Comoros, Greece, and Cambodia (the 'Mavi Marmara' incident) and all focusing on the gravity of the situation. In the first two of these decisions, only the first of which is directly relevant, Pre-Trial Chamber I in effect overruled the Prosecutor. Although this first decision formally enunciates a deferential standard of review to be applied by the Pre-Trial Chamber, in substance both reflect intense judicial scrutiny amounting in effect to de novo assessment of whether there existed a reasonable basis to proceed with an investigation into the situation. The third decision, according with the subsequent guidance of the Appeals Chamber as to the reviewability of the Prosecutor's assessment of gravity, acknowledged the limited power of the Pre-Trial Chamber to review questions of fact and the application of the law to the facts.

3.2.1.2.2 In detail

Following the referral by The Comoros in 2013 of the situation on the registered vessels of The Comoros, Greece, and Cambodia, the Prosecutor published a report under Article 53(1) declining to initiate an investigation into the situation, including on the ground that the gravity requirement in Article 17(1)(*d*) was not met.[14] In accordance with Article 53(3)(*a*), the referring state requested the Pre-Trial Chamber to review the Prosecutor's conclusion on several grounds, including that the Prosecutor had wrongly applied the gravity criterion in her assessment of admissibility under Article 53(1)(*b*).[15] In its decision of 2015, the Pre-Trial

---

[13] Rule 108(2) of the RPE requires that the Prosecutor on the request of the Pre-Trial Chamber under Article 53(3)(*a*) reconsider his or her decision 'as soon as possible'. Rule 108(3) requires further that he or she notify the Pre-Trial Chamber of his or her 'final decision' whether to proceed with the investigation.

[14] The Prosecutor also considered that the policy indication in relation to war crimes in Article 8(1) was not met. Article 8(1) confers jurisdiction over war crimes 'in particular when committed as part of a plan or policy or as part of a large-scale commission of such crimes'. Article 53(1) Report, Office of the Prosecutor, 6 November 2014, para 137.

[15] *Situation on the Registered Vessels of the Union of the Comoros, the Hellenic Republic and the Kingdom of Cambodia*, ICC-01/13-3-Red, Government of the Union of the Comoros, Application for Review Pursuant to Article 53(3)(a) of the Prosecutor's Decision of 6 November 2014 Not to Initiate an Investigation in the Situation, 29 January 2015.

86 GRAVITY AT THE INTERNATIONAL CRIMINAL COURT

Chamber ruled that the Prosecutor had erred in several ways in her assessment of gravity[16] and requested her to reconsider her decision 'as soon as possible'.[17]

In elaborating what it saw as the appropriate standard of review, the Pre-Trial Chamber sought to draw a distinction between its powers of review under Article 53(3)(a) and Article 15(4) respectively, characterizing the former as 'fundamentally different in that it is triggered only by the existence of a disagreement between the Prosecutor (who decides not to open an investigation) and the referring entity (which wishes that such an investigation be opened), and is limited by the parameters of this disagreement'.[18] On the basis of this distinction, the Pre-Trial Chamber suggested that Article 53(3)(a) did not require a de novo or correctness-based review of the Prosecutor's decision that there was no reasonable basis to proceed with an investigation. Instead, the Court was to determine only whether the Prosecutor's decision was 'materially affected by ... an error of procedure, an error of law, or an error of fact'.[19]

When addressing, however, whether the Prosecutor's application of the gravity threshold in Article 17(1)(d) was materially affected by any such error, the Pre-Trial Chamber (Judge Kovács dissenting) applied what in substance was a far more stringent standard of review. The majority asserted that Article 53(1)(b) imposed

[16] In addition to finding the Prosecutor's application of various indicators of gravity within the meaning of Article 17(1)(d) problematic (see later), the Pre-Trial Chamber considered that all facts other than those that were 'manifestly false' should have contributed to the Prosecutor's gravity assessment under Article 53(1)(b), including allegations marred by conflicting accounts. *Situation on the Registered Vessels of the Union of the Comoros, the Hellenic Republic and the Kingdom of Cambodia*, ICC-01/13-34, Pre-Trial Chamber I, Decision on the Request of the Union of the Comoros to Review the Prosecutor's Decision Not to Initiate an Investigation, 16 July 2015 (hereafter '*Situation on the Registered Vessels of the Union of the Comoros, the Hellenic Republic and the Kingdom of Cambodia*, Pre-Trial Chamber Decision 2015') para 35. In her 'Final Decision' in 2017, the Prosecutor countered that 'a "reasonable" conclusion is more than a possible, conceivable, or hypothetical inference'. *Situation on the Registered Vessels of the Union of the Comoros, the Hellenic Republic and the Kingdom of Cambodia*, ICC-01/13-57/Anx1, Office of the Prosecutor, Final Decision of the Prosecutor concerning the 'Article 53(1) Report' (ICC-01/13-6-AnxA), dated 6 November 2014, 29 November 2017 (hereafter '*Situation on the Registered Vessels of the Union of the Comoros, the Hellenic Republic and the Kingdom of Cambodia*, Final Decision of the Prosecutor 2017') para 22. The Chamber's approach is problematic as the admissibility threshold in Article 53(1)(b) would be rendered ineffective if satisfied by allegations without some affirmative basis in fact. See ME Cross, 'The Standard of Proof in Preliminary Examinations' in C Stahn and M Bergsmo (eds), *Quality Control in Preliminary Examinations: Volume 2* (Torkel Opsahl Academic EPublisher 2018) 238; KJ Heller, 'The Comoros Declination—and Remarkable Footnote 20', Opinio Juris, 4 December 2019, http://opiniojuris.org/2019/12/04/the-comoros-declination-and-remarkable-footnote-20/?utm_source=feedburner&utm_medium=email&utm_campaign=Feed%3A+opinioju risfeed+%28Opinio+Juris%29, accessed 14 March 2023. It also restricts the exercise of the Prosecutor's function of 'analysing and assessing the available evidence'. A Whiting, 'The ICC Prosecutor Should Reject Judges' Decision in Mavi Marmara Incident', Just Security, 20 July 2015, www.justsecurity.org/24778/icc-prosecutor-reject-judges-decision-mavi-marmara, accessed 14 March 2023.

[17] See Rule 108(2), RPE. *Situation on the Registered Vessels of the Union of the Comoros, the Hellenic Republic and the Kingdom of Cambodia*, Pre-Trial Chamber Decision 2015 (n 16) para 50.

[18] Nothing in the text of Article 53(3)(a) requires that the Pre-Trial Chamber limit its review to the grounds raised by the referring entity. *Situation on the Registered Vessels of the Union of the Comoros, the Hellenic Republic and the Kingdom of Cambodia*, Pre-Trial Chamber Decision 2015 (n 16) para 9.

[19] *Situation on the Registered Vessels of the Union of the Comoros, the Hellenic Republic and the Kingdom of Cambodia*, Pre-Trial Chamber Decision 2015 (n 16) para 12.

'exacting legal requirements' on the Prosecutor[20] and, contradicting in substance its prior statement that its task was not to review the Prosecutor's decision de novo, examined in detail the manner in which the Prosecutor applied the gravity threshold before arriving at its own findings. The Pre-Trial Chamber found that the Prosecutor had erred in her application of the various indicators of gravity within the meaning of Article 17(1)(d).[21] In dissent, Judge Kovács disagreed with the standard of review effectively applied by the majority. For him, a 'full-fledged review' of this kind was 'neither a duty nor automatic'.[22] Adopting a more deferential standard, he recognized that the Prosecutor enjoyed a degree of discretion in the application of Article 53(1). For him, the role of the Pre-Trial Chamber was only 'to ensure that the Prosecutor ha[d] not abused her discretion in arriving at her decision not to initiate an investigation'.[23]

Appealing the Pre-Trial Chamber's decision, the Prosecutor echoed Judge Kovács' 'abuse of discretion' standard, contending that the majority's approach threatened 'the careful balance ... between prosecutorial independence and accountability'.[24] While the Appeals Chamber declined in the event to comment on

---

[20] ibid para 14.

[21] Confirming The Comoros' view that the number of victims satisfied the requirement of scale, the Chamber concluded that the Prosecutor had committed a material error in her own evaluation that it did not. When addressing the nature of the crimes, even in the absence of information establishing a reasonable basis to believe that the war crimes of torture or inhuman treatment had been committed, the Chamber considered that the Prosecutor should have concluded that there was a reasonable basis to believe that these crimes had been committed, and on that basis that a finding of sufficient gravity was justified. This raises the question whether the Pre-Trial Chamber may, on the basis of additional crimes it has identified, deem admissible a situation that the Prosecutor has considered to be inadmissible. The approach is less problematic in the exercise of review under Article 15(4), in which context the Pre-Trial Chamber's inclusion of additional crimes would only reinforce the Prosecutor's affirmative finding as to the admissibility of the situation. Conversely, the identification of additional crimes by the Pre-Trial Chamber under Article 53(3)(a) interferes with the Prosecutor's preliminary examination of the situation. Finally, contradicting the Prosecutor's assessment of the impact of the alleged crimes, the Pre-Trial Chamber found the impact on the victims and their families to be a sufficient indicator of 'sufficient gravity', and that the Prosecutor had failed to account for the significant impact of the alleged crimes on the people of Gaza. See *Situation on the Registered Vessels of the Union of the Comoros, the Hellenic Republic and the Kingdom of Cambodia*, Pre-Trial Chamber Decision 2015 (n 16) paras 22–23, 26, 28–30, 47–48. See also M Longobardo, 'Everything Is Relative, Even Gravity' (2016) 14 Journal of International Criminal Justice 1011.

[22] He argued that the use of the term 'may' in Article 53(3)(a) indicated that the Pre-Trial Chamber was not obliged to review a prosecutorial decision merely because a referring entity had requested it. *Situation on the Registered Vessels of the Union of the Comoros, the Hellenic Republic and the Kingdom of Cambodia*, ICC-01/13-34-Anx-Corr, Pre-Trial Chamber I, Partly Dissenting Opinion of Judge Péter Kovács, 16 July 2015 (hereafter '*Situation on the Registered Vessels of the Union of the Comoros, the Hellenic Republic and the Kingdom of Cambodia* 2015') paras 2–3.

[23] ibid paras 7–8. In support, see KJ Heller, 'The Pre-Trial Chamber's Dangerous Comoros Review Decision', Opinio Juris, 17 July 2015, http://opiniojuris.org/2015/07/17/the-pre-trial-chambers-problematic-comoros-review-decision, accessed 14 March 2023; Whiting (n 16). Judge Kovács also considered that the majority had erred in 'enter[ing] new findings under jurisdiction ... instead of reviewing the existing ones'. *Situation on the Registered Vessels of the Union of the Comoros, the Hellenic Republic and the Kingdom of Cambodia*, Kovács Partial Dissent 2015 (n 22) para 11.

[24] *Situation on the Registered Vessels of the Union of the Comoros, the Hellenic Republic and the Kingdom of Cambodia*, ICC-01/13-35, Office of the Prosecutor, Notice of Appeal of 'Decision on the Request of the Union of the Comoros to Review the Prosecutor's Decision Not to Initiate an Investigation', 27 July 2015, para 17.

88   GRAVITY AT THE INTERNATIONAL CRIMINAL COURT

the standard of review applied by the Pre-Trial Chamber and dismissed the appeal *in limine*,[25] it nonetheless drew a distinction between Pre-Trial Chamber review under Article 53(3)(*a*) and (*b*),[26] noting that Article 53(3)(*a*) reflected 'a conscious decision on the part of the drafters to preserve a higher degree of prosecutorial discretion regarding decisions not to investigate' based on considerations of admissibility.[27]

Following the publication by the Prosecutor of a 'Final Decision' in which she refused, upon reconsideration, to initiate an investigation into the situation,[28] the Pre-Trial Chamber at the request of the referring entity issued in 2018 a second decision in which it found that the Prosecutor had been required to and had failed to 'comply with' its earlier decision of 2015.[29] Judge Kovács partially dissented, this time on the basis that the Prosecutor retained the discretion not to proceed with an investigation. In his view, reconsideration 'does not mean *per se* that the Prosecutor is obliged to reach a different conclusion than the one she initially reached'.[30]

[25] Observing that the Pre-Trial Chamber had requested the Prosecutor only to 'reconsider' her initial assessment under Article 53(3)(*a*) and could not, under that provision, compel her to investigate, the Appeals Chamber concluded that the Pre-Trial Chamber's decision was not one pertaining to admissibility for the purpose of Article 82(1)(*a*), the provision permitting appeal of admissibility decisions. *Situation on the Registered Vessels of the Union of the Comoros, the Hellenic Republic and the Kingdom of Cambodia*, ICC-01/13-51, Appeals Chamber, Decision on the Admissibility of the Prosecutor's Appeal Against the 'Decision on the Request of the Union of the Comoros to Review the Prosecutor's Decision Not to Initiate an Investigation', 6 November 2015 (hereafter '*Situation on the Registered Vessels of the Union of the Comoros, the Hellenic Republic and the Kingdom of Cambodia*, Appeals Chamber Decision 2015') para 60. For their part, dissenting Judges Fernández de Gurmendi and van den Wyngaert believed that the Prosecutor's appeal was justified by the fact that, when reconsidering her initial admissibility assessment, the Prosecutor would no doubt be guided by the Pre-Trial Chamber's decision. *Situation on the Registered Vessels of the Union of the Comoros, the Hellenic Republic and the Kingdom of Cambodia*, ICC-01/13-51-Anx, Appeals Chamber, Joint Dissenting Opinion of Judge Silvia Fernández de Gurmendi and Judge Christine van den Wyngaert, 6 November 2015 (hereafter '*Situation on the Registered Vessels of the Union of the Comoros, the Hellenic Republic and the Kingdom of Cambodia*, Fernández de Gurmendi and Wyngaert Dissent 2015') para 35.

[26] Pursuant to Article 53(3)(*b*), the Prosecutor's decision 'shall be effective only if confirmed by the Pre-Trial Chamber'. *Situation on the Registered Vessels of the Union of the Comoros, the Hellenic Republic and the Kingdom of Cambodia*, Appeals Chamber Decision 2015 (n 25) para 58.

[27] ibid para 59.

[28] See *Situation on the Registered Vessels of the Union of the Comoros, the Hellenic Republic and the Kingdom of Cambodia*, Final Decision of the Prosecutor 2017 (n 16).

[29] *Situation on the Registered Vessels of the Union of the Comoros, the Hellenic Republic and the Kingdom of Cambodia*, ICC-01/13-68, Pre-Trial Chamber I, Decision on the 'Application for Judicial Review by the Government of the Union of the Comoros', 15 November 2018, para 96. The concerns of the dissenting judges of the Appeals Chamber were validated in the proceedings that followed the Prosecutor's publication of her 'Final Decision'. Notwithstanding the Appeals Chamber's observation that the final decision lay with the Prosecutor, the Pre-Trial Chamber's de novo review of the Prosecutor's admissibility assessment in 2015, combined with its insistence in 2018 that the Prosecutor's reconsideration be based on that decision, restricted the Prosecutor's discretion to arrive at any conclusion that deviated from the Pre-Trial Chamber's own conclusion as to the requirement of 'sufficient gravity' in Article 17(1)(*d*). P Urs, 'Some Concerns with the Pre-Trial Chamber's Second Decision in Relation to the Mavi Marmara Incident', EJIL Talk!, 5 December 2018, www.ejiltalk.org/some-concerns-with-the-pre-trial-chambers-second-decision-in-relation-to-the-mavi-marmara-incident, accessed 14 March 2023.

[30] *Situation on the Registered Vessels of the Union of the Comoros, the Hellenic Republic and the Kingdom of Cambodia*, ICC-01/13-68-Anx, Pre-Trial Chamber I, Partly Dissenting Opinion of Judge Péter Kovács, 15 November 2018, para 16.

Appealing the Pre-Trial Chamber's second decision, the Prosecutor raised among others the question 'whether the Prosecutor, in carrying out a reconsideration ... [wa]s obliged to accept particular conclusions of law or fact contained in the Pre-Trial Chamber's request'.[31] Issuing its decision in 2019, the Appeals Chamber clarified that the Pre-Trial Chamber could not, in the exercise of its review under Article 53(3)(*a*), 'direct the Prosecutor as to the *result* of her reconsideration'.[32] Drawing a distinction between questions of law and questions of fact, the Appeals Chamber considered that while the Prosecutor had been obliged to follow the Pre-Trial Chamber's interpretation on questions of law, including the articulation by the Pre-Trial Chamber of the standard of review under Article 53(3)(*a*),[33] Pre-Trial Chamber scrutiny of questions of fact in respect of the Prosecutor's gravity assessment was more limited. The latter required a review only of whether the Prosecutor had accounted for 'certain available information' in her assessment of gravity.[34] This did not include 'direct[ing] the Prosecutor as to how to assess this information and which factual findings she should reach'.[35] Thus, while ultimately concluding that the Prosecutor had failed to reconsider her initial assessment on the basis of the Pre-Trial Chamber's 2015 decision, the Appeals Chamber considered that it had been 'inappropriate for the Pre-Trial Chamber to direct the Prosecutor as to ... what factual findings she should reach and to suggest the weight to be assigned to certain factors affecting the gravity assessment'.[36] Judges Eboe-Osuji and Ibáñez Carranza partially dissented, both disagreeing with the majority's restriction of Pre-Trial Chamber review of questions of fact.[37] When it came to gravity, Judge Ibáñez Carranza insisted on the Chamber's power 'to consider the

---

[31] *Situation on the Registered Vessels of the Union of the Comoros, the Hellenic Republic and the Kingdom of Cambodia*, ICC-01/13-69, Office of the Prosecutor, Request for Leave to Appeal the 'Decision on the "Application for Judicial Review by the Government of the Union of the Comoros"', 21 November 2018, para 13.

[32] *Situation on the Registered Vessels of the Union of the Comoros, the Hellenic Republic and the Kingdom of Cambodia*, ICC/01/13-98, Appeals Chamber, Judgment on the Appeal of the Prosecutor against Pre-Trial Chamber I's 'Decision on the "Application for Judicial Review by the Government of the Union of the Comoros"', 2 September 2019 (hereafter *Situation on the Registered Vessels of the Union of the Comoros, the Hellenic Republic and the Kingdom of Cambodia*, Appeals Chamber Decision 2019') para 76.

[33] ibid paras 78–79, 87–90.

[34] ibid para 80.

[35] ibid para 80. The Appeals Chamber referred, for example, to the Pre-Trial Chamber's disagreement with the Prosecutor as to the sufficiency of the scale and the impact of the alleged crimes. ibid para 93.

[36] ibid para 94.

[37] *Situation on the Registered Vessels of the Union of the Comoros, the Hellenic Republic and the Kingdom of Cambodia*, ICC-01/13-98-Anx, Appeals Chamber, Partly Dissenting Opinion of Judge Eboe-Osuji, 2 September 2019 (hereafter *Situation on the Registered Vessels of the Union of the Comoros, the Hellenic Republic and the Kingdom of Cambodia*, Eboe-Osuji Partial Dissent 2019') para 26; *Situation on the Registered Vessels of the Union of the Comoros, the Hellenic Republic and the Kingdom of Cambodia*, ICC-01/13-98-AnxI, Appeals Chamber, Separate and Partly Dissenting Opinion of Judge Luz del Carmen Ibáñez Carranza, 4 November 2019 (hereafter *Situation on the Registered Vessels of the Union of the Comoros, the Hellenic Republic and the Kingdom of Cambodia*, Ibáñez Carranza Partial Dissent 2019') paras 44, 62.

90 GRAVITY AT THE INTERNATIONAL CRIMINAL COURT

specific weight of factors such as the scale and impact of the crimes on victims in applying the law to the factual submissions of the parties'.[38]

Following the decision of the Appeals Chamber, the Prosecutor, on reconsideration, once again declined to initiate an investigation into the situation.[39] As before, that decision was reviewed by the Pre-Trial Chamber at the request of The Comoros, under Article 53(3)(a). When it came to the intensity of its review, the Pre-Trial Chamber asserted in its third decision, of 2020, that it 'must go beyond a mere "box-ticking" or "rubber-stamping" exercise and must be thorough, as opposed to cursory'.[40] With this in mind, the Chamber found that the Prosecutor had again committed several errors when reconsidering her decision, including in the application and weighing of all but one of the indicators of gravity.[41] Ultimately, however, the Pre-Trial Chamber did not request the Prosecutor to reconsider her decision, explaining that, the decisions of the Appeals Chamber notwithstanding, it remained unclear 'whether and to what extent it may request the Prosecutor to correct errors relat[ing] to ... the application of the law to the facts'[42] and 'relat[ing] to her assessment of the factors relevant to the gravity requirement'.[43]

3.2.1.2.3 Recapitulation

If only formally, the Pre-Trial Chamber's 2015 decision in relation to the Mavi Marmara incident recognized that the applicable standard of review under Article 53(3)(a) must be one that allows a degree of deference to the Prosecutor. The

---

[38] *Situation on the Registered Vessels of the Union of the Comoros, the Hellenic Republic and the Kingdom of Cambodia*, Ibáñez Carranza Partial Dissent 2019 (n 37) para 85.

[39] See *Situation on the Registered Vessels of the Union of the Comoros, the Hellenic Republic and the Kingdom of Cambodia*, ICC-01/13-99-Anx1, Office of the Prosecutor, Final Decision of the Prosecutor Concerning the 'Article 53(1) Report' (ICC-01/13-6-AnxA), Dated 6 November 2014, as Revised and Refiled in Accordance with the Pre-Trial Chamber's Request of 15 November 2018 and the Appeals Chamber's Judgment of 2 September 2019, 2 December 2019. Pointing to the limited scale of the crimes, and noting the absence of countervailing qualitative indicators of gravity that might militate in favour of the initiation of an investigation, the Prosecutor reiterated her earlier conclusion that 'no potential case in th[e] situation is sufficiently grave as to be admissible before the Court'. ibid para 91.

[40] See *Situation on the Registered Vessels of the Union of the Comoros, the Hellenic Republic and the Kingdom of Cambodia*, ICC-01/13-111, Pre-Trial Chamber I, Decision on the 'Application for Judicial Review by the Government of the Comoros', 16 September 2020 (hereafter '*Situation on the Registered Vessels of the Union of the Comoros, the Hellenic Republic and the Kingdom of Cambodia*, Pre-Trial Chamber Decision 2020') para 25.

[41] The Pre-Trial Chamber found that the Prosecutor had erred in her assessment of the nature of the alleged crimes, the manner of their commission, their impact, and the assessment of whether the potential case or cases implicated those bearing the greatest responsibility for the crimes. See *Situation on the Registered Vessels of the Union of the Comoros, the Hellenic Republic and the Kingdom of Cambodia*, Pre-Trial Chamber Decision 2020 (n 40) paras 34–45, 56–71, 76–83, 88–93. The Pre-Trial Chamber also considered that the Prosecutor's application of the gravity criterion had been 'in a manner ... inconsistent with its object and purpose'. ibid para 95. In the Chamber's view, gravity was not 'a criterion for the selection of the most serious situations and cases, as argued by the Prosecutor, but a requirement for the exclusion of (potential) cases of marginal gravity'. ibid para 96.

[42] *Situation on the Registered Vessels of the Union of the Comoros, the Hellenic Republic and the Kingdom of Cambodia*, Pre-Trial Chamber Decision 2020 (n 40) para 107.

[43] ibid para 110.

standard articulated by the majority of the Pre-Trial Chamber was one of material error, while Judge Kovács in his dissent preferred an even more deferential 'abuse of discretion' formulation. Both positions excluded de novo review by the Pre-Trial Chamber under Article 53(3)(*a*). The Appeals Chamber in its dictum of 2015 also effectively excluded the de novo application of Article 53(1)(*b*) by the Pre-Trial Chamber, recognizing the Prosecutor's particular discretion under that provision in relation to admissibility and affirming that the decision whether to investigate ultimately lay with her. In practice, however, the Pre-Trial Chamber's effective de novo review of the Prosecutor's decision in 2015 contradicted its professed deference to prosecutorial discretion and flew in the face of the Appeals Chamber's statement. The Appeals Chamber's decision of 2019, while not explicitly addressing the standard of review under Article 53(3)(*a*), clarified that Pre-Trial Chamber review under that provision did not include de novo review of the Prosecutor's application of the gravity criterion to the facts.

3.2.2 Pre-Trial Chamber Review under Article 15(4)

3.2.2.1 Article 15(4)

The initiation of an investigation into a situation by the Prosecutor *proprio motu* must be authorized by a Pre-Trial Chamber acting in accordance with Article 15(4) of the Rome Statute, which states:

> If the Pre-Trial Chamber, upon examination of the request and the supporting material, considers that there is a reasonable basis to proceed with an investigation, and that the case appears to fall within the jurisdiction of the Court, it shall authorize the commencement of the investigation, without prejudice to subsequent determinations by the Court with regard to the jurisdiction and admissibility of a case.[44]

Before making a request for authorization to initiate an investigation *proprio motu*, which Article 15(3) obliges her to do, the Prosecutor must herself have concluded—as indicated in Article 15(3), echoing Article 53(1), by reference to which the Prosecutor's decision whether or not to initiate an investigation *proprio motu* is actually taken[45]—that there exists a 'reasonable basis to proceed with

---

[44] The use of the term 'case' in this provision is an anomaly. The Pre-Trial Chambers have since 2010 applied the provision in relation to 'potential cases' arising out of the situation under consideration. Recall Chapter 2, Section 2.3.1.1.

[45] A prosecutorial decision to initiate an investigation *proprio motu* is taken under Article 53(1), the provision governing the initiation of investigations generally, while under Article 15(3) the existence of a 'reasonable basis to proceed' serves as a condition precedent to the Prosecutor's request for Pre-Trial Chamber authorization ('If the Prosecutor concludes that there is a reasonable basis to proceed ...'). In support, see Turone (n 12) 1147.

92   GRAVITY AT THE INTERNATIONAL CRIMINAL COURT

an investigation.[46] Just like Article 53(1), Article 15(1) and (2) specify that the Prosecutor have arrived at his or her conclusion on the basis of and having analysed the seriousness of information he or she has received pertaining to crimes within the jurisdiction of the Court.[47] Rule 48 of the Rules of Procedure and Evidence specifies further that the Prosecutor must, when assessing the existence or not of a reasonable basis to proceed with an investigation *proprio motu*, apply the criteria laid down in Article 53(1)(*a*)–(*c*), including the criterion of admissibility, and consequently of gravity, stipulated in Article 53(1)(*b*).[48]

Having examined the Prosecutor's request and supporting material, the Pre-Trial Chamber must then determine whether there is indeed a 'reasonable basis to proceed with an investigation'. Since both the Prosecutor as indicated in Article 15(3) and the Pre-Trial Chamber under Article 15(4) must conduct their assessments by reference to the same 'reasonable basis to proceed' standard, the Pre-Trial Chamber's assessment must by implication be by reference to the same criteria as those applied by the Prosecutor, namely those specified in Article 53(1)(*a*)–(*c*), including the criterion of admissibility, and thereby of gravity, in Article 53(1) (*b*).[49] The view is not shared by the Appeals Chamber, however, which, in its review in 2020 of the Pre-Trial Chamber's decision not to initiate an investigation into the situation in Afghanistan, sought to clarify what is required of the Pre-Trial Chamber under Article 15(4). While accepting that the Prosecutor is obliged to apply the criteria laid down in Article 53(1)(*a*)–(*c*) in her assessment under Article 15(3), and notwithstanding that both Article 15(3) and Article 15(4) require an assessment as to the existence or not of a 'reasonable basis to proceed' with an investigation, the Appeals Chamber held that a Pre-Trial Chamber acting under Article 15(4) is not required to consider the criteria enumerated in Article 53(1) (*a*)–(*c*).[50] Instead, the Pre-Trial Chamber must apply the 'separate factors' specified in Article 15(4),[51] which, in the view of the Appeals Chamber, requires the

---

[46] For the content of the Prosecutor's request, see Reg 49, Regulations of the Court 2004.

[47] The reference to 'seriousness' is not to the gravity criterion in Article 17(1)(*d*) of the Statute.

[48] See also *Situation in Afghanistan*, ICC-02/17-138, Appeals Chamber, Judgment on the Appeal against the Decision on the Authorisation of an Investigation into the Situation in the Islamic Republic of Afghanistan, 5 March 2020 (hereafter '*Situation in Afghanistan*, Appeals Chamber Decision 2020') para 35; Reg 29, Regulations of the Office of the Prosecutor 2009.

[49] *Situation in Kenya*, ICC-01/09-19, Pre-Trial Chamber II, Decision Pursuant to Article 15 of the Rome Statute on the Authorization on an Investigation into the Situation in the Republic of Kenya, 31 March 2010 (hereafter '*Situation in Kenya*, Pre-Trial Chamber Authorization Decision 2010') para 24; M Bergsmo, J Pejic, and D Zhu, 'Article 15' in O Triffterer and K Ambos (eds), *The Rome Statute of the International Criminal Court: A Commentary* (3rd edn, CH Beck 2016) 733, 735–36; KJ Heller, 'The Appeals Chamber Got One Aspect of the Afghanistan Decision Very Wrong', Opinio Juris, 9 March 2020, http://opiniojuris.org/2020/03/09/the-appeals-chamber-got-one-aspect-of-the-afghanistan-decision-very-wrong, accessed 14 March 2023; D Akande and T de Souza Dias, 'The ICC Pre-Trial Chamber Decision on the Situation in Afghanistan: A Few Thoughts on the Interests of Justice', EJIL Talk!, 18 April 2019, www.ejiltalk.org/the-icc-pre-trial-chamber-decision-on-the-situation-in-afghanistan-a-few-thoughts-on-the-interests-of-justice, accessed 14 March 2023.

[50] *Situation in Afghanistan*, Appeals Chamber Decision 2020 (n 48) para 35.

[51] ibid para 45.

Pre-Trial Chamber to consider only 'whether there is a reasonable factual basis to proceed with an investigation, in the sense of whether crimes have been committed, and whether potential case(s) arising from such investigation appear to fall within the Court's jurisdiction'.[52] Conversely, there is no requirement, in the view of the Appeals Chamber, that the Pre-Trial Chamber assess the admissibility, including the gravity, of a potential case or cases or the interests of justice.[53]

Although binding as a matter of law, the Appeals Chamber's exclusive focus on jurisdictional requirements is simply not supported by the text of Article 15(4), which requires the cumulative, if partially superfluous, consideration both of whether 'the case appears to fall within the jurisdiction of the Court' and whether there exists a 'reasonable basis to proceed' with an investigation, the latter including, by reference to Article 53(1)(a), the satisfaction of jurisdictional requirements.[54] Nor is there any reason to oblige the Prosecutor to apply the criteria under Article 53(1)(a)–(c) in choosing whether to initiate an investigation *proprio motu* but not the Pre-Trial Chamber in deciding whether to authorize the initiation of the investigation. On the contrary, limiting the role of the Pre-Trial Chamber under Article 15(4) to the authorization of an investigation based on the satisfaction only of relatively straightforward jurisdictional requirements makes light of the critical condition on which negotiating states agreed to confer on the Prosecutor the power to initiate investigations *proprio motu*. The inclusion of Pre-Trial Chamber authorization under Article 15(4) was decisive for states reluctant to confer upon the Prosecutor *proprio motu* power for the initiation of investigations.[55] By limiting the task of the Pre-Trial Chamber to the satisfaction of jurisdictional requirements only, Pre-Trial Chamber authorization under Article 15(4) becomes 'little more than a box-ticking exercise'.[56] The following discussion proceeds on the basis that the Pre-Trial Chamber acting under Article 15(4) must consider the same criteria as those applied by the Prosecutor under Article 15(3), namely the criteria specified in Article 53(1)(a)–(c), including the criterion of sufficient gravity.

In contrast to Article 53(3)(a), which permits the Pre-Trial Chamber to 'review [the] decision of the Prosecutor', Article 15(4) does not mention the Prosecutor's

---

[52] ibid para 34.

[53] When it comes to gravity, this implies that the Pre-Trial Chamber 'can no longer refuse to authorize an investigation because ... the [Prosecutor] is overestimating the gravity of the criminal conduct in question'. Heller, '*The Appeals Chamber Got One Aspect of the Afghanistan Decision Very Wrong*' (n 49).

[54] The former assessment is thus subsumed within the latter. Bergsmo, Pejic, and Zhu (n 49) 735–36. The redundancy of the requirement that 'the case appears to fall within the jurisdiction of the Court' can be explained by the fact that Articles 15 and 53 were drafted by different working groups of different committees at the Rome Conference. See *Situation in Kenya*, Pre-Trial Chamber Authorization Decision 2010 (n 49) para 67.

[55] Article 15(4) was included to allay the fears of states reluctant to confer on the Prosecutor the power to initiate an investigation in the absence of a referral by a state party or the Security Council. Recall Chapter 1, note 41. See also Heller, '*The Appeals Chamber Got One Aspect of the Afghanistan Decision Very Wrong*' (n 49).

[56] Heller, '*The Appeals Chamber Got One Aspect of the Afghanistan Decision Very Wrong*' (n 49).

94 GRAVITY AT THE INTERNATIONAL CRIMINAL COURT

decision, let alone specify that the Pre-Trial Chamber's task under the provision is to 'review' this decision. It states simply, in relevant part, that '[i]f the Pre-Trial Chamber considers ... that there is a reasonable basis to proceed with an investigation ... it shall authorise the commencement of an investigation'. This textual distinction could be taken to suggest that the Pre-Trial Chamber's task under Article 15(4) is not to review the Prosecutor's conclusion that there exists a reasonable basis to proceed with an investigation *proprio motu* but to conduct an independent assessment, without regard to the Prosecutor's, as to the existence of such a basis. This is the preferred approach of the Appeals Chamber.[57] On balance, however, the text and context of Article 15(4) indicate sufficiently persuasively that the Pre-Trial Chamber's task under Article 15(4) is, like its task under Article 53(3)(*a*), to review the Prosecutor's conclusion that there exists a reasonable basis to proceed with an investigation *proprio motu*. Article 15(4) requires that the Pre-Trial Chamber have examined the Prosecutor's request and its supporting material, which are tailored to disclose the situation's satisfaction, in the Prosecutor's opinion, of the 'reasonable basis to proceed' threshold; and, in accordance with the maxim of construction *expressio unius exclusio alterius*, the implication is that the Prosecutor's request and its supporting material are the only materials that the Pre-Trial Chamber is required to examine when determining under Article 15(4) whether there exists a reasonable basis to proceed with an investigation.[58] As the Appeals Chamber has acknowledged, a Pre-Trial Chamber engaging in an assessment of admissibility under Article 15(4) 'would have to rely on the Prosecutor, who considers that the case(s) would be admissible, to provide information that would allow it to form a view on issues of admissibility'.[59] Restriction of the material basis of the Pre-Trial

---

[57] *Situation in Afghanistan*, Appeals Chamber Decision 2020 (n 48) para 45.

[58] In accordance with Article 15(3) of the Statute and Rule 50(3) of the RPE, victims who have been informed by the Prosecutor of the request for authorization to initiate an investigation into the situation may make written representations to the Pre-Trial Chamber. There is no corresponding obligation on the Chamber to examine these representations, if any, in its decision under Article 15(4), although the Chamber is permitted, under Rule 50(4), to request additional information from the Prosecutor and any victims making representations. The inclusion of victims' participation in Article 15(3) compared with its exclusion from the text of Article 15(4) suggests a limited role for victims in support of the Prosecutor's request for authorization. This limited right of participation does not indicate that the task of the Pre-Trial Chamber under Article 15(4) is an assessment rather than a review. That victims' participation does not substantially affect the nature of the proceedings under Article 15(4) is evident from the decisions of the Pre-Trial Chambers, which have, more often than not, been taken 'on the exclusive basis of the information made available by the Prosecutor'. *Situation in Afghanistan*, ICC-02/17-33, Pre-Trial Chamber II, Decision Pursuant to Article 15 of the Rome Statute on the Authorisation of an Investigation into the Situation in the Islamic Republic of Afghanistan, 12 April 2019 (hereafter 'Situation in Afghanistan, Pre-Trial Chamber Authorization Decision 2019') para 30. See also *Situation in Bangladesh/Myanmar*, ICC-01/19-27, Pre-Trial Chamber III, Decision Pursuant to Article 15 of the Rome Statute on the Authorisation of an Investigation into the Situation in the People's Republic of Bangladesh/Republic of the Union of Myanmar, 14 November 2019 (hereafter 'Situation in Bangladesh/ Myanmar, Pre-Trial Chamber Authorization Decision 2019') para 19; *Situation in Afghanistan*, ICC-02/17-62, Pre-Trial Chamber II, Decision on the Prosecutor and Victims' Requests for Leave to Appeal the 'Decision Pursuant to Article 15 of the Rome Statute on the Authorisation of an Investigation into the Situation in the Islamic Republic of Afghanistan', 17 September 2019, paras 19–20.

[59] *Situation in Afghanistan*, Appeals Chamber Decision 2020 (n 48) para 40.

REVIEW OF THE ADMISSIBILITY OF 'SITUATIONS' 95

Chamber's determination under Article 15(4) to the Prosecutor's request and its supporting material suggests that what the Chamber is directed to do under Article 15(4) is to review the Prosecutor's conclusion, reached on the basis of the criteria in Article 53(1)(*a*)–(*c*), that there exists a reasonable basis to proceed with an investigation *proprio motu*. Such a characterization is lent further support by Rule 50(5) of the Rules of Procedure and Evidence, which requires that the Pre-Trial Chamber issue its decision 'with respect to all or any part of the request by the Prosecutor'.[60]

3.2.2.2 Pre-Trial Chamber Review to Date under Article 15(4)

3.2.2.2.1 Overview

With the exception of the Prosecutor's request in relation to the situation in Afghanistan, to date all of the Prosecutor's requests for authorization to initiate an investigation into a situation *proprio motu* have been granted by the Pre-Trial Chambers under Article 15(4). Relying on the text of the provision, all of the Pre-Trial Chambers except for the Chambers that authorized the initiation of investigations in Georgia, Bangladesh/Myanmar, and the Philippines have assessed de novo the existence or not of a reasonable basis to proceed with an investigation,[61] even if some individual judges have questioned this standard of review. When specifically addressing, however, the criterion of sufficient gravity, the Pre-Trial Chambers have not engaged in any serious de novo consideration, instead merely endorsing the Prosecutor's gravity analysis.[62]

---

[60] The related question whether the Pre-Trial Chamber is limited to the crimes identified by the Prosecutor in his or her request and supporting material or whether it is permitted to identify and direct the Prosecutor to investigate additional crimes depends on the characterization of the Pre-Trial Chamber's role under Article 15(4). The latter approach would be consistent with the articulation of the Pre-Trial Chamber's role under Article 15(4) as an independent assessment of the existence or not of a reasonable basis to proceed with an investigation *proprio motu*, but is less convincing if Article 15(4) is envisaged, as proposed here, as requiring a review of the Prosecutor's assessment, including his or her identification of alleged crimes.

[61] The Pre-Trial Chambers have done so in particular in assessments of whether there exists a 'reasonable basis to believe' that crimes within the jurisdiction *ratione materiae* of the Court have been committed under Article 53(1)(*a*). In this context, one commentator has instead characterized any extension by the Pre-Trial Chamber of the scope of the situation to include crimes additional to those articulated in the Prosecutor's request as an exercise of deference to the Prosecutor. L Poltronieri Rossetti, 'The Pre-Trial Chamber's Afghanistan Decision: A Step Too Far in the Judicial Review of Prosecutorial Discretion?' (2019) 17 Journal of International Criminal Justice 585, 588–89. While it is true that such an approach expands the scope of the Prosecutor's investigation, it is only through a de novo assessment that goes beyond the scope of the Prosecutor's more limited request that the Pre-Trial Chamber may do so.

[62] In requests for the authorization of investigations *proprio motu*, the Prosecutor has offered detailed gravity assessments, first in relation to the situation as a whole, as in Kenya, and then, on the instruction of the Pre-Trial Chamber that authorized the initiation of that investigation, in relation to potential cases within each situation. On the Pre-Trial Chambers' deferential approach to admissibility, see T Mariniello, 'Judicial Control over Prosecutorial Discretion at the International Criminal Court' (2019) 19 International Criminal Law Review 979, 984–85.

3.2.2.2.2 In detail

According to the Pre-Trial Chamber that authorized the initiation of the investigation into the situation in Kenya in 2010, the Prosecutor's first *proprio motu* investigation, Article 15(4) confers on the Pre-Trial Chamber 'a supervisory role over the *proprio motu* initiative of the Prosecutor'[63] that is intended to 'prevent the Court from proceeding with unwarranted, frivolous, or politically motivated investigations that could have a negative effect on its credibility'.[64] In the Chamber's view, the fulfilment of this objective requires a de novo assessment by reference to 'the exact standard on the basis of which the Prosecutor arrived at his conclusion' under Article 53(1), namely whether there is a 'reasonable basis to proceed' with an investigation.[65] Judge Kaul, while dissenting from the majority's authorization of the investigation, agreed with its de novo assessment, asserting that the Pre-Trial Chamber's determination under Article 15(4) 'is not of a mere administrative or procedural nature but requires a substantial and genuine examination'.[66] His disagreement with the majority's decision was in part due to what he saw in practice as its 'somewhat generous or only summary evaluation whereby any information, of even fragmentary nature, may satisfy the standard' of reasonableness in Article 15(4).[67]

In its subsequent first decision authorizing an investigation into post-election violence in Côte d'Ivoire since 2010, Pre-Trial Chamber III likewise assessed de novo the existence or not of a reasonable basis to proceed with an investigation into the situation, reiterating that the objective of Article 15(4) was to prevent 'unwarranted, frivolous or politically motivated investigations'.[68] It undertook an expansive examination of the Prosecutor's request, the material supporting it, and, for

---

[63] *Situation in Kenya*, Pre-Trial Chamber Authorization Decision 2010 (n 49) para 24.

[64] ibid para 32.

[65] ibid para 24. Confusingly, the Pre-Trial Chamber referred variously to its task under Article 15(4) as both 'assessment' and 'review'.

[66] *Situation in Kenya*, ICC-01/09-19, Pre-Trial Chamber II, Dissenting Opinion of Judge Hans-Peter Kaul, 31 October 2010, para 19.

[67] ibid para 15. Judge Kaul's dissent raises an issue that has also arisen in subsequent Pre-Trial Chamber decisions under Article 15(4) as well as in the Mavi Marmara proceedings under Article 53(3) (*a*); that is, if it is permissible for a Pre-Trial Chamber to justify the initiation of an investigation with a view to the clarification of relevant facts. Initiating an investigation on this basis would allow the Prosecutor greater investigative powers with which to establish relevant facts, but such an approach would in practice almost always favour the initiation of an investigation, calling into question the need for the Prosecutor's initial assessment of whether there exists a reasonable basis to proceed with an investigation. When invoked in the exercise of Pre-Trial Chamber review under Article 53(3)(*a*), such an approach would excessively limit the Prosecutor's discretion to decline to initiate an investigation under Article 53(1)(*b*), leaving little regard for the practical considerations that underlie the selectivity of the Prosecutor's investigations. Conversely, when applied by the Pre-Trial Chamber under Article 15(4), it would ease the Prosecutor's burden to an extent that would almost always favour the initiation of an investigation, frustrating the filtering mechanism in Article 15(4).

[68] *Situation in Côte d'Ivoire*, ICC-02/11-14, Pre-Trial Chamber III, Decision Pursuant to Article 15 of the Rome Statute on the Authorization of an Investigation into the Situation in the Republic of Côte d'Ivoire, 3 October 2011 (hereafter '*Situation in Côte d'Ivoire*, Pre-Trial Chamber Authorization Decision 2011') para 21.

REVIEW OF THE ADMISSIBILITY OF 'SITUATIONS'   97

good measure, victims' representations which went beyond the confines of the request to examine additional crimes and to conclude that there existed a reasonable basis to believe that these additional crimes had been committed.[69] Based on the Prosecutor's observation that Côte d'Ivoire had 'repeatedly experienced violence' even before 2010,[70] the Pre-Trial Chamber also ordered the Prosecutor to 'revert to the Chamber within one month with any additional information that [wa]s available to him on potentially relevant crimes committed between 2002 and 2010', authorizing in a second decision the expansion of the investigation to include additional crimes committed during this period.[71] Judge Fernández de Gurmendi dissented from the Pre-Trial Chamber's first decision in relation to the situation on the ground that the majority's application of Article 15(4) amounted to an unwarranted duplication of the Prosecutor's preliminary examination.[72] '[G]uided by the underlying purpose of providing a judicial safeguard against frivolous or politically-motivated charges', she warned that the Pre-Trial Chamber must limit itself to the supervisory role it purported to exercise.[73] Considering that Article 15(4) required the Pre-Trial Chamber to review the Prosecutor's decision and not to conduct an independent examination, she disagreed with the majority's de novo assessment, preferring an 'abuse of discretion' standard of review.[74]

Conversely, in the subsequent Pre-Trial Chamber decision authorizing an investigation into the situation in Georgia, it was the Chamber that adopted a 'strictly

[69] Contrary to the Prosecutor's assessment, the Pre-Trial Chamber found a reasonable basis to believe that additional crimes against humanity allegedly perpetrated by pro-Gbagbo forces and crimes against humanity allegedly perpetrated also by pro-Ouattara forces had been committed since the 2010 presidential election. See *Situation in Côte d'Ivoire*, Pre-Trial Chamber Authorization Decision 2011 (n 68) paras 83–86, 93–95.

[70] *Situation in Côte d'Ivoire*, ICC-02/11-3, Office of the Prosecutor, Request for Authorisation of Investigation Pursuant to Article 15, 23 June 2011, para 42.

[71] The Pre-Trial Chamber relied on Rule 50(4) of the RPE to do so. *Situation in Côte d'Ivoire*, Pre-Trial Chamber Authorization Decision 2011 (n 68) paras 183–85. The additional information submitted by the Prosecutor excluded any characterization of conduct as crimes within the jurisdiction of the Court. While not binding the Prosecutor to its characterization of conduct, it was the Pre-Trial Chamber that established, on the basis of the information supplied, a reasonable basis to believe that war crimes and crimes against humanity had been committed between 2002 and 2010. Notably, neither the Prosecutor in his submission of additional information nor the Pre-Trial Chamber in its second decision conducted a gravity assessment to support the broader scope of the investigation. *Situation in Côte d'Ivoire*, ICC-02/11-36, Pre-Trial Chamber III, Decision on the 'Prosecution's Provision of Further Information Regarding Potentially Relevant Crimes Committed Between 2002 and 2010', 22 February 2012, para 38.

[72] Judge Fernández de Gurmendi objected, for instance, to the majority's conclusion that there was a reasonable basis to believe that crimes against humanity had been committed by pro-Ouattara forces despite the fact that the Prosecutor had submitted that the information available to that point was insufficient to support such a conclusion. *Situation in Côte d'Ivoire*, ICC-02/11-15, Pre-Trial Chamber III, Separate and Partially Dissenting Opinion of Judge Silvia Fernández de Gurmendi, 3 October 2011 (hereafter '*Situation in Côte d'Ivoire*, Fernández de Gurmendi Partial Dissent 2011') paras 15, 41.

[73] *Situation in Côte d'Ivoire*, Fernández de Gurmendi Partial Dissent 2011 (n 72) para 16.

[74] ibid paras 12, 15–16. On this basis, she sought to clarify that the 'early and necessarily non-comprehensive identification of incidents serve[d] only as the basis for determining whether the requirements of Article 53 of the Statute [were] met'. ibid para 34. In her view, the determination in Article 15(4) related only to the Prosecutor's intention to investigate and not to the conduct of the preliminary examination, which was the exclusive competence of the Prosecutor. ibid paras 19–22, 35–38, 44–45.

98   GRAVITY AT THE INTERNATIONAL CRIMINAL COURT

limited' approach to Article 15(4), while a lone judge favoured more probing scrutiny. Pre-Trial Chamber I considered that Article 15(4) 'serves no other purpose than to prevent the abuse of power on the part of the Prosecutor'.[75] It consequently limited its assessment to the crimes specified in the Prosecutor's request, taking note of the Prosecutor's prerogative to investigate additional crimes and observing that 'it [was] unnecessary and inappropriate for the Chamber to go beyond the submissions in the request in an attempt to correct any possible error on the part of the Prosecutor'.[76] In his separate opinion, Judge Kovács found himself alone in the view that the Pre-Trial Chamber's mandate in Article 15(4) to 'consider', combined with its prerogative of requesting additional information,[77] demanded a more far-reaching examination.[78] Arguing that the Pre-Trial Chamber had a duty 'to reach its own conclusions on whether an investigation [was] warranted or not, and not merely examine the Prosecutor's conclusions',[79] he went beyond the crimes identified in the Prosecutor's request to find a reasonable basis to proceed with an investigation in relation to additional crimes.[80]

The Pre-Trial Chamber that subsequently authorized the initiation of an investigation in Burundi agreed that the objective of Article 15(4) was to prevent abuse of the Prosecutor's discretion in the initiation of investigations, but considered, as Judge Kovács did, that this required de novo assessment by the Pre-Trial Chamber.[81] As opposed to the Pre-Trial Chamber that authorized the investigation in Georgia, and resembling more closely the approach taken in relation to the situation in Côte d'Ivoire,[82] Pre-Trial Chamber III identified crimes additional to

---

[75] *Situation in Georgia*, ICC-01/15-12, Pre-Trial Chamber I, Decision on the Prosecutor's Request for Authorization of an Investigation, 27 January 2016 (hereafter '*Situation in Georgia*, Pre-Trial Chamber Authorization Decision 2016') para 3.

[76] This was notwithstanding the Chamber's observation that 'the Prosecutor ha[d] ... acted too restrictively and ha[d] imposed restrictions on the material that [could not] reasonably be met in the absence of an investigation'. *Situation in Georgia*, Pre-Trial Chamber Authorization Decision 2016 (n 75) para 35.

[77] Rule 50(4), RPE.

[78] *Situation in Georgia*, ICC-01/15-12-Anx1, Pre-Trial Chamber I, Separate Opinion of Judge Péter Kovács, 27 January 2016 (hereafter '*Situation in Georgia*, Kovács Separate Opinion 2016') para 5.

[79] ibid para 20.

[80] Judge Kovács found a reasonable basis to believe that the war crimes of indiscriminate or disproportionate attacks, rape, unlawful confinement, and hostage-taking and the crimes against humanity of imprisonment or other deprivation of liberty, rape, torture, and inhumane treatment had been committed. While ultimately arriving at the same conclusion as that of the majority, he considered that the majority's decision was insufficiently persuasive, preferring to have authorized the investigation on the broader basis he identified. Unlike the Pre-Trial Chamber that authorized the investigation in Côte d'Ivoire, however, Judge Kovács did not specify that the Prosecutor was obliged to investigate the additional crimes he had identified. *Situation in Georgia*, Kovács Separate Opinion 2016 (n 78) paras 17, 26–30, 34–36.

[81] *Situation in Burundi*, ICC-01/17-9-Red, Pre-Trial Chamber III, Public Redacted Version of 'Decision Pursuant to Article 15 of the Rome Statute on the Authorization of an Investigation into the Situation in the Republic of Burundi', 9 November 2017 (hereafter '*Situation in Burundi*, Pre-Trial Chamber Authorization Decision 2017') para 28.

[82] The decisions pertaining to Côte d'Ivoire and Burundi were both delivered by Pre-Trial Chamber III but different compositions of judges were responsible for each.

REVIEW OF THE ADMISSIBILITY OF 'SITUATIONS' 99

those enumerated in the Prosecutor's request in relation to Burundi.[83] It concluded that the Prosecutor had acted 'too restrictively' in limiting herself to crimes against humanity and obliged her also to 'enquire during her investigation whether a non-international armed conflict existed in Burundi during the relevant period and whether war crimes [had been] committed'.[84]

When in 2019 Pre-Trial Chamber II issued its unanimous decision refusing authorization for the Prosecutor's initiation of an investigation in Afghanistan, the Chamber undertook the first judicial assessment de novo of 'the interests of justice' within the meaning of Article 53(1)(c).[85] In doing so, it considered that its function under Article 15(4) was 'to set boundaries to and restrain the discretion of the Prosecution acting *proprio motu*, in order to avoid manifestly ungrounded investigations due to lack of adequate factual or legal fundaments'.[86] For the Pre-Trial Chamber, this required an assessment of the credibility of the information made available by the Prosecutor, including 'its completeness, relevance and consistency'.[87] Judge Mindua in his separate opinion endorsed the majority's de novo assessment,[88] the objective of which was, in his view, 'to limit extravagant politically motivated investigations'.[89] On an appeal by the Prosecutor,[90] the Appeals Chamber agreed that Article 15(4) required a de novo assessment by the Pre-Trial Chamber,[91] but found that the Pre-Trial Chamber had erred by considering itself bound to apply the criteria in Article 53(a)–(c).[92] The Appeals Chamber amended

---

[83] Having concluded that the threshold for a non-international armed conflict had not been established, the Prosecutor's request had excluded any characterization of conduct as war crimes and instead sought authorization only in relation to the alleged commission of crimes against humanity. *Situation in Burundi*, ICC-01/17-5-Red, Office of the Prosecutor, Public Redacted Version of 'Request for Authorisation of an Investigation Pursuant to Article 15', 6 September 2017, ICC-01/17-5-US-Exp, 15 November 2017, para 6.

[84] *Situation in Burundi*, Pre-Trial Chamber Authorization Decision 2017 (n 81) para 141.

[85] *Situation in Afghanistan*, Pre-Trial Chamber Authorization Decision 2019 (n 58) paras 34–35, 87.

[86] ibid para 32. The Pre-Trial Chamber claimed to limit its assessment to the Prosecutor's request and supporting material and, while ultimately rejecting the request, would have permitted the Prosecutor to investigate only those incidents specifically authorized by it under Article 15(4). ibid paras 30, 39–42. But see *Situation in Afghanistan*, ICC-02/17-33-Anx, Pre-Trial Chamber II, Concurring and Separate Opinion of Judge Antoine Kesia-Mbe Mindua, 31 May 2019 (hereafter '*Situation in Afghanistan*, Mindua Separate Opinion 2019') paras 6–10. The Appeals Chamber, in its authorization of the investigation, rejected the restrictive approach of the Pre-Trial Chamber, which it considered was not necessary for the fulfilment of the purpose of the authorization procedure under Article 15(4). In its view, such an approach would compromise the independence of the Prosecutor's investigation, and militated against considerations of judicial economy. *Situation in Afghanistan*, Appeals Chamber Decision 2020 (n 48) paras 61–63.

[87] *Situation in Afghanistan*, Pre-Trial Chamber Authorization Decision 2019 (n 58) para 38.

[88] *Situation in Afghanistan*, Mindua Separate Opinion 2019 (n 86) para 7.

[89] ibid para 6.

[90] The Prosecutor averred, first, that the Pre-Trial Chamber had committed an error of law 'by conditioning its determination under article 15(4) on reaching a positive assessment of the interests of justice'. *Situation in Afghanistan*, ICC-01/14-74, Office of the Prosecutor, Prosecution Appeal Brief, 30 September 2019, para 6. Second, the Prosecutor argued that the Pre-Trial Chamber had abused its discretion in its assessment of the interests of justice. ibid para 7.

[91] *Situation in Afghanistan*, Appeals Chamber Decision 2020 (n 48) para 45.

[92] ibid para 25.

the decision of the Pre-Trial Chamber to exclude its assessment of both admissibility and the interests of justice and, based on the satisfaction of jurisdictional requirements alone, authorized the initiation of the investigation.[93]

In contrast, Pre-Trial Chamber III in its authorization in 2019 of an investigation into the situation in Bangladesh/Myanmar undertook a deferential review of the Prosecutor's assessment.[94] Reiterating earlier decisions that had articulated the objective of Article 15(4) as preventing 'unwarranted, frivolous, or politically motivated investigations',[95] the Chamber considered that

> [t]his objective is achieved as soon as it can be established, based on the available information, that there is a reasonable basis to believe that 'at least one crime within the jurisdiction of the Court has been committed' and the potential case(s) are admissible ... If and once this is established, it can no longer be said that an investigation would be unwarranted or politically motivated.[96]

Accordingly, the Pre-Trial Chamber, limiting itself to the Prosecutor's application of the criteria in Article 53(1)(a)–(c) and the material supporting her request, authorized the investigation.[97]

Pre-Trial Chamber I, in its authorization in 2021 of an investigation into the situation in the Philippines, followed the guidance of the Appeals Chamber in the decision addressing the situation in Afghanistan. Declaring that its task under Article 15(4) was to 'curb[] any possible abuse of power' on the part of the Prosecutor, a task which did not, in the view of the Appeals Chamber, 'involve determinations on admissibility and interests of justice',[98] the Pre-Trial Chamber did no more than accept on its face the Prosecutor's declaration that 'potential cases which would likely arise from an investigation into the situation would be both admissible and sufficiently grave to justify further action by the Court'.[99]

---

[93] The approach of the Appeals Chamber to Pre-Trial Chamber authorization under Article 15(4) is problematic for several reasons. Recall Section 3.2.2.1.

[94] Exceptionally, the Pre-Trial Chamber, noting that the information available indicated the alleged commission of crimes before 9 October 2016, the date requested by the Prosecutor as the starting point for the proposed investigation, expanded the scope of the investigation to include crimes committed after 1 June 2010, the date of the entry into force of the Rome Statute for Bangladesh. *Situation in Bangladesh/Myanmar*, Pre-Trial Chamber Authorization Decision 2019 (n 58) para 131.

[95] ibid para 127.

[96] ibid para 127.

[97] ibid para 19. It is worth noting that the jurisdiction *ratione materiae* of the Court had already been addressed in an earlier decision of Pre-Trial Chamber I, which identified the crimes against humanity of deportation, persecution, and other inhumane acts as crimes committed in part on the territory of a state party and thus falling within the jurisdiction of the Court, all of which subsequently found their way into the Prosecutor's request for authorization under Article 15(3). See *Situation in Bangladesh/Myanmar*, ICC-RoC46(3)-01/18-37, Pre-Trial Chamber I, Decision on the 'Prosecution's Request for a Ruling on Jurisdiction under Article 19(3) of the Statute', 6 September 2018.

[98] *Situation in the Philippines*, ICC-01/21-12, Pre-Trial Chamber I, Decision on the Prosecutor's Request for Authorisation of an Investigation Pursuant to Article 15(3) of the Statute, 15 September 2021 (hereafter '*Situation in the Philippines*, Pre-Trial Chamber Authorization Decision 2021') para 15.

[99] ibid para 16.

Yet despite the fact that all but one of the Pre-Trial Chambers that have rendered decisions under Article 15(4) have purported to conduct their assessments by reference to the criteria in Article 53(1)(*a*)–(*c*), including admissibility, in practice they have rarely assessed de novo the criterion of gravity, the only exception being the Kenya authorization decision.[100] In the decisions relating to the situations in Côte d'Ivoire,[101] Georgia,[102] Burundi,[103] Afghanistan,[104] and Bangladesh/Myanmar,[105] the Pre-Trial Chambers all relied heavily on and in effect simply endorsed the Prosecutor's submissions in respect of gravity, turning only selectively to supporting materials and victims' representations. The same is true of the decision authorizing the investigation into the situation in the Philippines.[106]

3.2.2.2.3 Recapitulation

The majority of the Pre-Trial Chambers rendering decisions under Article 15(4) have claimed to assess de novo the existence or not of a 'reasonable basis to proceed' with an investigation into the situation. Only the Pre-Trial Chambers that authorized the investigations in Georgia, Bangladesh/Myanmar, and the Philippines, and Judge Fernández de Gurmendi in her partial dissent from the first decision authorizing the investigation in Côte d'Ivoire, have supported deferential review of the Prosecutor's conclusion, with each favouring an 'abuse of discretion' standard of review. When it has come, however, to admissibility and specifically to the criterion of gravity, most of the Pre-Trial Chambers have in practice merely rubber-stamped the Prosecutor's conclusion rather than undertake any genuine de novo assessment of gravity. Following the Appeals Chamber's decision pertaining to the situation in Afghanistan, moreover, authorization by the Pre-Trial Chamber of the investigation in the situation in the Philippines was given without any consideration as to the satisfaction or not of admissibility, including the criterion of gravity.

3.3 The Appropriate Limits of Pre-Trial Chamber Review in the Initiation of Investigations

In the absence of statutory guidance, the Pre-Trial Chambers have articulated different standards of judicial review under Articles 53(3)(*a*) and 15(4) respectively,

---

[100] By requiring that admissibility be assessed in relation to potential cases within the situation rather than the situation taken as a whole, it was necessary for the Pre-Trial Chamber not only to identify potential cases from the Prosecutor's request and supporting material but also to assess their gravity de novo. See *Situation in Kenya*, Pre-Trial Chamber Authorization Decision 2010 (n 49) paras 189–200.

[101] *Situation in Côte d'Ivoire*, Pre-Trial Chamber Authorization Decision 2011 (n 68) para 205.

[102] *Situation in Georgia*, Pre-Trial Chamber Authorization Decision 2016 (n 75) paras 52, 54–55.

[103] *Situation in Burundi*, Pre-Trial Chamber Authorization Decision 2017 (n 81) paras 185–88.

[104] *Situation in Afghanistan*, Pre-Trial Chamber Authorization Decision 2019 (n 58) paras 80–86.

[105] *Situation in Bangladesh/Myanmar*, Pre-Trial Chamber Authorization Decision 2019 (n 58) para 118.

[106] *Situation in the Philippines*, Pre-Trial Chamber Authorization Decision 2021 (n 98) para 16.

which in turn they have not applied in practice, at least in relation to the gravity of the situation. Under Article 53(3)(*a*), the Pre-Trial Chamber that reviewed the Prosecutor's decisions declining to investigate the Mavi Marmara incident purported to apply an error-based standard but effectively engaged in de novo review of the Prosecutor's gravity assessment. Conversely, under Article 15(4), the Pre-Trial Chambers have claimed to assess de novo the existence or not of a reasonable basis to proceed, but have been inconsistent in doing so in their application of the gravity criterion. This confused body of Pre-Trial Chamber practice under Articles 53(3)(*a*) and 15(4) poses the question as to what, subject to the text of the Rome Statute and any relevant Rules of Procedure and Evidence, ought to be the standard of review applied by the Pre-Trial Chamber when reviewing the Prosecutor's admissibility assessment under each provision. The answer in turn depends on the functions served in the context of the International Criminal Court (ICC, the Court) by prosecutorial discretion and by judicial scrutiny of its exercise, and on the respective competences of the Prosecutor and Pre-Trial Chamber. The task of selecting the most appropriate standard of review is assisted by the consideration of the justifications for judicial deference at other international courts, which may be equally applicable in this context.

3.3.1 Prosecutorial Discretion in the Initiation of Investigations

The Prosecutor's discretion to assess the existence or not of a 'reasonable basis to proceed' with an investigation under Articles 53(1) and 15(3) is justified in the first place by the Court's limited resources, which necessitate selectivity in the initiation of resource-intensive investigations into situations.[107] This discretion manifests itself in the application of the open-textured criterion of 'sufficient gravity', a component of the Prosecutor's admissibility assessment in relation to the situation under Article 53(1)(*b*).[108] As the Prosecutor explained in her 'Final Decision' declining to investigate the Mavi Marmara incident,

---

[107] S Fernández de Gurmendi, 'The Role of the International Prosecutor' in RS Lee (ed), *The International Criminal Court: The Making of the Rome Statute—Issues, Negotiations, Results* (Kluwer Law International 1999) 181; C Stahn, 'Damned If You Do, Damned If You Don't: Challenges and Critiques of Preliminary Examinations at the ICC' (2017) 15(3) Journal of International Criminal Justice 413, 432; WA Schabas, 'Victor's Justice: Selecting "Situations" at the International Criminal Court' (2010) 43 John Marshall Law Review 535, 541; H Olásolo, 'The Prosecutor of the ICC before the Initiation of Investigations: A Quasi-Judicial or a Political Body?' (2003) 3 International Criminal Law Review 87, 142–43. On the need for discretion in allocative decisions, see HK Woolf and others, *De Smith's Judicial Review* (8th edn, Sweet and Maxwell 2019) paras 1.041, 1.044–1.048. The Proposed Programme Budget for 2023 of the International Criminal Court confirms that investigations are 'the most resource-intensive activity' of the Office of the Prosecutor. Proposed Programme Budget for 2023, 30 September 2022, ICC-ASP/21/INF.2/Rev.1, para 21. See also S Ford, 'What Investigative Resources Does the International Criminal Court Need to Succeed: A Gravity-Based Approach' (2017) 16 Washington University Global Studies Law Review 1, 50–53.

[108] Recall Chapter 1, Section 1.2 and Chapter 2, Section 2.4.2. See also Turone (n 12) 1152; A Pues, 'Discretion and the Gravity of Situations at the International Criminal Court' (2017) 17 International

[a]ny investigation requires considerable investment of limited resources and operational assets which may not otherwise be used for other situations under investigation', where the article 53(1) standard was clearly met. Thus, although the drafters of the Statute did not expressly include the proper allocation of the Court's resources among the article 53(1) criteria, such considerations cannot be ignored when considering the merits of an expansive reading of article 53(1). Indeed, it may be in precisely this context, at least in part, that the 'sufficient gravity' requirement was included as an express criterion for initiating any investigation.[109]

As observed by the Independent Expert Review of the International Criminal Court and the Rome Statute System,[110] and as the recent practice of the Office of the Prosecutor demonstrates,[111] in the absence of this discretion the Prosecutor might be obliged to initiate an investigation into a situation even without the resources necessary to conduct the investigation.[112] Other practical considerations justifying

Criminal Law Review 960, 962. As Endicott explains, the use of open-textured legal language, or what he terms 'vagueness', 'always has this power-allocation function'. T Endicott, 'The Value of Vagueness' in A Marmor and S Soames (eds), *Philosophical Foundations of Language in the Law* (OUP 2011) 26.

[109] *Situation on the Registered Vessels of the Union of the Comoros, the Hellenic Republic and the Kingdom of Cambodia*, Final Decision of the Prosecutor 2017 (n 16) para 25.
[110] Final Report of the Independent Expert Review of the International Criminal Court and the Rome Statute System, 30 September 2020, para 642.
[111] The point is illustrated by the Prosecutor's decisions of 2020 in respect of the situations in Nigeria and Ukraine. In each context, following the preliminary examination of the situation, the Prosecutor concluded that there exists a 'reasonable basis to proceed' with an investigation. Yet, 'the operational capacity of the Office [of the Prosecutor] to roll out new investigations' and 'the fact that several preliminary examinations have reached or are approaching the same stage' prevented her from seeking Pre-Trial Chamber authorization to initiate an investigation *proprio motu*. Report on Preliminary Examination Activities, Office of the Prosecutor, 14 December 2020, paras 265, 289. Elsewhere, the Prosecutor has elaborated: '[t]he predicament we are confronted with due to capacity constraints underscores the clear mismatch between the resources afforded to my Office and the ever growing demands placed upon it'. See Statement of the Prosecutor, Fatou Bensouda, on the Conclusion of the Preliminary Examination in the Situation in Ukraine, 11 December 2020, www.icc-cpi.int/Pages/item. aspx?name=201211-otp-statement-ukraine, accessed 14 March 2023; Statement of the Prosecutor, Fatou Bensouda, on the Conclusion of the Preliminary Examination of the Situation in Nigeria, 11 December 2020, www.icc-cpi.int/Pages/item.aspx?name=201211-prosecutor-statement, accessed 14 March 2023. Similarly, the Proposed Programme Budget for 2023 of the International Criminal Court declares that the Prosecutor does not 'benefit from sufficient resources in order to effectively discharge its mandate with respect to the range of situations in relation to which it is currently engaged'. Proposed Programme Budget for 2023, 30 September 2022, ICC-ASP/21/INF.2/Rev.1, para 22.
[112] 'Once the Office [of the Prosecutor] reaches a finding that the conditions of article 53(1) are met, the Rome Statute requires the Prosecutor to open an investigation. At the same time, if multiple situations would reach the threshold at the same time, then it is, resource-wise, impossible to properly respond.' Strategic Plan 2019–2021, Office of the Prosecutor, 17 July 2019, 18. See also C Davis, 'Political Considerations in Prosecutorial Discretion at the International Criminal Court' (2015) 15 International Criminal Law Review 170, 174; L Poltronieri Rossetti, Prosecutorial Discretion and Its Judicial Review at the International Criminal Court: A Practice-Based Analysis of the Relationship between the Prosecutor and Judges (doctoral thesis, Università Degli Studi di Trento 2017–2018) 297–98. Rastan proposes that '[t]he reference to admissibility in the Article 53(1) stage should be viewed as a self-regulating procedure designed to encourage the Prosecutor to pre-emptively avoid challenges from competent jurisdictions so as to facilitate considerations as to viability and the optimal allocation of Court resources'. R Rastan, 'Situation and Case: Defining the Parameters' in C Stahn and M El Zeidy (eds), *The International Criminal Court and Complementarity* vol I (CUP 2011) 455–56.

104 GRAVITY AT THE INTERNATIONAL CRIMINAL COURT

discretion in the context of the Prosecutor's decisions whether to investigate include difficulties in securing states' cooperation and in the collection of evidence, both bearing on the feasibility of any eventual prosecution or prosecutions.[113]

During the Rome Conference, moreover, the conferral on the Prosecutor of the discretion to decide whether to initiate an investigation, including *proprio motu*, was deemed necessary to ensure the independence of his or her investigations from the political motivations of referring states parties and the Security Council.[114] Article 42(1) thus confers on the Prosecutor exclusive authority for the conduct of investigations, whether on referral or *proprio motu*,[115] with the Appeals Chamber confirming that '[m]anifestly, authority for the conduct of investigations vests in the Prosecutor'.[116] That it is the Prosecutor upon whom the discretion whether to initiate an investigation is conferred is evidenced by the Prosecutor's exclusive fact-finding mandate vis-à-vis the Pre-Trial Chamber and by the Prosecutor's application, in the first instance, of the criteria in Article 53(1)(*a*)–(*c*) when deciding whether there is a reasonable basis to proceed with an investigation.[117] This is notwithstanding the fact that the Pre-Trial Chamber may, to a limited extent, be able to itself secure relevant information from the Prosecutor.[118] Ultimately, it is the

[113] Cross (n 16) 235–37; G-JA Knoops and T Zwart, 'The *Flotilla Case* before the ICC: The Need to Do Justice While Keeping Heaven Intact' (2015) 15 International Criminal Law Review 1069, 1090–91.

[114] See eg the representations of Jordan and Malta. UN General Assembly, 'United Nations Diplomatic Conference of Plenipotentiaries on the Establishment of an International Criminal Court, Volume II' (15 June–17 July 1998) UN Doc A/CONF.183/13, 114–15; UN General Assembly, 'Report of the Preparatory Committee on the Establishment of an International Criminal Court, Volume I (Proceedings of the Preparatory Committee During March–April and August 1996)' (13 September 1996) UN Doc A/51/22, 49. See also L Moreno Ocampo, 'The International Criminal Court in Motion' in C Stahn and G Sluiter (eds), *The Emerging Practice of the International Criminal Court* (Martinus Nijhoff 2009) 15; M Brubacher, 'Prosecutorial Discretion within the International Criminal Court' (2004) 2 Journal of International Criminal Justice 71, 76; HB Jallow, 'Prosecutorial Discretion and International Criminal Justice' (2005) 3 Journal of International Criminal Justice 145, 154.

[115] *Situation in Côte d'Ivoire*, Fernández de Gurmendi Partial Dissent 2011 (n 72) paras 18–20; GM Pikis, *The Rome Statute of the International Criminal Court: Analysis of the Rome Statute, the Rules of Procedure and Evidence, the Regulations of the Court and Supplementary Instruments* (Martinus Nijhoff 2010) 243–44; KJ Heller, 'The Role of the International Prosecutor' in CP Romano, KJ Alter, and Y Shany (eds), *The Oxford Handbook of International Adjudication* (OUP 2013) 679; S de Smet, 'A Structural Analysis of the Role of the Pre-Trial Chamber in the Fact-Finding Process of the ICC' in C Stahn and G Sluiter (eds), *The Emerging Practice of the International Criminal Court* (Martinus Nijhoff 2009) 422–23.

[116] Clarifying the extent of victims' participation in judicial proceedings relation to investigations, the Appeals Chamber found that this right does not extend to participation in the investigation itself. *Situation in the Democratic Republic of the Congo*, ICC-01/04-556, Appeals Chamber, Judgment on Victim Participation in the Investigation Stage of the Proceedings in the Appeal of the OPCD against the Decision of Pre-Trial Chamber I of 7 December 2007 and in the Appeals of the OPCD and the Prosecutor against the Decision of Pre-Trial Chamber I of 24 December 2007, 19 December 2008, para 52.

[117] At the Rome Conference, the French proposal for judges to 'participate in investigating cases in cooperation with the Prosecutor from the preliminary stage' was rejected. UN General Assembly, 'United Nations Diplomatic Conference of Plenipotentiaries on the Establishment of an International Criminal Court, Volume II' (15 June–17 July 1998) UN Doc A/CONF.183/13, 101.

[118] Mariniello goes further in arguing that the Pre-Trial Chamber's determination of whether there exists a reasonable basis to proceed 'does not require direct evidence collected by the Prosecutor's own investigation, but can be satisfied merely by indirect, third party sources, such as reports of fact-finding commissions'. Mariniello (n 62) 990.

REVIEW OF THE ADMISSIBILITY OF 'SITUATIONS'   105

Prosecutor who must ascertain the facts by evaluating independently the information that is 'made available to him or her',[119] and who must apply the criteria in Article 53(1)(*a*)–(*c*) to those facts, including by selecting the potential cases to be weighed in the gravity assessment under Article 53(1)(*b*).

3.3.2 Judicial Review of Prosecutorial Discretion in the Initiation of Investigations

Under Article 53(3)(*a*), Pre-Trial Chamber review of the Prosecutor's exercise of discretion is tailored to give effect to the interest of the referring state party or the Security Council in the event that the Prosecutor has declined, including on the basis of inadmissibility under Article 53(1)(*b*), to initiate an investigation into the situation referred by it.[120] That this is the sole purpose underlying Pre-Trial Chamber review under Article 53(3)(*a*) has been confirmed by the Appeals Chamber in its 2015 decision relating to the Mavi Marmara incident.[121] The accountability of the Prosecutor in respect of a decision not to initiate an investigation into a situation is secured by allowing the Pre-Trial Chamber to review the sufficiency of the reasons underlying a prosecutorial decision not to proceed.[122] In other words, respect for the assessment of the referring state party or the Security Council in deciding to refer the situation supports the case for review of a prosecutorial decision to decline to investigate the referred situation. That being said, the limited extent to which the Rome Statute gives effect to this interest vis-à-vis prosecutorial independence is shown by the fact that the Pre-Trial Chamber reviewing the Prosecutor's admissibility assessment under Article 53(3)(*a*) cannot compel him or her to initiate an investigation into the situation.[123] Instead, it is for

[119] art 53(1), Rome Statute; see also art 15(1)–(2), Rome Statute. This includes the 'supporting documentation' supplied to the Prosecutor by a referring state party. See art 14(2), Rome Statute.

[120] *Situation on the Registered Vessels of the Union of the Comoros, the Hellenic Republic and the Kingdom of Cambodia*, Appeals Chamber Decision 2015 (n 25) para 9.

[121] ibid para 56.

[122] Stahn proposed that this '[i]nternal accountability might even serve [sic] protect the Prosecutor from claims of biased or partisan investigation or prosecution'. C Stahn, 'Judicial Review of Prosecutorial Discretion: Five Years On' in C Stahn and G Sluiter (eds), *The Emerging Practice of the International Criminal Court* (Martinus Nijhoff 2009) 255. In support, see *Situation on the Registered Vessels of the Union of the Comoros, the Hellenic Republic and the Kingdom of Cambodia*, Eboe-Osuji Partial Dissent 2019 (n 37) para 8; *Situation on the Registered Vessels of the Union of the Comoros, the Hellenic Republic and the Kingdom of Cambodia*, Ibáñez Carranza Partial Dissent 2019 (n 37) para 70; DDN Nsereko, 'Prosecutorial Discretion before National Courts and International Tribunals' (2005) 3 Journal of International Criminal Justice 124, 141–42; F Guarligia, 'Investigation and Prosecution' in RS Lee (ed), *The International Criminal Court: The Making of the Rome Statute—Issues, Negotiations, Results* (Kluwer Law International 1999) 230.

[123] Draft article 26(5) of the International Law Commission's 1994 draft statute for an international criminal court likewise mandated the reconsideration by the Prosecutor of a decision not to initiate an investigation into a situation, with the Commission noting in relation to that provision that any requirement that the Prosecutor initiate an investigation on the instruction of the Court would be inconsistent with prosecutorial independence. ILC, 'Report of the International Law Commission on the Work of Its Forty-Sixth Session' (2 May–22 July 1994) UN Doc A/49/10, 47.

106 GRAVITY AT THE INTERNATIONAL CRIMINAL COURT

the Prosecutor to 'reconsider', at the request of the Pre-Trial Chamber, whether to initiate an investigation.[124] As such, the Prosecutor retains, subject to the Pre-Trial Chamber's interpretations on question of law, broad discretion to decline to initiate an investigation into a situation on the basis of its inadmissibility.

When it comes to Article 15(4), the justification given by the Pre-Trial Chambers for what is at least said to be de novo assessment under Article 15(4) has been the putative object and purpose of the provision, namely to prevent the Court from proceeding with 'unwarranted, frivolous, or politically motivated investigations'.[125] Similarly, some Pre-Trial Chambers and individual judges have suggested that Pre-Trial Chamber review under Article 15(4) is intended to prevent abuse of the Prosecutor's discretion in the initiation of investigations *proprio motu*,[126] including through the initiation of 'manifestly ungrounded investigations'.[127] Crucially, as Judge Fernández de Gurmendi noted in her partial dissent from the Côte d'Ivoire authorization decision, the exercise of Pre-Trial Chamber review under Article 15(4) 'was not meant to affect ... the exclusive functions of the Prosecutor to investigate and prosecute under the Statute' and 'there is nothing in the terms of Article 15 (or any other provisions of the Statute) to suggest otherwise'.[128] The negative framing of the objectives underlying Article 15(4), moreover, noted by the Pre-Trial Chamber that authorized the initiation of an investigation in Bangladesh/Myanmar, suggests that the Pre-Trial Chamber must authorize the investigation as long as the Prosecutor has, in the exercise of his or her discretion, provided a reasonable basis to proceed.

In addition to the specific purposes underlying Pre-Trial Chamber oversight under Articles 53(3)(*a*) and 15(4) respectively, review under both provisions may be justified in more general terms by a desire for consistency and attendant predictability in the Prosecutor's assessment of admissibility, including in the application of the gravity criterion.[129] The limited powers of the Pre-Trial Chamber under

---

[124] Rule 108(3), RPE. While 'neither article 53(3)(*a*) nor rule 108(3) of the Rules preclude[s] a pretrial chamber from reviewing whether a decision of the Prosecutor that she considers to be "final" ... actually amounts to a proper "final decision"', the Appeals Chamber confirmed in its 2019 decision in relation to the Mavi Marmara proceedings that 'the "ultimate decision" as to whether to initiate an investigation is that of the Prosecutor'. *Situation on the Registered Vessels of the Union of the Comoros, the Hellenic Republic and the Kingdom of Cambodia*, Appeals Chamber Decision 2019 (n 32) paras 58–59.

[125] *Situation in Kenya*, Pre-Trial Chamber Authorization Decision 2010 (n 49) para 32. This objective was recalled by the Pre-Trial Chamber that authorized the initiation of an investigation in Côte d'Ivoire and by the Pre-Trial Chamber that refused authorization for an investigation in Afghanistan (including by Judge Mindua in his separate opinion in relation to the latter decision).

[126] The Pre-Trial Chambers that authorized the initiation of investigations into the situations in Georgia (including Judge Kovács in his separate opinion) and Burundi respectively invoked this objective. *Situation in Georgia*, Pre-Trial Chamber Authorization Decision 2016 (n 75) para 3; *Situation in Burundi*, Pre-Trial Chamber Authorization Decision 2017 (n 81) para 28.

[127] *Situation in Afghanistan*, Pre-Trial Chamber Authorization Decision 2019 (n 58) para 32.

[128] *Situation in Côte d'Ivoire*, Fernández de Gurmendi Partial Dissent 2011 (n 72) para 10.

[129] *Situation on the Registered Vessels of the Union of the Comoros, the Hellenic Republic and the Kingdom of Cambodia*, Pre-Trial Chamber Decision 2020 (n 40) para 101; A Pues, *Prosecutorial Discretion at the International Criminal Court* (Hart Publishing 2020) 80. See also Mariniello (n 62) 1002–03.

Article 53(3)(a) and Article 15(4) respectively, to review only certain decisions of the Prosecutor, suggests that the Pre-Trial Chamber's ability to fulfil this objective, whether under Article 53(3)(a) or Article 15(4), is limited.

3.3.3 Standards of Review under Article 53(3)(a) and Article 15(4)

In light of the various functions served by prosecutorial discretion in the initiation of investigations and of the more limited functions served by judicial review of that discretion under Articles 53(3)(a) and 15(4) respectively, it is sufficiently clear that some deference to the Prosecutor is required, excluding de novo review under both provisions.[130] As the decisions of the Pre-Trial Chambers to date attest, nor is there any reason to believe that the exercise of de novo review—effectively transferring the decision whether to investigate from the Prosecutor to the Pre-Trial Chamber—better fulfils the objectives of consistency and predictability.[131] On the contrary, the institutional competence of the Prosecutor vis-à-vis the Pre-Trial Chamber and considerations of judicial economy tend to support the case for deference.[132]

International courts, including international criminal courts, have expressed an overwhelming preference for deferential review in instances in which the primary decision-maker, in this context the Prosecutor, is in a better position to ascertain the facts and to apply the law to those facts.[133] Exclusive or superior fact-finding competence is a well-accepted justification for deference by international courts, in particular through the application of the 'margin of appreciation' doctrine in international human rights law, which the Appeals Chamber invoked in relation to the Prosecutor's application of the gravity criterion under Article 53(1)(b) in the Mavi Marmara proceedings.[134] So also there is wide agreement, including in international investment law and international trade law, that deference ought to be afforded to a primary decision-maker who is 'better placed to perform tasks

---

[130] National jurisdictions likewise exclude de novo review of administrative decisions out of respect for the discretion conferred on administrative authorities. H Wilberg, 'Judicial Review of Administrative Reasoning Processes' in P Cane and others (eds), *The Oxford Handbook of Comparative Administrative Law* (OUP 2020) 858.

[131] Mariniello (n 62) 1011–12; Poltronieri Rossetti, 'The Pre-Trial Chamber's Afghanistan Decision' (n 61) 595.

[132] As Shirlow notes, 'resourcing constraints ... may prompt international adjudicators to defer fact-heavy assessments to comparatively better-resourced domestic decision-makers'. E Shirlow, *Judging at the Interface: Deference to State Decision-Making Authority in International Adjudication* (CUP 2021) 24. The logic applies too in this context. See J de Hemptinne, 'The Creation of Investigating Chambers at the International Criminal Court: An Option Worth Pursuing?' (2007) 5 Journal of International Criminal Justice 402, 414.

[133] In international criminal law, see Mariniello (n 62) 1000–01.

[134] *Situation on the Registered Vessels of the Union of the Comoros, the Hellenic Republic and the Kingdom of Cambodia*, Appeals Chamber Decision 2019 (n 32) para 81.

108 GRAVITY AT THE INTERNATIONAL CRIMINAL COURT

such as gathering and evaluating complex information ... monitoring evolving situations, engaging in consultation and investigating alternative courses of action'.[135] These considerations all apply to the Prosecutor of the ICC in making the decision whether to initiate an investigation.[136] It is, in short, necessary 'to lean on the assessment of facts that are given by those in a better position to know about them'.[137] This justification for deference to the Prosecutor, which is independent of the reasons for any decision taken by him or her,[138] was shared by the Appeals Chamber in the context of the Mavi Marmara proceedings.[139] Considerations of judicial economy likewise support the case for deference in this context.[140] Deference does not imply, however, the abdication by the Pre-Trial Chamber of its judicial function.[141]

Under Article 53(3)(a), the relatively limited significance of the interests of the referring entity and the limits of the Pre-Trial Chamber's competence preclude the Pre-Trial Chamber from undertaking its own forensic analysis and characterization of conduct based on the limited information disclosed by the Prosecutor under Article 53(1).[142] By effectively exercising de novo review, or what has been

[135] C Henckels, 'The Role of the Standard of Review and the Importance of Deference in Investor-State Arbitration' in L Gruszczynski and W Werner (eds), *Deference in International Courts and Tribunals* (OUP 2014) 128. See also C Henckels, *Proportionality and Deference in Investor-State Arbitration* (CUP 2015) 38–41; Shirlow (n 132) 23; JH Fahner, *Judicial Deference in International Adjudication: A Comparative Analysis* (Hart Publishing 2020) 91–93; Y Shany, 'Toward a General Margin of Appreciation Doctrine in International Law?' (2006) 16(5) European Journal of International Law 907, 919; M Oesch, *Standards of Review in WTO Dispute Resolution* (OUP 2003) 128–29.

[136] As Shirlow notes, deference will need to be considered 'by *any* adjudicator confronted with overlapping and contested spheres of decision-making'. Shirlow (n 132) 240. 'The character of a regime cannot [] be used to expand or preclude a role for deference ex ante'. ibid.

[137] A Legg, *The Margin of Appreciation in International Human Rights Law: Deference and Proportionality* (OUP 2012) 26. That the widespread acceptance of deference by international courts is relevant to the question of the applicable standard of review under Article 53(3)(a) and Article 15(4) respectively of the Rome Statute is supported by Article 21 of the Statute, which articulates as a secondary source of the Court's applicable law 'principles and rules of international law', including general principles of international legal procedure, which are frequently articulated in the decisions of international courts.

[138] Shirlow (n 132) 18–19.

[139] *Situation on the Registered Vessels of the Union of the Comoros, the Hellenic Republic and the Kingdom of Cambodia*, Appeals Chamber Decision 2019 (n 32) paras 80–81. The former Prosecutor, Fatou Bensouda, advanced the same rationale for judicial deference, citing her role as the 'primary finder of fact' under Article 53(1) of the Rome Statute. *Situation on the Registered Vessels of the Union of the Comoros, the Hellenic Republic and the Kingdom of Cambodia*, Final Decision of the Prosecutor 2017 (n 16) para 58. In the context of the situation in Afghanistan, see A Kiyani, 'Afghanistan and the Surrender of International Criminal Justice', TWAIL Review, 2019, https://twailr.com/afghanistan-the-surrender-of-international-criminal-justice, accessed 14 March 2023.

[140] Shirlow (n 132) 20–23; Henckels, *Proportionality and Deference in Investor-State Arbitration* (n 135) 39.

[141] Shirlow (n 132) 240–41; Legg (n 137) 145–47; Henckels, *Proportionality and Deference in Investor-State Arbitration* (n 135) 187–88.

[142] Under Rule 107(2) of the RPE, the Pre-Trial Chamber may 'request the Prosecutor to transmit the information or documents in his or her possession, or summaries thereof, that the Chamber considers necessary for the conduct of the review'. This provision cannot be equated to the more comprehensive preliminary examination of the situation conducted by the Prosecutor under Article 53(1). But see Mariniello (n 62) 1008.

characterized as a 'correctness' standard of review,[143] the Pre-Trial Chamber in re-lation to the Mavi Marmara incident, showing no deference to the Prosecutor in her application of the gravity criterion, excessively restricted the Prosecutor's legit-imate exercise of her discretion under Article 53(1) to decline to initiate an inves-tigation into the situation under Article 53(1). As the Appeals Chamber stipulated in that context, 'it is primarily for the Prosecutor to evaluate the information made available to her and [to] apply the law ... to the facts found',[144] preventing the Pre-Trial Chamber from 'direct[ing] the Prosecutor as to what result she should reach in the gravity assessment or what weight she should assign to the individual factors'.[145] Nor is de novo review under Article 53(3)(*a*) justified on the ground that the ultimate decision whether to initiate an investigation remains with the Prosecutor. As Judges Fernández de Gurmendi and van den Wyngaert pointed out in relation to the Mavi Marmara incident, the exercise of de novo review re-stricts the Prosecutor's discretion under Article 53(1)(*b*) irrespective of whether the Pre-Trial Chamber's admissibility assessment is binding.[146] In other words, the Prosecutor should not be required to reconsider his or her decision under Article 53(1) merely because the Pre-Trial Chamber, in the exercise of the same discretion, would have arrived at a different conclusion as to the admissibility of the situation. That a deferential approach is required under Article 53(3)(*a*) was acknowledged not only by the Appeals Chamber but also by the Pre-Trial Chamber in relation to the Mavi Marmara incident, the latter's justification for the ostensible application of an error-based review being the limited function it ascribed to Article 53(3)(*a*), namely to satisfy the interest of the referring entity.[147]

Turning to Article 15(4), it is even less clear that de novo review is necessary to give effect to what the Pre-Trial Chambers have considered to be the object and purpose of that provision, namely to prevent the abuse of the Prosecutor's discre-tion through the initiation of unwarranted, frivolous, or politically motivated in-vestigations. Nor is the exercise of de novo review consistent with the institutional competences of the Prosecutor and Pre-Trial Chamber respectively in the initi-ation of investigations *proprio motu*.[148] When considering whether to initiate an

---

[143] Knoops and Zwart (n 113) 1078.

[144] *Situation on the Registered Vessels of the Union of the Comoros, the Hellenic Republic and the Kingdom of Cambodia*, Appeals Chamber Decision 2019 (n 32) para 80.

[145] ibid para 81. As Pues notes, it is the Prosecutor who is best placed to make the initial assessment of gravity. Pues, *Prosecutorial Discretion at the International Criminal Court* (n 129) 80.

[146] *Situation on the Registered Vessels of the Union of the Comoros, the Hellenic Republic and the Kingdom of Cambodia*, Fernández de Gurmendi and Wyngaert Dissent 2015 (n 25) para 35.

[147] *Situation on the Registered Vessels of the Union of the Comoros, the Hellenic Republic and the Kingdom of Cambodia*, Appeals Chamber Decision 2015 (n 25) para 59; *Situation on the Registered Vessels of the Union of the Comoros, the Hellenic Republic and the Kingdom of Cambodia*, Pre-Trial Chamber Decision 2015 (n 16) paras 9–10.

[148] In the context of the Pre-Trial Chamber's Afghanistan decision, Heller argued that Articles 53 and 15 'quite plainly assign primary responsibility for assessing the interests of justice to the [Office of the Prosecutor]' and that de novo review of the interests of justice is 'inconsistent with the structural inde-pendence of the [Office of the Prosecutor]'. The point applies equally to the assessment of admissibility, and thereby of gravity. KJ Heller, 'One Word for the PTC on the Interests of Justice: Taliban', Opinio

investigation into a situation *proprio motu*, it is the Prosecutor who must 'analyse' the seriousness of the information received.[149] Based on what is then distilled into the Prosecutor's request and supporting materials, the Pre-Trial Chamber must consider whether a reasonable basis to proceed with the investigation has been established. As Judge Fernández de Gurmendi rightly observed in her opinion in relation to the first Côte d'Ivoire authorization decision, the Chamber has 'no independent way to assess the reliability, credibility or completeness of the information available to it' and must exercise 'great caution ... in assessing the relevance and weight of the material provided'.[150] Indeed, any authorization by the Pre-Trial Chamber is based on the Prosecutor's assessment that there exists a reasonable basis to proceed, with 'the task of the Pre-Trial Chamber [being] to identify the outer parameters of the situation, not to fill in the individual pieces thereof'.[151] In other words, 'an appropriate measure of deference on factual matters' is warranted.[152] This might explain the deference the Pre-Trial Chambers acting under Article 15(4) have effectively accorded to the Prosecutor in respect of assessments of gravity. Viewed in the same light, the Pre-Trial Chamber's de novo assessment in relation to the situation in Afghanistan, which included considerations ranging from the effectiveness and feasibility of the proposed investigation to the 'complexity and volatility of the political climate' and the allocation of the Prosecutor's budget,[153] restricted the Prosecutor's discretion in the application of open-textured admissibility criteria, including gravity, under Article 15(4),[154] as did the decisions in relation to Côte d'Ivoire and Burundi. The intensity of the Pre-Trial Chamber's review must be suited to this allocation of responsibilities, excluding de novo review.

Having excluded de novo review under both Article 53(3)(*a*) and Article 15(4), the permissible standards of review that remain, from least to most deferential, are 'reasonableness' review, review for manifest error of law or fact, and 'abuse of discretion' review.[155] Identifying the applicable standards of review under Articles

Juris, 13 April 2019, https://opiniojuris.org/2019/04/13/one-word-for-the-ptc-on-the-interests-of-just ice-taliban, accessed 14 March 2023. See also Stahn, 'Judicial Review of Prosecutorial Discretion' (n 122) 255–57.

[149] See art 15(1)–(2), Rome Statute.

[150] *Situation in Côte d'Ivoire*, Fernández de Gurmendi Partial Dissent 2011 (n 72) paras 36–37.

[151] R Rastan, 'The Jurisdictional Scope of Situations before the International Criminal Court' (2012) 23 Criminal Law Forum 1, 27.

[152] Cross (n 16) 251.

[153] *Situation in Afghanistan*, Pre-Trial Chamber Authorization Decision 2019 (n 58) paras 89–90, 94–95.

[154] Heller, 'One Word for the PTC on the Interests of Justice: Taliban' (n 148); Poltronieri Rossetti, 'The Pre-Trial Chamber's Afghanistan Decision' (n 61) 598–99. But see Olásolo, *The Triggering Procedure of the International Criminal Court* (n 10) 68.

[155] This spectrum of standards of review is charted by reference to the various standards engaged at the national level to discipline the exercise of discretion by administrative authorities, including the exercise of prosecutorial powers. As Schill and Briese note, there is no principled reason why the same standards of review cannot govern the exercise of discretion at the national and international levels. S Schill and R Briese, ' "If the State Considers": Self-Judging Clauses in International Dispute Settlement'

53(3)(*a*) and 15(4) respectively requires consideration not only of the degree of deference to the Prosecutor warranted by the object and purpose of each provision but also of the institutional competence of the Pre-Trial Chamber to review, with the degree of scrutiny that each standard of review demands, the decision of the Prosecutor.

Under Article 53(3)(*a*), the Pre-Trial Chamber may, as Pre-Trial Chamber I claimed to do in relation to the Mavi Marmara incident, review against an error-based standard the commission by the Prosecutor of a manifest error of law or fact. It is necessary to distinguish, however, the commission by the Prosecutor of any such error, which relates more accurately to the satisfaction of jurisdictional requirements[156] and to the sufficiency of the evidence in support of the Prosecutor's conclusions as to facts relevant to the gravity analysis[157] from the legitimate exercise of the Prosecutor's discretion when assessing the gravity of the situation, which requires the application and weighing of relevant indicators of gravity in respect of potential cases selected by him or her.[158] The exercise of this discretion is not amenable to an error-based standard of review. In the absence of an objective threshold of 'sufficient gravity',[159] it is not clear what would constitute an 'error' in this respect. Alternatively, it may be that the Prosecutor's exercise of discretion in the application of gravity is better reviewed against a standard of reasonableness. 'Reasonableness' review permits degrees of judicial scrutiny ranging from the more deferential 'Wednesbury unreasonableness' standard, which requires the Pre-Trial Chamber only to determine whether the Prosecutor's decision was manifestly unreasonable, absurd, irrational, in bad faith, or arbitrary, to a more onerous formulation that warrants a finding as to whether the Prosecutor's decision fell within what the Chamber considers to be the range of reasonable decisions that might have been taken by a reasonable Prosecutor.[160] The Pre-Trial Chamber's ability to review

(2009) 13 Max Planck Yearbook of United Nations Law 61, 125. There is also 'broad consensus as regards the conceptual framework' for judicial review of administrative discretion across the common law and civil law traditions. ibid 135. In spite of their differences, both common law and civil law traditions are reflected in the standards of review discussed here. For an overview, see ibid 125–36; Wilberg (n 130).

[156] Under Article 53(1)(*a*), the Prosecutor must establish that '[t]he information available ... provides a reasonable basis to believe that a crime within the jurisdiction of the Court has been or is being committed'.

[157] *Situation on the Registered Vessels of the Union of the Comoros, the Hellenic Republic and the Kingdom of Cambodia*, Appeals Chamber Decision 2019 (n 32) para 80; M Fordham, *Judicial Review Handbook* (6th edn, Hart Publishing 2012) 508; Woolf and others (n 107) para 11.101.

[158] Recall Chapter 2, Section 2.4.1. The Pre-Trial Chamber's finding, for example, in its 2015 decision in relation to the Mavi Marmara incident that the Prosecutor had committed a 'material error' by considering that the number of victims was insufficient to satisfy the requirement of 'sufficient gravity' was an erroneous use of this standard of review. *Situation on the Registered Vessels of the Union of the Comoros, the Hellenic Republic and the Kingdom of Cambodia*, Pre-Trial Chamber Decision 2015 (n 16) para 26.

[159] Recall Chapter 2, Section 2.4.2.

[160] Woolf and others (n 107) paras 11.016, 11.019, 11.021–11.024, 11.093–11.099. In the interest of consistency, the application of a variable 'reasonableness' review is discouraged where more specific

the Prosecutor's decision against the latter, more demanding standard is limited by its capacity to determine, without undertaking its own preliminary examination of the situation, the range of permissible outcomes.[161] Judicial economy similarly supports the exclusion of 'reasonableness' review of this intensity. The more deferential 'Wednesbury unreasonableness', on the other hand, may be incorporated into an 'abuse of discretion' review of the kind contemplated by Judge Kovács, as the degree of judicial scrutiny it demands is compatible with the aim of preventing the abuse of the Prosecutor's discretion to decline to initiate an investigation into a situation referred to him or her by a state party or the Security Council, a discretion manifest in, inter alia, the criterion of 'sufficient gravity'.[162] This is not to say that the Prosecutor's exercise of discretion in the application of gravity is non-justiciable. Under Article 53(3)(a), an 'abuse of discretion' standard allows the Pre-Trial Chamber to determine to the satisfaction of the referring entity whether the Prosecutor abused his or her discretion by omitting to account for relevant indicators in the gravity analysis,[163] by failing to consider information that might support a finding of 'sufficient gravity'[164]—that is, the information supplied to him or her by the referring entity—or by arriving at the decision on the basis of extraneous considerations,[165] including by acting in bad faith or on improper motives.[166]

standards of scrutiny may be identified. Fordham (n 157) 569; DJ Galligan, *Discretionary Powers: A Legal Study of Official Discretion* (Clarendon Press 1990) 320; Henckels, 'The Role of the Standard of Review and the Importance of Deference in Investor-State Arbitration' (n 135) 117–20, 125; SR Tully, '"Objective Reasonableness" as a Standard for International Judicial Review' (2015) 6 Journal of International Dispute Settlement 546, 552; Fahner (n 135) 133–37.

[161] So also 'judges ought not to imagine themselves as being in the position of the competent authority when the decision was taken and then test the reasonableness of the decision against the decision they would have taken. To do that would involve the courts in a review of the merits of the decision, as if they were themselves the recipients of the power'. Woolf and others (n 107) para 11.016. See also Henckels, 'The Role of the Standard of Review and the Importance of Deference in Investor-State Arbitration' (n 135) 128.

[162] On the blurring of the line between Wednesbury unreasonableness and abuse of discretion, see Fordham (n 157) 491. Knoops and Zwart label this review for 'patent unreasonableness'. Knoops and Zwart (n 113) 1079–81.

[163] This does not include review of the weight accorded to relevant indicators of gravity unless 'the weight accorded ... has been manifestly excessive or inadequate', thereby rendering the Prosecutor's decision irrational. Wilberg (n 130) 859.

[164] *Situation on the Registered Vessels of the Union of the Comoros, the Hellenic Republic and the Kingdom of Cambodia*, Appeals Chamber Decision 2019 (n 32) para 80.

[165] This requires a determination of whether the impugned factors 'are extraneous to the objects or purposes of the statute under which the power is being exercised'. Woolf and others (n 107) para 11.019. See also MS Davis, 'Standards of Review: Judicial Review of Discretionary Decisionmaking' (2000) 2(1) Journal of Appellate Practice and Process 47, 54–55. It includes the exercise of discretion on discriminatory grounds, which would violate the obligation in Article 21(3) to apply the Rome Statute without adverse distinction as well as the Office of the Prosecutor's own commitment to act independently, impartially, and objectively. See Policy Paper on Preliminary Examinations, Office of the Prosecutor, 2013, 7–8. The civil law equivalent to review for improper purpose is review for abuse of power or *detournement de pouvoir*. Wilberg (n 130) 863; Schill and Briese (n 155) 131.

[166] Fordham (n 157) 491; Wilberg (n 130) 859. For the different view that an abuse of discretion warrants 'intrusive' judicial review of the kind carried out by the Pre-Trial Chamber in its 2015 review in respect of the Mavi Marmara proceedings, see Mariniello (n 62) 1000–02.

When determining whether there has been an abuse of the Prosecutor's discretion, the Pre-Trial Chamber may 'request the Prosecutor to transmit the information or documents in her or her possession, or summaries thereof', that it considers 'necessary for the conduct of the review'.[167] Not only is this 'abuse of discretion' review sufficient to balance the interest of the referring entity in securing prosecutorial accountability against prosecutorial discretion in the initiation of investigations under Article 53(3)(a) but it is also within the limits of the Pre-Trial Chamber's institutional capacity vis-à-vis the Prosecutor.[168]

Under Article 15(4), Pre-Trial Chamber review is intended to prevent the initiation by the Prosecutor of an investigation into a situation that does not satisfy the requirements of a reasonable basis to proceed, which the Pre-Trial Chambers have described as unwarranted, frivolous, or politically motivated investigations. The 'abuse of discretion' standard of review described above in relation to Article 53(3)(a) is tailored to fulfil this task of the Pre-Trial Chamber under Article 15(4), notwithstanding that what constitutes an abuse of discretion may differ in relation to Article 53(3)(a) and Article 15(4) respectively. An abuse of the Prosecutor's discretion under Article 15(3) includes the initiation by the Prosecutor—whether perfunctorily, without consideration of relevant indicators of gravity, or on the basis of politically motivated or other extraneous considerations—of an investigation into a situation that does not actually satisfy the requirement of 'sufficient gravity'. As with Article 53(3)(a), review for abuse of discretion under Article 15(4) is appropriate in light of the Prosecutor's independent and exclusive fact-finding mandate in the initiation of investigations and in light of the limited capability of the Pre-Trial Chamber, noted by Judge Fernández de Gurmendi,[169] to review the decision of the Prosecutor against a more onerous standard. In its review under Article 15(4), it is the Prosecutor's request and its supporting material that the Pre-Trial

---

[167] Rule 107(2), RPE.

[168] Conversely, Mariniello argues that by excluding the 'reassessment' by the Pre-Trial Chamber of the facts, this unjustifiably restricts the right of the referring state party or the Security Council under Article 53(3)(a). Mariniello (n 62) 1007–08. The basis for his argument in favour of the reassessment by the Pre-Trial Chamber of the facts is the Pre-Trial Chamber's prerogative of requesting, in accordance with Rule 107(2) of the RPE, additional information from the Prosecutor. For Mariniello, this supports the assessment by the Pre-Trial Chamber of questions of fact, presumably arising from the additional information supplied. See note 118. There is nothing to say, however, that additional information cannot be requested of the Prosecutor in order to determine whether there has been an abuse of his or her discretion in the making of the decision whether to investigate, for example through the omission of relevant facts. Pues objects to an 'abuse of discretion' review on the distinct ground that it minimizes the effectiveness of Pre-Trial Chamber oversight under Article 53(3)(a) in 'ensur[ing] consistency in the Prosecutor's application of gravity'. Pues, *Prosecutorial Discretion at the International Criminal Court* (n 129) 80. Any assessment of the effectiveness of Article 53(3)(a) must be by reference to the underlying purpose of the provision, which, as noted by the Appeals Chamber, is the protection of the interest of the referring entity. Were consistency in the application of the gravity criterion the primary function of review under Article 53(3)(a), the Pre-Trial Chamber might have been permitted to review the decision of the Prosecutor otherwise than at the request of the referring state party or the Security Council. That this is not the case is evidenced by the distinction between Pre-Trial Chamber review under Article 53(3)(a) and (b), with only the interests of justice being reviewable by the Chamber on its own initiative.

[169] *Situation in Côte d'Ivoire*, Fernández de Gurmendi Partial Dissent 2011 (n 72) para 10.

114 GRAVITY AT THE INTERNATIONAL CRIMINAL COURT

Chamber must examine. No provision is made for the Pre-Trial Chamber to look further to determine whether there has been an abuse of discretion on the part of the Prosecutor.[170] As under Article 53(3)(a), it does not preclude the identification by the Pre-Trial Chamber of a manifest error of law or fact on issues relevant to but nevertheless distinct from the Prosecutor's exercise of discretion in the application of the gravity criterion, such as the satisfaction of jurisdictional requirements or the sufficiency of the information in support of the Prosecutor's decision.[171]

For these reasons, some deference to the Prosecutor is required under Article 53(3)(a) and Article 15(4), excluding de novo review under both provisions and requiring that Pre-Trial Chamber review of the Prosecutor's admissibility assessment, whether under Article 53(3)(a) or Article 15(4), be limited to a highly deferential review for abuse of discretion, at least in respect of the application of the open-textured gravity criterion.

3.4 Conclusion

Whether under Article 53(3)(a) or Article 15(4) of the Rome Statute, the Pre-Trial Chambers have been inconsistent in their oversight of the Prosecutor's assessment of admissibility vis-à-vis a situation. Under Article 53(3)(a), the Pre-Trial Chamber in relation to the Mavi Marmara incident ostensibly applied a deferential standard of review but effectively reviewed de novo the Prosecutor's application of the gravity criterion, substituting its own assessment for that of the Prosecutor. Under Article 15(4), the opposite has been true. The Pre-Trial Chambers have claimed to assess de novo the existence or not of a reasonable basis to proceed with an investigation, but have ultimately reviewed the Prosecutor's gravity assessments against a less onerous standard, if at all. The Appeals Chamber has, for its part, also proposed a de novo assessment under Article 15(4), but its exclusion from the assessment of considerations of admissibility and the interests of justice suggests absolute deference to the Prosecutor's assessment of these requirements in the initiation of investigations *proprio motu*.[172]

By identifying the various considerations that underlie the balance between prosecutorial independence and prosecutorial accountability in the exercise of Pre-Trial Chamber review under Articles 53(3)(a) and 15(4) respectively, and with a view to the justifications for judicial deference by international courts generally, this chapter has illustrated the ways in which judicial review of the Prosecutor's

---

[170] This absence is in contrast with Rule 107(2) of the RPE, which permits the Pre-Trial Chamber to request the Prosecutor to 'transmit' to it 'the information or documents in his or her possession, or summaries therefore'. See also *Situation in Côte d'Ivoire*, Fernández de Gurmendi Partial Dissent 2011 (n 72) paras 36–37.

[171] Fordham (n 157) 508; Woolf and others (n 107) para 11.101.

[172] *Situation in Afghanistan*, Appeals Chamber Decision 2020 (n 48) para 25.

gravity assessments under each of these provisions has been problematic, whether by excessively restricting under Article 53(3)(*a*) the Prosecutor's discretion to decline to initiate an investigation into a situation on the basis of its inadmissibility or by inadequately scrutinizing under Article 15(4) his or her admissibility assessment when authorizing the initiation of an investigation *proprio motu*. For the reasons discussed, some of which pertain specifically to the distinct functions of Pre-Trial Chamber review under Article 53(3)(*a*) and Article 15(4), others of which go to the heart of the Pre-Trial Chamber's competence vis-à-vis the Prosecutor in the initiation of investigations and in the application of the gravity criterion, the chapter concludes that an 'abuse of discretion' standard of review is most suitable under both Article 53(3)(*a*) and Article 15(4). The view is supported by the jurisprudence of other international courts, which defer to the exercise of discretion by states or other decision-makers where they are better equipped to ascertain the facts and apply the law to them. That the task of the Pre-Trial Chamber under both Article 53(3)(*a*) and Article 15(4) of the Rome Statute is to review the Prosecutor's assessment of admissibility against a highly deferential 'abuse of discretion' standard suggests that the Prosecutor retains considerable discretion in his or her decision whether to initiate an investigation into a situation, whether on referral or *proprio motu*. This includes wide discretion in the application of Article 17(1)(*d*) in this context. This is not to endorse, however, the Appeals Chamber's exclusion of any oversight whatsoever under Article 15(4) of the Prosecutor's assessment of admissibility as part of his or her decision to initiate an investigation into a situation *proprio motu*.

4

Pre-Trial Chamber Review and Pre-Trial or Trial Chamber Determination of the Admissibility of 'Cases'

4.1 Introduction

The admissibility of a case, assessed by the Prosecutor as part of his or her decision whether to prosecute, may be subject to judicial oversight or independent judicial assessment under relevant provisions of the Rome Statute. In accordance with Article 53(2)(*b*) of the Statute, the Prosecutor may, having initiated an investigation into a situation, consider that a case arising out of the situation is inadmissible and, on that basis, conclude and notify the Pre-Trial Chamber and, where relevant, the referring state party or the United Nations (UN) Security Council that 'there is not a sufficient basis for a prosecution'.[1] As indicated in Article 53(2)(*b*), admissibility falls to be assessed by reference to the criteria specified in Article 17 of the Statute, among them the criterion of sufficient gravity found in Article 17(1)(*d*). Where a situation has been referred to the Prosecutor by a state party or the Security Council, any decision by the Prosecutor not to initiate a prosecution, including on the basis of inadmissibility, may be reviewed by the Pre-Trial Chamber at the request of the referring state or the Council, as provided for in Article 53(3)(*a*).[2]

A decision by the Prosecutor not to proceed with a case on the basis that 'there is not a sufficient basis for a prosecution' under Article 53(2) involves the exercise of his or her discretion, including in the application of the open-textured criterion of 'sufficient gravity' specified in Article 17(1)(*d*).[3] Pre-Trial Chamber review under Article 53(3)(*a*) is intended to discipline the exercise of this discretion. The Rome Statute, however, offers no indication as to the standard of review to be applied in the course of judicial oversight of the Prosecutor's exercise of discretion, including in respect of the admissibility of a case. As with the initiation of investigations,

---

[1] art 53(2), Rome Statute of the International Criminal Court 1998 (Rome Statute).
[2] Where the Prosecutor's decision not to initiate a prosecution is based solely on the interests of justice in Article 53(2)(*c*) of the Rome Statute, the decision may be reviewed at the initiative of the Pre-Trial Chamber under Article 53(3)(*b*) and 'shall be effective only if confirmed by the Pre-Trial Chamber'.
[3] Recall Chapter 1, Section 1.2 and Chapter 2, Section 2.4.2.

Gravity at the International Criminal Court. Priya Urs, Oxford University Press. © Priya Urs 2024.
DOI: 10.1093/oso/9780198882954.003.0004

the Statute does not expressly direct the Pre-Trial Chamber only to ask whether the Prosecutor's assessment constitutes an abuse of discretion or reflects a manifest error of law or fact or is reasonable or instead to go further and engage in de novo or ex novo assessment by reference to the legal test applied by the Prosecutor.[4] In the absence of any such explicit indication, it is left to the Pre-Trial Chambers themselves to articulate the appropriate standard of judicial review under Article 53(3)(*a*) of the Prosecutor's assessment of the admissibility of a case with which he or she does not wish to proceed, including on the basis of insufficient gravity.

Where, conversely, the Prosecutor wishes to proceed with a prosecution, the admissibility of the case may be determined by the Pre-Trial Chamber or, if the charges against the suspect[5] have been confirmed, by the Trial Chamber,[6] in accordance with one of three procedures articulated in Article 19(1), (2), and (3) respectively of the Rome Statute. Under Article 19(1), the Pre-Trial Chamber or the Trial Chamber may determine the admissibility of the case on its own motion. Under Article 19(2), the relevant Chamber may do so upon an admissibility challenge by a person against whom an arrest warrant or a summons to appear has been issued,[7] an accused,[8] a state with jurisdiction over the case, or '[a] state from which acceptance of jurisdiction is required'.[9] Under Article 19(3), the Pre-Trial Chamber or the Trial Chamber may determine the admissibility of the case at the request of the Prosecutor. As under Article 53(2)(*b*), the admissibility of a case with which the Prosecutor wishes to proceed is likewise assessed by reference to the criteria specified in Article 17, including the criterion of sufficient gravity in Article 17(1)(*d*).[10] Unlike Article 53(3)(*a*), which allows the Pre-Trial Chamber to review the Prosecutor's assessment of admissibility, the task of the Pre-Trial Chamber or the Trial Chamber under Article 19(1)–(3) is not to review the Prosecutor's admissibility assessment but to assess independently the admissibility of the case. The application of the gravity criterion under Article 19 is in this sense different from the Pre-Trial Chamber's review under Article 53(3)(*a*) of the Prosecutor's assessment of gravity in the context of his or her decision whether to prosecute a case.

---

[4] Recall Chapter 3, Section 3.2.1.1.

[5] The term 'suspect' is used in reference to proceedings before the confirmation of the charges under Article 61(7) of the Rome Statute. Where an arrest warrant or a summons to appear has been issued, the term 'person for whom a warrant of arrest or a summons to appear has been issued', which appears in Article 19(2)(*a*), is preferred.

[6] See art 19(6), Rome Statute.

[7] See art 58, Rome Statute.

[8] The 'accused' is the person formally charged with a crime following the confirmation of the charges under Article 61(7). An admissibility challenge by '[t]he accused' under Article 19(2)(*b*) will, in accordance with Article 19(6), be heard by the Trial Chamber. See also International Law Commission (ILC), 'Report of the International Law Commission on the Work of Its Forty-Sixth Session' (2 May–22 July 1994) UN Doc A/49/10 (hereafter 'ILC Report 1994') 47; M Klamberg 'Article 58' in M Klamberg (ed), *Commentary on the Law of the International Criminal Court* (Torkel Opsahl Academic EPublisher 2017) 426.

[9] See art 12(3), Rome Statute.

[10] Exceptionally, see art 19(2)(*b*), Rome Statute.

118 GRAVITY AT THE INTERNATIONAL CRIMINAL COURT

Distinct issues as to the application of Article 17(1)(*d*) arise in the context of the admissibility procedures under Article 19(1)–(3). The Rome Statute does not specify when the Pre-Trial Chamber or the Trial Chamber may undertake the assessment of admissibility under Article 19(1), (2) or (3). In particular, the Statute is silent as to whether the Pre-Trial Chamber may determine the admissibility of a case before it has issued a warrant of arrest or a summons to appear for the suspect under Article 58 of the Statute. In the absence of statutory guidance, the question of the permissibility of an assessment of admissibility, and thereby of gravity, before the issuance by the Pre-Trial Chamber of a warrant for the suspect's arrest or a summons for the suspect to appear under Article 58 is left to the determination of the Pre-Trial Chamber.[11]

In light of the two procedures outlined above, and with a view to distinguishing the application of the gravity criterion in the context of the Prosecutor's decision whether to prosecute a case from the Pre-Trial or Trial Chamber's application of the gravity criterion in its determination of the admissibility of a case with which the Prosecutor wishes to proceed, this chapter seeks to clarify the task of the Pre-Trial Chamber under Article 53(3)(*a*) and that of the Pre-Trial or Trial Chamber under Article 19(1)–(3) of the Rome Statute, both in respect of the application of the gravity criterion to a case.

Section 4.2 examines the Pre-Trial Chamber's virtually non-existent exercise to date of judicial review under Article 53(3)(*a*) in respect of a prosecutorial decision not to prosecute a case. It also answers the preliminary question whether the Prosecutor's obligation to notify the Pre-Trial Chamber of a decision not to proceed with a case arises in respect of every case with which he or she has decided not to proceed or only upon the closure of the investigation without having initiated any prosecutions.[12] On the basis of various relevant considerations, it then arrives at what it argues is the most appropriate standard of judicial review under Article 53(3)(*a*) of a prosecutorial decision not to proceed with a case on the basis of insufficient gravity. As with the Pre-Trial Chamber's review under Article 53(3) (*a*) of a prosecutorial decision not to initiate an investigation into a situation,[13] various considerations are weighed to strike a balance between prosecutorial independence and prosecutorial accountability in this context. On the one hand, judicial deference is supported by the subjective application of the open-textured criterion of 'sufficient gravity' in Article 17(1)(*d*),[14] which justifies the conferral of a broad discretion on the Prosecutor under Article 53(2)(*b*), and by the need to preserve the independence of the Prosecutor's investigation. The justifications for

---

[11] While the Trial Chamber may also assess the admissibility of a case under Article 19, the question of the permissibility of an assessment of admissibility before the issuance by the Pre-Trial Chamber of a warrant of arrest or a summons to appear is clearly addressed to the Pre-Trial Chamber.

[12] See Section 4.2.1.1.

[13] Recall Chapter 3, Section 3.3.

[14] Recall Chapter 1, Section 1.2 and Chapter 2, Section 2.4.2.

judicial deference to discretionary decision-makers by other international courts and across national criminal jurisdictions may also support the case for deference in this context. On the other hand, prosecutorial accountability and predictability in the application of Article 17(1)(*d*) warrant closer judicial scrutiny of the application of the gravity criterion and may equally be justified by the interest of the referring state party or the Security Council in the prosecution of one or more cases arising out of the situation it has referred to the Court. Whether the Prosecutor is bound to comply with the decision of the Pre-Trial Chamber under Article 53(3)(*a*) is also relevant to the analysis of their respective roles.

Section 4.3 scrutinizes the decisions of the Pre-Trial Chambers under Article 19 of the Statute issued during proceedings under Article 58 and, where these decisions have been appealed, the relevant decisions of the Appeals Chamber. It then answers the question of the permissibility of an assessment of admissibility, and specifically of gravity, in accordance with the various procedures provided in Article 19(1)–(3) before the issuance of a warrant of arrest or a summons to appear for the suspect under Article 58. It does so by reference to the authoritative decisions of the Appeals Chamber and by identifying the underlying interests at stake in the assessment of admissibility under Article 19(1)–(3). The conferral on the Pre-Trial Chamber of the discretion to decide when to undertake an assessment of admissibility may be justified by considerations of judicial economy, which warrant the dismissal of inadmissible cases as early as possible during the proceedings, including during proceedings under Article 58. The Prosecutor and other interested parties, including the states referred to under Article 19(2)(*b*)–(*c*), the referring state party or the Security Council, and victims, may also have an interest in confirming the admissibility of the case sooner rather than later. The assessment of the admissibility of a case during proceedings under Article 58 necessarily excludes the participation of the suspect in the proceedings.

4.2 Pre-Trial Chamber Review of the Prosecutor's Assessment of Admissibility

4.2.1 Pre-Trial Chamber Review under Article 53(3)(*a*) of the Statute

4.2.1.1 Article 53(3)(*a*)

Under Article 53(2)(*b*) of the Rome Statute, the Prosecutor may, 'upon [the] investigation' of the situation, consider that a case arising out of the situation is inadmissible and that there is as a result 'not a sufficient basis for a prosecution'. Unlike Article 53(1), which obliges the Prosecutor to initiate an investigation into a situation unless there is 'no reasonable basis to proceed', Article 53(2) requires only that the Prosecutor notify the Pre-Trial Chamber and, where relevant, the referring

120 GRAVITY AT THE INTERNATIONAL CRIMINAL COURT

state party or the Security Council of his or her conclusion that there is 'not a sufficient basis for a prosecution'.[15] In other words, the negative framing of Article 53(2) (*b*) suggests that there is no obligation on the Prosecutor to undertake the prosecution of every case with which he or she may consider that there is a sufficient basis to proceed.[16]

The text of Article 53(2) does not indicate when the Prosecutor's obligation of notification arises.[17] Put differently, the provision does not specify whether the Prosecutor is required to notify the Pre-Trial Chamber during the course of his or her investigation of every case in relation to which he or she has concluded that there is not a sufficient basis to prosecute or if the Prosecutor is obliged to notify the Pre-Trial Chamber only when he or she has concluded that there is not a sufficient basis to prosecute even a single case arising out of the investigation, resulting in the closure of the investigation without undertaking any prosecutions.[18]

---

[15] See Rule 106, Rules of Procedure and Evidence 1998 (RPE). The distinction between a 'sufficient basis for a prosecution' under Article 53(2) and a 'reasonable basis to proceed' under Article 53(1) is deliberate. See UN General Assembly, 'United Nations Diplomatic Conference of Plenipotentiaries on the Establishment of an International Criminal Court, Volume II' (15 June–17 July 1998) UN Doc A/CONF.183/13 (Vol. II) (hereafter 'Rome Conference II') 243; UN General Assembly, 'United Nations Diplomatic Conference of Plenipotentiaries on the Establishment of an International Criminal Court, Volume III' (15 June–17 July 1998) UN Doc A/CONF.183/13 (Vol. III) 292; K de Meester, 'Article 53' in M Klamberg (ed), *Commentary on the Law of the International Criminal Court* (Torkel Opsahl Academic EPublisher 2017) 395. The absence of a 'sufficient basis for a prosecution' may be based on a failure to satisfy jurisdictional requirements, the absence of evidence 'strong enough to make a conviction likely', the inadmissibility of the case, and the strength of potential defences. ILC Report 1994 (n 8) 47. See also WA Schabas, *The International Criminal Court: A Commentary on the Rome Statute* (2nd edn, OUP 2016) 839.

[16] A McDonald and R Haveman, 'Prosecutorial Discretion—Some Thoughts on "Objectifying" the Exercise of Prosecutorial Discretion by the Prosecutor of the ICC', Office of the Prosecutor, 15 April 2003, https://asp.icc-cpi.int/iccdocs/asp_docs/library/organs/otp/mcdonald_haveman.pdf, accessed 15 March 2023, 5; AM Danner, 'Enhancing the Legitimacy and Accountability of Prosecutorial Discretion at the International Criminal Court' (2003) 97 American Journal of International Law 510, 520–21; AKA Greenawalt, 'Justice without Politics? Prosecutorial Discretion and the International Criminal Court' (2007) 39 New York University Journal of International Law and Politics 583, 610–11; C Stahn, 'Judicial Review of Prosecutorial Discretion: Five Years On' in C Stahn and G Sluiter (eds), *The Emerging Practice of the International Criminal Court* (Martinus Nijhoff 2009) 249; D Akande, 'Is There Still a Need for Guidelines for the Exercise of ICC Prosecutorial Discretion?', EJIL Talk!, 28 October 2009, www.ejiltalk.org/is-there-still-a-need-for-guidelines-for-the-exercise-of-icc-prosecutorial-discretion, accessed 15 March 2023.

[17] Stahn outlines four possibilities: '(i) a decision not to prosecute a specific individual; (ii) a decision not to prosecute a certain group of persons in a given situation; (iii) a decision not to prosecute certain crimes; or (iv) a decision not to prosecute at all'. Stahn, 'Judicial Review of Prosecutorial Discretion' (n 16) 270–71.

[18] One commentator goes so far as to suggest that a decision to prosecute one case constitutes an 'implicit decision' not to prosecute others, thereby triggering the Prosecutor's obligation of notification under Article 53(2). M El Zeidy, 'The Gravity Threshold under the Statute of the International Criminal Court' (2008) 19 Criminal Law Forum 35, 56. See also A Pues, *Prosecutorial Discretion at the International Criminal Court* (Hart Publishing 2020) 202, arguing that Article 53(2) 'should be interpreted in such a way that it allows a review of cases that are not being prosecuted even if other prosecutions are under way'. Others disagree. See K Ambos and I Stegmiller, 'Prosecuting International Crimes at the International Criminal Court: Is There a Coherent and Comprehensive Prosecution Strategy?' (2013) 59 Crime, Law and Social Change 415, 419; Schabas, *The International Criminal Court* (n 15) 832; G Turone, 'Powers and Duties of the Prosecutor' in A Cassese, P Gaeta, and JRWD Jones (eds), *The Rome Statute of the International Criminal Court* (OUP 2002) 1172.

DETERMINATION OF THE ADMISSIBILITY OF 'CASES' 121

The former, case-specific approach ought to be excluded in order to preserve the independence of the Prosecutor's investigations, as guaranteed by Article 42(1) of the Statute.[19] As one commentator observes, 'if the Prosecutor was required to inform the Pre-Trial Chamber and the referring party every time she determined that a particular person could not be prosecuted ... she would no longer be acting independently but under an intrusive form of supervision'.[20] The use of the term 'upon investigation' to preface Article 53(2) might also be taken to suggest that the Prosecutor's obligation of notification arises only upon the completion of an investigation from which no prosecutions arise.[21] The Prosecutor's obligation to notify the Pre-Trial Chamber and, where relevant, the referring state party or the Security Council that there is not a sufficient basis for a prosecution is therefore better seen as arising only when he or she concludes that there is not a sufficient basis for even a single prosecution.

Where the situation was referred to the Prosecutor by a state party or the Security Council, any decision by the Prosecutor that there is not a sufficient basis for a prosecution, including on the basis of inadmissibility, may be subject to judicial review under Article 53(3)(*a*), which provides:

> At the request of the State making a referral under article 14 or the Security Council under article 13, paragraph (b), the Pre-Trial Chamber may review a decision of the Prosecutor under paragraph 1 or 2 not to proceed and may request the Prosecutor to reconsider that decision.[22]

[19] The view is shared by the Office of the Prosecutor. Policy Paper on Case Selection and Prioritisation, Office of the Prosecutor, 15 September 2016, paras 17–18; Policy on Situation Completion, Office of the Prosecutor, 15 June 2021, paras 53–54. The 2020 report of the Independent Expert Review of the International Criminal Court and the Rome Statute System agrees that '[t]here is ... no comprehensive assessment of the OTP's [Office of the Prosecutor's] progress in each situation, including the determination of the appropriate number of cases per situation'. Final Report, Independent Expert Review of the International Criminal Court and the Rome Statute, 30 September 2020 (hereafter 'Independent Expert Review') para 683.

[20] ME Cross, 'The Standard of Proof in Preliminary Examinations' in C Stahn and M Bergsmo (eds), *Quality Control in Preliminary Examinations: Volume 2* (Torkel Opsahl Academic EPublisher 2018) 226, footnote 40. Others from the Office of the Prosecutor agree that '[m]ere disagreement as to where the [P]rosecutor is focusing her investigative and prosecutorial efforts fall squarely outside the scope of judicial review'. F Guariglia and E Rogier, 'Selection of Situations and Cases by the OTP of the ICC' in C Stahn (ed), *The Law and Practice of the International Criminal Court* (OUP 2015) 363. See also F Guariglia, 'The Selection of Cases by the Office of the Prosecutor of the International Criminal Court' in C Stahn and G Sluiter (eds), *The Emerging Practice of the International Criminal Court* (Martinus Nijhoff 2009) 216.

[21] This view was also taken by the ILC, which in the commentary to its 1994 draft statute for an international criminal court considered that 'the Prosecutor must ... decide whether or not there is a sufficient basis to proceed with a prosecution' '[f]ollowing the investigation'. ILC Report 1994 (n 8) 47. In support, see Cross (n 20) 225–26; Turone (n 18) 1171; Schabas, *The International Criminal Court* (n 15) 843.

[22] As with the review of a prosecutorial decision not to initiate an investigation, Turone argues that any decision by the Prosecutor not to proceed with a prosecution on the ground of insufficient gravity is reviewable not only at the request of a referring state party or the Security Council under Article 53(3)(*a*) but also at the initiative of the Pre-Trial Chamber under Article 53(3)(*b*). Turone (n 18) 1174. On the contrary, it is the Prosecutor's assessment of the interests of justice under Article 53(2)(*c*),

As with the initiation of investigations,[23] Article 53(3)(*a*) does not specify the standard of review that the Pre-Trial Chamber is expected to apply when reviewing the Prosecutor's assessment of admissibility under Article 53(2)(*b*) as part of his or her decision 'that there is not a sufficient basis for a prosecution' and when determining whether to request that he or she reconsider his or her decision 'as soon as possible'.[24] Where an investigation into the situation is initiated by the Prosecutor *proprio motu*, there is no comparable provision for judicial review of a decision by the Prosecutor that there is not a sufficient basis for a prosecution.

4.2.1.2 Pre-Trial Chamber Review to Date under Article 53(3)(*a*)
4.2.1.2.1 *Overview*
To date, the Prosecutor has not notified the Pre-Trial Chamber of any decision not to proceed with the prosecution of a case under Article 53(2), whether on the basis of inadmissibility or otherwise. This has not prevented, however, various parties from requesting Pre-Trial Chamber review under Article 53(3)(*a*), whether as a means of procuring information from the Prosecutor about the status of ongoing investigations or as a route to challenging the Prosecutor's selection of charges against a suspect. For their part, the Pre-Trial Chambers have consistently held that the Prosecutor's obligation of notification under Article 53(2), and therefore the possibility of Pre-Trial Chamber review under Article 53(3)(*a*), is triggered only upon the completion of the entire investigation. Since the Prosecutor has not closed any investigations to date,[25] the Pre-Trial Chambers have not exercised their power of review under Article 53(3)(*a*) and have thus not had the occasion to articulate what they consider to be the appropriate standard of review under Article

---

which includes, inter alia, consideration of 'the gravity of the crime', that is reviewable by the Pre-Trial Chamber under Article 53(3)(*b*). The requirement of 'sufficient gravity' in relation to the case is a discrete admissibility criterion under Article 53(2)(*b*) that cannot be equated with 'the gravity of the crime', an indicator of the interests of justice, under Article 53(2)(*b*). In accordance with the maxim *expressio unius exclusio alterius*, moreover, the express mention of Article 53(2)(*c*), but not Article 53(2)(*b*), in Article 53(3)(*b*) can be taken to exclude review of the Prosecutor's admissibility assessment under Article 53(2)(*b*) at the initiative of the Pre-Trial Chamber under Article 53(3)(*b*). Recall Chapter 1, Section 1.5.2 and Chapter 3, note 12.

[23] Recall Chapter 3, Section 3.2.1.1.
[24] See Rule 108(2), RPE.
[25] In 2022, the Prosecutor announced the conclusion of the respective 'investigation phases', rather than the investigations themselves, of the situations in the Central African Republic and Georgia, having initiated the prosecution of several cases arising out of each situation. *Situation in CAR I and II*, Office of the Prosecutor, The Prosecutor of the International Criminal Court, Karim A.A. Khan KC, Announces Conclusion of the Investigation Phase in the Situation in the Central African Republic, 16 December 2022, www.icc-cpi.int/news/prosecutor-international-criminal-court-karim-aa-khan-kc-announces-conclusion-investigation-0, accessed 15 March 2023; *Situation in Georgia*, Office of the Prosecutor, The Prosecutor of the International Criminal Court, Karim A.A. Khan KC, Announces Conclusion of the Investigation Phase in the Situation in Georgia, 16 December 2022, www.icc-cpi.int/news/prosecutor-international-criminal-court-karim-aa-khan-kc-announces-conclusion-investigation, accessed 15 March 2023.

DETERMINATION OF THE ADMISSIBILITY OF 'CASES' 123

53(3)(a) of a prosecutorial decision not to proceed with a prosecution, including on the basis of inadmissibility under Article 53(2)(b).

4.2.1.2.2 In detail
The first occasion on which a Pre-Trial Chamber addressed the Prosecutor's obligation of notification under Article 53(2) of the Statute was in respect of the situation in Uganda, referred to the Prosecutor by Uganda itself in 2004. At the request of the Ugandan government, Pre-Trial Chamber II directed the Prosecutor to clarify certain conflicting statements he had made about whether the investigation into the situation had been completed.[26] Convening a status conference to resolve the matter, the Pre-Trial Chamber requested the Prosecutor 'to promptly inform the Chamber in writing of ... any decision concluding that "there is not a sufficient basis for a prosecution under Article 53, paragraph 2" '.[27] The Prosecutor's response was that, since he had not notified the Pre-Trial Chamber of a decision not to prosecute under Article 53(2), the investigation was ongoing and the possibility of Pre-Trial Chamber review was foreclosed.[28] There was, in other words, no prosecutorial decision for the Pre-Trial Chamber to review.

Similarly, in 2007, the legal representative of a number of victims in the situation in the Democratic Republic of the Congo (DRC) sought review of what he characterized as the Prosecutor's 'implicit decision' under Article 53(2) not to prosecute Thomas Lubanga Dyilo for certain crimes allegedly committed by him during the armed conflict in Ituri.[29] The Prosecutor had in fact sought an arrest warrant for Lubanga, but had decided for various reasons 'to temporarily suspend the further investigation in relation to other potential charges',[30] all the while being careful to clarify that 'his decision [did] not exclude that he may continue his investigation into crimes allegedly committed' by Lubanga.[31] Finding that the Prosecutor's

---

[26] *Situation in Uganda*, ICC-02/04-01/05-68, Pre-Trial Chamber II, Decision to Convene a Status Conference on the Investigation in the Situation in Uganda in Relation to the Application of Article 53, 2 December 2005 (hereafter '*Situation in Uganda*, Pre-Trial Chamber Decision to Convene a Status Conference 2005') paras 7–9.

[27] *Situation in Uganda*, ICC-02/04-01/05-52, Pre-Trial Chamber II, Decision on the Prosecutor's Application for Unsealing of the Warrants of Arrest, 13 October 2005, para 32. The Pre-Trial Chamber justified its direction by reference to the consequences that attach to a prosecutorial conclusion based solely on the interests of justice under Article 53(2)(c). Were the Prosecutor to arrive at a decision not to prosecute on that basis, his or her decision would have been effective 'only if confirmed by the Pre-Trial Chamber' under Article 53(3)(b). *Situation in Uganda*, Pre-Trial Chamber Decision to Convene a Status Conference 2005 (n 26) para 13.

[28] *Situation in Uganda*, ICC-02/04-01/05-76, Office of the Prosecutor, OTP Submissions Providing Information on Status of the Investigation in Anticipation of the Status Conference to be Held on 13 January 2006, 11 January 2006, paras 6, 8.

[29] The request having been made by reference to the interests of justice in Article 53(2)(c), Pre-Trial Chamber review was sought under Article 53(3)(b). *Situation in the Democratic Republic of the Congo*, ICC-01/04-399, Pre-Trial Chamber I, Decision on the Requests of the Legal Representative for Victims VPRS 1 to VPRS 6 regarding 'Prosecutor's Information on Further Investigation', 26 September 2007 (hereafter '*Situation in the Democratic Republic of the Congo*, Pre-Trial Chamber Decision 2007') 2.

[30] *Situation in the Democratic Republic of the Congo*, ICC-01/04-01/06-170, Office of the Prosecutor, Prosecutor's Information on Further Investigation, 28 June 2006, para 7.

[31] ibid para 10.

124 GRAVITY AT THE INTERNATIONAL CRIMINAL COURT

statements did not amount to a conclusion that 'there [was] not a sufficient basis for a prosecution' under Article 53(2), Pre-Trial Chamber I found that the investigation was ongoing and that there was, as a result, no basis for a review under Article 53(3)(a).[32] The same Pre-Trial Chamber made a similar assessment when the Women's Initiatives for Gender Justice sought leave to participate in the proceedings in part on the basis that the Prosecutor's exclusion of gender-based crimes in the arrest warrant for Lubanga amounted to a decision that there was not a sufficient basis to prosecute those crimes under Article 53(2).[33] Since the investigation into the situation was ongoing, the Chamber rejected the request, noting that the Prosecutor 'ha[d] not foreclosed the possibility of bringing additional charges against other persons'.[34]

In the absence of a prosecutorial decision to close the investigation of a situation on the basis that there is 'not a sufficient basis for a prosecution' under Article 53(2), on none of these occasions did the Pre-Trial Chamber engage in a review of any assessment of admissibility that may have been undertaken by the Prosecutor. Accordingly, nor did the Pre-Trial Chambers identify what they believed to be the applicable standard of review of a prosecutorial decision that there was not a sufficient basis for a prosecution under Article 53(2), whether on the basis of insufficient gravity or otherwise.

4.2.1.2.3 Recapitulation

To date, the Pre-Trial Chambers have considered that the Prosecutor's obligation of notification in respect of a decision under Article 53(2) is triggered only upon the Prosecutor's completion of the investigation into a situation without undertaking any prosecutions whatsoever. The Pre-Trial Chambers' consistent approach in this regard, combined with the Prosecutor's implicit decisions to date not to close any investigations, has so far forestalled Pre-Trial Chamber review under Article 53(3)(a). As long as an investigation is ongoing, any assessment of admissibility undertaken by the Prosecutor as part of his or her decision whether to proceed with the prosecution of a case remains beyond judicial scrutiny.[35] As a result, the Pre-Trial Chambers have not yet articulated what they believe to be the appropriate standard of review of the Prosecutor's assessment of admissibility, and therefore of gravity, under Article 53(3)(a).

---

[32] *Situation in the Democratic Republic of the Congo*, Pre-Trial Chamber Decision 2007 (n 29) 5.

[33] *Situation in the Democratic Republic of the Congo*, ICC-01/04-01/06-403, Women's Initiatives for Gender Justice, Request Submitted Pursuant to Rule 103(1) of the Rules of Procedure and Evidence for Leave to Participate as Amicus Curiae in the Article 61 Confirmation Proceedings, 7 September 2006, para 19.

[34] *Situation in the Democratic Republic of the Congo*, ICC-01/04-373, Pre-Trial Chamber I, Decision on the Request Submitted Pursuant to Rule 103(1) of the Rules of Procedure and Evidence, 17 August 2007, para 5.

[35] In the words of one commentator, 'in the absence of prosecutorial notification', Pre-Trial Chamber review under Article 53(3)(a) in respect of the Prosecutor's initiation or not of prosecutions remains 'largely academic'. Stahn, 'Judicial Review of Prosecutorial Discretion' (n 16) 271–72.

4.2.2 The Appropriate Limits of Pre-Trial Chamber Review in the Initiation of Prosecutions

The text of Article 53(3)(*a*) of the Rome Statute offers no indication as to the intensity of Pre-Trial Chamber scrutiny of the Prosecutor's assessment of the admissibility of a case under Article 53(2)(*b*). Nor to date has there been any practice under Article 53(3)(*a*) in relation to a prosecutorial decision not to proceed with the prosecution of a case. Nonetheless, the appropriate standard of judicial review of the Prosecutor's assessment of admissibility, and thereby of gravity, under Article 53(2)(*b*) may be discerned by reference to the functions served in the context of the International Criminal Court (ICC, the Court) by prosecutorial discretion and by judicial scrutiny of its exercise. To the extent that the same functions are served by prosecutorial discretion and by judicial scrutiny of its exercise in the assessment under Article 53(1)(*b*) of admissibility vis-à-vis a situation, reference can be made to the previous discussion of Pre-Trial Chamber review under Article 53(3) (*a*) of the Prosecutor's assessment of admissibility in relation to a situation.[36] This includes, where relevant, reference to the authoritative statements of the Appeals Chamber bearing on the intensity of Pre-Trial Chamber review under Article 53(3)(*a*). Additional reference is made to the justifications for judicial deference to discretionary decision-making by international courts in the areas of international human rights law, international investment law, and international trade law, and to the striking of the balance between prosecutorial independence and prosecutorial accountability by national criminal courts.

4.2.2.1 Prosecutorial Discretion in the Initiation of Prosecutions

Prosecutorial discretion in the initiation of prosecutions, which, as per the negative framing of Article 53(2), includes the discretion not to undertake any prosecutions at all,[37] is necessitated first and foremost by the limited resources at the disposal of the Prosecutor.[38] The resultant selectivity of prosecutions at the ICC was anticipated during the discussions leading up to the drafting of the Rome Statute, with the International Law Commission (ILC) expressing concern during

---

[36] Recall Chapter 3, Section 3.3.

[37] R O'Keefe, *International Criminal Law* (OUP 2015) 536.

[38] Guariglia, 'The Selection of Cases by the Office of the Prosecutor of the International Criminal Court' (n 20) 212; A Kiyani, 'Re-Narrating Selectivity' in MM deGuzman and V Oosterveld (eds), *The Elgar Companion to the International Criminal Court* (Edward Elgar Publishing 2020) 323. According to Pues, 'disturbing th[is] process ... would infringe on the Prosecutor's authority to manage the Office [of the Prosecutor] and the resources available to it'. Pues (n 18) 114. In addition to the allocation of scarce resources, this discretion allows the Prosecutor to decide what charges to bring and to test the strength of each potential case. 'Preliminary Proceedings' (2017) 46 Georgetown Law Journal Annual Review of Criminal Procedure 269, 269, footnote 679; A Whiting, 'Dynamic Investigative Practice at the International Criminal Court' (2013) 76 Law and Contemporary Problems 163, 174–79. The Office of the Prosecutor has further suggested that it permits 'expeditious trials while aiming to represent the entire range of victimization'. Policy Paper on Victims' Participation, Office of the Prosecutor, 2010, 8.

126 GRAVITY AT THE INTERNATIONAL CRIMINAL COURT

its drafting of a statute for an international criminal court that without relevant admissibility criteria 'the court might be swamped by peripheral complaints'.[39] This selectivity is evidenced in the Rome Statute, with neither Article 53(2) nor any other provision of the Statute obliging the Prosecutor to prosecute every case in respect of which there may be 'a sufficient basis for a prosecution'.[40] Had such an obligation been imposed under Article 53(2), the text of the provision would have mirrored that of Article 53(1), which contrariwise obliges the Prosecutor to initiate an investigation into a situation 'unless ... there is no reasonable basis to proceed'.[41] That the decision whether to prosecute a case at the ICC involves the exercise of discretion has been recently noted by the Independent Expert Review of the International Criminal Court and the Rome Statute (Independent Expert Review), which in its report of 2020 emphasized that the ICC 'cannot, and should not, be expected to prosecute each individual responsible for the commission of Rome Statute crimes'.[42] The Prosecutor thus enjoys, according to the Independent Expert Review, 'considerable discretion over the selection and prioritization of ... cases'.[43]

The Prosecutor's discretion whether to prosecute a case, based on his or her assessment under Article 53(2) of whether there exists 'a sufficient basis for a prosecution', manifests itself in part in the assessment of the admissibility of the case under Article 53(2)(*b*), in particular in the application of the open-textured criterion of 'sufficient gravity' specified in Article 17(1)(*d*).[44] When the gravity criterion was first introduced by the ILC, albeit in slightly different form from that eventually adopted in Article 17(1)(*d*), it was intended to 'ensur[e] that the court would deal solely with the most serious crimes' and 'adapt its caseload to the resources available'.[45] The same rationale is reflected in the Regulations of the Office of the Prosecutor, which explain that the Prosecutor's selection of cases is driven

---

[39] ILC, 'Summary Records of the Meetings of the Forty-Sixth Session' (2 May–22 July 1994) UN Doc A/CN.4/SER.A/1994, 9. See also UN General Assembly, 'Report of the Ad Hoc Committee on the Establishment of an International Criminal Court, General Assembly, Fiftieth Session' (6 September 1995) UN Doc A/50/22, para 12; ILC, 'Report of the International Law Commission on the Work of its Forty-Sixth Session (1994), Topical Summary of the Discussion Held in the Sixth Committee of the General Assembly during Its Forty-Ninth Session Prepared by the Secretariat, Addendum' (22 February 1995), UN Doc A/CN.4/464/Add.1, para 15.

[40] See Section 4.2.1.1.

[41] R Rastan, 'Comment on Victor's Justice and Ex Ante Standards' (2010) 43 John Marshall Law Review 569, 589; WA Schabas, 'Selecting Situations and Cases' in C Stahn (ed), *The Law and Practice of the International Criminal Court* (OUP 2015) 377.

[42] Independent Expert Review (n 19) para 633.

[43] ibid para 660. See also Schabas, 'Selecting Situations and Cases' (n 41) 378.

[44] Turone (n 18) 1173. Also recall Chapter 1, Section 1.2 and Chapter 2, Section 2.4.2. On the 'power-allocation' function of open-textured legal language, see T Endicott, 'The Value of Vagueness' in A Marmor and S Soames (eds), *Philosophical Foundations of Language in the Law* (OUP 2011) 26.

[45] ILC Report 1994 (n 8) 52. Notwithstanding the limits of the proposed court's jurisdiction *ratione materiae*, it was thus accepted that 'there could still be cases in which no action was warranted'. J Crawford, 'The ILC Adopts a Statute for an International Criminal Court' (1995) 89 American Journal of International Law 404, 413. But see Pues (n 18) 112, arguing that to ensure consistency, the assessment of admissibility, and thereby of gravity, must be made 'regardless of the caseload of the Court and solely on the merits of the individual case'.

DETERMINATION OF THE ADMISSIBILITY OF 'CASES' 127

primarily by the need to 'identify the most serious crimes committed within the situation'.[46] Indeed, the Office has consistently identified gravity as 'the predominant case selection criteri[on]', even if it has sought to distinguish this criterion for case selection from the admissibility requirement of sufficient gravity in Article 17(1)(*d*) of the Statute.[47] More recently, the Independent Expert Review, in light of ongoing concerns over the allocation of limited investigative resources, endorsed the prioritization of gravity as the criterion 'of highest importance' during case selection.[48] That the assessment of gravity involves the exercise of discretion has been confirmed by the Appeals Chamber, which in 2019 explained that 'the assessment of gravity involves ... the evaluation of numerous factors and information relating thereto, which the Prosecutor has to balance in reaching her decision'.[49] A comparable discretion is afforded to prosecutors, in one form or another, across the common law and civil law traditions, since 'it is essentially impossible' that selective prosecution does not occur.[50] Both traditions frequently assign an allocative function to the gravity or seriousness of a crime or a case to guide the exercise of prosecutorial discretion in determining whether to initiate a prosecution. In the common law tradition, in which the decision whether to prosecute is governed by the principle of opportunity, seriousness is a criterion for assessing whether the prosecution of a case is in the public interest.[51] In the civil law tradition, the

[46] Reg 33, Regulations of the Office of the Prosecutor 2009 (OTP Regs).

[47] Policy Paper on Case Selection and Prioritisation, Office of the Prosecutor, 15 September 2016, para 6. In its Policy Paper on Case Selection and Prioritisation, the Office of the Prosecutor considered the two criteria it proposed as being 'assessed similarly', while noting that '[g]ravity of crime(s) as a case selection criterion' may involve the application of a 'stricter test' than the gravity criterion for admissibility. See ibid para 36. As one commentator from the Office of the Prosecutor notes, '[g]ravity is an overarching consideration and a critical admissibility factor which must be analysed before any decision to ... prosecute is made'. Guariglia, 'The Selection of Cases by the Office of the Prosecutor of the International Criminal Court' (n 20) 213. See also P Seils, 'The Selection and Prioritization of Cases by the Office of the Prosecutor of the ICC' in M Bergsmo (ed), *Criteria for Prioritizing and Selecting Core International Crimes Cases* (Torkel Opsahl Academic EPublisher 2010) 77. For a more detailed assessment of the policy consideration of 'relative gravity' proposed by some commentators, see Chapter 5, Sections 5.3.2.1 and 5.3.3.1.

[48] Independent Expert Review (n 19) para R230. On the Prosecutor's resource constraints, see ibid para 634.

[49] *Situation on the Registered Vessels of the Union of the Comoros, the Hellenic Republic and the Kingdom of Cambodia*, ICC/01/13-98, Appeals Chamber, Judgment on the Appeal of the Prosecutor against Pre-Trial Chamber I's 'Decision on the "Application for Judicial Review by the Government of the Union of the Comoros"', 2 September 2019 (hereafter '*Situation on the Registered Vessels of the Union of the Comoros, the Hellenic Republic and the Kingdom of Cambodia*, Appeals Chamber Decision 2019') para 81.

[50] R Cryer, *Prosecuting International Crimes: Selectivity and the International Criminal Law Regime* (CUP 2005) 192. See also K Ligeti, 'The Place of the Prosecutor in Common Law and Civil Law Jurisdictions' in DK Brown and others (eds), *The Oxford Handbook of Criminal Process* (OUP 2019) 150–53; MM deGuzman and WA Schabas, 'Initiation of Investigations and Selection of Cases' in S Zappalà and others (eds), *International Criminal Procedure: Principles and Rules* (OUP 2013) 157–63.

[51] In England and Wales, this includes an assessment of the seriousness of the offence and the harm caused to the victim. See Code for Crown Prosecutors, www.cps.gov.uk/publication/code-crown-pros ecutors, accessed 15 March 2023, para 4.14(*a*)–(*g*). Similarly, prosecutorial guidelines in Canada provide that 'the more serious the offence, the more likely the public interest will require that a prosecution be pursued'. Public Prosecution Service of Canada Deskbook, The Federal Prosecution Service Deskbook, www.ppsc-sppc.gc.ca/eng/pub/fpsd-sfpg/fps-sfp/fpd/ch15.html#section15_3_2, accessed 15 March 2023, para 15.3.2. Cf Danner (n 16) footnote 285. See also Ligeti (n 50) 152–54.

128   GRAVITY AT THE INTERNATIONAL CRIMINAL COURT

insufficient gravity of a crime may provide a justifiable exception to the principle of legality, which otherwise calls for mandatory prosecutions.[52]

In addition to the need to limit the number of prosecutions at the Court, the conferral on the Prosecutor of the discretion whether or not to prosecute a case is further justified by a desire to preserve the independence of his or her investigations, as enshrined in Article 42(1) of the Rome Statute, and 'which is ultimately based on the interest of impartial justice'.[53] Prosecutorial independence during the investigation of a situation is also reflected in the Rome Statute's allocation exclusively to the Prosecutor of various investigative powers and duties.[54] As commentators point out, the independent exercise of prosecutorial discretion during an investigation is necessary to 'insulate the Prosecutor from the political interests of states',[55] including those which may have referred a situation to him or her.[56] The Pre-Trial Chamber's reading to date of Article 53(2) as obliging the Prosecutor to notify the Pre-Trial Chamber only of a decision not to prosecute any cases within a situation supports the independent exercise of this discretion while an investigation is ongoing. When it comes, moreover, to the notification by the Prosecutor of 'the reasons for [his or her] conclusion' that there is not a sufficient basis for a prosecution under Article 53(2), the Prosecutor enjoys the additional discretion to decide, in situations in which multiple cases have been investigated, which cases to include in his or her notification to the Pre-Trial Chamber. As the Appeals

---

[52] The various exceptions in German law to the overarching principle of legality, or *Legalitätsprinzip*, for example, include the possibility of dismissing a case involving a less serious offence 'if the offender's guilt is considered to be minor and there is no public interest in the prosecution'. Section 153, StPO, English translation, www.gesetze-im-internet.de/englisch_stpo/englisch_stpo.pdf, accessed 15 March 2023.

[53] M Bergsmo, P Kruger, and O Bekou, 'Article 53' in O Triffterer and K Ambos (eds), *Rome Statute of the International Criminal Court: A Commentary* (3rd edn, CH Beck 2016) 1367. See also P Webb, 'The ICC Prosecutor's Discretion Not to Proceed in the "Interests of Justice"' (2005) 50 Criminal Law Quarterly 305, 307.

[54] See art 54, Rome Statute. For Stahn, it is this 'division of roles between the judges and the Prosecutor in international criminal proceedings' that justifies the conferral of prosecutorial discretion. Stahn, 'Judicial Review of Prosecutorial Discretion' (n 16) 255. See also Greenawalt (n 16) 599.

[55] MR Brubacher, 'Prosecutorial Discretion within the International Criminal Court' (2004) 2 Journal of International Criminal Justice 71, 76. See also F Mégret, 'Three Dangers for the International Criminal Court: A Critical Look at a Consensual Project' (2001) 12 Finnish Yearbook of International Law 193, 213; HB Jallow, 'Prosecutorial Discretion and International Criminal Justice' (2005) 3 Journal of International Criminal Justice 145, 154. The Office of the Prosecutor has adopted independence, impartiality, and objectivity as key principles during case selection. See Policy Paper on Case Selection and Prioritisation, Office of the Prosecutor, 15 September 2016, 7–9.

[56] As others clarify, however, judicial scrutiny of the exercise of prosecutorial discretion under Article 53(2) does not increase the risk of political interference. In Stahn's view, '[i]nternal accountability might even serve [sic] protect the Prosecutor from claims of biased or partisan investigation or prosecution'. Stahn, 'Judicial Review of Prosecutorial Discretion' (n 16) 255. See also DDN Nsereko, 'Prosecutorial Discretion before National Courts and International Tribunals' (2005) 3 Journal of International Criminal Justice 124, 141–42; F Guariglia, 'Investigation and Prosecution' in RS Lee (ed), *The International Criminal Court: The Making of the Rome Statute—Issues, Negotiations, Results* (Kluwer Law International 1999) 230.

DETERMINATION OF THE ADMISSIBILITY OF 'CASES' 129

Chamber has confirmed, therefore, '[m]anifestly, authority for the conduct of investigations vests in the Prosecutor.'[57]

4.2.2.2 Judicial Review of Prosecutorial Discretion in the Initiation of Prosecutions

It is only at the request of the referring state party or the Security Council, as the case may be, that the Prosecutor's assessment of the admissibility of a case under Article 53(2)(b) is reviewable by the Pre-Trial Chamber under Article 53(3)(a).[58] As this indicates, the availability of Pre-Trial Chamber review under Article 53(3)(a), whether of a prosecutorial decision not to initiate an investigation into a situation or not to prosecute a case, serves to acknowledge the interest of the referring state party or the Security Council in the outcome of the Prosecutor's decision. As Pre-Trial Chamber I noted in relation to the Mavi Marmara proceedings, '[t]he object and purpose of article 53(3)(a) is to give the referring entity the opportunity to challenge ... the validity of the Prosecutor's decision.'[59]

The Statute's acknowledgement of the interest of the referring entity in the outcome of the Prosecutor's decision is, however, only limited. First, and at least as applied to date by the Pre-Trial Chambers, Article 53(2) obliges the Prosecutor to notify the referring state party or the Security Council, as the case may be, only of a decision not to prosecute any cases within a situation, excluding review under Article 53(3)(a) while an investigation is ongoing of any prosecutorial decision not to proceed with the prosecution of one or more cases.[60] Second, under Article 53(3)(a), the most the Pre-Trial Chamber can do upon review of the Prosecutor's decision is to request the Prosecutor to reconsider his or her decision.[61] The 'final

---

[57] *Situation in the Democratic Republic of the Congo*, ICC-01/04-556, Appeals Chamber, Judgment on Victim Participation in the Investigation Stage of the Proceedings in the Appeal of the OPCD against the Decision of Pre-Trial Chamber I of 7 December 2007 and in the Appeals of the OPCD and the Prosecutor against the Decision of Pre-Trial Chamber I of 24 December 2007, 19 December 2008, para 52.

[58] This is in stark contrast to Article 53(3)(b), which allows the Pre-Trial Chamber to review the Prosecutor's assessment of the 'interests of justice', specified under Article 53(2)(c), on its own initiative. During the Mavi Marmara proceedings, the Appeals Chamber explained that Article 53(3)(a), considered in contrast with Article 53(3)(b), reflects 'a conscious decision on the part of the drafters to preserve a higher degree of prosecutorial discretion' in relation to admissibility. *Situation on the Registered Vessels of the Union of the Comoros, the Hellenic Republic and the Kingdom of Cambodia*, ICC-01/13-51, Appeals Chamber, Decision on the Admissibility of the Prosecutor's Appeal Against the 'Decision on the Request of the Union of the Comoros to Review the Prosecutor's Decision Not to Initiate an Investigation', 6 November 2015 (hereafter '*Situation on the Registered Vessels of the Union of the Comoros, the Hellenic Republic and the Kingdom of Cambodia*, Appeals Chamber Decision 2015') para 59.

[59] *Situation on the Registered Vessels of the Union of the Comoros, the Hellenic Republic and the Kingdom of Cambodia*, ICC-01/13-34, Pre-Trial Chamber I, Decision on the Request of the Union of the Comoros to Review the Prosecutor's Decision Not to Initiate an Investigation, 16 July 2015, para 9.

[60] In the case against Jean-Pierre Bemba Gombo (*Bemba*), for example, Judge Trendafilova remarked that 'the issue of selection of cases by the Prosecutor and that of prosecutorial policy ... are not dealt with by the Chamber'. *Prosecutor v Bemba*, ICC-01/05-01/08-453, Pre-Trial Chamber II, Decision on Request for Leave to Submit *Amicus Curiae* Observations Pursuant to Rule 103 of the Rules of Procedure and Evidence, 17 July 2009, para 10.

[61] Draft article 26(5) of the ILC's 1994 draft statute for an international criminal court also permitted the Prosecutor to reconsider a decision not to initiate an investigation into a situation, with the

130 GRAVITY AT THE INTERNATIONAL CRIMINAL COURT

decision' is reserved for the Prosecutor.[62] As explained by the ILC, 'for the [Pre-Trial Chamber] to direct a prosecution would be inconsistent with the independence of the Prosecutor, and would raise practical difficulties given that responsibility for the conduct of the prosecution is a matter for the Prosecutor'.[63]

More generally, Pre-Trial Chamber review under Article 53(3)(*a*) may be justified by a desire for consistency and predictability in the application by the Prosecutor of the gravity criterion to a case.[64] The limited power of the Pre-Trial Chamber under Article 53(3)(*a*), however, to review only a decision by the Prosecutor not to prosecute any cases arising out of a situation, and that too only at the request of the referring entity, coupled with the complete absence of any power to review a decision by the Prosecutor not to prosecute any cases arising out of an investigation initiated *proprio motu*, suggests a limited competence to ensure consistency and predictability in the assessment by the Prosecutor of admissibility, and thereby of gravity.[65]

4.2.2.3 Standard of Review under Article 53(3)(*a*)

The limits on Pre-Trial Chamber oversight under Article 53(3)(*a*) indicate that the Rome Statute accords greater importance to the Prosecutor's discretion in his or her assessment under Article 53(2)(*b*) of whether there is a sufficient basis for a prosecution, including on the ground of admissibility and thereby of gravity, than to the interest of the referring state party or Security Council in the outcome of the Prosecutor's decision. Due acknowledgement of this comparative importance calls for the Pre-Trial Chamber to conduct any review under Article 53(3) (*a*) of a prosecutorial decision under Article 53(2)(*b*) as to the inadmissibility of a case, including on the ground of insufficient gravity, with a degree of deference.[66] This suggests that stringent, de novo review of the Prosecutor's assessment under Article 53(2)(*b*) is inappropriate. All the more inappropriate would be requiring the Prosecutor to 'reconsider' his or her decision by giving effect to the Pre-Trial Chamber's own assessment of admissibility.[67] As the Appeals Chamber has noted

Commission noting that any requirement that the Prosecutor initiate an investigation on the instruction of the Court would be inconsistent with prosecutorial independence. ILC Report 1994 (n 8) 47.

[62] See Rule 108(3), RPE. Conversely, under Article 53(3)(*b*), 'the decision of the Prosecutor shall only be effective if confirmed by the Pre-Trial Chamber'.

[63] ILC Report 1994 (n 8) 47. See also Nsereko (n 56) 137.

[64] Pues (n 18) 79.

[65] Proposals for widening the powers of the Pre-Trial Chambers in this respect recognize that this would require the amendment of the Rome Statute. See J de Hemptinne, 'The Creation of Investigating Chambers at the International Criminal Court: An Option Worth Pursuing?' (2007) 5 Journal of International Criminal Justice 402.

[66] Stahn, 'Judicial Review of Prosecutorial Discretion' (n 16) 255. National jurisdictions likewise exclude de novo review of administrative decisions out of respect for the discretion conferred on administrative authorities. H Wilberg, 'Judicial Review of Administrative Reasoning Processes' in P Cane and others (eds), *The Oxford Handbook of Comparative Administrative Law* (OUP 2020) 858.

[67] *Situation on the Registered Vessels of the Union of the Comoros, the Hellenic Republic and the Kingdom of Cambodia*, ICC-01/13-51-Anx, Appeals Chamber, Joint Dissenting Opinion of Judge Silvia

DETERMINATION OF THE ADMISSIBILITY OF 'CASES'   131

in relation to the admissibility of a situation, Pre-Trial Chamber review under Article 53(3)(*a*) 'cannot lead to a determination of admissibility that would have the effect of obliging the Prosecutor to initiate an investigation, the final decision in this regard being reserved for the Prosecutor'.[68] The same logic could be said to apply to the review itself under Article 53(3)(*a*) of the Prosecutor's assessment of the admissibility of a case.

In the absence of investigative powers comparable to those exercisable by the Prosecutor, the Pre-Trial Chamber would in any event be ill-equipped to undertake de novo review of whether or not there exists 'a sufficient basis for a prosecution', including on the basis of an assessment of the admissibility of one or more cases brought to its attention by the Prosecutor. While the Prosecutor's decision that there is 'not a sufficient basis for a prosecution' under Article 53(2) is taken 'upon investigation', the information at the disposal of the Pre-Trial Chamber is only that made available by the Prosecutor in his or her notification under that provision and any additional information supplied by him or her at the request of the Chamber.[69] As such, the information that is available to the Pre-Trial Chamber under Article 53(3)(*a*) remains only a fraction of the information considered by the Prosecutor during the course of his or her investigation. In the assessment of gravity, therefore, 'it is primarily for the Prosecutor to evaluate the information made available to her and apply the law … to the facts found'.[70] This 'margin of appreciation', recognized by the Appeals Chamber,[71] and by international criminal courts generally,[72] necessarily excludes de novo review at least of the assessment of gravity under Article 53(3)(*a*).[73]

This is not to say, however, that the exercise of the Prosecutor's discretion ought to escape Pre-Trial Chamber scrutiny altogether. To avoid the redundancy of the provision, some measure of review is obviously warranted under Article 53(3)(*a*). The deferential standards of review that could be applied under Article 53(3)(*a*) in respect of a case are the same as those discussed previously in respect of a

---

Fernández de Gurmendi and Judge Christine van den Wyngaert, 6 November 2015, para 35. As Pues notes, 'this would duplicate the work of the different organs of the Court and would diminish the scope for "reconsideration" [by] the Prosecutor'. Pues (n 18) 80. See also Schabas, *The International Criminal Court* (n 15) 843.

[68] *Situation on the Registered Vessels of the Union of the Comoros, the Hellenic Republic and the Kingdom of Cambodia*, Appeals Chamber Decision 2015 (n 58) para 64.

[69] See Rule 107(2), RPE.

[70] *Situation on the Registered Vessels of the Union of the Comoros, the Hellenic Republic and the Kingdom of Cambodia*, Appeals Chamber Decision 2019 (n 49) para 80.

[71] ibid para 81.

[72] See T Mariniello, 'Judicial Control over Prosecutorial Discretion at the International Criminal Court' (2019) 19 International Criminal Law Review 979, 1000–01. According to Jallow, judges at international criminal courts are not equipped to make the decision whether to prosecute a case, which requires the comparison of two or more potential cases. Jallow (n 55) 155.

[73] See E Shirlow, *Judging at the Interface: Deference to State Decision-Making Authority in International Adjudication* (CUP 2021) 30.

situation.[74] From least to most deferential, these are 'reasonableness' review, review for manifest error of law or fact, and review for abuse of discretion. As with judicial review of prosecutorial discretion during the initiation of investigations, these standards of review are identified by reference to the standards of review that may be applicable to the exercise of discretion by administrative authorities at the national level, including the exercise of prosecutorial powers.[75] When it comes to the initiation of prosecutions, a comparison between judicial review of prosecutorial discretion at the national level and at the ICC is apposite. Similar rationales underpin the exercise of prosecutorial discretion in both contexts, even if the precise justification for the exercise of discretion and its breadth differ as between the national and international levels, and as between different national legal systems. In both contexts, it is ultimately the rule of law, including the equal application of the law, that must be balanced against respect for prosecutorial independence and other underlying justifications for selective prosecutions. The appropriate standard of review under Article 53(3)(a) must be selected from among the various standards on the basis of the functions served by prosecutorial discretion under Article 53(2)(b) and by judicial scrutiny of its exercise, as well as of the institutional competence of the Pre-Trial Chamber to review, with the degree of scrutiny that each standard demands, the decision of the Prosecutor.

Just as in relation to the assessment of gravity vis-à-vis a situation,[76] the exercise of the Prosecutor's discretion to assess the gravity of a case is unamenable to an error-based standard of review. The Prosecutor's exercise of discretion when assessing the case's satisfaction or not of the requirement of 'sufficient gravity' under Article 17(1)(d) requires the subjective application and weighting of various indicators of the gravity of the alleged crimes to the case under consideration for prosecution.[77] In the absence of an objective requirement of 'sufficient gravity', it is open to question what might constitute an 'error' in the Prosecutor's assessment. This would not prevent, however, the identification by the Pre-Trial Chamber of a manifest error of law or fact when reviewing the case's satisfaction or not of jurisdictional requirements[78] and the sufficiency of the evidence in support of the Prosecutor's conclusions as to facts relevant to the gravity analysis.[79]

---

[74] Recall Chapter 3, Section 3.3.3.

[75] As Schill and Briese demonstrate, there is 'broad consensus as regards the conceptual framework' for judicial review across the common law and civil law traditions. S Schill and R Briese, '"If the State Considers": Self-Judging Clauses in International Dispute Settlement' (2009) 13 Max Planck Yearbook of United Nations Law 61, 135. See also Wilberg (n 66) 858. As such, the standards of review discussed here are reflective of both common law and civil law traditions. See Schill and Briese, ibid 125–36; Wilberg (n 66).

[76] Recall Chapter 3, Section 3.3.3.

[77] Recall Chapter 2, Section 2.4.2.

[78] See art 53(2)(a), Rome Statute.

[79] See M Fordham, *Judicial Review Handbook* (6th edn, Hart Publishing 2012) 508; HK Woolf and others, *De Smith's Judicial Review* (8th edn, Sweet and Maxwell 2019) para 11.101.

Instead of error-based review of the Prosecutor's assessment of gravity, the Pre-Trial Chamber could choose to conduct a review for 'reasonableness' of the Prosecutor's assessment, a standard of review that admits of varied intensity. In its more stringent form, review for reasonableness would require a determination as to whether the Prosecutor's decision fell within what the Chamber considers to be the range of reasonable decisions that might have been taken by a reasonable Prosecutor.[80] With neither its own investigative powers nor sufficient access to the entirety of the Prosecutor's independent investigation, the Pre-Trial Chamber's institutional competence to identify the range of reasonable decisions that the Prosecutor might have taken during the course of the investigation would be limited and the exercise burdensome, which tends to rule out judicial scrutiny of this intensity.[81] 'Reasonableness' review in its more deferential form, however, frequently referred to as 'Wednesbury unreasonableness', asks whether the Prosecutor's decision was 'so unreasonable that no reasonable authority could ever come to it'.[82] This limited review for reasonableness may be more appropriate in light of the function of Article 53(3)(a). It would take appropriately weighted account of the interest of the referring state party or the Security Council in the Prosecutor's decision by indicating not whether that decision was incorrect or even unreasonable as such but whether it was manifestly unreasonable, absurd, irrational, in bad faith, or arbitrary.[83] Across national jurisdictions and international law, this minimal standard of unreasonableness is frequently elided with the most deferential standard of review that may be applied, namely review for abuse of discretion, already identified[84] as the most suitable standard of review under Article 53(3)(a) of a prosecutorial decision not to initiate an investigation into a situation based on considerations of gravity.[85] In the context of review of the Prosecutor's assessment of the gravity of a

---

[80] Woolf and others (n 79) paras 11.016, 11.019, 11.021–11.024, 11.093–11.099.

[81] At the Rome Conference, the French proposal for judges to 'participate in investigating cases in cooperation with the Prosecutor' was rejected. Rome Conference II (n 15) 101. Instead, as specified in Rule 107(2) of the RPE, the Pre-Trial Chamber may 'request the Prosecutor to transmit the information or documents in his or her possession, or summaries thereof, that the Chamber considers necessary for the conduct of the review'. Additionally, Regulation 48 of the Regulations of the Court, adopted by the judges of the Court in 2004, states that '[t]he Pre-Trial Chamber may request the Prosecutor to provide specific or additional information or documents in his or her possession, or summaries thereof, that the Pre-Trial Chamber considers necessary in order to exercise the functions and responsibilities set forth in article 53, paragraph 3(b)'. The conspicuous exclusion of Article 53(3)(a) from Regulation 48 might be taken to suggest that the judges did not consider its application necessary in the exercise of a more deferential review under Article 53(3)(a).

[82] *Associated Provincial Picture House Ltd. v Wednesbury Corporation* [1948] 1 KB 233, 229–30 (Greene LJ).

[83] Woolf and others (n 79) paras 11.016, 11.019, 11.021–11.024, 11.093–11.099. Indeed, states parties to the Rome Statute 'can expect' that any discretion conferred under the treaty 'will be exercised reasonably and in good faith'. Schill and Briese (n 75) 127.

[84] Recall Chapter 3, Section 3.3.3.

[85] On the blurring of the line between Wednesbury unreasonableness and abuse of discretion, see Fordham (n 79) 491. As in Chapter 3, review for abuse of discretion is preferred here as being more specific than a broad review for reasonableness. On the need for specificity in setting standards of review, see ibid 569; DJ Galligan, *Discretionary Powers: A Legal Study of Official Discretion* (Clarendon Press 1990) 320; SR Tully, '"Objective Reasonableness" as a Standard for International Judicial Review' (2015)

case, the 'abuse of discretion' standard would allow the Pre-Trial Chamber to assess, at the request of the referring entity, whether the Prosecutor abused his or her discretion by omitting to consider relevant indicators in the analysis of the gravity of the case,[86] by failing to account for information that may be relevant to the assessment of gravity, where information relating to the investigation is made available to the Pre-Trial Chamber,[87] or by arriving at the decision on the basis of extraneous considerations,[88] including by acting in bad faith or on improper motives.[89] The 'abuse of discretion' is the most appropriate standard of review of the Prosecutor's assessment of the gravity of a case under Article 53(3)(a). It implies wide discretion for the Prosecutor in the application of the gravity criterion in the context of his or her decision whether to prosecute a case.

4.3 Pre-Trial or Trial Chamber Determination of Admissibility

4.3.1 Pre-Trial or Trial Chamber Decision under Article 19 of the Statute

4.3.1.1 Article 19

The admissibility of a case with which the Prosecutor wishes to proceed may be assessed by the Pre-Trial Chamber or, where the charges against the suspect have

---

6 Journal of International Dispute Settlement 546, 552; C Henckels, 'The Role of the Standard of Review and the Importance of Deference in Investor-State Arbitration' in L Gruszczynski and W Werner (eds), *Deference in International Courts and Tribunals* (OUP 2014) 125. Conversely, Pues rejects a review for abuse of discretion as insufficient on the basis that it would 'render the work of the different organs of the Court ineffective'. Pues (n 18) 80–81.

[86] The Pre-Trial Chamber may oblige the Prosecutor to 'take into account certain factors'. *Situation on the Registered Vessels of the Union of the Comoros, the Hellenic Republic and the Kingdom of Cambodia*, Appeals Chamber Decision 2019 (n 49) para 81. This does not include, however, review of the weight accorded to relevant indicators of gravity unless 'the weight accorded ... has been manifestly excessive or inadequate', thereby rendering the Prosecutor's decision irrational. Wilberg (n 66) 859.

[87] See Rule 107(2), RPE. According to the Appeals Chamber, the Pre-Trial Chamber may, under Article 53(3)(a), request the Prosecutor 'to take into account certain available information when determining whether there is a sufficient factual basis to initiate an investigation'. *Situation on the Registered Vessels of the Union of the Comoros, the Hellenic Republic and the Kingdom of Cambodia*, Appeals Chamber Decision 2019 (n 49) para 81. The same logically applies to review of the Prosecutor's assessment of whether there is a sufficient basis for a prosecution under Article 53(2).

[88] This requires a determination of whether the Prosecutor's consideration of the impugned factors was illegal 'because they are extraneous to the objects or purposes of the statute under which the power is being exercised'. Woolf and others (n 79) para 11.019. See also MS Davis, 'Standards of Review: Judicial Review of Discretionary Decisionmaking' (2000) 2(1) Journal of Appellate Practice and Process 47, 54–55. It includes the exercise of discretion on discriminatory grounds, which would violate the obligation in Article 21(3) to apply the Rome Statute without adverse distinction as well as the Office of the Prosecutor's own commitment to act independently, impartially, and objectively. See Policy Paper on Case Selection and Prioritisation, Office of the Prosecutor, 15 September 2016, 7–9. The civil law equivalent to review for improper purpose is review for abuse of power or *detournement de pouvoir*. Wilberg (n 66) 863; Schill and Briese (n 75) 131.

[89] Fordham (n 79) 491; Rastan, 'Comment on Victor's Justice and Ex Ante Standards' (n 41) 589; Danner (n 16) 521.

DETERMINATION OF THE ADMISSIBILITY OF 'CASES'   135

been confirmed, by the Trial Chamber,[90] in accordance with one of three proced-ures specified in Article 19(1), (2), and (3) respectively of the Rome Statute:

1. ... The Court may, on its own motion, determine the admissibility of a case in accordance with article 17.
2. Challenges to the admissibility of a case on the grounds referred to in article 17 or challenges to the jurisdiction of the Court may be made by:
   (a) An accused or a person for whom a warrant of arrest or a summons to appear has been issued under article 58;
   (b) A State which has jurisdiction over a case, on the ground that it is investigating or prosecuting the case or has investigated or prosecuted; or
   (c) A State from which acceptance of jurisdiction is required under article 12.
3. The Prosecutor may seek a ruling from the Court regarding a question of jurisdiction or admissibility. In proceedings with respect to jurisdiction or admissibility, those who have referred the situation under article 13, as well as victims, may also submit observations to the Court.[91]

As provided in the text of the provision, the assessment of admissibility under Article 19 must be made by reference to the criteria specified in Article 17 of the Statute, which include the criterion of sufficient gravity found in Article 17(1)(d). At the same time, a state with jurisdiction over the case which seeks under Article 19(2)(b) to challenge the case's admissibility is prevented from challenging the gravity of the case, since such a state may bring a challenge only on the ground that it is investigating or prosecuting the case or has done so.[92] A challenge to the gravity of the case by any of the other parties mentioned in Article 19(2) must be made 'prior to or at the commencement of trial'.[93]

Where the Prosecutor has chosen to proceed with the prosecution of a case, he or she must seek a warrant of arrest or a summons to appear in accordance with Article 58(1) and (7) respectively of the Rome Statute. The text of Article 58 makes no mention of admissibility. Nowhere is it specified in the provision or indeed else-where that the Prosecutor is obliged, in an application pursuant to Article 58, to demonstrate the admissibility of the case. Article 58(2)(d) provides only that the

---

[90] See art 19(6), Rome Statute.

[91] See also Rule 58(2) of the RPE, specifying that the relevant Chamber 'shall decide on the procedure to be followed' under Article 19.

[92] Rejecting a literal reading of Article 19(2)(b) and (c), Schabas suggests that it is 'implausible' and likely an oversight that a state with jurisdiction over a case, under Article 19(2)(b), has a right to chal-lenge the admissibility of a case on the sole basis of an ongoing or completed national investigation or prosecution, while a state from which acceptance of jurisdiction is required under Article 19(2)(c) enjoys the additional right to challenge the gravity of the case and also the jurisdiction of the Court. Schabas, *The International Criminal Court* (n 15) 492–93.

[93] art 19(4), Rome Statute. In other words, an admissibility challenge by any of the parties listed under Article 19(2) 'at the commencement of a trial, or subsequently with the leave of the Court, may be based only on article 17, paragraph 1(c)'. ibid.

Prosecutor must submit '[a] summary of the evidence and any other information which establish reasonable grounds to believe that the person committed th[e] crimes'. Nor does Article 58 require the Pre-Trial Chamber, upon its examination of 'the application and the evidence or other information', to establish the admissibility of the case before issuing a warrant of arrest or a summons to appear. The purpose of the procedures specified in Article 58(1) and (7), in the words of one Pre-Trial Chamber, is simply to determine 'the sufficiency of evidence and material presented by the Prosecutor in establishing reasonable grounds to believe that the conditions provided for in [A]rticle 58 of the Statute have been met'.[94] The distinction made in Article 53(2) between the existence or not of 'a sufficient legal or factual basis to seek a warrant or summons', under Article 53(2)(*a*), and the Prosecutor's conclusion as to the admissibility of the case, under Article 53(2)(*b*), confirms the irrelevance of admissibility to either the Prosecutor's application for or the Pre-Trial Chamber's issuance of a warrant of arrest or a summons to appear under Article 58.

Yet although Article 58 itself imposes no requirement in relation to the admissibility of the case, the question arises whether a judicial assessment of admissibility may nevertheless be undertaken during Pre-Trial Chamber proceedings pertaining to the issuance of a warrant of arrest or a summons to appear under Article 58(1) and (7) respectively in accordance with any of the procedures specified in Article 19(1)–(3).[95] A Pre-Trial Chamber determination of the admissibility of a case at this stage of the proceedings would effectively condition the issuance of a warrant of arrest or a summons to appear on the admissibility of the case, which the Prosecutor would, in his or her request for a warrant or a summons, be required to demonstrate. The title of Article 19 ('Challenges to ... the Admissibility of a Case') and the consistent threading of the term 'case' throughout its text impose as a minimum requirement that an admissibility assessment under Article 19

---

[94] *Situation in Kenya*, ICC-01/09-42, Pre-Trial Chamber II, Decision on the 'Application for Leave to Participate in the Proceedings before the Pre-Trial Chamber relating to the Prosecutor's Application under Article 58(7)', 11 February 2011, para 10. The ICC's Pre-Trial Practice Manual, prepared by the judges of the Pre-Trial Chambers, also notes in respect of proceedings under Article 58 that '[a]ny detailed discussion of the evidence or analysis of legal questions is premature at this stage and should be avoided'. Pre-Trial Practice Manual 2015, 5. As Cross suggests, thus, 'Article 58 is not concerned with examining the entirety of the Prosecutor's case against the suspect, but only in verifying that there is *a* case against the suspect'. Cross (n 20) 232.

[95] The need to clarify the timing of the admissibility assessment in relation to a case was briefly highlighted in the Preparatory Committee on the Establishment of an International Criminal Court (Preparatory Committee). UN General Assembly, 'Report of the Preparatory Committee on the Establishment of an International Criminal Court, Volume I (Proceedings of the Preparatory Committee During March–April and August 1996)' (13 September 1996) UN Doc A/51/22 (hereafter 'Preparatory Committee Report 1996') para 235. Admissibility provisions which appeared in earlier drafts of the Rome Statute would have permitted assessments of admissibility 'at all stages of the proceedings', an expression that was ultimately removed from the text of Article 19. The Preparatory Committee's draft article 17, for instance, provided that '[a]t all stages of the proceedings, the Court ... may, on its own

pertain to a 'case'.[96] Neither the provision nor the Statute more broadly stipulates, however, whether a 'case' comes into existence prior to or upon the conclusion of proceedings under Article 58. That said, the text of Article 19(2)(*a*) indicates that an admissibility challenge under at least that subclause is conditioned by the requirement that the person making the challenge be either '[a]n accused' or 'a person for whom a warrant of arrest or a summons to appear has been issued'. This logically precludes a judicial assessment of admissibility under Article 19(2)(*a*) prior to the issuance of a warrant of arrest or a summons to appear under Article 58. It is unclear on the face of Article 19, however, whether this restriction on the application of Article 19(2)(*a*) equally conditions by implication the application of the other admissibility procedures in Article 19.[97] In other words, Article 19 itself does not settle whether a judicial assessment of admissibility under Article 19(1), (2)(*b*) or (*c*), or (3) is equally impermissible absent the existence of 'a person for whom a warrant of arrest or a summons to appear has been issued'—that is, prior to the issuance of a warrant of arrest or a summons to appear under Article 58. Prima facie, therefore, a judicial assessment of admissibility under Article 19(1), (2)(*b*)–(*c*), and (3), including the assessment of gravity under Article 19(1), (2)(*c*), and (3), may be undertaken during proceedings under Article 58.

4.3.1.2 Pre-Trial Chamber Decisions to Date under Article 19

4.3.1.2.1 Overview

The Pre-Trial Chambers have on several occasions undertaken assessments of admissibility under Article 19 during proceedings pertaining to the issuance of an arrest warrant under Article 58. Three of these occasions, namely in the *Lubanga* and *Ntaganda* cases, both arising out of the situation in the DRC, and in the *Al Hassan* case, arising out of the situation in Mali, have featured ex parte assessment of the gravity of the case by reference to Article 17(1)(*d*), while a fourth decision, in *Bemba*, arising out of the first situation in the Central African Republic (CAR), has not. While several of the Pre-Trial Chamber's decisions have been appealed, including the Pre-Trial Chamber's decisions in *Ntaganda* and *Al Hassan*, the Appeals Chamber has only twice addressed the question of the permissibility of

---

motion, determine the admissibility of the case'. UN General Assembly, 'United Nations Diplomatic Conference of Plenipotentiaries on the Establishment of an International Criminal Court, Report of the Preparatory Committee on the Establishment of an International Criminal Court, Addendum' (14 April 1998) UN Doc A/CONF.183/2/Add.1, 43. The ILC in its 1994 draft statute for an international criminal court similarly suggested in its draft article 35 that admissibility may be assessed 'at any time prior to the commencement of the trial'.

[96] CK Hall, DDN Nsereko, and MJ Ventura, 'Article 19' in O Triffterer and K Ambos (eds), *Rome Statute of the International Criminal Court: A Commentary* (3rd edn, CH Beck 2016) 875, footnote 121.

[97] Rule 58(3) of the RPE guarantees '[a] person ... who has been surrendered to the Court or who has appeared voluntarily or pursuant to a summons' the right to submit observations in relation to an admissibility 'request' or 'application' under Article 19(2)(*b*)–(*c*) and (3) respectively, but this does not bar an assessment of admissibility before the person has appeared before the Court.

138   GRAVITY AT THE INTERNATIONAL CRIMINAL COURT

an assessment of admissibility during proceedings under Article 58.[98] In addition to *Ntaganda*, the issue was addressed by the Appeals Chamber as obiter dictum in *Kony and others*, arising out of the situation in Uganda.

4.3.1.2.2 In detail

When in 2005 Pre-Trial Chamber II issued the Court's first ever set of arrest warrants, pertaining to crimes allegedly committed by members of the Lord's Resistance Army in Uganda, its only statement on admissibility was that 'the case ... [fell] within the jurisdiction of the Court and appear[ed] to be admissible'.[99] Accordingly, warrants were issued for Joseph Kony, Vincent Otti, Raska Lukwiya, Okot Odhiambo, and Dominic Ongwen (*Kony and others*).

The permissibility of assessing admissibility during proceedings under Article 58 came before Pre-Trial Chamber I later that year when, acting ostensibly under Article 19(2)(a), ad hoc counsel for the Defence raised the admissibility of any potential cases arising out of the situation in the DRC.[100] The Pre-Trial Chamber

---

[98] A Pre-Trial Chamber decision as to the admissibility of a case under Article 19 is appealable to the Appeals Chamber under Article 19(6) read in conjunction with Article 82(1)(a) of the Statute. Nowhere does the Statute specify the standard of Appeals Chamber review of the Pre-Trial Chamber's decision, leaving its articulation, including when it comes to the review of the Pre-Trial Chamber's assessment of gravity, to the determination of the Appeals Chamber. G Boas and others, 'Appeals, Reviews and Reconsideration' in G Sluiter and others (eds), *International Criminal Procedure: Principles and Rules* (OUP 2013) 969. In practice, the Appeals Chamber has been consistent in articulating what it considers to be the applicable standard of review of the Pre-Trial Chamber's assessment of admissibility, imposing a deferential review of the Pre-Trial Chamber's decision and, where the Pre-Trial Chamber's assessment involved the exercise of discretion, a review for abuse of discretion. See *Situation in the Democratic Republic of the Congo*, ICC-01/04-169, Appeals Chamber, Judgment on the Prosecutor's Appeal against the Decision of Pre-Trial Chamber I entitled 'Decision on the Prosecutor's Application for Warrants of Arrest, Article 58', 13 July 2006 (hereafter '*Situation in the Democratic Republic of the Congo*, Appeals Chamber Decision 2006') paras 34–35; *Prosecutor v Kony and others*, ICC-02/04-01/05-408, Appeals Chamber, Judgment on the Appeal of the Defence against the 'Decision on the Admissibility of the Case under Article 19 of the Statute' of 10 March 2009, 16 September 2009 (hereafter '*Kony and others*, Appeals Chamber Decision 2009') paras 79–80; *Prosecutor v Ruto and others*, ICC-01/09-01/11-307, Appeals Chamber, Judgment on the Appeal of the Republic of Kenya against the Decision of Pre-Trial Chamber II of 30 May 2011 Entitled 'Decision on the Application by the Government of Kenya Challenging the Admissibility of the Case Pursuant to Article 19(2)(b) of the Statute', 30 August 2011 (hereafter '*Ruto and others*, Appeals Chamber Decision 2011') para 89; *Prosecutor v Al Hassan*, ICC-01/12-01/18-601-Red, Appeals Chamber, Judgment on the Appeal of Mr Al Hassan Against the Decision of Pre-Trial Chamber I Entitled 'Décision relative a l'exception d'irrecevabilité pour insufficiance de gravité de l'affaire soulevée par la défense', 19 February 2020 (hereafter '*Al Hassan*, Appeals Chamber Decision 2020') para 39, citing *Prosecutor v Kenyatta*, ICC-01/09-02/11-1032, Appeals Chamber, Judgment on the Prosecutor's Appeal against Trial Chamber V(B)'s 'Decision on Prosecution's Application for a Finding of Non-Compliance under Article 87(7) of the Statute', 19 August 2015 (hereafter '*Kenyatta*, Appeals Chamber Decision 2015') para 22. According to the Appeals Chamber, an abuse of discretion 'will occur when the decision is so unfair or unreasonable as to "force the conclusion that the Chamber failed to exercise its discretion judiciously"' and if the Chamber 'gave weight to extraneous or irrelevant considerations or failed to give weight or sufficient weight to relevant considerations in exercising its discretion'. *Kenyatta*, Appeals Chamber Decision 2015, ibid para 25. See also *Kony and others*, Appeals Chamber Decision 2009, ibid para 80.

[99] *Situation in Uganda*, ICC-02/04-01/05-1-US-Exp, Pre-Trial Chamber II, Decision on the Prosecutor's Application for Warrants of Arrest under Article 58, 8 July 2005, 2.

[100] The Prosecutor had sought measures relating to a special investigative opportunity in respect of the situation under Article 56 of the Rome Statute. Among its objections to the measures, the Defence raised the issue of admissibility. *Situation in the Democratic Republic of the Congo*, ICC-01/04-93, Pre-Trial Chamber I, Decision Following the Consultation Held on 11 October 2005 and the Prosecution's Submission on Jurisdiction and Admissibility Filed on 31 October 2005, 9 November 2005, 2, footnote 1.

declined to address the question of admissibility on the ground that an admissibility challenge could be made under Article 19(2)(*a*) only by '[a]n accused' or 'a person for whom a warrant of arrest or summons to appear has been issued', of which at that point there was neither.[101] While noting that an admissibility challenge under Article 19(2)(*a*) was limited in this way by definition, the Pre-Trial Chamber proceeded to define a 'case' for the purpose of Article 19 as a whole as involving 'proceedings that take place after the issuance of a warrant of arrest or a summons to appear',[102] a definition later confirmed by the Appeals Chamber in a different context.[103] Since, in the Pre-Trial Chamber's view, a case was not yet in existence, ad hoc counsel for the Defence lacked standing to raise an admissibility challenge under Article 19(2)(*a*).

An identically composed Pre-Trial Chamber I, however, when subsequently considering whether to issue warrants for the arrest of Thomas Lubanga Dyilo (*Lubanga*) and Bosco Ntaganda (*Ntaganda*) for their involvement in the situation in the DRC, relied on Pre-Trial Chamber II's sparse decision in *Kony and others* to conclude that an affirmative finding of admissibility was necessary before arrest warrants could be issued for the suspects.[104] The Chamber appeared to consider an assessment of admissibility a prerequisite for a determination under Article 58, but it relied ultimately on Article 19(1), under which the Pre-Trial Chamber 'may, on its own motion, determine the admissibility of a case'.[105] In short, contradicting the approach previously taken by it in response to the admissibility challenge by ad hoc

[101] ibid 4.

[102] ibid 4. For a clearer articulation of this position by the same Pre-Trial Chamber, see *Situation in the Democratic Republic of the Congo*, ICC-01/04-101-tEN-Corr, Pre-Trial Chamber I, Decision on the Applications for Participation in the Proceedings of VPRS 1, VPRS 2, VPRS 3, VPRS 4, VPRS 5, and VPRS 6, 17 January 2006, para 65.

[103] *Ruto and others*, Appeals Chamber Decision 2011 (n 98) para 39. Similarly, in 2019, when the Prosecutor invoked Article 19(3) to seek a ruling on the Court's jurisdiction over the alleged deportation of the Rohingya people from Myanmar to Bangladesh before initiating an investigation into the situation, Judge Perrin de Brichambaut partially dissented based on the inapplicability in his view of Article 19(3) before the commencement of a 'case' following proceedings under Article 58. *Situation in Bangladesh/Myanmar*, ICC-RoC46(3)-01/1-Anx-ENG, Pre-Trial Chamber I, Partially Dissenting Opinion of Judge Marc Perrin de Brichambaut, 6 September 2018, paras 5, 9–12. Nor was the majority convinced of the applicability during a preliminary examination of Article 19(3), relying instead on its inherent power to determine its jurisdiction as the basis for its decision. *Situation in Bangladesh/Myanmar*, ICC-RoC46(3)-01/18-37, Pre-Trial Chamber I, Decision on the 'Prosecution's Request for a Ruling on Jurisdiction under Article 19(3) of the Statute', 6 September 2018, para 33. More recently, however, in respect of the situation in Palestine, a differently composed Pre-Trial Chamber I held that Article 19(3) was applicable 'before a case emanates from a situation'. *Situation in Palestine*, ICC-01/18-143, Pre-Trial Chamber I, Decision on the 'Prosecution Request pursuant to Article 19(3) for a Ruling on the Court's Territorial Jurisdiction in Palestine', 5 February 2021, para 68. In addition to its inconsistency with the prior decision of the Appeals Chamber, the Pre-Trial Chamber's reliance on the text and context of Article 19(3) to support its position is unconvincing. The reference to a 'case' in the title to and in various clauses of Article 19 suggests that Article 19(3) must likewise be applicable to a 'case'. See ibid paras 69–86; Hall, Nsereko, and Ventura (n 96) 875, footnote 121.

[104] *Situation in the Democratic Republic of the Congo*, ICC-01/04-02/06-20-Anx2, Pre-Trial Chamber I, Decision on Prosecutor's Application for Warrants of Arrest, Article 58, 10 February 2006, para 18.

[105] ibid para 19. In the event, the Pre-Trial Chamber declared the case against Lubanga admissible and the case against Ntaganda inadmissible, the latter on the basis that it did not satisfy the threshold of sufficient gravity in Article 17(1)(*d*). Recall Chapter 2, Section 2.3.2.2.2.

140 GRAVITY AT THE INTERNATIONAL CRIMINAL COURT

counsel for the Defence, the Pre-Trial Chamber assessed admissibility on its own motion, under Article 19(1), even before a 'case', as per its own definition, existed.

When the Prosecutor appealed the Pre-Trial Chamber's finding of inadmissibility in *Ntaganda*, the Appeals Chamber examined in detail the Pre-Trial Chamber's decision to assess the admissibility of the 'case' in proceedings under Article 58(1) for the issue of a warrant for the suspect's arrest. The majority of the Appeals Chamber held, first, that a determination of admissibility was not required for the issuance of a warrant of arrest under Article 58.[106] To begin with, Article 58(1), which lists exhaustively the criteria for the Pre-Trial Chamber's decision, did not include any requirement that the case be admissible.[107] Nor was the Prosecutor obliged to supply the Pre-Trial Chamber with information relating to the admissibility of the case and, in the absence of any such information, any determination of admissibility by the Pre-Trial Chamber would be considerably more difficult and the proceedings likely prolonged.[108] Turning to whether an assessment of admissibility in proceedings under Article 58, while not required, was permitted, the Appeals Chamber disagreed with the Pre-Trial Chamber's exercise in the proceedings at issue of its discretion under Article 19(1) to assess the admissibility of the case on its own motion, since such an assessment before the issue of a warrant of arrest did not sufficiently account for the suspect's interests.[109] The Pre-Trial Chamber had considered that, had the case against Ntaganda been held admissible, the latter's interests would have been preserved through his opportunity to challenge the admissibility of the case at a later stage of the proceedings in his capacity as 'a person for whom a warrant of arrest or a summons to appear ha[d] been issued' under Article 19(2)(*a*). For the Appeals Chamber, however, this safeguard fell short of what was required, as any *ex parte* decision as to the admissibility of the case during proceedings under Article 58 would be detrimental to a suspect who was not yet before the Court.[110] Even if, as in *Ntaganda*, the Pre-Trial Chamber had found the case to be inadmissible, its decision could have been reversed on appeal, leaving the suspect at an even greater disadvantage when subsequently challenging

---

[106] Judge Pikis, in his partly dissenting opinion, agreed that 'the Pre-Trial Chamber [wa]s not under duty to satisfy itself *ab initio* that [the] case [wa]s admissible'. *Situation in the Democratic Republic of the Congo*, ICC-01/04-169, Appeals Chamber, Separate and Partly Dissenting Opinion of Judge Georghios M. Pikis, 13 July 2006 (hereafter '*Situation in the Democratic Republic of the Congo*, Pikis Partial Dissent 2006') paras 4–6.

[107] *Situation in the Democratic Republic of the Congo*, Appeals Chamber Decision 2006 (n 98) para 44.

[108] ibid para 45. Had the Pre-Trial Chamber declined to exercise its discretion to determine the admissibility of the case, moreover, its decision whether to issue the warrant of arrest would have been based on the more limited grounds provided in Article 58(1), the satisfaction of which would have led to the issuance of a warrant. ibid para 84.

[109] ibid para 48.

[110] ibid para 51. This was notwithstanding its broad view of Article 19(2)(*a*), which permitted an admissibility challenge 'even before the person is arrested and surrendered to the Court'. ibid para 51. The related question arises whether the participation of the suspect is permissible subsequent to the issuance of a warrant of arrest or a summons to appear under Article 58 but before the appearance before the Court of the suspect. In a series of subsequent decisions not pertaining to the assessment of gravity,

the admissibility of the case under Article 19(2)(a).[111] Nor could it be said that the Pre-Trial Chamber's use of Article 19(1) in proceedings under Article 58 was itself in order to protect the interests of the suspect, which were safeguarded specifically by way of Article 19(2)(a).[112] Accordingly, the Appeals Chamber restricted when the Pre-Trial Chamber may exercise during proceedings under Article 58 its discretion to determine the admissibility of a case under Article 19(1) to 'only when it is appropriate in the circumstances of the case, bearing in mind the interests of the suspect'.[113] Such circumstances could include 'where a case is based on the established jurisprudence of the Court, [on] uncontested facts that render a case clearly inadmissible or [on] an ostensible cause impelling the exercise of *proprio motu* review'.[114] Any determination of admissibility in such circumstances had to 'bear[] in mind the rights of other participants'.[115] The Appeals Chamber did not address, however, the extent to which these various exceptional considerations might justify the assessment specifically of gravity during proceedings under Article 58.[116]

Subsequently, the Pre-Trial Chambers have on occasion undertaken assessments of admissibility during proceedings under Article 58. In 2008, Pre-Trial Chamber III, tasked with determining whether to issue a warrant of arrest under Article 58 against Jean-Pierre Bemba Gombo (*Bemba*) for his alleged involvement in the first

---

the Pre-Trial Chambers went beyond the wording of Rule 58(3) of the RPE to permit the participation in admissibility proceedings of suspects whose appearance before the Court was prevented by a state's unwillingness to execute an outstanding arrest warrant or, where a suspect was already in the custody of a state, to surrender the suspect to the Court. See *Prosecutor v Gaddafi and Al-Senussi*, ICC-01/11-01/11-129, Pre-Trial Chamber I, Decision on OPCD Requests, 27 April 2012, paras 11–12; *Prosecutor v Gaddafi and Al-Senussi*, ICC-01/11-01/11-134, Pre-Trial Chamber I, Decision on the Conduct of Proceedings Following the 'Application on Behalf of the Government of Libya Pursuant to Article 19 of the Statute', 4 May 2012, para 11; *Prosecutor v Gaddafi and Al-Senussi*, ICC-01/11-01/11-325, Pre-Trial Chamber I, Decision on the Conduct of the Proceedings Following the 'Application on Behalf of the Government of Libya Relating to Abdullah Al-Senussi Pursuant to Article 19 of the ICC Statute', 26 April 2013, para 8; *Prosecutor v Simone Gbagbo*, ICC-02/11-01/12-15, Pre-Trial Chamber I, Decision on the Conduct of the Proceedings Following Côte d'Ivoire's Challenge to the Admissibility of the Case against Simone Gbagbo, 15 November 2013, para 8.

[111] *Situation in the Democratic Republic of the Congo*, Appeals Chamber Decision 2006 (n 98) para 50.
[112] ibid para 51.
[113] ibid para 52.
[114] ibid para 52. Judge Pikis, drawing attention to Rules 58 and 59 of the RPE, agreed on limiting the exercise of the Pre-Trial Chamber's discretion to assess admissibility under Article 19(1) 'by reference to such factors as in justice have a bearing on the decision', which to his mind included the participation of the suspect and of the referring entity and victims. *Situation in the Democratic Republic of the Congo*, Pikis Partial Dissent 2006 (n 106) para 6. In the absence of such factors there were 'strong grounds to refrain from ruling on admissibility'. ibid.
[115] *Situation in the Democratic Republic of the Congo*, Appeals Chamber Decision 2006 (n 98) para 52. In the event, owing to the *ex parte* nature of the proceedings, the Appeals Chamber restricted the right of the referring entity and of victims to submit observations under Article 19(3), concluding that 'even if this right is applicable it must out of necessity be restricted in its enforcement'. ibid para 30.
[116] Ultimately, owing to the confidential and *ex parte* nature of the proceedings, the Appeals Chamber declined to rule itself on admissibility and remanded the matter to the Pre-Trial Chamber for reconsideration. *Situation in the Democratic Republic of the Congo*, Appeals Chamber Decision 2006 (n 98) para 54. The Pre-Trial Chamber, obliging, chose not to address the admissibility of the case upon

142 GRAVITY AT THE INTERNATIONAL CRIMINAL COURT

situation in the CAR, chose first to address the admissibility of the case, presumably to determine whether it was being investigated by national authorities.[117] The Pre-Trial Chamber did not articulate, however, the legal basis on which it undertook this assessment, leaving it unclear whether it was relying on Article 19(1).[118]

In 2009, Pre-Trial Chamber II, proceeding under Article 19(1) in *Kony and others*, in which the arrest warrants of 2005 remained outstanding, determined the admissibility of the case, in particular whether it was being prosecuted at the

---

reconsideration, stating simply that 'none of the factors provided for in article 17 of the Statute [wa] s relevant, including the gravity threshold'. *Prosecutor v Ntaganda*, ICC-01/04-02/06-1-Red-tENG, Pre-Trial Chamber I, Decision on the Prosecution Application for a Warrant of Arrest, 6 March 2007, para 15. Its *ex parte* finding in favour of admissibility in *Lubanga*, which had not been subjected to Appeals Chamber review, was not similarly reconsidered. The Defence for Lubanga did appeal the Pre-Trial Chamber's decision affirming the admissibility of the case, but later discontinued the appeal. See *Situation in the Democratic Republic of the Congo*, ICC-01/04-01/06-57-Corr-tEN, Defence, Appeal by Duty Counsel for the Defence against Pre-Trial Chamber I's Decision of 10 February 2006 on the Prosecutor's Application for a Warrant of Arrest, Article 58, 24 March 2006; *Situation in the Democratic Republic of the Congo*, ICC-01/04-01/06-75-tEN, Defence, Brief Filed under Regulation 64 in Support of the Appeal of 27 March 2006, 10 April 2006, para 2.3.

[117] art 17(1)(*a*), Rome Statute; *Prosecutor v Bemba*, ICC-01/05-01/08-14-tENG, Pre-Trial Chamber III, Decision on the Prosecutor's Application for a Warrant of Arrest against Jean-Pierre Bemba Gombo, 10 June 2008 (hereafter '*Bemba*, Pre-Trial Chamber Decision 2008') para 21. See also Hall, Nsereko, and Ventura (n 96) 856–57. The Pre-Trial Chamber, making no mention of the gravity criterion, declared the case admissible. The proceedings that followed highlight the potential adverse consequences for the Defence of an affirmation of admissibility during proceedings under Article 58. In 2010, after Pre-Trial Chamber II had confirmed the charges under Article 61(7) of the Statute and the Trial Chamber had been constituted to hear the merits of the case, the Defence challenged, inter alia, the gravity of the case. Given that an admissibility challenge under Article 19(2)(*a*) must take place 'prior to or at the commencement of trial', the Trial Chamber was required first to determine whether, following the confirmation of the charges and the constitution of the Trial Chamber to hear the case, the admissibility challenge was permissible. The Trial Chamber considered that the 'natural and normal' meaning of Article 19(4) required that the trial commence only once 'the evidence in the case is called and counsel—by speeches, submissions, statements and questioning—address the merits of the [case]'. The Defence was thus entitled to its challenge. *Prosecutor v Bemba*, ICC-01/05-01/08-802, Trial Chamber III, Decision on the Admissibility and Abuse of Process Challenges, 24 June 2010, para 210. Despite elaborate Defence and Prosecution submissions on gravity, the Trial Chamber declined to apply the gravity criterion, assuming that Pre-Trial Chamber II had already done so when confirming the charges. *Prosecutor v Bemba*, ICC-01/05-01/08-802, Trial Chamber III, Decision on the Admissibility and Abuse of Process Challenges, 24 June 2010, para 249. Pre-Trial Chamber II, however, had not assessed the gravity of the case, having relied instead on Pre-Trial Chamber III's affirmation of admissibility in its decision issuing the warrant for Bemba's arrest. *Prosecutor v Bemba*, ICC-01/05-01/08-424, Pre-Trial Chamber II, Decision Pursuant to Article 61(7)(*a*) and (*b*) of the Rome Statute on the Charges of the Prosecutor against Jean-Pierre Bemba Gombo, 15 June 2009, para 25. As already noted, neither did that decision disclose the application, by Pre-Trial Chamber III, of the gravity criterion under Article 17(1)(*d*). As such, the Trial Chamber rejected the Defence's challenge to the gravity of the case under Article 19(2)(*a*) by relying on two earlier decisions in which neither Pre-Trial Chamber actually articulated its assessment as to the case's satisfaction of the gravity criterion.

[118] Indeed, the possibility cannot be excluded that the Pre-Trial Chamber invoked an inherent power to assess the admissibility of the case. Support for this characterization is offered by the Pre-Trial Chamber's statements on jurisdiction, in which context it claimed that 'irrespective of the terms of article 19(1) of the Statute, every international court has the power to determine its own jurisdiction, even when there is no explicit provision to that effect'. *Bemba*, Pre-Trial Chamber Decision 2008 (n 117) para 11. See also R Rastan, 'What Is a "Case" for the Purpose of the Rome Statute?' (2008) 19

DETERMINATION OF THE ADMISSIBILITY OF 'CASES' 143

national level, on its own motion.[119] Warrants of arrest having been issued for the suspects, the decision is not relevant to the question whether a judicial assessment of admissibility may be undertaken under Article 58. On an appeal of that decision by ad hoc counsel for the Defence, however, the Appeals Chamber nevertheless sought to clarify its earlier statements in *Ntaganda* on the permissibility of an assessment of admissibility under Article 19(1), including during proceedings under Article 58.[120] It suggested that it was only an assessment of gravity, and not of complementarity, which would be prejudicial to a suspect who could not participate in the proceedings. In the Appeals Chamber's view, this was because, unlike complementarity,

> a Chamber determines the gravity of a case only once in the course of the proceedings because the facts underlying the assessment of gravity are unlikely to change and a party may therefore be unable to raise the same issue again in future admissibility challenges.[121]

More recently, in 2018, Pre-Trial Chamber I again invoked Article 19(1) following the Prosecutor's request for the issuance of a warrant under Article 58 for the arrest of Al Hassan Ag Abdoul Aziz Ag Mohamed Ag Mahmoud (*Al Hassan*) in connection with the alleged commission of crimes against humanity and war crimes in Mali. Although the Pre-Trial Chamber's initiative was, as in previous cases, motivated by considerations of complementarity,[122] its assessment of admissibility included a consideration of the gravity of the case, leading to a finding of 'sufficient

---

Criminal Law Forum 435–48, footnote 21. Similarly, Pre-Trial Chamber II in *Kony and others* suggested that 'la compétence de la compétence' includes a 'binding determination on the admissibility of a given case'. *Prosecutor v Kony and others*, ICC-02/04-01/05-377, Pre-Trial Chamber II, Decision on the Admissibility of the Case under Article 19(1) of the Statute, 10 March 2009 (hereafter '*Kony and others*, Pre-Trial Chamber Decision 2009') paras 31, 45. It is questionable whether this is so, particularly since Article 19(1) expressly provides for the assessment of admissibility. Rastan, ibid footnote 21.

[119] *Prosecutor v Kony and others*, ICC-02/04-01/05-320, Pre-Trial Chamber II, Decision Initiating Proceedings under Article 19, Requesting Observations and Appointing Counsel for the Defence, 21 October 2008. The Pre-Trial Chamber declared the case admissible without addressing the question of gravity, which it held was not at issue. *Kony and others*, Pre-Trial Chamber Decision 2009 (n 118) para 36.

[120] Ad hoc counsel for the Defence had objected, inter alia, to the assessment of admissibility 'pending proper implementation of the defendants' rights to effectively participate in the proceedings' in accordance with the Appeals Chamber's guidance in *Ntaganda*. *Situation in Uganda*, ICC-02/04-01/05-379, Defence, Defence Appeal against 'Decision on the Admissibility of the Case under Article 19(1) of the Statute' dated 10 March 2009, 16 March 2009, para 31. Since the proceedings in *Kony and others* were not *ex parte* but public and ad hoc counsel had been appointed to represent the interests of the Defence, the Appeals Chamber found that there had been no prejudice to the suspects of the kind identified by the Appeals Chamber in *Ntaganda*. *Kony and others*, Appeals Chamber Decision 2009 (n 98) para 85.

[121] *Kony and others*, Appeals Chamber Decision 2009 (n 98) para 85. Since the gravity of the case was not at issue, the Appeals Chamber found no error in the Pre-Trial Chamber's exercise of its discretion to assess the admissibility of the case under Article 19(1).

[122] *Prosecutor v Al Hassan*, ICC-01/12-01/18-35-Red2-tENG, Pre-Trial Chamber I, Decision on the Prosecutor's Application for the Issuance of a Warrant of Arrest for Al Hassan Ag Abdoul Aziz Ag Mohamed Ag Mahmoud, 22 May 2018, para 23.

144 GRAVITY AT THE INTERNATIONAL CRIMINAL COURT

gravity' and ultimately of admissibility.[123] The Pre-Trial Chamber, upon a subsequent challenge by the Defence to the admissibility of the case under Article 19(2) (a),[124] confirmed its earlier findings.[125] On appeal by the Defence, the Appeals Chamber, in a decision of 2020,[126] did not review the Pre-Trial Chamber's earlier decision to assess the gravity of the case *ex parte* under Article 19(1) during proceedings under Article 58.

4.3.1.2.3 Recapitulation

In *Ntaganda*, the Appeals Chamber restricted the circumstances in which the Pre-Trial Chamber may exercise its discretion to undertake an assessment of admissibility under Article 19(1) during proceedings under Article 58 for the issuance of a warrant for the arrest of the suspect or a summons for the suspect to appear. Its justification for the restriction was the *ex parte* nature of the proceedings under Article 58, which excluded the participation of the suspect whose right subsequently to challenge the admissibility of the case under Article 19(2)(a) might be prejudiced by a prior determination as to its admissibility. According to the Appeals Chamber, any invocation of Article 19(1) by the Pre-Trial Chamber during proceedings under Article 58 must account for, among other things, the interest of the suspect in the question of admissibility and is permissible only in instances in which 'a case is based on the established jurisprudence of the Court, uncontested facts ... render a case clearly inadmissible or an ostensible cause impel[s] the exercise of *proprio motu* review'.[127] In *Kony and others*, the Appeals Chamber added that it is the *ex parte* assessment specifically of gravity, including during proceedings under Article 58, that may be prejudicial to a suspect who is not yet before the Court. In its view, 'the facts underlying the assessment of gravity [being] unlikely to change', the assessment is likely to take place only once, thereby limiting the ability of the Defence to 'raise the same issue again in future admissibility challenges'.[128]

4.3.2 Assessment of Admissibility under Article 19 of the Statute

4.3.2.1 Assessment of Admissibility during Proceedings under Article 58

The decision of the Appeals Chamber in *Ntaganda* goes some way towards clarifying the circumstances in which the Pre-Trial Chamber may assess the

---

[123] ibid para 38.

[124] *Situation in Mali*, ICC-01/12-01/18-394-Red, Defence, Public Redacted Version of 'Submissions for the Confirmation of Charges', 9 July 2019, para 258.

[125] See *Prosecutor v Al Hassan*, ICC-01/12-01/18-459-tENG, Pre-Trial Chamber I, Decision on the Admissibility Challenge Raised by the Defence for Insufficient Gravity of the Case, 27 September 2019, paras 49–58.

[126] See *Al Hassan*, Appeals Chamber Decision 2020 (n 98).

[127] *Situation in the Democratic Republic of the Congo*, Appeals Chamber Decision 2006 (n 98) para 52.

[128] *Kony and others*, Appeals Chamber Decision 2009 (n 98) para 85.

admissibility of a case during proceedings under Article 58 of the Statute. In neither its decision in *Ntaganda* nor its later dictum on gravity in *Kony and others*, however, did the Appeals Chamber articulate the circumstances in which the assessment specifically of gravity is permitted in *ex parte* or public proceedings under Article 58. Moreover, since both decisions relate to the assessment of admissibility at the initiative of the Pre-Trial Chamber under Article 19(1),[129] the question remains whether the assessment of admissibility, and thereby of gravity, in proceedings under Article 58 is permissible under any of the remaining admissibility procedures in Article 19, namely upon a challenge under Article 19(2)(*c*) by a state from which acceptance of jurisdiction is required or at the request of the Prosecutor under Article 19(3).[130]

Whether under Article 19(1), (2)(*c*), or (3), the conferral on the Pre-Trial Chamber of a wide discretion to assess the admissibility of a case in proceedings under Article 58 may be justified in broad terms by considerations of judicial economy. The state specified under Article 19(2)(*c*), the Prosecutor, the referring state party or the Security Council, and victims may also have an interest in an early finding as to the admissibility of a case. Conversely, as laid down by the Appeals Chamber in *Ntaganda*, the Pre-Trial Chamber's discretion under at least Article 19(1) to determine the admissibility of a case during proceedings under Article 58 is circumscribed by the countervailing consideration of the suspect's interest in the determination, which may be prejudiced by his or her absence from the proceedings. The permissibility of an assessment of the admissibility of a case, including its gravity, during proceedings under Article 58 rightly depends on the balancing of these various considerations.

4.3.2.1.1 *Judicial economy and related considerations*
As agreed during the various stages of the drafting of the Rome Statute, issues pertaining to the admissibility of a case should 'normally be dealt with as soon as possible'.[131] An early confirmation of admissibility promotes judicial economy[132] and is warranted to minimize resort to admissibility procedures 'for purposes of delay or destruction'.[133] The state party that referred the situation to the Court, or in relevant cases the Security Council, and victims may also be said to have an interest

---

[129] Recall also *Al Hassan*, Appeals Chamber Decision 2020 (n 98).

[130] The discussion excludes the consideration of Article 19(2)(*a*) and (*b*) since, as already noted, the text of the former provision logically excludes a challenge to the admissibility of a case during proceedings under Article 58 by '[a]n accused or a person for whom a warrant of arrest or a summons to appear has been issued', and the latter provision precludes a gravity-based challenge by a state having jurisdiction over the case.

[131] Rome Conference II (n 15) 214. See also Preparatory Committee Report 1996 (n 95) para 249; ILC Report 1994 (n 8) 53; M Abdou, 'Article 19' in M Klamberg (ed), *Commentary on the Law of the International Criminal Court* (Torkel Opsahl Academic EPublisher 2017) 226.

[132] C Stahn, 'Admissibility Challenges before the ICC: From Quasi-Primacy to Qualified Deference?' in C Stahn (ed), *The Law and Practice of the International Criminal Court* (OUP 2015) 246; Y Shany, *Questions of Jurisdiction and Admissibility before International Courts* (CUP 2015) 151.

[133] Rome Conference II (n 15) 214. See also Hall, Nsereko, and Ventura (n 96) 860.

146 GRAVITY AT THE INTERNATIONAL CRIMINAL COURT

in the early assessment of admissibility. In the words of one Pre-Trial Chamber, Article 19 is 'clearly aimed at avoiding challenges to admissibility needlessly hindering or delaying the proceedings'.[134] Considered alone, this might justify the conferral on the Pre-Trial Chamber of a broad discretion to assess admissibility, whether on its own motion under Article 19(1) or upon an application or request under Article 19(2)(c) or Article 19(3) respectively, even before the issuance of a warrant of arrest or a summons to appear. Indeed, Rule 58(2) of the Court's Rules of Procedure and Evidence grants the Pre-Trial Chamber the discretion to 'decide on the procedure to be followed' in any determination of admissibility under Article 19. A comparison of Article 19 with earlier drafts of the Rome Statute, however, which would have permitted assessments of admissibility 'at all stages of the proceedings', suggests that the Pre-Trial Chamber's discretion to undertake an assessment of admissibility is not without its limits.[135]

When it comes to the assessment of gravity, these purposes will be best served through the assessment of the gravity of a case sooner rather than later. Additionally, as noted by the Appeals Chamber in *Kony and others*, 'the facts underlying the assessment of gravity are unlikely to change', suggesting that an evolving factual situation is not a valid reason to delay the assessment of gravity.[136]

4.3.2.1.2 Interest of the suspect in the question of admissibility

Considerations of judicial economy and the like, which tend to support the assessment of admissibility during proceedings under Article 58, must be balanced against the suspect's interest in the assessment of admissibility, which, as the Appeals Chamber emphasized in *Ntaganda*, is at stake irrespective of the outcome of the assessment.[137] This interest is safeguarded primarily through the right of '[the] person for whom a warrant of arrest or a summons to appear has been issued' to challenge the admissibility of the case under Article 19(2)(a).[138] Where the suspect has not challenged the admissibility of the case under Article 19(2)(a), his or her interest in the outcome of any assessment of admissibility is acknowledged

---

[134] *Prosecutor v Katanga and Ngudjolo*, ICC-01/04-01/07-1213-tENG, Trial Chamber II, Reasons for the Oral Decision on the Motion Challenging the Admissibility of the Case (Article 19 of the Statute), 16 June 2009, para 44.

[135] See note 95.

[136] *Kony and others*, Appeals Chamber Decision 2009 (n 98) para 85.

[137] *Situation in the Democratic Republic of the Congo*, Appeals Chamber Decision 2006 (n 98) para 51. In support, see M El Zeidy, 'Some Remarks on the Question of the Admissibility of a Case during Arrest Warrant Proceedings before the International Criminal Court' (2006) 19 Leiden Journal of International Law 741, 749.

[138] The precise formulation of Article 19(2)(a) was the subject of debate at the Rome Conference. Delegations were divided over whether both an accused and a 'suspect' should be entitled to challenge admissibility, ultimately substituting for 'suspect' 'a person for whom a warrant of arrest or a summons to appear has been issued'. Rome Conference II (n 15) 213–21. See also Hall, Nsereko, and Ventura (n 96) 866. Article 19(2)(a) was construed by the Appeals Chamber in *Ntaganda* to permit a person for whom a warrant of arrest has been issued to challenge the admissibility of the case prior to his or her arrest and surrender to the Court. See note 110.

DETERMINATION OF THE ADMISSIBILITY OF 'CASES' 147

by way of a limited right of participation in admissibility proceedings initiated by others. Referring to a challenge to admissibility by a state under Article 19(2) (*b*) or (*c*) and to the seeking by the Prosecutor of a ruling on admissibility under Article 19(3), Rule 58(3) of the Rules of Procedure and Evidence obliges the Court to transmit a request or application for an assessment of admissibility 'to the person … who has been surrendered to the Court or who has appeared voluntarily or pursuant to a summons' and to 'allow [him or her] to submit written observations [on] the request or application.'[139]

Rule 58(3) does not guarantee a right of participation in respect of admissibility proceedings initiated before the suspect's surrender to or voluntary appearance or appearance pursuant to a summons before the Court. Although this suggests that the assessment of admissibility during proceedings under Article 58 cannot be excluded by the fact of the absence from the proceedings of the suspect, the Pre-Trial Chambers have not infrequently gone beyond the wording of Rule 58(3) to permit the participation in admissibility proceedings of a suspect whose arrest or appearance before the Court is contingent on the decision of a state in which or in whose custody he or she may be.[140] Some commentators go further in asserting a right for suspects to participate in the proceedings even beyond the ambit of Rule 58(3).[141] Not dissimilarly, although the participation of the suspect is likewise not guaranteed in proceedings initiated under Article 19(1) by the Pre-Trial Chamber on its own motion, the Appeals Chamber in *Ntaganda* asserted that the absence from the proceedings of the suspect was likely to prejudice his or her right subsequently to challenge the admissibility of the case:

> [I]f the Pre-Trial Chamber makes a determination that the case against a suspect is admissible without the suspect participating in the proceedings, and the suspect at a later stage seeks to challenge the admissibility of a case pursuant to article 19(2)(*a*) of the Statute, he or she comes before a Pre-Trial Chamber that has

---

[139] The distinction made in Rule 58(3) between a person 'who has been surrendered to the Court', which seems not to require that the person have appeared before the Court, and a person 'who has appeared voluntarily or pursuant to a summons', which requires, by definition, that the person have appeared before the Court, is of limited practical significance. That a person 'who has been surrendered to the Court' must also have appeared before it is implied by the parity of reasoning with a person 'who has appeared voluntarily or pursuant to a summons' and by the fact that a person 'who has been surrendered to the Court' appears before it in effect immediately. See Guariglia, 'Investigation and Prosecution' (n 56) 236.

[140] See note 110.

[141] For Hall, Nsereko, and Ventura, the exercise of the Pre-Trial Chambers' discretion to permit the participation in the proceedings of the suspect before his or her appearance before the Court offers insufficient protection of the suspect's interest in the determination of the admissibility of the case. In their view, 'both common sense and due process concerns' require the inclusion of a right to participate in admissibility proceedings before the suspect's appearance before the Court, without which the assessment of admissibility 'has the potential to lead to further breaches of procedural fairness'. Hall, Nsereko, and Ventura (n 96) 873.

148   GRAVITY AT THE INTERNATIONAL CRIMINAL COURT

already decided the very same issue to his or her detriment. A degree of predetermination is inevitable.[142]

As the Appeals Chamber observed in *Kony and others*, this is especially so with respect to the assessment of the gravity of a case, which need be assessed no more than once.

The concern raised by the Appeals Chamber for the interests of the suspect is not limited to the assessment of admissibility on the motion of the Pre-Trial Chamber under Article 19(1). It arguably extends also to the assessment of admissibility absent the participation of the suspect in proceedings initiated under Article 19(2)(*c*) and (3). The inability of the suspect to participate in the proceedings, noted by the Appeals Chamber, militates against the assessment of admissibility during proceedings under Article 58, whether under Article 19(1), (2)(*c*), or (3).

4.3.2.1.3 *The permissibility of the assessment of admissibility under Article 19(2)(c) and (3)*

In *Ntaganda*, the Appeals Chamber held that the Pre-Trial Chamber's power under Article 19(1) to assess the admissibility of a case on its own motion was qualified by the need to protect the suspect from being prejudiced by an assessment of

---

[142] *Situation in the Democratic Republic of the Congo*, Appeals Chamber Decision 2006 (n 98) para 51. In support, see El Zeidy, 'Some Remarks on the Question of the Admissibility of a Case' (n 137) 749. As explained by the Prosecutor, moreover, 'to permit admissibility proceedings, with participation of victims and referring entities, at the stage of issuance of an arrest warrant would produce absurd results. On the one hand, if victims and referring entities are permitted to submit observations, but the suspect is not, then this would seem a curious and unfair process wherein various observers are allowed to participate but the person most concerned is not. On the other hand, if the suspect is permitted to submit observations, then the ICC would have a very curious system wherein suspects are permitted to comment on their own arrest warrants before they are issued'. *Situation in the Democratic Republic of the Congo*, ICC-01/04-136, Office of the Prosecutor, Prosecutor's Supplementary Submissions in Compliance of the Appeals Chamber's 29 March 2006 'Order Pursuant to Regulation 28 of the Regulations of the Court for the Prosecutor to Respond to Questions', 5 April 2006, para 30. The right of the referring state party or the Security Council and victims to participate, provided for in the second sentence of Article 19(3), is itself open to question. On its face, the provision may be taken to suggest that their participation is predicated on a request by the Prosecutor, in accordance with the first sentence of Article 19(3), for a ruling on admissibility. The provision makes sufficiently clear, however, that the participation of the referring entity and of victims is not so limited, guaranteeing their participation broadly '[i]n proceedings with respect to jurisdiction or admissibility'. As one commentator notes, moreover, '[t]here is nothing in the Official Records of the Rome Conference to indicate that placement of the final sentence of paragraph 3 in such a way as to imply that it only applies to that paragraph was anything but inadvertent'. Schabas, *The International Criminal Court* (n 15) 493. Rule 59(3) of the RPE elaborates that the referring state party or the Security Council and victims may, upon notification, 'make representation in writing to the competent Chamber'. That the respective interests in the admissibility proceedings of the referring entity and of victims are not to be dispensed with lightly is supported by Judge Pikis' dictum in *Ntaganda* that 'the lack of amenity to hear the entities and persons specified in article 19(3) of the Statute … on the issue of admissibility may provide strong grounds to refrain from ruling on admissibility'. *Situation in the Democratic Republic of the Congo*, Pikis Partial Dissent 2006 (n 106) para 6. Similarly, the ILC considered in relation to draft article 36 of its 1994 draft statute for an international criminal court at least that 'the complainant State ha[s] the right to be heard' during an admissibility challenge. ILC Report 1994 (n 8) 52–53.

admissibility in his or her absence. It was insufficient protection, in the Appeals Chamber's view, that the suspect retained the right subsequently to challenge the admissibility of the case.[143] A prior assessment of admissibility would 'likely limit the scope' of any later challenge.[144] On this view, the balance between judicial economy and related considerations, on the one hand, and the interests of the suspect in the assessment of admissibility, on the other, is tilted in favour of the latter, limiting the circumstances in which admissibility may be assessed under Article 19(1) in the course of proceedings under Article 58. The question, however, is how this balance is to be struck in respect of the distinct procedures under Article 19(2)(c) and (3) respectively by which an assessment of admissibility can be triggered.

The procedure for challenging the admissibility of a case provided for in Article 19(2)(c) recognizes the interest in the question of admissibility of a state from which acceptance of jurisdiction is required. Yet although Article 19(2)(c) entitles such a state to challenge the admissibility of a case on grounds, including gravity, broader than those in Article 19(2)(b) on which a state having jurisdiction over a case may do the same,[145] the participation in admissibility proceedings of a state from which acceptance of jurisdiction is required is not guaranteed where the proceedings are initiated otherwise than under Article 19(2)(c). Neither is the Court obliged to notify a state entitled to challenge the admissibility of the case under Article 19(2)(c) of an assessment of admissibility triggered otherwise than in accordance with that provision. Both things indicate that the interest in the question of admissibility protected by Article 19(2)(c) is not indispensable.[146] Nor is the interest in admissibility of a state referred to in Article 19(2)(c) time-bound, so as to call specifically for the assessment of admissibility during proceedings under Article 58. All in all, it is doubtful whether this limited interest underlying the admissibility procedure in Article 19(2)(c) overrides the suspect's interest, recognized by the Appeals Chamber, in participating in the proceedings. In this light, the better position would be to restrict any assessment of admissibility initiated under Article 19(2)(c) in the course of proceedings under Article 58 to the exceptional circumstances outlined by the Appeals Chamber in *Ntaganda*, namely where 'a case is based on the established jurisprudence of the Court, uncontested facts ... render a case clearly inadmissible or an ostensible cause impel[s] the exercise of *proprio motu* review'.[147]

---

[143] *Situation in the Democratic Republic of the Congo*, Appeals Chamber Decision 2006 (n 98) para 51. See also El Zeidy, 'Some Remarks on the Question of the Admissibility of a Case' (n 137) 749.

[144] Hall, Nsereko, and Ventura (n 96) 875.

[145] Article 19(2)(c) is also broader than might have been the case had the suggestion during the drafting of the Rome Statute that it be limited to states parties only been accepted. See W Burke-White and S Kaplan, 'Shaping the Contours of Domestic Justice: The International Criminal Court and an Admissibility Challenge in the Uganda Situation' in C Stahn and G Sluiter (eds), *The Emerging Practice of the International Criminal Court* (Martinus Nijhoff 2009) 96–98; Schabas, *The International Criminal Court* (n 15) 486.

[146] Abdou (n 131) 227.

[147] *Situation in the Democratic Republic of the Congo*, Appeals Chamber Decision 2006 (n 98) para 52.

150 GRAVITY AT THE INTERNATIONAL CRIMINAL COURT

As for a request by the Prosecutor under Article 19(3) for a ruling on admissibility, Article 19(3) gives effect to the Prosecutor's evident interest in an affirmative finding of admissibility, without which he or she is prevented from proceeding with the prosecution of the case. The participation of the Prosecutor in admissibility proceedings initiated otherwise than under Article 19(3) is also guaranteed, since the judicial assessment of the admissibility of a case is based first and foremost on the information supplied by him or her.[148] The Prosecutor's interest in the assessment of admissibility specifically before the issuance of a warrant of arrest or a summons to appear for a suspect under Article 58, rather than at a later stage in the proceedings, is supported by his or her investment in the case of limited prosecutorial resources.[149] Although this is a compelling justification for the assessment of admissibility before the issuance of a warrant of arrest or a summons to appear, the Appeals Chamber's assertion in *Ntaganda* that the assessment of admissibility during proceedings under Article 58 'bear[] in mind the interests of the suspect'[150] arguably extends to the assessment of admissibility at the request of the Prosecutor under Article 19(3). Accordingly, any decision to assess the admissibility of a case during proceedings under Article 58 at the request of the Prosecutor must equally account for the suspect's interest in participating in the proceedings. As with the assessment of admissibility under Article 19(1) and (2)(*c*), the assessment of admissibility under Article 19(3) should be permitted during proceedings under Article 58 only if 'a case is based on the established jurisprudence of the Court, uncontested facts ... render a case clearly inadmissible or an ostensible cause impel[s] the exercise of *proprio motu* review'.[151]

4.3.2.2 Assessment of Gravity during Proceedings under Article 58

The question might be asked whether the Appeals Chamber's guidance in *Ntaganda*, applied not only to admissibility proceedings initiated by the Pre-Trial Chamber on its own motion under Article 19(1) but also to proceedings initiated in accordance with the procedures specified in Article 19(2)(*c*) and (3) respectively, justifies the assessment specifically of gravity under Article 19(1), (2)(*c*), or

---

[148] Rule 58(3), RPE. It is likely for this reason that Article 19(10) of the Rome Statute entitles the Prosecutor to request the Pre-Trial Chamber to review a finding of inadmissibility 'when he or she is fully satisfied that new facts have arisen which negate the basis on which the case had previously been found inadmissible under article 17'.

[149] *Situation in Bangladesh/Myanmar*, ICC-RoC46(3)-01/18-1, Office of the Prosecutor, Prosecution's Request for a Ruling on Jurisdiction under Article 19(3) of the Statute, 9 April 2018, para 54; Stahn, 'Judicial Review of Prosecutorial Discretion' (n 16) 257–58.

[150] *Situation in the Democratic Republic of the Congo*, Appeals Chamber Decision 2006 (n 98) para 52.

[151] ibid.

DETERMINATION OF THE ADMISSIBILITY OF 'CASES' 151

(3) in the course of proceedings under Article 58 for the issuance of a warrant of arrest or a summons to appear.[152]

As specifically regards the criterion of the gravity of the case embodied in Article 17(1)(d) of the Statute, there are a number of reasons to exclude its assessment by the Pre-Trial Chamber during proceedings under Article 58 for the issuance of a warrant of arrest or a summons to appear. To begin with, the Appeals Chamber's decision in *Ntaganda* suggests that the balance among the various relevant interests, including those of a state from which consent to jurisdiction is required and those of the Prosecutor, as safeguarded under Article 19(2)(c) and (3) respectively, weighs in favour of the suspect. The exclusion of an *ex parte* assessment of gravity in that decision was on the basis that it would 'seriously impair' the right of the suspect subsequently to bring an admissibility challenge, including as to the case's satisfaction of the gravity criterion.[153] The Appeals Chamber's later dictum on gravity in *Kony and others* lends further support to the view that the assessment specifically of gravity should not be undertaken without the participation in the proceedings of the suspect. The outcome of the gravity assessment being unlikely to change over the course of the proceedings, a suspect who seeks to challenge the gravity of a case is prejudiced by the prior assessment of gravity absent his or her participation in the proceedings.[154] As the Appeals Chamber noted in *Ntaganda*, '[a] degree of predetermination is inevitable'.[155]

Indeed, whether an assessment of the gravity of the case should be undertaken during proceedings under Article 58 even in circumstances in which, in the words of the Appeals Chamber in *Ntaganda*, 'a case is based on the established jurisprudence of the Court, uncontested facts ... render a case clearly inadmissible or an ostensible cause impel[s] the exercise of *proprio motu* review'[156] merits closer scrutiny. To begin with, that 'a case is based on the established jurisprudence of the Court' is not a compelling reason to undertake an assessment of gravity during proceedings under Article 58. The gravity of any

---

[152] Nothing in the Rome Statute obliges the Pre-Trial Chamber, when choosing to assess the admissibility of a case during proceedings under Article 58, to undertake the assessment of all the admissibility criteria specified in Article 17. On the contrary, it may be the case that the narrow set of circumstances identified by the Appeals Chamber in *Ntaganda* justifies the assessment of some admissibility criteria but not others during proceedings under Article 58. Such an approach is supported by the dictum of the Appeals Chamber in *Kony and others*, in which the Appeals Chamber suggested that the answer to the question of the permissibility of an assessment of admissibility, including during proceedings under Article 58, may differ in respect of the assessment of complementarity and gravity respectively.

[153] *Situation in the Democratic Republic of the Congo*, Appeals Chamber Decision 2006 (n 98) para 50.

[154] It is only the assessment of complementarity that is accurately described as an 'ongoing process throughout the pre-trial phase, the outcome of which is subject to review depending on the evolution of the relevant factual scenario'. *Kony and others*, Pre-Trial Chamber Decision 2009 (n 118) para 28. See also Hall, Nsereko, and Ventura (n 96) 857.

[155] *Situation in the Democratic Republic of the Congo*, Appeals Chamber Decision 2006 (n 98) para 52.

[156] ibid.

case is assessed on a case-by-case basis and involves the nuanced application to the specific facts of the case of relevant indicators of gravity.[157] The outcome of this assessment cannot be determined by algorithmic reference to the established jurisprudence of the Court. Nor, for that matter, is the Pre-Trial Chamber bound by the outcome of any assessment of gravity in a previous case. Similarly, the assessment of gravity *ex parte* or absent the participation in the proceedings of the suspect is hard to justify on the basis of 'uncontested facts' which 'render [the] case clearly admissible'. Again, the assessment of the gravity of a case involves the subtle, weighted application of the law to the facts. That those facts are 'uncontested' does not suffice to render the case 'clearly inadmissible', although this exceptional justification may carry weight where the application of none of the relevant indicators supports a finding of 'sufficient gravity'. Finally, while the assessment of gravity under Article 58 may in principle be warranted by an 'ostensible cause impelling the exercise of *proprio motu* review', it is difficult to conceive in practice of any such causes relevant specifically to gravity. On the contrary, as noted by the Appeals Chamber in *Kony and others*, the outcome of the Pre-Trial Chamber's gravity analysis is unlikely to change over the course of the proceedings, making a later assessment no different to this extent from an earlier one.[158] In sum, as specifically regards the gravity of the case as a criterion of admissibility, it is not evident that the factors identified by the Appeals Chamber in *Ntaganda* could ever outweigh the interest of the suspect in participating in the proceedings, even if the possibility cannot be excluded.

4.4 Conclusion

When it comes to the admissibility of a case, a distinction must be made between the assessment of admissibility in the context of the Prosecutor's decision whether to prosecute a case under Article 53(2), which the Pre-Trial Chamber may be called upon to review at the request of the referring state party or the Security Council under Article 53(3)(*a*), and the Pre-Trial or Trial Chamber's own determination as to the admissibility of the case in accordance with the procedures specified in Article 19(1)–(3). Different considerations are relevant to the assessment in each

---

[157] Recall Chapter 2, Section 2.4.

[158] The only exception to this position is the amendment of the charges by the Prosecutor under Article 61(4) of the Statute prior to the confirmation of the charges against the suspect, as a result of which the outcome of the gravity assessment may differ. See Cross (n 20) 232. This does not justify, however, the assessment of gravity during proceedings under Article 58.

context of admissibility, and thereby of gravity, by the Prosecutor and the Chamber respectively.

In the absence of sufficient case-law to date, the appropriate standard of judicial review under Article 53(3)(*a*) of the Rome Statute of the Prosecutor's assessment of the gravity of a case, which forms part of his or her assessment of the admissibility of the case under Article 53(2)(*b*), must be identified chiefly[159] by reference to the principled considerations that inform the balance under the Statute between prosecutorial discretion and prosecutorial accountability. These considerations, in particular the independent exercise by the Prosecutor of his or her investigative function and the considerable discretion whether to prosecute that is conferred on him or her, suggest the preferability of the Pre-Trial Chamber's application of a highly deferential 'abuse of discretion' standard when reviewing under Article 53(3)(*a*) the Prosecutor's assessment of the gravity of a case. Even more so than in the initiation of investigations, the limited intensity of Pre-Trial Chamber review under Article 53(3)(*a*) implies that the Prosecutor enjoys substantial discretion in the application of the gravity criterion in Article 17(1)(*d*) in the context of his or her decision whether to prosecute a case. The wide scope of the Prosecutor's discretion in the assessment of the gravity of a case in his or her decision whether to prosecute is further supported, in the context of an investigation initiated by the Prosecutor *proprio motu*, by the absence from the Rome Statute of a provision for judicial review comparable to Article 53(3)(*a*). Similar considerations are used to justify deference by national criminal courts, across the civil law and common law traditions, to prosecutorial decisions on case selection. Exclusive fact-finding capacity is also a common justification for judicial deference at other international courts.

When it comes to the Pre-Trial Chamber's or the Trial Chamber's assessment under Article 19(1)–(3) of the admissibility of a case, the assessment does not involve the review of any prior assessment of admissibility by the Prosecutor. In this context, the distinct question arises whether an assessment of gravity is permissible during proceedings under Article 58 for the issuance of a warrant of arrest or a summons to appear. The guidance provided by the Appeals Chamber in *Ntaganda* and the significance of the interest of the suspect in the question when compared to countervailing considerations lead to the conclusion that an assessment of gravity

---

[159] To the extent that the Appeals Chamber has pronounced on the role of the Pre-Trial Chamber under Article 53(3)(*a*) in respect of the Prosecutor's decision whether to initiate an investigation into a situation, its authoritative statements on the respective competences of the Prosecutor and the Pre-Trial Chamber must also obviously be considered.

under Article 19(1), (2)(*c*), or (3) is difficult to justify in proceedings under Article 58 in anything but the most exceptional of cases. Indeed, it is unlikely that the exceptional circumstances outlined by the Appeals Chamber in *Ntaganda* that might justify the assessment of the admissibility of a case during proceedings under Article 58 for the issuance of a warrant of arrest or a summons to appear could justify the assessment specifically of gravity.

5

The Function of the Gravity Criterion for Admissibility in Article 17(1)(*d*) of the Rome Statute

5.1 Introduction

This book has so far sought to clarify the application of the admissibility criterion of the sufficient gravity of a case in Article 17(1)(*d*) of the Rome Statute in the context of the Prosecutor's decisions whether to investigate and whether to prosecute. Having ascertained how the criterion of sufficient gravity has been applied in practice, it has suggested, where necessary, a more coherent application of the criterion in the selection of investigations and prosecutions by the Prosecutor. The analysis has included a clarification of the respective roles of the Prosecutor and the Pre-Trial Chamber in the assessment of gravity under relevant provisions. In addition, the book has sought to lend clarity to the application by the Pre-Trial Chamber or the Trial Chamber of the gravity criterion as part of the distinct determination of the admissibility of a case with which the Prosecutor has decided to proceed.

The answer to how to apply Article 17(1)(*d*) in the context of the Prosecutor's decisions whether to investigate and whether to prosecute bears in turn on the function of the gravity criterion in this context.[1] Against the backdrop of Chapters 2, 3, and 4, and with a view to the ongoing debates in practice and in the existing literature as to how to justify the selectivity of investigations and prosecutions at the Court, this chapter presents what it argues is ultimately the function of the gravity criterion in this context: the allocation of scarce investigative and prosecutorial resources. It concludes with a discussion of the implications of this function for the investigation and prosecution of international crimes at the International Criminal Court (ICC, the Court) and beyond.

Section 5.2 recapitulates the analysis undertaken in Chapters 2, 3, and 4 to support this chapter's overall argument for a recalibration of the application and ultimately a reconsideration of the function of the criterion of the sufficient gravity of a case in Article 17(1)(*d*) in the context of the Prosecutor's decisions whether to investigate and prosecute respectively. It recalls the relevant indicators of the gravity

---

[1] See Section 5.3.

Gravity at the International Criminal Court. Priya Urs, Oxford University Press. © Priya Urs 2024.
DOI: 10.1093/oso/9780198882954.003.0005

156 GRAVITY AT THE INTERNATIONAL CRIMINAL COURT

of a potential case or case and the argument for a subjective and discretionary assessment of sufficient gravity under Article 17(1)(*d*) of the Statute, whether by the Prosecutor or the Pre-Trial Chamber.[2] When it comes specifically to the assessment by the Prosecutor of sufficient gravity, it argues that a subjective and discretionary approach facilitates the judicious allocation of scarce investigative and prosecutorial resources. Section 5.2 also recounts the respective roles of the Prosecutor and the Pre-Trial Chamber in the application of the gravity criterion in the context of the decisions whether to initiate an investigation and whether to prosecute a case.[3] It shows how a wide discretion is conferred on the Prosecutor in making these decisions compared with the limited powers of judicial oversight conferred on the Pre-Trial Chamber.

Against this backdrop, Section 5.3 recalls the function of the gravity criterion articulated by the Appeals Chamber, namely the exclusion of 'marginal cases only',[4] and considers the recommendation of the Independent Expert Review of the International Criminal Court and the Rome Statute System (Independent Expert Review) in its report of 2020 that the Prosecutor apply a 'higher threshold' of sufficient gravity with a view to the allocation of scarce resources.[5] It also examines suggestions in the existing scholarship for the use of criteria other than the admissibility criterion of the sufficient gravity of a case in Article 17(1)(*d*) to facilitate the allocation of investigative and prosecutorial resources. As a contribution to the ongoing debate over how to justify the selectivity of investigations and prosecutions at the Court, Section 5.3 rejects the various suggestions advanced in the existing scholarship and, in common with the Independent Expert Review, reiterates that the wide discretion available to the Prosecutor in the application of the gravity criterion in the context of the decisions whether to investigate and prosecute respectively facilitates the allocation of scarce investigative and prosecutorial resources.[6] This calls for a recalibration of the Court's understanding of the function of the gravity criterion in the context of the Prosecutor's decisions whether to investigate and whether to prosecute. The function of the gravity criterion in this context is the allocation of resources.

Section 5.4 distils key recommendations for the practice of the ICC going forward and considers the potential utility of a comparable admissibility criterion of gravity or seriousness at other international or national criminal courts tasked

---

[2] Recall Chapter 2.

[3] Recall Chapters 3 and 4.

[4] *Prosecutor v Al Hassan*, ICC-01/12-01/18-601-Red, Appeals Chamber, Judgment on the Appeal of Mr Al Hassan Against the Decision of Pre-Trial Chamber I Entitled 'Décision relative a l'exception d'irrecevabilité pour insufficiance de gravité de l'affaire soulevée par la défense', 19 February 2020 (hereafter '*Al Hassan*, Appeals Chamber Decision 2020') para 53.

[5] Final Report of the Independent Expert Review of the International Criminal Court and the Rome Statute System, 30 September 2020 (hereafter 'Independent Expert Review') para R227. See further ibid paras 647, 650.

[6] Recall Chapter 2, Section 2.4.2.

with the investigation and prosecution of international crimes. It compares the use of such a criterion with other devices for the division of the tasks of investigation and prosecution, namely the restriction of the jurisdiction *ratione materiae* of international criminal courts and the use of case referral procedures between international criminal courts and national criminal courts or between ordinary and specialized criminal courts at the national level.

5.2 The Application of the Gravity Criterion in Article 17(1)(*d*) of the Rome Statute and the Initiation of Investigations and Prosecutions

5.2.1 The Appropriate Indicators of Gravity and the Subjective Nature of the Gravity Assessment under Article 17(1)(*d*)

When it comes to the Prosecutor's decisions whether to investigate and whether to prosecute, the Pre-Trial Chambers and the Appeals Chamber have in principle considered relevant to the open-textured criterion of the sufficient gravity of a case in Article 17(1)(*d*) of the Rome Statute the four indicators articulated by the Office of the Prosecutor, namely scale, nature, manner of commission, and impact of the alleged crimes.[7] With respect to the initiation of investigations specifically, the Pre-Trial Chambers have also required the additional consideration, as a fifth indicator of gravity, of whether the situation under consideration implicates the person or persons who bear the greatest responsibility for the alleged crimes.[8] The inconsistency in the application in practice of these various indicators raises the question of their suitability to the assessment of gravity. Closer scrutiny of each indicator suggests that only the scale, manner of commission, and impact of the alleged crimes are relevant indicators of gravity, whether in relation to a situation or a case.[9] Conversely, the nature of the alleged crimes and any requirement that a potential case or case implicate the person or persons bearing greatest responsibility for the alleged crimes are irrelevant to the assessment of gravity under Article 17(1)(*d*), although they may be considered as a matter of prosecutorial prioritization.[10]

The subjective application of the qualitative indicators of the manner of commission and impact of the alleged crimes, and their balancing alongside the quantitative indicator of the scale of the alleged crimes, call for the exercise of discretion. This discretionary application of the indicators suggests that the assessment of gravity in respect of both a situation[11] and a

---

[7] Recall Chapter 2, Sections 2.3.1.2 and 2.3.2.2.

[8] Recall Chapter 2, Section 2.3.1.2.2.5.

[9] Recall Chapter 2, Section 2.4.1.

[10] Recall Chapter 2, Sections 2.4.1.2 and 2.4.1.5.

[11] *Situation on the Registered Vessels of the Union of the Comoros, the Hellenic Republic and the Kingdom of Cambodia*, ICC/01/13-98, Appeals Chamber, Judgment on the Appeal of the Prosecutor

case[12] is in turn a subjective and discretionary endeavour. In the specific context of the Prosecutor's decisions whether to investigate and whether to prosecute, the subjective application and weighing of the relevant indicators of gravity facilitate the allocation by the Prosecutor of investigative and prosecutorial resources. That is, the Prosecutor's application of the gravity criterion to compare the situation or case before him or her with others that might also draw on available resources reflects his or her choices as to the allocation of those resources. Not only is a subjective and discretionary assessment of gravity a necessary consequence of the multi-factored assessment of gravity endorsed by the Appeals Chamber,[13] it is also preferable, for several reasons, to an objective assessment of gravity.[14] In particular, it is warranted by the necessary selectivity of investigations and prosecutions in the face of scarce investigative and prosecutorial resources.

When undertaken in good faith, the application of the indicators of scale, manner of commission, and impact of the alleged crimes restricts the otherwise unlimited discretion in the application of the open-textured criterion of the sufficient gravity of a case specified in Article 17(1)(*d*). This lends greater consistency and predictability to the application of the provision, whether by the Prosecutor or the Pre-Trial Chamber.[15] In the specific context of the Prosecutor's decisions whether to investigate and whether to prosecute, this application also provides a legal basis on which to justify the Prosecutor's decisions, and serves ultimately as a legal justification for selective investigations and prosecutions at the Court.

That the Prosecutor enjoys wide discretion in the application of the gravity criterion for admissibility under Article 17(1)(*d*) of the Statute is reinforced by the assessment of the relationship between the Prosecutor and the Pre-Trial Chamber in the context of the decisions whether to investigate and to prosecute.

5.2.2 Prosecutorial Discretion and Pre-Trial Chamber Review during the Initiation of Investigations

A prosecutorial decision whether to initiate an investigation into a situation, under Article 53(1) alone or by additional reference to Article 15(3), is reviewable by the Pre-Trial Chamber under Articles 53(3)(*a*) and 15(4) respectively of the Rome Statute. Review under each provision is intended to discipline the exercise of the

---

against Pre-Trial Chamber I's 'Decision on the "Application for Judicial Review by the Government of the Union of the Comoros"', 2 September 2019 (hereafter '*Situation on the Registered Vessels of the Union of the Comoros, the Hellenic Republic and the Kingdom of Cambodia*, Appeals Chamber Decision 2019') para 81.

[12] *Al Hassan*, Appeals Chamber Decision 2020 (n 4) para 53.
[13] Recall Chapter 2, Section 2.4.2.1.
[14] Recall Chapter 2, Section 2.4.2.2.
[15] ibid.

Prosecutor's discretion in assessing whether there is a reasonable basis to proceed with an investigation, including in the assessment of admissibility and thereby of gravity. The limited powers of judicial review conferred on the Pre-Trial Chamber under Articles 53(3)(*a*) and 15(4) respectively and arguments supporting a highly deferential standard of review in each context, namely for abuse of discretion only, militate in favour of due acknowledgement of the wide discretion enjoyed by the Prosecutor in the application of the gravity criterion in the context of his or her decision whether to initiate an investigation into a situation. The justifications for judicial deference to discretionary decision-makers by other international courts, such as those addressing international human rights law, international investment law, and international trade law, also support the case for wide discretion in this context.

The review under Article 53(3)(*a*) of a prosecutorial decision not to initiate an investigation into a situation owing to the inadmissibility in the Prosecutor's opinion of one or more potential cases arising out of the situation gives effect to the interest of the referring state party or the United Nations Security Council in the initiation of an investigation into the situation referred by it. Compared with the limited interest of the referring state or the Council, prosecutorial discretion in the initiation of investigations is crucial in preserving the independence of the Prosecutor's decisions whether to investigate. Discretion is also justified by the necessary selectivity, owing to limited resources, of investigations. The balancing of these and other relevant considerations weighs in favour of prosecutorial discretion in the initiation of investigations,[16] which suggests the appropriateness of review only for abuse of discretion under Article 53(3)(*a*).[17] When it comes to the assessment of gravity, this requires the Pre-Trial Chamber to determine whether the Prosecutor failed to consider information that might have supported a finding of sufficient gravity,[18] omitted to account for relevant indicators of gravity, or arrived at the decision not to proceed with an investigation on the basis of politically motivated or other extraneous considerations,[19] such as bad faith or impropriety.[20]

Pre-Trial Chamber review under Article 15(4) of a decision by the Prosecutor that there exists a reasonable basis to proceed with the investigation *proprio motu* of a situation, including a finding as to the admissibility of one or more potential cases arising out of the situation, is intended to prevent the Prosecutor from

---

[16] Recall Chapter 3, Section 3.3.

[17] Recall Chapter 3, Section 3.3.3.

[18] *Situation on the Registered Vessels of the Union of the Comoros, the Hellenic Republic and the Kingdom of Cambodia*, Appeals Chamber Decision 2019 (n 11) para 80.

[19] HK Woolf and others, *De Smith's Judicial Review* (8th edn, Sweet and Maxwell 2019) para 11.019. See also MS Davis, 'Standards of Review: Judicial Review of Discretionary Decisionmaking' (2000) 2(1) Journal of Appellate Practice and Process 47, 54–55.

[20] M Fordham, *Judicial Review Handbook* (6th edn, Hart Publishing 2012) 491.

160 GRAVITY AT THE INTERNATIONAL CRIMINAL COURT

proceeding with 'unwarranted, frivolous, or politically motivated investigations'[21] and to prevent the abuse of his or her discretion in the initiation of investigations *proprio motu*.[22] When balanced against the need to preserve the independence of the Prosecutor in choosing to initiate an investigation *proprio motu*, the fulfilment of these objectives warrants review only for abuse of discretion.[23] This highly deferential standard of review is equally supported by the limited competence of the Pre-Trial Chamber to review the Prosecutor's assessment against a more demanding standard. When it comes to the Prosecutor's assessment of gravity, contrary to the view of the Appeals Chamber, which excludes any review of admissibility, the better view is that the task of the Pre-Trial Chamber under Article 15(4) is to consider whether the Prosecutor has abused his or her discretion by failing to account for information which might have supported a finding of insufficient gravity, by excluding the consideration of relevant indicators of gravity, or by arriving at a decision to proceed on the basis of politically motivated or other extraneous considerations,[24] including bad faith or improper motives.[25]

5.2.3 Prosecutorial Discretion and Pre-Trial Chamber Review during the Initiation of Prosecutions

As for the initiation of prosecutions, it is only a decision by the Prosecutor not to prosecute even a single case arising out of a situation that is reviewable by the Pre-Trial Chamber under Article 53(3)(*a*),[26] at the request of the state party or the Security Council that referred the situation to the Court. The interest of the referring state or the Council in the prosecution of one or more cases arising out of the situation, compared with the Rome Statute's guarantee of an independent investigation,[27] suggests the conferral on the Prosecutor considerable discretion in choosing which cases, if any, to prosecute.[28] Indeed, the Prosecutor is not obliged to prosecute every admissible case.[29] As in the initiation of investigations, prosecutorial discretion in the initiation of prosecutions is also necessitated by the limited

---

[21] *Situation in Bangladesh/Myanmar*, ICC-01/19-27, Pre-Trial Chamber III, Decision Pursuant to Article 15 of the Rome Statute on the Authorisation of an Investigation into the Situation in the People's Republic of Bangladesh/Republic of the Union of Myanmar, 14 November 2019, para 127.

[22] *Situation in Georgia*, ICC-01/15-12, Pre-Trial Chamber I, Decision on the Prosecutor's Request for Authorization of an Investigation, 27 January 2016, para 3; *Situation in Burundi*, ICC-01/17-9-Red, Pre-Trial Chamber III, Public Redacted Version of 'Decision Pursuant to Article 15 of the Rome Statute on the Authorization of an Investigation into the Situation in the Republic of Burundi', 9 November 2017, para 28.

[23] Recall Chapter 3, Section 3.3.3.

[24] Woolf and others (n 19) para 11.019. See also Davis (n 19) 54–55.

[25] Fordham (n 20) 491.

[26] Recall Chapter 4, Section 4.2.1.1.

[27] See art 42(1), Rome Statute of the International Criminal Court 1998 (Rome Statute).

[28] Recall Chapter 4, Section 4.2.2.

[29] See art 53(2), Rome Statute.

resources available to the Prosecutor, which call for selective prosecution.[30] When it comes to a prosecutorial decision not to prosecute any case arising out of a situation, the balancing of these and other relevant considerations supports review for abuse of discretion only under Article 53(3)(a).[31] As for the Prosecutor's assessment of the gravity of one or more cases, the 'abuse of discretion' standard would allow the Pre-Trial Chamber to assess whether the Prosecutor omitted to consider relevant indicators of gravity,[32] failed to account for information that may be relevant to the assessment of gravity,[33] or arrived at the decision on the basis of extraneous considerations,[34] including bad faith or improper motives.[35] Even more so than in the context of the initiation of an investigation, the limited power of the Pre-Trial Chamber to review only a prosecutorial decision not to prosecute any cases arising out of a situation ensures a wide discretion for the Prosecutor in the application of the gravity criterion in the context of his or her decision whether to prosecute a case. This is not only consistent with the deferential approaches to discretionary decision-makers by international courts but also supported by the discretion conferred on prosecutors across the common law and civil law traditions.

In contrast with what is required of it in its review under Article 53(3)(a) of the Prosecutor's application of the gravity criterion in deciding to prosecute no cases at all, in its determination of the admissibility of a case in accordance with the procedures specified in Article 19(1)–(3) the Pre-Trial Chamber or, exceptionally, the Trial Chamber is required itself to apply the gravity criterion. Unlike the Prosecutor, whose mandate is the management of prosecutorial resources, the Pre-Trial or Trial Chamber is not required to examine the allocative implications of the assessment of gravity.[36] Instead, the question in this context is whether an assessment by the relevant Chamber of the admissibility of a case, including an assessment of gravity, is permissible during proceedings for the issuance of a warrant of arrest or a summons to appear under Article 58.[37] The Appeals Chamber's guidance in *Ntaganda* and a comparison of the interest of the suspect with countervailing considerations lead to the conclusion that an assessment of gravity under

[30] Recall Chapter 4, Section 4.2.2.1.
[31] Recall Chapter 4, Section 4.2.2.3.
[32] *Situation on the Registered Vessels of the Union of the Comoros, the Hellenic Republic and the Kingdom of Cambodia*, Appeals Chamber Decision 2019 (n 11) para 81.
[33] ibid. The same logically applies to review of the Prosecutor's assessment of whether there is a sufficient basis for a prosecution under Article 53(2).
[34] Woolf and others (n 19) para 11.019; Davis (n 19) 54–55.
[35] Fordham (n 20) 491; R Rastan, 'Comment on Victor's Justice and Ex Ante Standards' (2010) 43 John Marshall Law Review 569, 589; AM Danner, 'Enhancing the Legitimacy and Accountability of Prosecutorial Discretion at the International Criminal Court' (2003) 97 American Journal of International Law 510, 521; S Schill and R Briese, '"If the State Considers": Self-Judging Clauses in International Dispute Settlement' (2009) 13 Max Planck Yearbook of United Nations Law 61, 128–33.
[36] Recall Chapter 2, Section 2.4.2.2.
[37] Recall Chapter 4, Section 4.3.

162   GRAVITY AT THE INTERNATIONAL CRIMINAL COURT

the relevant subclauses of Article 19 is justifiable only in the most exceptional of circumstances.[38]

5.3 The Function of the Gravity Criterion in Article 17(1)(*d*) of the Rome Statute and the Initiation of Investigations and Prosecutions

What remains to be seen is how these various clarifications as to the application of the criterion of the sufficient gravity of a case in Article 17(1)(*d*), in the context of the Prosecutor's decisions whether to investigate and whether to prosecute, implicate the function of the gravity criterion in this context. According to the Appeals Chamber in *Al Hassan*, the purpose of the gravity criterion is, in all contexts, the exclusion of cases 'of marginal gravity only'.[39] In contrast, the Independent Expert Review, noting the limited resources at the disposal of the Prosecutor, recommended the application by the Prosecutor of 'a higher threshold for the gravity of the crimes alleged to have been perpetrated' in the context of his or her decisions whether to investigate and whether to prosecute.[40] As the Independent Expert Review seems to suggest, the subjective and discretionary application of the gravity criterion in the context of the Prosecutor's decisions whether to investigate and prosecute respectively facilitates the allocation of investigative and prosecutorial resources.[41] This calls for a reconsideration in this context of what the Appeals Chamber has considered to be the purpose of the gravity criterion, namely the exclusion of only marginal cases from investigation and prosecution at the Court. In contrast, no allocative function is performed by the assessment of gravity by the Pre-Trial or Trial Chamber as part of its determination of the admissibility of a case with which the Prosecutor wishes to proceed.

The following discussion affirms that the purpose of the gravity criterion, when applied in the context of the Prosecutor's decisions whether to investigate and prosecute respectively, is the allocation of investigative and prosecutorial resources. It does so by examining the recommendation of the Independent Expert Review and alternative proposals in the existing scholarship as to how to address the problem of the selectivity of investigations and prosecutions at the Court. None of the suggestions advanced in the existing scholarship is found to be persuasive. In the end, the analysis of the application of the gravity criterion in the context of the Prosecutor's decisions whether to investigate and prosecute respectively suggests

---

[38] Recall Chapter 4, Section 4.3.2.2.
[39] *Al Hassan*, Appeals Chamber Decision 2020 (n 4) para 53.
[40] Independent Expert Review (n 5) para R227. See also ibid paras 647, 650.
[41] Recall Chapter 2, Section 2.4.2.2.

5.3.1 The Independent Expert Review

The Independent Expert Review, established by the ICC Assembly of States Parties, noted in its report of 2020 the Prosecutor's inability to initiate investigations into all situations in which there may be a reasonable basis to proceed or to prosecute all cases in respect of which there may be a sufficient basis for a prosecution.[42] Observing that 'the current situation is unsustainable having regard to the limited resources available',[43] the report suggested the application of 'a higher threshold for the gravity of the crimes alleged to have been perpetrated' as part of the Prosecutor's decision whether to initiate an investigation into a situation.[44] The Independent Expert Review justified its approach by reference to the considerable discretion enjoyed by the Prosecutor in the assessment of gravity,[45] a discretion which should in its view be exercised with a view to initiating fewer investigations.[46] On the face of it, the application of this 'higher threshold' of gravity seems to call for an objective approach to the assessment of gravity.[47] It is unclear, however, whether the allocation of scarce resources, noted by the Independent Expert Review, necessarily requires the application under Article 17(1)(*d*) of a 'higher [objective] threshold' of gravity, which would call for the mechanistic application of quantifiable indicators of gravity requiring constant revision in light of fluctuating resources. Instead, in accordance with a subjective approach to the assessment of gravity, endorsed by the Appeals Chamber, the recommendation of the Independent Expert Review is better understood as leaving to the discretion of the Prosecutor the subjective assessment of gravity in accordance with available resources. Indeed, the Independent Expert Review itself noted the wide discretion available to the Prosecutor in the assessment of gravity. In times of resource scarcity, this might call for the application by the Prosecutor of a 'higher threshold' of gravity so called. The subjective assessment by the Prosecutor of gravity, coupled with limited Pre-Trial Chamber review under relevant provisions, facilitates the allocation by the Prosecutor of scarce resources even without any 'higher [objective] threshold' of gravity.

---

[42] Independent Expert Review (n 5) paras 642–43.
[43] ibid para 646.
[44] ibid para R227.
[45] ibid paras 649, 660–61.
[46] ibid para 644. Similarly, the report suggested the application of this 'higher gravity' criterion as part of the Prosecutor's decision whether to initiate a preliminary examination into a situation. ibid para 650.
[47] Recall Chapter 2, Section 2.4.2.1.

164   GRAVITY AT THE INTERNATIONAL CRIMINAL COURT

When it came to the initiation of prosecutions, gravity was identified by the Independent Expert Review as the criterion 'of highest importance',[48] the practical application of which was likewise criticized 'for being set at too low a threshold'.[49] Ultimately, however, owing to the considerable discretion enjoyed by the Prosecutor in the initiation of prosecutions, the report did not consider that the Prosecutor's approach to the assessment of the gravity of a case required reconsideration.[50]

Underpinning the recommendation of the Independent Expert Review is the view that the purpose of the gravity criterion in Article 17(1)(d), when applied in the context of the Prosecutor's decisions whether to investigate and prosecute respectively, is not merely the exclusion of marginal cases from investigation and prosecution at the Court. It is the allocation of scarce resources to some situations and cases and not others.

5.3.2 The Existing Scholarship

In contrast with the recommendation of the Independent Expert Review, other attempts to justify the selectivity of investigations and prosecutions at the Court have all rejected the proposition that the allocation of scarce resources is facilitated by the application in the context of the Prosecutor's decisions whether to investigate and whether to prosecute of the criterion of the sufficient gravity of a case in Article 17(1)(d). Commentators have preferred a more limited role for the gravity criterion in this context, akin to that articulated by the Appeals Chamber in *Al Hassan*.[51] They instead suggest that the allocation of investigative and prosecutorial resources, which commentators all acknowledge as being a necessary part of the Prosecutor's decisions whether to investigate and prosecute respectively, is or must be situated elsewhere.

5.3.2.1 A Policy Criterion of 'Relative Gravity'
Some commentators propose facilitating the allocation of limited resources during the initiation of investigations and prosecutions through a 'dual-use of gravity'.[52]

---

[48]   Independent Expert Review (n 5) para R230.

[49]   ibid para 663.

[50]   Rather, it was the Prosecutor's focus on prosecuting 'the person or persons who appear to be the most responsible' that required reconsideration. See Reg 34(1), Regulations of the Office of the Prosecutor 2009. On the Prosecutor's wide discretion in the initiation of prosecutions, recall Chapter 4, Section 4.2.2.1.

[51]   *Al Hassan*, Appeals Chamber Decision 2020 (n 4) para 53.

[52]   A Pues, 'Discretion and the Gravity of Situations at the International Criminal Court' (2017) 17 International Criminal Law Review 960, 982. The proposal has been affirmed by the ICC in its 'overall response' to the report of the Independent Expert Review. See Overall Response of the International Criminal Court to the 'Independent Expert Review of the International Criminal Court and the Rome Statute System—Final Report': Preliminary Analysis of the Recommendations and Information

The first such use is the application by the Prosecutor of the admissibility criterion of sufficient gravity in Article 17(1)(*d*), presumably to exclude only marginal cases in accordance with the approach of the Appeals Chamber in *Al Hassan*.[53] The second use, meant to facilitate resource allocation, is the application by the Prosecutor of a policy criterion of 'relative gravity' as the basis for selecting 'among the pool of admissible cases'.[54] The Office of the Prosecutor has also drawn such a distinction in relation to the decision whether to prosecute, although not in relation to the prior decision whether to investigate.[55] By excluding resource considerations from the assessment of admissibility, one commentator suggests, this approach prioritizes consistency in the application of Article 17(1)(*d*).[56] Others likewise support the application by the Prosecutor of Article 17(1)(*d*) to exclude only marginal cases, thereby minimizing in their view any allocative effects of the assessment of sufficient gravity, but on grounds similar to those raised by the Appeals Chamber in *Ntaganda*, namely that potential cases or cases rendered inadmissible owing to resource considerations will effectively restrict the Court's jurisdiction *ratione materiae* and reduce its ability to deter.[57] The application by the Prosecutor of the additional policy criterion of 'relative gravity', it is argued, avoids these consequences and allows the Prosecutor to allocate resources based on what commentators propose should be a clear articulation of his or her priorities.[58]

5.3.2.2 The Interests of Justice

Another suggestion is that resource allocation be facilitated through the application by the Prosecutor of the 'interests of justice' criterion under Article 53(1)(*c*) and (2)(*c*) of the Rome Statute.[59] For some, this requires, as part of the Prosecutor's

---

on Relevant Activities undertaken by the Court, 14 April 2021 (hereafter 'Overall Response to the Independent Expert Review') para 411.

[53] *Al Hassan*, Appeals Chamber Decision 2020 (n 4) para 53.

[54] Pues (n 52) 982. See also MM deGuzman, 'Gravity and the Legitimacy of the International Criminal Court' (2008) 32(5) Fordham International Law Journal 1400, 1432–35; MM deGuzman, *Shocking the Conscience of Humanity: Gravity and the Legitimacy of International Criminal Law* (OUP 2020) 131–34; S SáCouto and K Cleary, 'The Gravity Threshold of the International Criminal Court' (2007) 23(5) American University International Law Review 807, 813–14; I Stegmiller, 'The Gravity Threshold under the ICC Statute: Gravity Back and Forth in *Lubanga* and *Ntaganda*' (2009) 9 International Criminal Law Review 547, 557.

[55] In its 2016 Policy Paper on Case Selection and Prioritisation, the Office of the Prosecutor distinguished '[g]ravity of crime(s) as a case selection criterion' and 'gravity as a factor for admissibility'. Policy Paper on Case Selection and Prioritisation, Office of the Prosecutor, 2016, para 36.

[56] Pues (n 52) 983.

[57] For deGuzman, '[a] substantial gravity threshold would threaten the legitimacy of international criminal law by limiting its ability to accomplish its central goal of crime prevention'. deGuzman, *Shocking the Conscience of Humanity* (n 54) 120. See further deGuzman, 'Gravity and the Legitimacy of the International Criminal Court' (n 54) 1433; Stegmiller (n 54) 557.

[58] deGuzman, *Shocking the Conscience of Humanity* (n 54) 131–32.

[59] P Webb, 'The ICC Prosecutor's Discretion Not to Proceed in the "Interests of Justice"' (2005) 50 Criminal Law Quarterly 305, 340–42; C Davis, 'Political Considerations in Prosecutorial Discretion at the International Criminal Court' (2015) 15 International Criminal Law Review 170, 182; deGuzman, *Shocking the Conscience of Humanity* (n 54) 136; G Turone, 'Powers and Duties of the Prosecutor' in A

166 GRAVITY AT THE INTERNATIONAL CRIMINAL COURT

assessment of the interests of justice, the selection of 'the gravest situations from among admissible situations'.[60] Put differently, it has been argued that the assessment of the interests of justice under Article 53(1)(c) and (2)(c) allows the Prosecutor the discretion to decline to initiate investigations and prosecutions in order to 'privilege the prosecution of major cases and to discourage the prosecution of minor cases'.[61] Others qualify this suggestion by proposing that resource considerations 'should be a criterion in assessing the "interests of justice"' but should not be 'a decisive criterion'.[62]

5.3.3 Rejecting the Approaches in the Existing Scholarship

The various suggestions as to how to address the Prosecutor's resource constraints in the initiation of investigations and prosecutions, all of which exclude the facilitation of resource allocation through the application of the admissibility criterion of the sufficient gravity of a case under Article 17(1)(d), are unconvincing or offer only partial solutions. In the end, it is the wide discretion associated with the Prosecutor's assessment of the sufficient gravity of a case under Article 17(1)(d) in the context of his or her decisions whether to investigate and prosecute respectively that best facilitates the allocation of investigative and prosecutorial resources.

5.3.3.1 A Policy Criterion of 'Relative Gravity'
To begin with, the allocation of limited resources through the application of an additional policy criterion of 'relative gravity' is contingent on the availability of such an additional discretion under the Rome Statute. When it comes to the initiation of investigations, however, Article 53(1), the provision governing the initiation of investigations generally,[63] obliges the Prosecutor to initiate an investigation into

Cassese, P Gaeta, and JRWD Jones (eds), *The Rome Statute of the International Criminal Court* (OUP 2002) 1174.

[60] deGuzman, *Shocking the Conscience of Humanity* (n 54) 136. See also MM deGuzman and WA Schabas, 'Initiation of Investigations and Selection of Cases' in S Zappalà and others (eds), *International Criminal Procedure: Principles and Rules* (OUP 2013) 146.

[61] Turone (n 59) 1174.

[62] Webb (n 59) 342.

[63] Conversely, deGuzman draws a distinction between the initiation of investigations on referral, which is governed by Article 53(1), and the initiation of investigations *proprio motu*, which she considers to be governed not by Article 53(1) but by Article 15(3). Recognizing that Article 53(1) obliges the Prosecutor to initiate an investigation where there is a reasonable basis to proceed, deGuzman concedes that the proposed policy criterion of 'relative gravity' would only be applicable in the exercise of the Prosecutor's discretion whether to initiate an investigation *proprio motu*, under Article 15(3). This offers only a partial solution to the problem of the allocation of scarce resources, and one that prioritizes investigations on referral over investigations initiated *proprio motu*. deGuzman, 'Gravity and the Legitimacy of the International Criminal Court' (n 54) 1430–31; deGuzman and Schabas (n 60) 143–44. See also Overall Response to the Independent Expert Review (n 52) para 412. With respect, deGuzman's approach is also based on an inaccurate characterization of the relationship between Article 53(1) and Article 15(3). The Prosecutor's decision whether to initiate an investigation into a situation *proprio motu*

every situation in respect of which he or she has concluded that there is a reasonable basis to proceed. That is, once the requirements of Article 53(1)(*a*)–(*c*) are met, the Prosecutor is not permitted any additional discretion to decline to investigate, whether through the consideration of 'relative gravity' or on any other basis. There is thus no foundation in Article 53(1) or indeed elsewhere in the Statute on which to justify the exercise by the Prosecutor of the additional discretion to decline to initiate an investigation into a situation through the application of a policy criterion of 'relative gravity'. The Prosecutor's choices as to the allocation of resources must be reflected in the application of one or more of the criteria specified in Article 53(1)(*a*)–(*c*), namely jurisdictional and admissibility requirements, including gravity, and the interests of justice.

Conversely, when it comes to the initiation of prosecutions, the Prosecutor enjoys considerable discretion to decline to prosecute a case. Under Article 53(2), the Prosecutor is not obliged to undertake the prosecution of every case in respect of which he or she has concluded that there is a 'sufficient basis for a prosecution'.[64] Whether as part of the assessment of gravity under Article 53(2)(*b*) or through the application of an additional policy criterion of 'relative gravity', the Prosecutor's selection of cases reflects his or her choices as to the allocation of investigative and prosecutorial resources.[65] In this light, in the context of the initiation of prosecutions, the distinction commentators seek to draw between the admissibility assessment of gravity and the additional policy assessment of 'relative gravity' is ultimately inconsequential.

Next, proposing an additional policy criterion of 'relative gravity' in order to ensure consistency in the application of the gravity criterion for admissibility prioritizes consistency in the application of Article 17(1)(*d*) over consistency in the Prosecutor's ultimate decisions whether to investigate and whether to prosecute, to which the consideration of resource constraints in any event contributes. Accordingly, even if such an approach reduces the Prosecutor's discretion, and therefore potential inconsistencies, in the application of Article 17(1)(*d*), it does not guarantee any greater consistency in the overall decisions whether to investigate and whether to prosecute. In fact, transparency in the allocation of limited resources would be better ensured through the application of the admissibility criterion of gravity specified in Article 17(1)(*d*), which is subject to judicial review,

---

is not taken under Article 15(3) but under Article 53(1). Under Article 15(3), the existence of a 'reasonable basis to proceed' is only a condition precedent to the Prosecutor's request for Pre-Trial Chamber authorization ('If the Prosecutor concludes that there is a reasonable basis to proceed ...'). The point is clarified in Rule 48 of the Rules of Procedure and Evidence (RPE), which specifies that the Prosecutor must, when assessing the existence or not of a reasonable basis to proceed with an investigation *proprio motu*, apply the criteria laid down in Article 53(1)(*a*)–(*c*). Recall Chapter 3, Section 3.2.2.1.

[64] Recall Chapter 4, Section 4.2.1.1.
[65] This is also why the Independent Expert Review did not ultimately consider the Prosecutor's assessment of the gravity of a case as requiring revision.

168   GRAVITY AT THE INTERNATIONAL CRIMINAL COURT

than through leaving it to the vagaries of prosecutorial prioritization.[66] The inconsistency with which commentators are concerned is also unlikely to be reduced by the use of the policy criterion of 'relative gravity', the application of which, unlike that of Article 17(1)(*d*), is not subject to judicial review.

Lastly, that the facilitation of resource allocation through the application of Article 17(1)(*d*) effectively restricts the Court's jurisdiction *ratione materiae* and its ability to deter is a valid contention only if Article 17(1)(*d*) is understood as calling for an objective assessment of gravity. When Article 17(1)(*d*) is conceived, however, as it has been by the Appeals Chamber, as calling for a subjective assessment of gravity,[67] the characterization of a potential case or case as insufficiently grave does not have the effect of narrowing the Court's jurisdiction *ratione materiae* or its deterrent effect. A subjective approach to the assessment of gravity does not require that a situation or case be as serious as any which has already been investigated or prosecuted. The assessment of gravity is not binding as a matter of law. In accordance with a subjective approach to the assessment of gravity, the facilitation of the allocation of limited resources through the application of Article 17(1)(*d*) restricts neither the Court's jurisdiction *ratione materiae* nor its ability to deter in the future.

5.3.3.2 The Interests of Justice

Nor is it clear that the allocation of investigative and prosecutorial resources is facilitated through the assessment of the interests of justice. Even assuming a wider understanding of the interests of justice than that currently adopted by the Office of the Prosecutor,[68] it is not at all evident how the assessment of the interests of justice, which is not tailored to the performance of an allocative function but is instead a countervailing consideration, might facilitate the allocation of scarce resources. As one commentator concedes, '[t]his is admittedly not the most intuitive reading' of the criterion.[69] Perhaps it is in acknowledgement of this concern that others propose subsuming the admissibility assessment of sufficient gravity within the assessment of the interests of justice. That position, which elides the distinct criteria of admissibility and the interests of justice in the context of the Prosecutor's decisions whether to investigate and whether to prosecute, is unpersuasive, since Article 53 clearly outlines different procedures for Pre-Trial Chamber review of the Prosecutor's assessments of admissibility and the interests of justice respectively.[70]

---

[66] Webb (n 59) 312.

[67] Recall Chapter 2, Section 2.4.2.1.

[68] See generally Policy Paper on Interests of Justice, Office of the Prosecutor, 2007; Policy Paper on Preliminary Examinations, Office of the Prosecutor, 2013, para 69; Policy Paper on Case Selection and Prioritisation, Office of the Prosecutor, 2016, para 33. For a wider reading of the interests of justice, see eg Webb (n 59); T de Souza Dias, ' "Interests of Justice": Defining the Scope of Prosecutorial Discretion in Article 53(1)(c) and (2)(c) of the Rome Statute of the International Criminal Court' (2017) 30 Leiden Journal of International Law 731; Davis (n 59).

[69] deGuzman, *Shocking the Conscience of Humanity* (n 54) 136.

[70] Recall the distinction drawn in Chapter 1, Section 1.5.2.

That a prosecutorial decision not to proceed with an investigation or prosecution in the interests of justice, reviewable by the Pre-Trial Chamber on its own initiative, is in the event of such a review effective only 'if confirmed by the Pre-Trial Chamber'[71] also tends to exclude the allocation of resources through the assessment of the interests of justice. Were the notion of the interests of justice to be used this way, it would ultimately be the Pre-Trial Chamber which would determine the allocation of investigative and prosecutorial resources, thereby infringing on their independent management by the Office of the Prosecutor guaranteed under Article 42 of the Statute.

In the end, there is little disagreement that the Prosecutor's decisions whether to investigate and whether to prosecute are allocative in nature. It is through the exercise of prosecutorial discretion in making these decisions that selective investigation and prosecution may be justified. Among the various criteria the Prosecutor is required to apply in the context of his or her respective decisions whether to investigate and to prosecute,[72] it is the admissibility criterion of the sufficient gravity of a case in Article 17(1)(d) whose application involves the exercise of the discretion best suited to facilitate the allocation of scarce investigative and prosecutorial resources.[73] At the same time, the mandatory application by the Prosecutor to potential cases and cases of the admissibility criterion of gravity provides a consistent criterion for resource allocation, bringing greater consistency to the decisions whether to investigate and prosecute respectively.

---

[71] art 53(3)(b), Rome Statute.

[72] When it comes to the initiation of investigations under Article 53(1), the application of Article 53(1)(a), which addresses the satisfaction of jurisdictional requirements, is non-discretionary, since it requires 'a rational and objective assessment'. Turone (n 59) 1152. Likewise, the application of the principle of complementarity as part of the assessment of admissibility under Article 53(1)(b) does not admit of the kind of discretion necessary to justify the allocation of investigative and prosecutorial resources. This leaves only the 'fully discretionary' assessment of gravity under Article 53(1)(b). ibid. See also F Mégret, 'Three Dangers for the International Criminal Court: A Critical Look at a Consensual Project' (2001) 12 Finnish Yearbook of International Law 193, 213; Pues (n 52) 962. The facilitation of resource allocation through the application of the 'interests of justice' criterion in Article 53(1)(c) is also unconvincing. Recall Section 5.3.3.2. As with the Prosecutor's decision whether to initiate an investigation under Article 53(1), when it comes to the Prosecutor's decision whether to initiate a prosecution, under Article 53(2), it is only the application of the gravity criterion as part of the assessment of admissibility under Article 53(2)(b) that admits of the kind of discretion necessary to allocate investigative and prosecutorial resources. As with Article 53(1)(a), the satisfaction of the jurisdictional requirements in Article 53(2)(a) is a non-discretionary exercise. Turone (n 59) 1172–73. Likewise, the application of the principle of complementarity under Article 53(2)(b) is non-discretionary. ibid 1173. As under Article 53(1)(c), the facilitation of resource allocation through the application of the 'interests of justice' criterion under Article 53(2)(c) is also to be excluded. Recall again Section 5.3.3.2.

[73] For Danner, owing to its 'primary focus on the crimes committed', gravity also 'afford[s] the surest foundation for impartial prosecutorial decision making'. Danner (n 35) 544.

5.4 Recommendations for Practice

5.4.1 At the ICC

The application to date of the admissibility criterion of the sufficient gravity of a case in Article 17(1)(*d*) of the Rome Statute has, generally speaking, been characterized by inconsistency. This is true not only in the context of the Prosecutor's respective decisions whether to investigate and to prosecute but also in the context of the Pre-Trial Chamber's assessment of gravity as part of the determination of the admissibility of a case with which the Prosecutor has chosen to proceed. On the basis of this assessment of the relevant practice, and with a particular view to a more coherent application of Article 17(1)(*d*) in the context of the Prosecutor's decisions whether to investigate and prosecute respectively, several proposals for reform might be advanced.

First, the subjective and discretionary nature of the gravity assessment under Article 17(1)(*d*) of the Statute, which in the context of the Prosecutor's respective decisions whether to investigate and to prosecute facilitates the allocation of investigative and prosecutorial resources, necessitates the recalibration in this context of what has so far been considered to be the function of the gravity criterion. The function of the Prosecutor's assessment of gravity in this context is not merely the exclusion of marginal cases, as has been suggested by the Appeals Chamber in *Al Hassan*. It is the allocation of scarce resources and, ultimately, a justification in legal terms for the selectivity of investigations and prosecutions at the ICC. Accepting this role for the gravity criterion in Article 17(1)(*d*) will assist the Prosecutor and indeed the Court in deflecting criticisms of inconsistency, bias, or politicization in the decisions whether to investigate and to prosecute respectively. This use of the gravity criterion is neither to endorse impunity nor to say that cases of insufficient gravity are not deserving of investigation and prosecution; such cases may be investigated or prosecuted elsewhere.

In practical terms, the allocation of resources through the use of Article 17(1)(*d*) contributes to ongoing discussions around the effective use of the budget of the Office of the Prosecutor—part of an overarching narrative of efficiency at the Court.[74] Within the ICC, the Prosecutor has 'full authority over the management and administration of the Office', including independence in the use of the prosecutorial budget.[75] Yet the constraints of a limited budget suggest that even where

---

[74] See R Clements, *Governing International Criminal Justice: Managerial Practices and the International Criminal Court* (doctoral thesis, University of Cambridge, 2019) 112–58. On the sometimes misplaced focus on efficiency at the Court, see R Clements, 'From Bureaucracy to Management: The International Criminal Court's Internal Progress Narrative' (2019) 21 Leiden Journal of International Law 149.

[75] art 42(2), Rome Statute. See also J O'Donohue, 'Towards a Fully Functional International Criminal Court: The Adoption of the 2004 Budget' (2004) 17 Leiden Journal of International Law 579, 586–89; J O'Donohue, 'The 2005 Budget of the International Criminal Court: Contingency, Insufficient Funding

investigations or prosecutions have formally commenced, the Prosecutor is unable to 'immediately and fully start' these activities, requiring 'a reasonable degree of prioritization' that may imply 'an insufficient response to the demand'.[76] The Proposed Programme Budget for 2023 of the ICC, for example, declares that 'the [Office of the Prosecutor] does not presently benefit from sufficient resources in order to effectively discharge its mandate with respect to the range of situations in relation to which it is currently engaged'.[77] The allocative use of the gravity criterion when deciding whether to investigate and whether to prosecute, which is logically prior to prioritization and other measures of efficiency during any eventual investigation or prosecution, also plays a role in the management of a limited budget. At that point, the Prosecutor must assess 'sufficient gravity' by comparing the situation or case before him or her with others that might also draw on his or her limited resources.[78] Should more substantial funds be allocated to the Prosecutor in years to come, the need for selectivity in the tasks of investigation and prosecution may be reduced.

Second, the examination of the various indicators considered relevant to the assessment of gravity by the Office of the Prosecutor and the Chambers of the Court leads to the conclusion that only the indicators of scale, manner of commission, and impact of the alleged crimes are relevant to the assessment of gravity, whether in the Prosecutor's decisions on the initiation of investigations and prosecutions respectively or in the determination by the Pre-Trial Chamber or the Trial Chamber of the admissibility of a case.[79] These indicators must be applied consistently to potential cases or cases, maintaining both the distinction between a situation and a case and the distinction between jurisdiction *ratione materiae* and admissibility. Although the application of these indicators supports a subjective and discretionary assessment of gravity, clarity as to the relevant indicators of gravity and the exclusion of irrelevant considerations promotes consistency and predictability in the application of Article 17(1)(*d*), whether by the Prosecutor or the relevant Chamber.

Third, the clarification of the respective roles of the Prosecutor and the Pre-Trial Chamber in the decisions whether to investigate and whether to prosecute suggests a broad discretion on the part of the Prosecutor in the assessment of gravity under Article 17(1)(*d*) in each of these contexts and a much more limited role for the Pre-Trial Chamber. Any answer to how to apply the gravity criterion in Article

in Key Areas and the Recurring Question of the Independence of the Prosecutor' (2005) 18 Leiden Journal of International Law 591, 594–95.

[76] Report of the Court on the Basic Size of the Office of the Prosecutor, 17 September 2015, ICC-ASP/14/21, para 11.

[77] Proposed Programme Budget for 2023, 30 September 2022, ICC-ASP/21/INF.2/Rev.1, para 22.

[78] Recall Chapter 2, Section 2.4.2.2.

[79] Recall Chapter 2, Section 2.4.1.

172 GRAVITY AT THE INTERNATIONAL CRIMINAL COURT

17(1)(*d*) in the context of the Prosecutor's decisions whether to investigate and prosecute respectively must account for this breadth of the Prosecutor's discretion in making these decisions. The mere fact of the exercise of this discretion does not imply, however, that the application by the Prosecutor of the gravity criterion is necessarily arbitrary or constitutes an abuse of discretion. In their oversight of prosecutorial discretion, the Pre-Trial Chambers must account for the discretionary nature of the assessment.

Fourth, in the light of the respective roles of the Prosecutor and the Pre-Trial Chamber in the initiation of investigations and prosecutions, the most suitable standard of judicial review of the Prosecutor's application of the gravity criterion under the various provisions is a highly deferential one.[80] For different reasons in each context, the balancing of relevant considerations suggests that the Pre-Trial Chamber ought to review a prosecutorial decision not to initiate an investigation into a situation or not to prosecute a case, under Article 53(3)(*a*), as well as a prosecutorial decision to proceed with an investigation into a situation *proprio motu*, under Article 15(4), against an 'abuse of discretion' standard.[81] The limited intensity of Pre-Trial Chamber review in each context would reflect the importance of the considerable discretion afforded the Prosecutor, compared with competing considerations, including the interest of the referring state party or the Security Council, where relevant, and the desire for prosecutorial accountability. In each context, a limited review for abuse of discretion is equally supported by the limited competence of the Pre-Trial Chamber to review the decision of the Prosecutor against a more demanding standard of review. The view is consistent with the practice of international courts vis-à-vis discretionary decision-makers and the deference accorded to prosecutors across the common law and civil law traditions.

As a final ancillary point, the Rome Statute and its supporting instruments do not specifically provide for victims' representation during the initiation of investigations and prosecutions. Yet victims are undoubtedly at the core of the Prosecutor's assessments of gravity and any representations made by them to the Prosecutor must inevitably contribute to any eventual decision whether to investigate and whether to prosecute. A Pre-Trial Chamber reviewing the Prosecutor's assessment of gravity, whether in relation to a situation or a case, may also permit the participation in the proceedings of victims when determining whether there has been an abuse of the Prosecutor's discretion.[82]

---

[80] Recall Chapter 3, Section 3.3.3 and Chapter 4, Section 4.2.2.3.

[81] As explained in Chapter 3, Section 3.2.2.1, this is not to endorse the Appeals Chamber's exclusion, based on a dubious reading of the Rome Statute, of any Pre-Trial Chamber review whatsoever of the Prosecutor's assessment of admissibility in the context of a situation under Article 15(4).

[82] When it comes to the initiation of an investigation *proprio motu*, Article 15(3) of the Statute and Rule 50(3) of the RPE provide that victims who have been informed by the Prosecutor of the request for authorization to initiate an investigation into the situation may make written representations to the Pre-Trial Chamber. There is no corresponding obligation on the Chamber to examine these representations, if any, but the Chamber may, under Rule 50(4), request additional information from any victims making representations. Although not explicitly provided for in the context of Article 53(3)(*a*), the Pre-Trial

5.4.2 At Other International and National Criminal Courts

The ICC is neither the first nor the only court with jurisdiction over international crimes to use considerations of gravity or seriousness to allocate investigative and prosecutorial resources. Other international and national criminal courts have used or use varying notions of gravity to allocate the task of investigation and prosecution between international and national criminal courts or, at the national level, between ordinary and specialized criminal courts. This allocative function may be performed in more ways than one.

First, like the ICC, international criminal courts such as the International Criminal Tribunal for the former Yugoslavia (ICTY) and the International Criminal Tribunal for Rwanda (ICTR) used gravity to restrict their respective jurisdictions *ratione materiae*.[83] The implication is that not every international crime is to be prosecuted by the relevant international criminal court, leaving less grave crimes to be prosecuted elsewhere, likely before relevant national criminal courts. So also, at the national level, gravity has been used to restrict the jurisdictions *ratione materiae* of specialized criminal courts, like the Kosovo Specialist Chambers,[84] and special panels in ordinary criminal courts, as with the District Court of Dili in East Timor.[85]

In addition to the restriction of the jurisdiction *ratione materiae* of an international or a national criminal court, gravity may be used in other ways to effectively divide the tasks of investigation and prosecution. In some contexts, gravity has been a criterion for the referral of cases to other courts. Such a referral procedure was included in the completion strategy of the ICTY, which provided for the referral of cases to relevant national jurisdictions on the basis of 'the gravity of

Chamber may, in accordance with Rules 89(1) and 92(2) of the RPE, permit victims to participate in its review of a prosecutorial decision not to initiate an investigation or not to prosecute a case. Victims do not have a right to participate in the investigation of a situation. See *Situation in the Democratic Republic of the Congo*, ICC-01/04-556, Appeals Chamber, Judgment on Victim Participation in the Investigation Stage of the Proceedings in the Appeal of the OPCD against the Decision of Pre-Trial Chamber I of 7 December 2007 and in the Appeals of the OPCD and the Prosecutor against the Decision of Pre-Trial Chamber I of 24 December 2007, 19 December 2008, para 52.

[83] See art 1, Statute of the International Criminal Tribunal for the former Yugoslavia 1993; art 1, Statute of the International Criminal Tribunal for Rwanda 1994; art 1(1), Statute of the Special Court for Sierra Leone 2002; art 5, Rome Statute.

[84] The jurisdiction *ratione materiae* of the Kosovo Specialist Chambers includes crimes against humanity, war crimes, and 'other crimes under Kosovo law'. See arts 13–15, Law No 05/L-053 on Specialist Chambers and Specialist Prosecutor's Office (3 August 2015).

[85] The special panels in the District Court of Dili in East Timor had exclusive jurisdiction over 'serious criminal offences', which were defined to include genocide, war crimes, crimes against humanity, murder, sexual offences, and torture. In contrast, the Commission for Reception, Truth and Reconciliation in East Timor was responsible for the reintegration of individuals responsible for 'the commission of minor criminal offences and other harmful acts'. Section 3(1)(*h*), UNTAET Regulation No 2001/10 (13 July 2001).

174 GRAVITY AT THE INTERNATIONAL CRIMINAL COURT

the crimes charged'.[86] Conversely, in the case of the ICTR, a national criminal court was required to defer a case to it if '[t]he seriousness of the offences' warranted it.[87] Similar procedures were put in place at the Kosovo Specialist Chambers[88] and the special panels in the District Court of Dili,[89] although without explicit reference to gravity or seriousness.

Gravity as a criterion for admissibility in Article 17(1)(*d*) of the Rome Statute stands apart from both limits on jurisdiction *ratione materiae* and the use of referral procedures, neither of which is likely to constitute a sufficient mechanism for filtering cases. The wide discretion available to the Prosecutor in the application of Article 17(1)(*d*), which is supported by both the open-textured nature of the provision[90] and the institutional balance between the Prosecutor and the Pre-Trial Chambers of the Court, suggests a role for gravity in justifying highly selective investigations and prosecutions. These considerations may support the use of an admissibility criterion of gravity at other international or national criminal courts with jurisdiction over international crimes where—due to fears of case overload or underfunding or, in the case of international criminal courts, out of deference to national jurisdictions—investigations and prosecutions are intended to be highly selective. That said, an international criminal court or a specialized criminal court at the national level whose jurisdiction is geographically and perhaps also temporally restricted to one situation, or which is otherwise limited to certain crimes or cases, may not face the same need for discrimination in investigations and prosecutions, calling for necessary adjustments in the application by their respective prosecutors of relevant indicators of gravity. The assessment of gravity as part of the decisions whether to investigate and whether to prosecute at such courts may also depend on whether ordinary criminal courts at the national level have jurisdiction over the conduct.

---

[86] Rule 11bis(C), Rules of Procedure and Evidence of the International Criminal Tribunal for the former Yugoslavia 1994 (as amended in 2009).

[87] Rule 9(ii)(*a*), Rules of Procedure and Evidence of the International Criminal Tribunal for Rwanda 1995 (as amended in 1997).

[88] The Chamber has the power to 'order the transfer of proceedings within its jurisdiction from any other prosecutor or any other court in the territory of Kosovo'. art 10(2), Law No 05/L-053 on Specialist Chambers and Specialist Prosecutor's Office (3 August 2015).

[89] Like the Specialist Chambers in Kosovo, the special panels in the District Court of Dili enjoyed the power to require other panels or courts in East Timor to defer to them in the prosecution of a case. Section 1, UNTAET Regulation No 2000/15 (6 June 2000). The Commission for Reception, Truth and Reconciliation in East Timor could also refer 'matters of serious criminal offences' to 'the appropriate authority', presumably the special panels. Section 38(1), UNTAET Regulation No 2001/10 (13 July 2001).

[90] Recall Chapter 1, Section 1.2.

5.5 Conclusion

Looking back on twenty years of the ICC's practice, there is no doubt now, if there ever was any, that the investigation and prosecution of international crimes at the Court are highly selective exercises. Not only is the selectivity of investigations and prosecutions incorporated into relevant provisions of the Rome Statute but it is also supported by the consideration of the limited resources, mainly in the form of state party contributions, made available to the Court and therefore the Prosecutor.[91] With a view to the management both of resources and of expectations amongst various quarters of the Court, due regard for this selectivity calls for more cautious characterization of the Court's role in ensuring that 'the most serious crimes of concern to the international community as a whole must not go unpunished'.[92] The role of the ICC in meeting this objective and, indeed, various underlying objectives—amongst others, retribution, deterrence, and the protection of the interests of victims—is much more limited than the Rome Statute's preambular language suggests.

In the end, the relevant legal question in this context is how best to justify, consistently with the Rome Statute and its supporting instruments, the selection of situations and cases by a Prosecutor faced with limited resources and under constant public scrutiny. In the absence of statutory guidance, the doctrinal assessment of the application and function of the gravity criterion for admissibility in Article 17(1)(d) in this book reveals extensive support for the conclusion that the discretionary application of this open-textured criterion facilitates the allocation of scarce resources, and that it does so more convincingly than other criteria relevant to the decisions whether to investigate and whether to prosecute. Along the way, the book has also clarified, often in the face of highly inconsistent practice and at times questionable legal reasoning, the respective roles of the Prosecutor and the Pre-Trial Chambers and Trial Chambers in the initiation of investigations and prosecutions. These various clarifications may serve as guidance in ensuring greater consistency in the decisions whether to investigate and whether to prosecute international crimes at other international and national criminal courts. They may also indicate how a comparable criterion of gravity may be used as a device to divide the tasks of investigation and prosecution amongst other international or national criminal courts.

Viewed through the widest lens, the book contributes to the rich scholarship in public international law on the interaction between international courts and discretionary decision-makers. Whether due to a tendency to classify international criminal courts as 'criminal' courts rather than 'international' courts, or because the existing literature is concerned chiefly with judicial deference to states, as in

---

[91] See art 115, Rome Statute.
[92] Para 4, preamble, Rome Statute.

international human rights law, international investment law, and international trade law, international criminal courts have been conspicuously absent from these discussions. The book's examination of the role of the ICC vis-à-vis its Prosecutor in the assessment of the admissibility criterion of gravity draws substantial support from this literature and, in so doing, shows that the deference conferred on states by international courts need not always be justified by respect for the role of states in public international law. The justifications for deference that rely on the competence and fact-finding capabilities of discretionary decision-makers extend equally to other entities, such as the organs of international courts themselves, in this case the Prosecutor of the ICC. At the same time, the allocative function performed by the discretionary application by the ICC Prosecutor of the gravity criterion distinguishes this context from the treatment of discretionary decision-making at other international courts. By teasing apart these similarities and differences, it is hoped that this book enriches the existing literature further by setting out the distinct case for judicial deference by international criminal courts.

Bibliography

Books

Bos M, *A Methodology of International Law* (North-Holland 1984)

Cherif Bassiouni M, *Introduction to International Criminal Law* (Martinus Nijhoff 2013)

Cryer R, *Prosecuting International Crimes: Selectivity and the International Criminal Law Regime* (CUP 2005)

deGuzman MM, *Shocking the Conscience of Humanity: Gravity and the Legitimacy of International Criminal Law* (OUP 2020)

Fahner JH, *Judicial Deference in International Adjudication: A Comparative Analysis* (Hart Publishing 2020)

Fordham M, *Judicial Review Handbook* (6th edn, Hart Publishing 2012)

Galligan DJ, *Discretionary Powers: A Legal Study of Official Discretion* (Clarendon Press 1990)

Hart HLA, *The Concept of Law* (3rd edn, OUP 2012)

Henckels C, *Proportionality and Deference in Investor-State Arbitration* (CUP 2015)

Kolb R, *Interprétation et Création du Droit International* (Editions Bruylant 2006)

Legg A, *The Margin of Appreciation in International Human Rights Law: Deference and Proportionality* (OUP 2012)

McNair A, *The Law of Treaties* (OUP 1986)

O'Keefe R, *International Criminal Law* (OUP 2016)

Oesch M, *Standards of Review in WTO Dispute Resolution* (OUP 2003)

Olásolo H, *The Triggering Procedure of the International Criminal Court* (Martinus Nijhoff 2005)

Pikis GM, *The Rome Statute of the International Criminal Court: Analysis of the Rome Statute, the Rules of Procedure and Evidence, the Regulations of the Court and Supplementary Instruments* (Martinus Nijhoff 2010)

Pues A, *Prosecutorial Discretion at the International Criminal Court* (Hart Publishing 2020)

Schabas WA, *The International Criminal Court: A Commentary on the Rome Statute* (2nd edn, OUP 2016)

Shany Y, *Questions of Jurisdiction and Admissibility before International Courts* (CUP 2015)

Shirlow E, *Judging at the Interface: Deference to State Decision-Making Authority in International Adjudication* (CUP 2021)

Stahn C, *Justice as Message: Expressivist Foundations of International Criminal Justice* (OUP 2020)

Woolf HK and others, *De Smith's Judicial Review* (8th edn, Sweet and Maxwell 2019)

Zakerhossein MH, *Situation Selection Regime at the International Criminal Court: Law, Policy, Practice* (Intersentia 2017)

Book Chapters

Abdou M, 'Article 19' in Klamberg M (ed), *Commentary on the Law of the International Criminal Court* (Torkel Opsahl Academic EPublisher 2017)

Bergsmo M, Pejic J, and Zhu D, 'Article 15' in Triffterer O and Ambos K (eds), *Rome Statute of the International Criminal Court: A Commentary* (3rd edn, CH Beck 2016)

Boas G and others, 'Appeals, Reviews and Reconsideration' in Sluiter G and others (eds), *International Criminal Procedure: Principles and Rules* (OUP 2013)

Burke-White W and Kaplan S, 'Shaping the Contours of Domestic Justice: The International Criminal Court and an Admissibility Challenge in the Uganda Situation' in Stahn C and Sluiter G (eds), *The Emerging Practice of the International Criminal Court* (Martinus Nijhoff 2009)

Cassese A, 'The International Criminal Court Five Years On: *Andante* or *Moderato*?' in Stahn C and Sluiter G (eds), *The Emerging Practice of the International Criminal Court* (Martinus Nijhoff 2009)

Cross ME, 'The Standard of Proof in Preliminary Examinations' in Stahn C and Bergsmo M (eds), *Quality Control in Preliminary Examinations: Volume 2* (Torkel Opsahl Academic EPublisher 2018)

deGuzman MM and Schabas WA, 'Initiation of Investigations and Selection of Cases' in Zappalà S and others (eds), *International Criminal Procedure: Principles and Rules* (OUP 2013)

de Meester K, 'Article 53' in Klamberg M (ed), *Commentary on the Law of the International Criminal Court* (Torkel Opsahl Academic EPublisher 2017)

de Smet S, 'A Structural Analysis of the Role of the Pre-Trial Chamber in the Fact-Finding Process of the ICC' in Stahn C and Sluiter G (eds), *The Emerging Practice of the International Criminal Court* (Martinus Nijhoff 2009)

Emrah Bozbayindir A, 'The Venture of the Comoros Referral at the Preliminary Examination Stage' in Stahn C and Bergsmo M (eds), *Quality Control in Preliminary Examinations Volume 1* (Torkel Opsahl Academic EPublisher 2018)

Endicott T, 'The Value of Vagueness' in Marmor A and Soames S (eds), *Philosophical Foundations of Language in the Law* (OUP 2011)

Fernández de Gurmendi S, 'The Role of the International Prosecutor' in Lee RS (ed), *The International Criminal Court: The Making of the Rome Statute—Issues, Negotiations, Results* (Kluwer Law International 1999)

Greenawalt AKA, 'Admissibility as a Theory of International Criminal Law' in deGuzman MM and Oosterveld V (eds), *The Elgar Companion to the International Criminal Court* (Edward Elgar 2020)

Guariglia F, 'Investigation and Prosecution' in Lee RS (ed), *The International Criminal Court: The Making of the Rome Statute—Issues, Negotiations, Results* (Kluwer Law International 1999)

—— 'The Selection of Cases by the Office of the Prosecutor of the International Criminal Court' in Stahn C and Sluiter G (eds), *The Emerging Practice of the International Criminal Court* (Martinus Nijhoff 2009)

—— and Rogier E, 'The Selection of Situations and Cases by the OTP of the ICC' in Stahn C (ed), *The Law and Practice of the International Criminal Court* (OUP 2015)

Hall CK, Nsereko DDN, and Ventura MJ, 'Article 19' in Triffterer O and Ambos K (eds), *Rome Statute of the International Criminal Court: A Commentary* (3rd edn, CH Beck 2016)

Heller KJ, 'Situational Gravity under the Rome Statute' in Stahn C and van den Herik L (eds), *Future Perspectives on International Criminal Justice* (TM Asser Press 2010)

—— 'The Role of the International Prosecutor' in Romano CP, Alter KJ, and Shany Y (eds), *The Oxford Handbook of International Adjudication* (OUP 2013)

Henckels C, 'The Role of the Standard of Review and the Importance of Deference in Investor-State Arbitration' in Gruszczynski L and Werner W (eds), *Deference in International Courts and Tribunals* (OUP 2014)

Jacobs D and Naouri J, 'Making Sense of the Invisible: The Role of the "Accused" during Preliminary Examinations' in Stahn C and Bergsmo M (eds), *Quality Control in Preliminary Examinations Volume 2* (Torkel Opsahl Academic EPublisher 2018)

Kersten M, 'Taking the Opportunity: Prosecutorial Opportunism and the International Criminal Court' in deGuzman M and Oosterveld V (eds), *The Elgar Companion to the International Criminal Court* (Edward Elgar 2020)

Klamberg M, 'Article 58' in Klamberg M (ed), *Commentary on the Law of the International Criminal Court* (Torkel Opsahl Academic EPublisher 2017)

Ligeti K, 'The Place of the Prosecutor in Common Law and Civil Law Jurisdictions' in Brown DK and others (eds), *The Oxford Handbook of Criminal Process* (OUP 2019)

Moreno Ocampo L, 'The International Criminal Court in Motion' in Stahn C and Sluiter G (eds), *The Emerging Practice of the International Criminal Court* (Martinus Nijhoff 2009)

Nouwen SMH and Lewis DA, 'Jurisdictional Arrangements and International Criminal Procedure' in Sluiter G and others (eds), *International Criminal Procedure: Principles and Rules* (OUP 2013)

Rastan R, 'Situation and Case: Defining the Parameters' in Stahn C and El Zeidy M (eds), *The International Criminal Court and Complementarity* (CUP 2011)

Schabas WA, 'Prosecutorial Discretion and Gravity' in Stahn C and Sluiter G (eds), *The Emerging Practice of the International Criminal Court* (Martinus Nijhoff 2009)

—— 'Selecting Situations and Cases' in Stahn C (ed), *The Law and Practice of the International Criminal Court* (OUP 2015)

—— and El Zeidy MM, 'Article 17' in Triffterer O and Ambos K (eds), *The Rome Statute of the International Criminal Court: A Commentary* (3rd edn, CH Beck 2016)

Scheffer D, 'False Alarm about the *Proprio Motu* Prosecutor' in Minow M, True-Frost C, and Whiting A (eds), *The First Global Prosecutor* (University of Michigan Press 2015)

Seils P, 'The Selection and Prioritization of Cases by the Office of the Prosecutor' in Bergsmo M (ed), *Criteria for Prioritizing and Selecting Core International Crimes* (Torkel Opsahl Academic EPublisher 2010)

Stahn C, 'Admissibility Challenges before the ICC: From Quasi-Primacy to Qualified Deference?' in Stahn C (ed), *The Law and Practice of the International Criminal Court* (OUP 2015)

—— 'Judicial Review of Prosecutorial Discretion: Five Years On' in Stahn C and Sluiter G (eds), *The Emerging Practice of the International Criminal Court* (Martinus Nijhoff 2009)

—— and Sluiter G, 'From "Infancy" to Emancipation? A Review of the Court's First Practice' in Stahn C and Sluiter G (eds), *The Emerging Practice of the International Criminal Court* (Martinus Nijhoff 2009)

Stegmiller I, 'Article 15' in Klamberg M (ed), *Commentary on the Law of the International Criminal Court* (Torkel Opsahl Academic EPublisher 2017)

Triffterer O, Bergsmo O, and Ambos K, 'Preamble' in Triffterer O and Ambos K (eds), *The Rome Statute of the International Criminal Court: A Commentary* (3rd edn, CH Beck 2016)

Turone G, 'Powers and Duties of the Prosecutor' in Cassese A, Gaeta P, and Jones JRWD (eds), *The Rome Statute of the International Criminal Court* (OUP 2002)

180 BIBLIOGRAPHY

Vasiliev S, 'The Making of International Criminal Law' in Brölmann C and Radi Y (eds), *Research Handbook on the Theory and Practice of International Lawmaking* (Edward Elgar 2016)

von Hebel H and Robinson D, 'Crimes within the Jurisdiction of the Court' in Lee RS (ed), *The International Criminal Court: The Making of the Rome Statute—Issues, Negotiations, Results* (Kluwer Law International 1999)

Wilberg H, 'Judicial Review of Administrative Reasoning Processes' in Cane P and others (eds), *The Oxford Handbook of Comparative Administrative Law* (OUP 2020)

Zappalà S, 'Judicial Activism v. Judicial Restraint in International Criminal Justice' in Cassese A and others (eds), *The Oxford Companion to International Criminal Justice* (OUP 2009)

Articles

'Preliminary Proceedings' (2017) 46 Georgetown Law Journal Annual Review of Criminal Procedure 269

Ambos K and Stegmiller I, 'Prosecuting International Crimes at the International Criminal Court: Is There a Coherent and Comprehensive Prosecution Strategy?' (2013) 59 Crime, Law and Social Change 415

Arbour L, 'The Need for an Independent and Effective Prosecutor in the Permanent International Criminal Court' (1999) 17 Windsor Yearbook of Access to Justice 207

Bekou O, 'Rule 11 BIS: An Examination of the Process of Referrals to Nationals Courts in ICTY Jurisprudence' (2009) 33 Fordham International Law Journal 723

Berman F, 'International Treaties and British Statutes' (2005) 26 Statute Law Review 1

Brubacher M, 'Prosecutorial Discretion within the International Criminal Court' (2004) 2 Journal of International Criminal Justice 71

Burke-White W, 'Proactive Complementarity: The International Criminal Court and National Courts in the Rome System of International Justice' (2008) 49 Harvard International Law Journal 53

Clements R, 'From Bureaucracy to Management: The International Criminal Court's Internal Progress Narrative' (2019) 21 Leiden Journal of International Law 149

Cowell F, 'Inherent Imperialism: Understanding the Legal Roots of Anti-Imperialist Criticism of the International Criminal Court' (2017) 15 Journal of International Criminal Justice 667

Crawford J, 'The ILC Adopts a Statute for an International Criminal Court' (1995) 89 American Journal of International Law 404

Damaška M, 'What Is the Point of International Criminal Justice?' (2008) 83 Chicago-Kent Law Review 329

Danner AM, 'Enhancing the Legitimacy and Accountability of Prosecutorial Discretion at the International Criminal Court' (2003) 97 American Journal of International Law 510

Davis C, 'Political Considerations in Prosecutorial Discretion at the International Criminal Court' (2015) 15 International Criminal Law Review 170

Davis MS, 'Standards of Review: Judicial Review of Discretionary Decisionmaking' (2000) 2 Journal of Appellate Practice and Process 47

deGuzman MM, 'Gravity and the Legitimacy of the International Criminal Court' (2008) 32 Fordham International Law Journal 1400

—— 'Gravity Rhetoric: The Good, the Bad, and the "Political"' (2013) American Society of International Law Proceedings 421

—— 'The International Criminal Court's Gravity Jurisprudence at Ten' (2013) 12 Washington University Global Studies Law Review 475

de Hemptinne J, 'The Creation of Investigating Chambers at the International Criminal Court: An Option Worth Pursuing?' (2007) 5 Journal of International Criminal Justice 402

de Souza Dias T, '"Interests of Justice": Defining the Scope of Prosecutorial Discretion in Article 53(1)(c) and (2)(c) of the Rome Statute of the International Criminal Court' (2017) 30 Leiden Journal of International Law 731

del Ponte C, 'Prosecuting the Individuals Bearing the Highest Level of Responsibility' (2004) 2 Journal of International Criminal Justice 516

Delmas-Marty M, 'Interactions between National and International Criminal Law in the Preliminary Phase of Trial at the ICC' (2006) 4 Journal of International Criminal Justice 2

El Zeidy M, 'Some Remarks on the Question of the Admissibility of a Case During Arrest Warrant Proceedings before the International Criminal Court' (2006) 19 Leiden Journal of International Law 741

—— 'The Gravity Threshold under the Statute of the International Criminal Court' (2008) 19 Criminal Law Forum 35

Ezennia CN, 'The Modus Operandi of the International Criminal Court System: An Impartial or a Selective Justice Regime?' (2016) 16 International Criminal Law Review 448

Ford S, 'What Investigative Resources Does the International Criminal Court Need to Succeed? A Gravity-Based Approach' (2017) 16 Washington University Global Studies Law Review 1

Goldston JA, 'More Candour about Criteria' (2010) 8 Journal of International Criminal Justice 383

Greenawalt AKA, 'Justice without Politics? Prosecutorial Discretion and the International Criminal Court' (2007) 39 New York University Journal of International Law and Politics 583

Jalloh CC, 'Regionalizing International Criminal Law?' (2009) 9 International Criminal Law Review 445

Jallow HB, 'Prosecutorial Discretion and International Criminal Justice' (2005) 3 Journal of International Criminal Justice 145

Kiyani A, 'Group-Based Differentiation and Local Repression: The Custom and Curse of Selectivity' (2016) 14 Journal of International Criminal Justice 939

Knoops G-JA, 'The Legitimacy of Initiating Contemporary International Criminal Proceedings: Rethinking Prosecutorial Discretionary Powers from a Legal, Ethical and Political Perspective' (2004) 1 International Studies Journal 1

—— and Zwart T, 'The Flotilla Case before the ICC: The Need to Do Justice While Keeping Heaven Intact' (2015) 15 International Criminal Law Review 1069

Kotecha B, 'The International Criminal Court's Selectivity and Procedural Justice' (2020) 18 Journal of International Criminal Justice 107

Longobardo M, 'Everything Is Relative, Even Gravity' (2016) 14 Journal of International Criminal Justice 1011

—— 'Factors Relevant for the Assessment of Sufficient Gravity in the ICC: Proceedings and the Elements of International Crimes' (2016) 33 Questions of International Law 21

López R, 'The Law of Gravity' (2020) 58 Columbia Journal of Transnational Law 565

Mariniello T, 'Judicial Control over Prosecutorial Discretion at the International Criminal Court' (2019) 19 International Criminal Law Review 979

Mégret F, 'Three Dangers for the International Criminal Court: A Critical Look at a Consensual Project' (2001) 12 Finnish Yearbook of International Law 193

BIBLIOGRAPHY

—— 'Beyond "Gravity": For a Politics of International Criminal Prosecutions' (2013) American Society of International Law Proceedings 428

—— 'The Anxieties of International Criminal Justice' (2016) 29 Leiden Journal of International Law 197

Meloni C, 'The ICC Preliminary Examination of the Flotilla Situation: An Opportunity to Contextualise Gravity' (2016) 33 Questions of International Law 3

Murphy R, 'Gravity Issues and the International Criminal Court' (2006) 17 Criminal Law Forum 281

Nouwen SMH and Werner WG, 'Doing Justice to the Political: The International Criminal Court in Uganda and Sudan' (2011) 21 European Journal of International Law 941

Nsereko DDN, 'Prosecutorial Discretion before National Courts and International Tribunals' (2005) 3 Journal of International Criminal Justice 124

O'Donohue J, 'Towards a Fully Functional International Criminal Court: The Adoption of the 2004 Budget' (2004) 17 Leiden Journal of International Law 579

—— 'The 2005 Budget of the International Criminal Court: Contingency, Insufficient Funding in Key Areas and the Recurring Question of the Independence of the Prosecutor' (2005) 18 Leiden Journal of International Law 591

O'Keefe R, 'The ILC's Contribution to International Criminal Law' (2006) 49 German Yearbook of International Law 201

—— 'Interpretation versus Application of Treaties: A Question of Character' (forthcoming)

Olásolo H, 'The Prosecutor of the ICC Before the Initiation of Investigations: A Quasi-Judicial or a Political Body?' (2003) 3 International Criminal Law Review 87

—— 'The Lack of Attention to the Distinction between Situations and Cases in National Laws on Co-operation with the International Criminal Court with Particular Reference to the Spanish Case' (2007) 20 Leiden Journal of International Law 193

Orentlicher D, 'Remarks of Diane Orentlicher' (2013) American Society of International Law Proceedings 425

Poltronieri Rossetti L, 'The Pre-Trial Chamber's Afghanistan Decision: A Step Too Far in the Judicial Review of Prosecutorial Discretion?' (2019) 17 Journal of International Criminal Justice 585

Pues A, 'Discretion and the Gravity of Situations at the International Criminal Court' (2017) 17 International Criminal Law Review 960

Rastan R, 'What Is a "Case" for the Purpose of the Rome Statute?' (2008) 19 Criminal Law Forum 435

—— 'Comment on Victor's Justice and Ex Ante Standards' (2010) 43 John Marshall Law Review 569

—— 'The Jurisdictional Scope of Situations before the International Criminal Court' (2012) 23 Criminal Law Forum 1

Reynolds J and Xavier S, '"The Dark Corners of the World": TWAIL and International Criminal Justice' (2016) 14 Journal of International Criminal Justice 959

Robinson D, 'Inescapable Dyads: Why the International Criminal Court Cannot Win' (2015) 28 Leiden Journal of International Law 323

Rogers J, 'Restructuring the Exercise of Prosecutorial Discretion in England' (2006) 26 Oxford Journal of Legal Studies 775

Ruys T, 'Criminalizing Aggression: How the Future of the Law on the Use of Force Rests in the Hands of the ICC' (2018) 29 European Journal of International Law 887

SáCouto S and Cleary K, 'The Gravity Threshold of the International Criminal Court' (2007) 23 American University International Law Review 807

Schabas WA, 'Victor's Justice: Selecting "Situations" at the International Criminal Court' (2010) 43 John Marshall Law Review 535

Schill S and Briese R, ' "If the State Considers": Self-Judging Clauses in International Dispute Settlement' (2009) 13 Max Planck Yearbook of United Nations Law 61

Shany Y, 'Toward a General Margin of Appreciation Doctrine in International Law?' (2006) 16 European Journal of International Law 907

Smith SE, 'Inventing the Laws of Gravity: The ICC's Initial Lubanga Decision and its Regressive Consequences' (2008) 8 International Criminal Law Review 331

Stahn C, 'The Future of International Criminal Justice' (2009) 4 Hague Justice Journal 257

—— 'Damned If You Do, Damned If You Don't: Challenges and Critiques of Preliminary Examinations at the ICC' (2017) 15 Journal of International Criminal Justice 413

Stegmiller I, 'The Gravity Threshold under the ICC Statute: Gravity Back and Forth in Lubanga and Ntaganda' (2009) 9 International Criminal Law Review 547

Tully SR, ' "Objective Reasonableness" as a Standard for International Judicial Review' (2015) 6 Journal of International Dispute Settlement 546

Urs P, 'Judicial Review of Prosecutorial Discretion in the Initiation of Investigations into Situations of "Sufficient Gravity" ' (2020) 18 Journal of International Criminal Justice 851

Ventura MJ, 'The "Reasonable Basis to Proceed" Threshold in the Kenya and Côte d'Ivoire Proprio Motu Investigation Decisions: The International Criminal Court's Lowest Evidentiary Standard?' (2013) 12 The Law and Practice of International Courts and Tribunals 49

Vest H, 'Problems of Participation—Unitarian, Differentiated Approach, or Something Else?' (2014) 12 Journal of International Criminal Justice 295

Waldron J, 'Vagueness in Law and Language: Some Philosophical Issues' (1994) 82 California Law Review 509

Webb P, 'The ICC Prosecutor's Discretion Not to Proceed in the "Interests of Justice" ' (2005) 50 Criminal Law Quarterly 305

Whiting A, 'Dynamic Investigative Practice at the International Criminal Court' (2013) 76 Law and Contemporary Problems 163

—— 'A Program for the Next ICC Prosecutor' (2020) 52 Case Western Reserve Journal of International Law 479

Williams S, 'ICTY Referrals to National Jurisdictions: A Fair Trial or a Fair Price?' (2006) 17 Criminal Law Forum 177

Zakerhossein MH, 'A Concept without Consensus: Conceptualisation of the "Situation" Notion in the Rome Statute' (2018) 18 International Criminal Law Review 686

Doctoral Theses

Clements R, Governing International Criminal Justice: Managerial Practices and the International Criminal Court (doctoral thesis, University of Cambridge 2019)

Hacking M, The Law of Gravity: The Role of Gravity in International Criminal Law (doctoral thesis, University of Cambridge 2014)

Poltronieri Rossetti L, Prosecutorial Discretion and Its Judicial Review at the International Criminal Court: A Practice-Based Analysis of the Relationship between the Prosecutor and Judges (doctoral thesis, Università Degli Studi di Trento 2017–2018)

184 BIBLIOGRAPHY

Online Sources

Akande D, 'Is There Still a Need for Guidelines for the Exercise of ICC Prosecutorial Discretion?' (*EJIL Talk!*, 28 October 2009) www.ejiltalk.org/is-there-still-a-need-for-gui delines-for-the-exercise-of-icc-prosecutorial-discretion

—— and de Souza Dias T, 'The ICC Pre-Trial Chamber Decision on the Situation in Afghanistan: A Few Thoughts on the Interests of Justice' (*EJIL Talk!*, 18 April 2019) www. ejiltalk.org/the-icc-pre-trial-chamber-decision-on-the-situation-in-afghanistan-a-few-thoughts-on-the-interests-of-justice

Ambos K, ' "Solid Jurisdictional Basis"? The ICC's Fragile Jurisdiction for Crimes Allegedly Committed in Palestine' (*EJIL Talk!*, 2 March 2021) www.ejiltalk.org/solid-jurisdictio nal-basis-the-iccs-fragile-jurisdiction-for-crimes-allegedly-committed-in-palestine/ ?utm_source=mailpoet&utm_medium=email&utm_campaign=ejil-talk-newsletter-post-title_2

Heller KJ, 'Could the ICC Investigate Israel's Attack on the Mavi Marmara?' (*Opinio Juris*, 14 May 2013) http://opiniojuris.org/2013/05/14/could-the-icc-investigate-the-mavi-marm ara-incident

—— 'The Pre-Trial Chamber's Dangerous Comoros Review Decision' (*Opinio Juris*, 17 July 2015) http://opiniojuris.org/2015/07/17/the-pre-trial-chambers-problematic-comoros-review-decision

—— 'A Potentially Serious Problem with the Final Decision Concerning Comoros' (*Opinio Juris*, 1 December 2017) http://opiniojuris.org/2017/12/01/33365

—— 'Three Cautionary Thoughts on the OTP's Rohingya Request' (*Opinio Juris*, 9 April 2018) http://opiniojuris.org/2018/04/09/some-thoughts-on-the-otps-rohingya-request

—— 'One Word for the PTC on the Interests of Justice: Taliban' (*Opinio Juris*, 13 April 2019) https://opiniojuris.org/2019/04/13/one-word-for-the-ptc-on-the-interests-of-justice-taliban

—— 'The Comoros Declination—and Remarkable Footnote 20' (*Opinio Juris*, 4 December 2019) http://opiniojuris.org/2019/12/04/the-comoros-declination-and-remarka ble-footnote-20/?utm_source=feedburner&utm_medium=email&utm_campaign= Feed%3A+opiniojurisfeed+%28Opinio+Juris%29

Jacobs D, 'The Comoros Referral to the ICC of the Israel Flotilla Raid: When a "Situation" Is Not Really a "Situation" ' (*Spreading the Jam*, 15 May 2013) https://dovjacobs.com/2013/ 05/15/the-comoros-referral-to-the-icc-of-the-israel-flotilla-raid-when-a-situation-is-not-really-a-situation

—— 'The Gaza Flotilla, Israel and the ICC: Some Thoughts on Gravity and the Relevant Armed Conflict' (*Spreading the Jam*, 11 November 2014) https://dovjacobs.com/2014/ 11/11/the-gaza-flotilla-israel-and-the-icc-some-thoughts-on-gravity-and-the-relevant-armed-conflict

—— 'ICC Judges Ask the Prosecutor to Reconsider Decision Not to Investigate Israeli Gaza Flotilla Conduct' (*Spreading the Jam*, 20 July 2015) https://dovjacobs.com/2015/07/20/ icc-judges-ask-the-prosecutor-to-reconsider-decision-not-to-investigate-israeli-gaza-flotilla-conduct

Kiyani A, 'Afghanistan and the Surrender of International Criminal Justice' (TWAIL Review, 2019) https://twailr.com/wp-content/uploads/2019/09/Kiyani-Afghanistan-the-Surren der-of-International-Criminal-Justice.pdf

McDonald A and Haveman R, 'Prosecutorial Discretion—Some Thoughts on "Objectifying" the Exercise of Prosecutorial Discretion by the Prosecutor of the ICC', Office of the

Prosecutor (15 April 2003) https://asp.icc-cpi.int/iccdocs/asp_docs/library/organs/otp/mcdonald_haveman.pdf

O'Donohue J, 'ICC Prosecutor Symposium: Wanted—International Prosecutor to Deliver Justice Successfully across Multiple Complex Situations with Inadequate Resources' (*Opinio Juris*, 14 April 2020) http://opiniojuris.org/2020/04/14/icc-prosecutor-symposium-wanted-international-prosecutor-to-deliver-justice-successfully-across-multiple-complex-situations-with-inadequate-resources/?utm_source=feedburner&utm_medium=email&utm_campaign=Feed%3A+opiniojurisfeed+%28Opinio+Juris%29

Osiel M, 'How Should the ICC Office of the Prosecutor Choose Its Cases? The Multiple Meanings of "Situational Gravity"' (*The Hague Justice Portal*, 5 March 2009) www.haguejusticeportal.net/index.php?id=10344

Urs P, 'Some Concerns with the Pre-Trial Chamber's Second Decision in Relation to the Mavi Marmara Incident' (*EJIL Talk!*, 5 December 2018) www.ejiltalk.org/some-concerns-with-the-pre-trial-chambers-second-decision-in-relation-to-the-mavi-marmara-incident

van Sliedregt E, 'The ICC Ntaganda Appeals Judgment: The End of Indirect Co-perpetration?' (*Just Security*, 14 May 2021) www.justsecurity.org/76136/the-icc-ntaganda-appeals-judgment-the-end-of-indirect-co-perpetration

Whiting A, 'The ICC Prosecutor Should Reject Judges' Decision in Mavi Marmara Incident' (*Just Security*, 20 July 2015) www.justsecurity.org/24778/icc-prosecutor-reject-judges-decision-mavi-marmara

—— 'What to Look for in the Next ICC Prosecutor' (*Justice in Conflict*, 17 April 2020) https://justiceinconflict.org/2020/04/17/what-to-look-for-in-the-next-icc-prosecutor

Miscellaneous

'Improving the Operations of the ICC Office of the Prosecutor: Reappraisal of Structures, Norms, and Practices', Outcome Report and Recommendations, Open Society Justice Initiative and Amsterdam Center for International Law/Department of Criminal Law, Amsterdam Law School, 15 April 2020

SáCouto S and Cleary K, 'The Relevance of a "Situation" to the Admissibility and Selection of Cases before the International Criminal Court', War Crimes Research Office, 2009

Index

For the benefit of digital users, indexed terms that span two pages (e.g., 52–53) may, on occasion, appear on only one of those pages.

Abu Garda (Bahr Idriss Abu Garda) 54–55, 60–61
admissibility
  as assessed during Article 58
    proceedings 135–37, 144–50
  as assessed during confirmation of
    charges 142n.117
  of a case 48–50
    as assessed by the Prosecutor 119–21
    as assessed by the Pre-Trial or Trial
      Chamber 134–37
    as distinct from jurisdiction *ratione
      materiae* 18, 52–54, 65
  of a situation 29–35, 83–84, 91–92
Afghanistan 39–40, 42, 43–44, 45, 46, 92–95, 99–100, 101, 109–10
African Union Mission in Sudan 60–61
Al Hassan (Al Hassan Ag Abdoul Aziz Ag
    Mohamed Ag Mahmoud) 28, 49–50,
    54–55, 56–57, 58–61, 73–74, 143–44,
    164–65
Al-Werfalli (Mahmoud Mustafa Busayf
    Al-Werfalli) 58–59, 61
application of law 11–14, 51–52
arrest warrant *see* warrant of arrest

Banda (Abdallah Banda Abakaer
    Nourain) 55n.144, 60–61
Bangladesh *see* Myanmar
Bemba (Jean-Pierre Bemba Gombo) 58n.161,
    129n.60, 137–38, 141–42
Blé Goudé (Charles Blé Goudé) 50n.118, 54–55,
    56, 58–59
Burundi 39–40, 41–42, 46, 64–65, 98–99, 101,
    109–10

Cambodia *see* Mavi Marmara incident
case 21–22
Central African Republic 36–37, 137–38,
    141–42
  see also Bemba (Jean-Pierre Bemba Gombo)

civil law 2–3, 8n.42, 110–11n.155, 112n.165,
    126–28, 132n.75, 134n.88, 153, 160–61,
    172
common law 2–3, 8n.42, 110–11n.155, 126–28,
    132n.75, 153, 160–61, 172
Comoros, The *see* Mavi Marmara incident
complementarity 5, 26n.7, 37n.52, 142–44,
    169n.72
confirmation of charges 49–50
Côte d'Ivoire 27–28, 30n.29, 38–40, 41–42n.73,
    43–44, 46, 54–55, 96–97, 101, 109–10
  see also Blé Goudé (Charles Blé Goudé)

Darfur *see* Sudan
Democratic Republic of the Congo (DRC) 36–
    37, 123–24, 138–39
  see also Lubanga (Thomas Lubanga Dyilo);
    Ntaganda (Bosco Ntaganda)
District Court of Dili 4–5, 173–74

East Timor *see* District Court of Dili
Eboe-Osuji (Chile Eboe-Osuji) 89–90
expressio unius exclusio alterius 26–27, 84n.12,
    93–95, 122n.24

Fernández de Gurmendi (Silvia Fernández de
    Gurmendi) 88n.25, 96–97, 101, 106,
    108–10, 113–14
Forces Patriotiques pour la Libération du
    Congo 52nn.127–28

Gaza *see* Palestine; Mavi Marmara incident
Gaza Flotilla incident *see* Mavi Marmara incident
Georgia 39–40, 41–42n.73, 45, 46, 95, 97–99,
    101
gravity
  as admissibility criterion
    assessment during Article 58
      proceedings 150–52
    assessment of gravity beyond jurisdictional
      scope of situation 34–35

188 INDEX

gravity (*cont.*)
    'marginal gravity' 11, 13–14, 28, 162
    objective approach 53, 54, 63, 72–74,
      77n.252, 79–80, 157–58, 163, 168
    open-texture of 'sufficient gravity' in Article
      17(1)(*d*) of the Rome Statute 7–8, 12–13,
      102, 109–10, 114, 126–28, 157–58, 174, 175
    of a potential case 29–34
    purpose 8–11, 15–16, 26–28, 162–69
    'relative gravity' 13–14, 164–65, 166–68
    'situational gravity' 32–33
    subjective approach 13–15, 53, 63, 72–79,
      157–58, 162, 163, 168, 170, 171
    in assessment of 'interests of justice' 19,
      84n.12
    of a crime 4–5
    as factor in sentencing 20
    in jurisdiction *ratione materiae* of the ICC 17–18
    gravity-based hierarchy of crimes 41n.70, 65
Greece *see* Mavi Marmara incident

Hussein Ali (Mohammed Hussein Ali) *see*
    Kenyatta (Uhuru Muigai Kenyatta)

Ibáñez Carranza (Luz del Carmen Ibáñez
    Carranza) 89–90
Independent Expert Review of the International
    Criminal Court and the Rome Statute
    System (Independent Expert Review) 3–
    4, 11, 67n.208, 71–72, 77, 125–28, 162–64
interests of justice 13–14, 15–16, 19, 39–40,
    92–93, 99–100, 165–66, 168–69
International Criminal Court (ICC)
    Elements of Crimes 17–18
    jurisdiction
      jurisdiction *ratione materiae* 1–2n.6, 4–5,
        8–10, 17–18, 27–28, 52–54, 64–65, 79,
        95n.61, 100n.97, 126n.45, 164–65, 168,
        171, 173, 174
      jurisdiction *ratione personae* 69–70, 79
    Rome Statute
      drafting of 2n.6, 8–10, 8n.41, 20–21, 27–28,
        27n.8, 28n.14, 69n.213, 76–77, 83–84,
        87–88, 93n.54, 102–5, 120n.15, 125–26,
        129–30n.61, 136–37n.95, 145–46,
        146n.138, *see also* International Law
        Commission
    Rules of Procedure and Evidence 20, 39–40,
      43, 54–55, 81n.1, 83–84, 91–92, 93–95,
      101–2, 145–48
International Criminal Tribunal for Rwanda
    (ICTR) 2–3, 4–5, 173

International Criminal Tribunal for the former
    Yugoslavia (ICTY) 2–3, 4–5, 173
international human rights law 14, 60, 61,
    67–68, 107–8, 125, 175–76
international investment law 14, 103, 107–8,
    125, 175–76
International Law Commission (ILC) 8–10,
    125–28, 129–30
    draft statute for an international criminal
      court 8–10, 27n.8, 27n.12, 28n.14,
      76n.246, 105n.123, 121n.21, 129–30n.61,
      136–37n.95, 148n.142
    reception in the Sixth Committee of the UN
      General Assembly 9n.50
international trade law 14, 107–8, 125, 175–76
interpretation of law 11–14, 51–52
Iraq 35n.44, 37
Israel Defense Forces 34–35, 43
Ituri *see* Democratic Republic of the
    Congo (DRC)

Jerbo (Saleh Mohammed Jerbo Jamus) 60–61
judicial economy 14, 67, 71, 99n.86, 107–8,
    111–13, 145–46, 148–49
judicial review
    judicial deference 14, 16, 107–14, 130–34
    standard of review
      abuse of discretion 7–8, 86–88, 90–91,
        96–97, 101, 110–14, 131–32, 133–34,
        138n.98, 153, 158–62
      arbitrariness 7–8, 74–75, 111–13, 133–34,
        171–72
      bad faith *see* good faith
      de novo assessment or review 85–87,
        95–100, 101, 107–10, 130–31
      good faith 73, 75, 111–13, 133–34, 158,
        159–61
      manifest error of law or fact 110–14,
        131–32
      margin of appreciation 107–8, 131
      reasonableness 96, 110–13, 131–32, 133–34
      'Wednesbury unreasonableness' 111–13,
        133–34

Kenya 27–28, 29–32, 35–36, 38–40, 41–42, 43,
    45–46, 59, 96, 101
    see also Kenyatta (Uhuru Muigai Kenyatta)
Kenyatta (Uhuru Muigai Kenyatta) 59, 138n.98
Kony (Joseph Kony) 137–40, 142–45, 146, 148,
    151–52, 151n.152
Kosovo *see* Kosovo Specialist Chambers
Kosovo Specialist Chambers 4–5, 173–74

INDEX

Kovács (Peter Kovács) 34–35, 38–39, 46–47, 86–88, 90–91, 97–99, 111–13

Libya see Al-Werfalli (Mahmoud Mustafa Busayf Al-Werfalli)
Lubanga (Thomas Lubanga Dyilo) 27–28, 50–52, 123–24, 137–38, 139–40, 141–42n.116
Lukwiya (Raska Lukwiya) see Kony (Joseph Kony)

Mali 28, 50–51, 137–38, 143–44
  see also Al Hassan (Al Hassan Ag Abdoul Aziz Ag Mohamed Ag Mahmoud)
Mavi Marmara incident 28, 31–32, 34–35, 38–39, 41, 43, 44–45, 46–47, 48, 64–65, 68, 72–73, 85–91, 102–3, 107–9, 111–13, 129
Mindua (Antoine Kesia-Mbe Mindua) 99–100
most responsible see those who bear the greatest responsibility
Muthaura (Francis Kirimi Muthaura) see Kenyatta (Uhuru Muigai Kenyatta)
Myanmar 31–32, 34–35, 39–40, 46, 49n.112, 95, 100, 101, 106, 139n.103

Ntaganda (Bosco Ntaganda) 27–28, 50–54, 61–62, 68–70, 72–73, 137–38, 139–41, 144–45, 147–52, 161–62, 164–65

Odhiambo (Okot Odhiambo) see Kony (Joseph Kony)
Office of the Prosecutor of the ICC
  Policy Paper on Case Selection and Prioritisation 50–51, 54
  Policy Paper on Preliminary Examinations 35–36, 38, 47
  Regulations of the Office of the Prosecutor 35–36, 37, 47, 50–51, 54, 126–28
Ongwen (Dominic Ongwen) see Kony (Joseph Kony)
open-texture of legal language 7–8, 12–14
  see also gravity; open texture of 'sufficient gravity' in Article 17(1)(d) of the Rome Statute
Otti (Vincent Otti) see Kony (Joseph Kony)

Palestine 34–35, 44–45, 49n.112, 85–91, 139n.103
Philippines 95, 100–1
Pikis (Georghios Pikis) 53n.133, 54, 140n.106, 141n.114, 148n.142
preliminary examination 37n.52, 82–83, 87n.21, 96–97, 103n.111, 108n.142, 111–13
  see also International Criminal Court (ICC); Office of the Prosecutor; Policy Paper on Preliminary Examinations

prosecutorial discretion
  see also International Criminal Court; Office of the Prosecutor
  abuse of discretion see judicial review; abuse of discretion
  in the assessment of gravity 75
  during investigation 2–3, 102–5, 158–60
  during prosecution 2–3, 125–29, 160–62
  fact-finding competence 107–8, 113–14, 153
  prosecutorial accountability see judicial review
  prosecutorial budget 102n.107, 103n.111, 170–71
  prosecutorial independence 70, 104–6, 120–21, 128–30, 159–60, 170–71
  resource allocation 8–10, 13–16, 33–34, 64, 68, 71–72, 76–79, 102–4, 125–28, 150, 162–69

referral of situation to the International Criminal Court
  by state party 34–35, 85–86, 104–6, 113n.168, 119–21, 129–31, 133–34, 148n.142
  by UN Security Council 6, 14, 20–21, 24, 33n.37, 36–37, 81, 84, 104–6, 113n.168, 116, 118–21, 129–31, 133–34, 145–46, 148n.142, 152–53, 159, 160–61, 172
Rome Statute see International Criminal Court (ICC)
Rwanda see International Criminal Tribunal for Rwanda (ICTR)

Sierra Leone see Special Court for Sierra Leone (SCSL)
situation 20–21
South Ossetia see Georgia
Special Court for Sierra Leone (SCSL) 2–3
Sudan 36–37, 54–55, 60–61
  see also Abu Garda (Bahr Idriss Abu Garda); Jamus (Saleh Mohammed Jerbo Jamus); Nourain (Abdallah Banda Abakaer Nourain)
sufficient gravity see gravity
summons to appear 21–22, 49–50, 117–18, 135–44, 150

those who bear the greatest responsibility 45–47, 51–54, 61, 68–72
Timbuktu see Mali
Timor Leste see District Court of Dili
truth and reconciliation mechanisms 4–5, 15–16, 173n.85, 174n.89

190 INDEX

Uganda 36–37, 123, 137–38
  see also Kony (Joseph Kony)
Union des Patriotes Congolais 52nn.127–28

van den Wyngaert (Christine van den
  Wyngaert) 88n.25, 108–9
victims 1, 14, 15–16, 37, 38–45, 48, 54–55,
  56–62, 64–68, 87n.21, 94n.58, 97–98,
  101, 104n.116, 123–24, 141nn.114–15,
  145–46, 148n.142, 172

warrant of arrest 21–22, 49–50, 117–18, 135–44,
  148n.142, 150

Yugoslavia *see* International Criminal Tribunal
  for the former Yugoslavia (ICTY)